HINDUISM RECONSIDERED

SOUTH ASIA INSTITUTE, NEW DELHI BRANCH
HEIDELBERG UNIVERSITY
SOUTH ASIAN STUDIES NO. XXIV

Hinduism Reconsidered

Edited by

GÜNTHER-DIETZ SONTHEIMER
HERMANN KULKE

MANOHAR
1997

ISBN 81-7304-198-9

First published 1989
Reprinted 1991, 1994
Revised edition 1997

Published by
Ajay Kumar Jain for
Manohar Publishers & Distributors
2/6 Ansari Road, Daryaganj
New Delhi 110 002

Typeset by
A J Software Publishing Co. Pvt. Ltd.
305, Durga Chambers, 1333 D.B. Gupta Road
Karol Bagh, New Delhi 110 005

Printed at
Replika Press Pvt. Ltd.
Plot No. A-229, DSIDC Narela Indl. Park
Delhi 110040

CONTENTS

PREFACE TO SECOND EDITION

The first edition published in 1989 contained thirteen papers presented at the IXth European Conference of Modern South Asian Studies at Heidelberg in 1986. Reprints were published in 1991 and 1994. The present revised and enlarged edition contains the original papers, some of which have been slightly revised by their authors, and four new contributions. They complete certain aspects of the discourse of the first edition (Anncharlott Eschmann, Gaya Charan Tripathi) and enlarge its scheme in view of recent developments in India (Romlia Thapar). Aditya Malik's paper replaces D. Shulman's short introductory note to the first edition.

Since the publication of the first edition, its co-editor Günther-Dietz Sontheimer, as well as Richard Burghart and Horst Krüger, who contributed important papers to it, have died. This second edition is dedicated to their memory.

THE EDITORS

PREFACE TO FIRST EDITION

This volume is based on papers delivered during the IXth European Conference of Modern South Asian Studies at Heidelberg in 1986. The editors were substantially helped in their editorial work by Mr. Martin Brandtner and Mr. Tilman Frasch, both of the Dept. of History, South Asia Institute, University of Heidelberg. We are most grateful to them as well as to Mr. Aditya Malik of the Dept. of Indology of the South Asia Institute who has taken special efforts in bringing the different articles into a uniform shape, compiling the indexes, and preparing a camera-ready copy. The publication of the book in the South Asia Series of the branch of South Asia Institute, New Delhi, was supported financially by the "Verein der Förderer des Südasien-Instituts" in Heidelberg. We also wish to thank Dr. Claus Peter Zoller, New Delhi and the publishers for their cooperation.

THE EDITORS

INTRODUCTION

This second, enlarged edition of *Hinduism Reconsidered* contains four new papers in addition to the thirteen papers which had been presented in a panel of the IXth European Conference of Modern South Asian Studies held at Wilhelmsfeld near Heidelberg in 1986 and which were already published in 1989 in the first edition. The idea of holding the panel "Hinduism Reconsidered" was to evaluate critically current concepts and analytical frameworks used by scholars in their studies on Hinduism. The participants of the panel were therefore invited to contribute papers which either focus critically on theoretical approaches to Hinduism or illustrate their analytical parameters and concepts of Hinduism by a case study based on field work or literary sources.

Several issues arose from the papers and accordingly dominated the often rather heated and controversial discussions. Several papers define present-day Hinduism strictly as an "etic" construct. Von Stietencron calls into question from the point of view of comparative history of religions the very existence of Hinduism as one single religion. Thapar contrasts the diversity of religious sects of premodern Hinduism with the contemporary attempt to create a monolith religion and Frykenberg deals with the nineteenth century development of an "indigenous" concept of Hinduism and the, mostly external, factors which fostered this development. The second and largest group of papers approach the cosmos of Hindu beliefs and our notion of them through detailed micro-studies of specific institutions and cults and their religious and social contexts. It was this group of papers which brought Hinduism most directly and unfiltered by conceptual frameworks into the conference. A third group of contributions attempts to define Hinduism in "etic" terms which however are derived mainly from their own 'emic' studies on Hinduism.

Malik presents in his introductory paper a critical analysis of several recent "approaches" to Hinduism and distinguishes between two groups of theories. One tries to construct a "unity within Hinduism" even though its proponents differ in some cases quite radically in the way and extent to which they try to define this unity. Another group of non-essentialist theories emphasizes "historicity and multiplicity of meaning". Malik stresses the "somewhat dubious dimension" of this discourse as it forms "an integral part of a transcultural project of understanding and analysing non-western religions, societies and civilizations" which is still dominated by the perspective of the "West". The perpetuation of this cultural and cognitive hegemony may be partly due to the fact that non-western scholars participate in this discourse without creating "indigenous interpretative frameworks that contest those from the west". He concludes with the cautious warning that "plural worlds are tacitly sacrificed for the sake of a unitary, inter-civilizational language and culture" as the disciplines of the sciences and the humanities "tend to represent a single dominant tradition". In a global perspective Malik thus raises a similar point as Thapar does in her paper in the Indian context when she warns against a "Syndicated Hinduism" and its attempts to create a uniform and monolithic Hinduism at the cost of the diversity of India's cultures.

Von Stietencron's paper "Hinduism: on the proper use of a deceptive term" is certainly the most radical reconsideration of Hinduism in this volume. Denying that even the most important "essentials" of Hinduism, e.g. recognition of the Vedas, belief in reincarnation, the doctrine of *karman*, and the hierarchical caste structure apply to all sections of Hinduism, he argues that "Hinduism *in toto*, with various contradicting systems and all the resulting inconsistencies, certainly does not meet the fundamental requirements for a historical religion of being a coherent system; but its distinct entities [the so-called 'sects'] do. They are indeed religions, while Hinduism is not." He concludes that "what we call 'Hinduism' is a geographically defined group of distinct but related religions". Lumping together these different religions in one religion in our preconceived Western/Christian notion would be tantamount to combination of Judaism, Christianity and Islam which too are "cognate but distinct religions united by origin in the same region".

Romila Thapar's paper on "Syndicated Hinduism" is a critical evaluation of the attempts to restructure the indigenous religions of India "into a monolithic, uniform religion, paralleling some features of Semitic religions" which is tantamount to "fundamental departure" from the essentials of Hindu religions. These forces were operating at two historically interlinked levels. In the nineteenth century they defended, redefined and created Hinduism on the model of Christianity with an equivalent of monotheistic God, congregational worship, etc. In more recent times these endeavours culminated in the attempt to "bring into politics a uniform monolithic Hinduism" which Thapar calls *Syndicated Hinduism* and which is "projected by some vocal and politically powerful segments of what is referred to as the Hindu community". Thapar regards the changes which are caused and striven for by these forces as alarming because "the major asset of what we call Hinduism of the premodern period was that it was not a uniform monolithic religion" but a diversity of different religious movements which are deeply rooted in India's history. A major emphasis of her paper is therefore "to briefly review what might be called Hinduism through history and observe the essentials of the earliest beginnings and the innovations introduced over time".

Frykenberg, too, points out in his paper on "the emergence of modern 'Hinduism' as a concept and as an institution" that "there has never been [in pre-colonial times] any such thing as a single 'Hinduism' for all of India". But in contrast to von Stietencron he accepts the existence of a contemporary system of one corporate Hinduism. Therefore he emphasizes that the origins of "Hinduism" and its application as metaphysical instrument for socio-religious realities in India need to be better understood. According to Frykenberg "modern Hinduism is the product of a socio-political process—a process of reification which has evolved during the past two centuries and which lead to syndicated (R. Thapar) or organized religion". Of crucial importance were missionaries and their institutions, state sponsored Hinduism during colonial period and revivalist and fundamentalist movements. Frykenberg illustrates his thesis with detailed references to the development of modern Hinduism in south India.

Eschmann's paper deals with the so-called sects in Hinduism which were of crucial importance for the development of medieval Hinduism and its definition in modern times. Although it was published several years before Said's *Orientalism* it is an important contribution to the Orientalism discourse. It shows that the term "sect" was introduced into India in the heydays of early nineteenth century Orientalism. It was applied to the various *sampradāyas* of Hinduism which however were manifestations of orthodox Hinduism rather than heretical communities "cut off" from orthodoxy. Dividing Hinduism into countless "sects" stigmatized and weakened Hinduism in its encounter with the monotheistic Semitic religions. On the other hand, Eschmann points out that the model of Protestant sects as a "subsidiary organization of the churches" with all their educational, social and missionary activities had a deep impact on the formation of "Neo-Hinduism" and its various institutions, e.g. Brahmo Samaj and Arya Samaj. Their endeavour to create a uniform Hinduism with a monastic and "church-like" organization has to be regarded as another indirect result of wrongly labelling India's *sampradāyas* as sects.

Tripathi's paper is a critique of western views on Hinduism. As a major obstacle for a fruitful debate between Hinduism and Western religions he criticized the "self-invented" Eurocentric parameters and to define, e.g. religious system as "a true religion". These western criteria are largely responsible for the various Western misconceptions of Hinduism. Tripathi points out that most of the Western views on Hinduism (e.g. on caste system, polytheism and idolatry, etc.) are based either on ignorance or pre-conceived notions and "theories". At the same time Tripathi's paper holds up a mirror to Western religions and their (not so different) institutions and belief systems. A major emphasis of his paper is placed on the irrelevance of the polytheism *versus* monotheism controversy in the context of the various attempts to define Hinduism. Since Vedic times Indians believed "that there is only one single abstract source for the origin of this world". This spiritual monism is open to different expressions of faith and practice which gives Hinduism its enormous richness to "satisfy the needs and religious sentiments of all temperaments and all strata of society".

Wagle's paper on "Hindu-Muslim interactions in medieval Maharashtra" partly contradicts von Stietencron's and Frykenberg's theses. It proves the existence of a strong awareness of Hindu distinctiveness already in sixteenth century Maharashtra. Eknath's "Hindu-Turk debate" contains a vivid picture of what Eknath, one of the most famous Marathi bhakti poets, regarded as the essentials of

Hinduism. These were the Vedas and the Śāstras as highest authorities, image worship, the dominant role of the sādhus, rigid *jātī*/caste rules, prohibition of commensality between different castes and the fear of pollution. Wagle's paper demonstrates the enormous social and religious flexibility of Hinduism under Muslim rule. In this connection Wagle's analysis of late medieval Marathi historical writing is of particular interest. Texts like the *Paraśarāma caritra* show the Hindu writers of the eighteenth century tried to accommodate the nearly 400 years of Muslim rule in Maharashtra into the traditional system of Hindu Yugas, depicting some Muslim rulers even as benevolent protectors of Hindu temples. But Wagle's paper also confirms partly von Stietencron's and Frykenberg's theses, as it shows that even in Maharashtra with its strong "Hindu" awareness, a term like Hinduism never occurred. Instead *Mahārāṣṭra dharma* is mentioned in several contemporary texts.

The importance of Orientialist studies as a central factor in the emergence of modern Hinduism was often emphasized in the panel. In his paper "The concept of the ideal Brahman as an Indological construct", van der Veer criticizes the Orientialist perspective in the context of his studies of Ayodhya *tīrtha purohits* and Parry's study of Mahabrahmans of Benares. In Ayodhya, van der Veer was unable "to discern anything having the faintest connection with the cultural model of an 'ideal Brahman'", thus questioning the dominant historical role of Brahmans and their institutions as one of the major props of the perception of Hinduism.

The independence movement is yet another important factor which influenced the development of modern Hinduism. In his paper "Hinduism and liberation movement in India" Krüger points out that even the activities of socialist workers' unions led to a further strengthening of modern Hinduism. Certain values and taboos had to be mobilized in order to organize strikes by trade unions and even "radical agitators worked among the masses more on the basis of religious sentiments than on class issues". The outcome was the attempt to create a synthesis between socialist ideas and often extremely nationalistic, strongly Hindu revivalist thoughts,—an ideological blending unknown in earlier decades which, however, is still prevalent in certain circles of political Hinduism.

Bouez approaches Hinduism through an analysis of the cult of the snake goddess Manasa in Bengal. Questioning Dumont's strict construct of a pure/impure dichotomy he shows that the very concept of the goddess intertwines both levels through transgression. Manasa is at the same time a *devī* and a *rākṣasī*, a divine mother and a whore, exactly in the same way as blood sacrifices are very efficient and very impure. "Religious love", as known from many folk legends, is characterized by the same ambivalence as the one embedded in power and sacrifice: impurity is attached to them, yet life and regeneration are possible only through them. Bouez sees an equivalence between intense devotion to the divine *mā* and the ritualized transgression of kinship prohibition. Some of the most popular poets in Bengal owed their fame to a deliberately transgressive behaviour of their poetic figures.

Vertovec's paper on "Hinduism in diaspora" is a an interesting and necessary extention of the South Asia focus of the panel as it reminds us that Hinduism, though still an "ethnic religion", has become a world religion in the literal sense, extending from South Asia to South-East Asia and the Pacific and to South Africa, Europe and America. On the one hand, Hinduism in the diaspora apparently tends to produce new "regional varieties" of Hinduism largely depending on the origin of the majority of its Indian members. On the other hand, there is a general tendency of homogenization towards all-Indian or greater regional traditions at the cost of the many "little traditions" which had been carried into diaspora. Vertovec concludes that the phenomenon of Hinduism in diaspora represents an almost laboratory-like situation for analysing processes of retention and change. Time will show whether these changes are exemplary for future changes in India, too.

Three case studies follow. Mallison discusses the devotional songs of the Khojās, who are an offshoot of Nizārī Ismā'īlī sect. The songs were composed between the thirteenth century and the beginning of the twentieth century. They point to a remarkable capacity of Ismā'īlism to adapt the religious currents of their environment and show that the idea of "inclusivism" (P. Hacker) was not confined to Hinduism in medieval times. In the field of religion Hinduism formed what the author calls an "open culture". Agglutination to the Hindu social system was possible and acceptable to the Khojās. It was this Hinduism with which the Khojās seemed to have been more comfortable than with orthodox Islam. Hidden away in a footnote Mallison notices, however, modern readjustments of the Khojās towards Islamic expression in songs and prayers.

Vaudeville's study of the Lord of Govardhan is in line with her earlier insightful investigations of the Kṛṣṇa cult in Braj and Rajasthan. It is based on field research combined with evidence from a wide range of sources, such as iconography, the Purāṇas, the sectarian literature of the Vallabhites. The study reveals the complex and multi-layered history of a single cult which can, as she shows, be profitably compared with parallels in other parts of India. Vaudeville makes full use of the folk traditions and her study shows their importance in the making of a cult and, for that matter, in the making of Hinduism. Folk traditions are generally ignored, perhaps because they do not reflect on themselves for the benefit of outsiders, or are just not considered prestigious by sectarians and "modern" Hindus, whereas folklorists tend to study them in isolation.

Horstmann, in her study on *bhakti* and monasticism, dwells on the basic theological and ontological incompatibility of *saṃnyāsa* (salvation through complete cessation from the world) and *bhakti* (salvation bestowed through God's grace). Her point of departure is Louis Dumont's celebrated observation: renunciation is transcended by *bhakti* and internalized. The renouncer is socially absorbed in the life of the man-in-the-world. She finds that as far as the central concept of *bhakti* is concerned this statement is correct, but that it does not correspond to the reality of *bhakti*. At least *bhakti* in the individual struggle of the mystics is compatible neither with the communal life of the householder nor with that of the monastic order. Her arguments touch the pervasive tension in Hinduism, namely between involvement in the world and abstraction from it, and deserve to be explored in different contexts. For the ordinary devotee not bound by rigidity, institutionalized sectarianism and monasticism, the high claim of this goal may stimulate him to observe certain rules of renunciation, perhaps periodically, and combine it with his love for God and the hope for God's grace. This may bestow on him salvation, if not spontaneously "here and now", at least at the time of death.

In an attempt to avoid monolithic conceptualization and to include the whole spectrum of Hinduism, Sontheimer speaks of "components of Hinduism" which themselves are not monolithic, but form a continuum. He lists five: (1) The work and teaching of the Brahmans, (2) asceticism and renunciation, (3) tribal religion, (4) folk religion, and (5) bhakti. Hinduism cannot come within the purview of one discipline nor can it be explained on the basis of indigenous self-image of one group including those of the modern fundamentalists. Each component has to be seen for the time being in its own right and one has to examine which component dominates in a particular case, e.g. in a particular cult. Thus, for example, the Khaṇḍobā cult in Maharashtra mirrors the five components, and for that matter Hinduism, but it is folk religion which is emphasized in this particular case. The dynamic interrelationship between the components, which can take many forms, has existed over many centuries and has produced a religious network binding tribal religion as well as the highest philosophy into it. This network can hardly be denied the label "Hinduism" even if it does not fit a Western definition of religion.

If definitions of Hinduism have failed, do we have to reject the term Hinduism or deny it the status of religion? Eichinger Ferro-Luzzi puts the blame not on Hinduism, but on the "Western" conviction that all concepts can be defined, because they must have common attributes and clear-cut boundaries. After reviewing various more-or-less idiosyncratic statements of what Hinduism means, she proceeds to base her arguments on Wittgenstein's discovery that concepts are held together by a "complicated network of similarities overlapping and criss-crossing", in other words that "a family resemblance" may exist among their members. These polythetic concepts cannot be defined but only exemplified. Disparate aspects of Hinduism can thus be held together by sporadic overlapping similarities rather than by a common denominator at a higher or deeper level of analysis. The polythetic concept may be vague and the author supplements it with the concept of prototype. Prototype refers to a collection of the most frequent features reducing the vagueness of polythetic notion. Some characteristic features of Hinduism are prototypical in the sense of combining high frequency of occurrence and prestige.

Burghart sees "translation" as central to our scholarly understanding of Hinduism as well as to the perpetuation of Hinduism by Hindus themselves. Translation by Hindu ritual spokesmen like Brahmans or ascetics takes on a particular character in a specifically Indian structure of tradition. Their translation undercuts historiography by a notion of ontic identity. Other systems of belief and practice are brought into relation as successive or variant instances of an ever-present or central ontic source, namely Brahman. Conflict occurs not on the existence of the absolute, but on its identity, e.g. whether *nirguṇa* or *saguṇa*, its manifestation, and the relative value of the ways of attaining it. Translation by observers of Hinduism may be rather different. Scholarly understanding more or less accurately re-words the metaphysics of Hinduism, but in gaining access through texts to divine knowledge, scholars disregard the metaphysics of Hindu religious methodology. Objectivity, not divinity, facts, not divine realization, govern the codes of their translation. Their judgements and presuppositions can reversely be taken up by Hindu ritual spokesmen. The result is that Hinduism has acquired a human source of authority and appears in various guises, e.g. in the self-definition of Hinduism as the "timeless spiritual culture" of a people. The essential ("modern") characteristics of Hinduism, e.g. reverence of the cow, tolerance, etc., mark a people in their capacity as subjects of a culture. "Culture", rather than *dharma* has become the meta-term governing Hinduism's relation with the West.

Most of the authors show the flexibility of traditional Hinduism which may result in *coincidentiae oppositorum* or, rather, a delicate balance between opposites. They seem to presuppose that there is something like a common ground which may be an ontic source from the point of view of the Hindu ritual spokesmen. This common ground may have been created by the constant interaction between the different components of a religion. On the other hand, however, some authors point to discontinuities amounting nevertheless to a commonality of things *Indian.* Complete reversals of values can lead to an equivalence between the extremely high and the extremely low. Meaning used to be common and transcultural, as when Nepalese poets switch to Maithili to evoke an aesthetic feeling rather than a different meaning. Perhaps the very strength of Hinduism lies in the fact that it cannot be forced into watertight, inflexible categories.

Kiel HERMANN KULKE
November 1996

HINDUISM OR THREE-THOUSAND-THREE-HUNDRED-AND-SIX WAYS TO INVOKE A CONSTRUCT

Aditya Malik

I

Preliminaries

At the beginning of his introduction to the recently published Princeton University Reader on Indian Religions,[1] Richard Davis cites a famous dialogue from the *Bṛhadaraṇyaka Upaniṣad* as an example of one of the earliest statements on theological plurality found in Hinduism:[2]

> Then Vidagdha Śākalya questioned him, saying:
> "How many gods are there, Yājñavalkya?"
>
> He answered by (reciting) this invocatory formula:
>
> "As many as are mentioned in the invocatory formula in the hymn to the All-gods, —three hundred and three thousand and three (= 3306)".
>
> "Yes", he said, "but how many gods are there really (*eva*), Yājñavalkya?"
>
> "Thirty-three".
>
> "Yes", he said, "but how many gods are there really, Yājñavalkya?"
>
> "Six".
>
> "Yes", he said, "but how many gods are there really, Yājñavalkya?"
>
> "Three".
>
> "Yes", he said, "but how many gods are there really, Yājñavalkya?"
>
> "Two".
>
> "Yes", he said, "but how many gods are there really, Yājñavalkya?"

"One and a half".

"Yes", he said, "but how many gods are there really, Yājñavalkya?"

"One".

"Yes", he said, "but which are those three hundred and three and those three thousand and three?"

(*Bṛhadaraṇyaka Upaniṣad*: III, ix)[3]

This brief, but significant passage, not only appositely describes theological multiplicity, it also in many ways characterizes our understanding of Hinduism: it encapsulates the well-known theme of "unity in diversity" that has been nurtured and cherished by Indologists and laymen alike for decades. Simultaneously, it can be taken as a metaphor for the range and variety of "approaches" that have been postulated in the past for understanding Hinduism, and Indian Civilization. While some theories thus envision Hinduism in terms of "deep" or "overarching" structures played out by the workings of a single, dominant "theme" such as "caste", or *bhakti*, others see divergence, dissent, fracture and amorphism as decisive. Whereas some approaches stress the continuity of social and religious patterns and symbols through time, others emphasize disjuncture, historicity, and "context-sensitivity". Indeed, the pendulum of theories swings back and forth like the passage quoted above. Bewildered by variety we tend to use our modern versions of Occam's razor to trim the many thousand manifestations down to one, only then to revert back and ask: "but which are those three hundred and three and those three thousand and three?"

These "problems" not only face scholars attempting to arrange their materials, but also anyone trying to marshall together the diverse theories that have taken root since the late 50s.[4] In fact to write a review of "approaches" to Hinduism is almost as much of a challenging, if not daunting and perplexing task as is the study of Hinduism itself. In what manner are the multitude of materials, theories and methodologies native to the Sociology, Anthropology, Archaeology, "Indology" and History of India to be understood, reflected upon, "ordered" and "classified"? Is there coherence and agreement underlying the different perspectives? Or do the approaches diverge radically from one another?[5] Is coherence something to be sought after at all?[6] Which approaches have been central and which peripheral to the understanding of Hinduism—of Indian Civilization?

Given the abundance of approaches to Hinduism, I too, like the authors of diverse theories, must choose and select in my attempt to critically grasp and evaluate the "data". The purpose of this article thus is to provide a review of a *selection* of relatively recent formulation on Hinduism, and not a comprehensive survey of the literature.[7] Moreover, the structure of this article draws inspiration from the reflexive nature of Indian textual tradition.[8] While reflecting on "other" texts I also critically reflect on the text of which this article forms a part. What follows then has something of the substance of a "counter-text", and a "meta-text", that comments on its own "parent" text.[9]

But beyond various approaches—the merits and demerits of which can be weighed in a relatively forthright manner—the study of Hinduism has another, somewhat larger, and, at times, somewhat dubious aspect.[10] It forms an integral part of a *transcultural* project of understanding, analysing, and comparing religions, societies, and civilizations. In the latter context, approaches to Hinduism are bracketed within a framework of cultural, cognitive, and ideological encounters between the "West"[11] and India. This of course is not simply a "neutral", curiosity bound, "context-free", "scientific" endeavour. Rather, it is irrevocably anchored in a long-standing, on-going process of projecting, mirroring, confronting, eluding, denying, asserting—in short—fabricating the self and its other. As part of this larger "plot" of understanding and constructing non-Western religions, approaches to Hinduism often take for granted that categories such as "god, rite, myth, belief, essence, cult, sacrifice, worship" are universally valid. There is a tendency here to explain that which is alien through a framework which itself is alien to the "object" that demands making sense of. However, in a *phenomenology* of religion an alternative aim emerges: "to explain religion in terms, wherever possible, that the religion has developed for its own self-description and simultaneously to explain the religion to the external observer in his terms" (Piatigorsky 1985: 215). The challenge of studying Hinduism with these goals in mind is accentuated by the fact that "Indian religion is probably the only religion in the world which has been able to produce and develop within itself its own theoretical awareness of itself ... we are dealing with an object which has, as it were, already been investigated by itself" (Piatigorsky 1985: 252).

The study of Hinduism therefore implies a dual movement. On

the one hand it concerns approaches, theoretical models, and data pertaining to academic disciplines. On the other hand, it implicitly involves an evaluation of a non-Western religious tradition from the perspective of the "West". It entails an appraisal of the West's own and its "Other's" religious, cultural, and civilizational identity. In the context of the latter "Project", it remains to be seen whether Yājñavalkya's revelationary insight into the plurality of perspectives will win ground within the discourse of anthropological and Indological knowledge about India.[12]

II

APPROACHES AND DEFINITIONS

Approaches to Hinduism can sometimes explicitly or implicitly entail a definition of Hinduism. In this section I discuss four such perspectives on Hinduism. Two approaches are taken from this volume (von Stietencron and Sontheimer).[13] Two belong to recent and not so recent studies of Hinduism (B.K. Smith and M. Biardeau). What binds the work of these scholars together is their concern with constructing a unity within Hinduism. How they go about doing this differs significantly.[14] Their understanding of Hinduism diverges vastly although each make reference to similar terms and materials: *Bhakti*, Veda, "Brahmanism", *Tantra, Saṃnyāsa, Saṃpradāyas,* etc. Although Sontheimer, Biardeau, and Smith can be said to develop an holistic vision of Hinduism, they digress in terms of its structure and constituents. Von Stietencron while denying Hinduism existence as a single entity, asserts the coherent nature of individual religious traditions.

Biardeau's position is unequivocally stated in the first pages of her monograph: "Hinduism: The anthropology of a civilization" (1981/1994).[15] Her aim is to present a "unified account" of the culture and history of India, which according to her, is "a particularly favourable case for an undertaking of this sort" (p. 1). She continues to describe this "undertaking" as consisting in "taking literally the desire of a whole society ... to present itself as a well ordered whole.... Unity is sought at a deeper level ... on the basis of the explicit or implicit norms which every Hindu carries in his head ..." (pp. 2/16).[16] These "explicit or implicit norms" and "deeper" unity have their source in the Veda:

If he [the Hindu] mentions the Veda ... it is not as a corpus of very ancient texts, but above all as a universal reference ... it is around the [Vedic] revelation that we shall see taking shape a Hinduism which draws from it different readings.... So, without denying change over the centuries, one is nonetheless sent back to the complex, stable system of values, beliefs and practices that still underlines the surface variations and which alone makes them comprehensible. (pp. 14/16)

Biardeau's position is essentially non-historical and structuralist. The emphasis on the Veda as a "universal reference" brings her perspective closest to that of B.K. Smith's, who, in two publications (1989, 1994) conjointly states and builds on a "working" definition of Hinduism. The definition of Hinduism proposed by Smith simultaneously provides for an explanation of the internal ordering and workings of Hinduism. Hinduism, according to Smith, is less of an essence and more of a process whose referential base is the Veda:

Hinduism is the religion of those humans who create, perpetuate, and transform tradition with legitimizing reference to the authority of the Veda. (1989: 13f.)

This "legitimizing reference" is expressed through a "variety of strategies":

reflection (this is the Veda); restatement (this is based on the Veda); reduction (this is the *simplified* Veda); reproduction (this *enlarges* the Veda); recapitulation (this is the *condensed* essence of the Veda); and even reversal (the Veda is *based* on this).... The Veda is the prototypical canon that lends its authority to resembling counterparts. It is here, as we shall see, that some interesting possibilities open for rethinking Hinduism as a set of "Vedic" traditions. (1989: 29)

There is no denying that Smith's strategies of resemblance are valuable in tracing the development and nature of a specific body of texts found within the Hindu tradition. But does the corpus of written texts and philosophical perspectives cover all of Hinduism? Is Hinduism wholly encompassed by *Śrauta Sūtras, Gṛhya Sūtras*, Upaniṣads, Brahmaṇas, and the Sanskrit epics? Surely this is an astoundingly top-heavy perspective on the many-layered religious traditions of Hinduism, some of which take no note at all, whether consciously or unconsciously of the Veda, let alone use it a point of "legitimizing reference".

Moreover, Smith's "working" definition of Hinduism is strangely distanced from the social and historical contexts in which the texts he discusses arose. And, for some reason, he disregards the abundantly rich and complex streams of folk and tribal Hinduism with their oral literature, ritual performances, and forms of worship.[17] Do they all consistently refer to the Veda? Certainly one can talk of a continuum, but is the continuum structured by the options given by Smith? While a number of studies are careful to show the Vedic "antecedents" underlying the texts and rituals of certain folk cults,[18] they also emphasize that this feature is more part of a process of transformation of the structure of Hindu religion, rather than a conscious attempt at "legitimizing". It is the scholar who establishes the connections and disjunctures, not the devotee or the participant herself/himself. While Smith's work is undoubtedly valuable for understanding the conscious establishment of relations between outwardly unrelated entities (in this case texts) through the Vedic notion of equivalences, it does not account for qualitative aspects of folk worship and narrative that may represent a transformation of Vedic ritual and myth.

Two other approaches which are also tantamount to definitions of Hinduism are published in this volume. The articles I have in mind are, as previously mentioned, those of Heinrich von Stietencron and Günther-Dietz Sontheimer. By occupying the beginning and end of this book, they are not only spatially apart from one another—they deviate distinctly in their vision of Hinduism.

Von Stietencron begins by pointing out that generations of scholars "have struggled in vain to arrive at an acceptable definition of this religion or at least to outline the 'essential core' of Hinduism". The problem, according to him, lies in the false assumption that we are dealing with one religion: "our problems would vanish if we took Hinduism to denote a socio-cultural unit or civilization which contains a plurality of distinct religions"[19] (1989: 11). By doing so Hinduism would be cleansed of its seeming contradictions, inconsistencies, paradoxes and general obscurity. Later on, von Stietencron talks about the meaning of "our term religion" which "as a concept presumes cross-cultural universals in human nature". Furthermore, "it can only be applied to corporately shared *coherent systems* of world explanation and values; and the human actions directly related to these systems" (1989: 20). This definition is both derivative and applicable to Judaism, Christianity, Buddhism and Islam. Hinduism, however, "does not meet the fundamental requirement for a historical religion of being a coherent system; but its distinct religious entities do".[20]

Laudable as von Stietencron's intention is to place Hinduism on level with other "World Religions" so as to minimize confusion and facilitate communication, it still inadvertently falls within the previously mentioned framework of inventing (or, in this case, reinventing) the other in terms of one's own system of reference.[21] Rather than encountering Hinduism through its own categories and terms, von Stietencron assumes the universality of Western, Judeo-Christian concepts such as religion, culture, civilization, etc.[22] The result of this pursuit is, in my opinion, the fragmentation and compartmentalization of a many-layered, complex, and in Ramanujan's words, "context-sensitive" civilization.[23] By redefining Hinduism within the framework mentioned above, von Stietencron bypasses the opportunity provided by the hermeneutic enterprise which is true dialogue, and the creation of an authentic alternative to traditions of Western situated *Religionswissenschaft*, or for that matter anthropology, and Indology.[24]

The other "definitional" approach to Hinduism in this volume is that of Günther-Dietz Sontheimer. Rather than splitting up Hinduism into discrete religions, Sontheimer suggests a theory of constituent elements or components, as he calls them, that collectively make up Hinduism. Similar to von Stietencron, Sontheimer begins by stating that there is "no comparable theology or religious conceptual framework or even terminology in Western religions which completely fits what we call Hinduism" (1989:187). Radically different from von Stietencron he does not thereafter trim and cut Hinduism to suit the categories of Western civilization. Sontheimer's approach is "holistic" in a particular sense: it perceives *all* phenomena within the category of Hinduism as made up of "dynamic and fluid" interrelationship between the constituent components. His approach is not holistic in the sense Biardeau's is, who perceives of a *single* "deep structure" operating at all levels of tradition through the ideology of *Bhakti*. Of the five components[25] Sontheimer mentions, the most important in the context of the bulk of his later work is perhaps the category of folk religion. This emphasis arose—among other things—from a lack of interest in that area of Hinduism in the academic programme of Indology in Germany. Sontheimer was engaged in creating a new paradigm for Indological studies the implications of which meant a fresh formulation of what constitutes Hinduism. Turning away from a vertical, hierarchical placement of folk religion at the lower end of the scale which has classical religion at is pinnacle, Sontheimer urges us to view folk religion as an independent yet interactive domain of Hinduism:

> Once we have admitted the simultaneous order of the components we can proceed to investigate a particular institution of Hinduism or Hinduism as a whole in terms of dynamic interrelations among the components.

Sontheimer's approach is, like Biardeau's, ahistorical, since it postulates the existence of these components from the very inception of Hinduism.[26] Even less convincing, however, is his attempt to provide a structure to Hinduism by connecting social and religious categories of different kinds as though they belonged to the same level of discourse. Whereas the work and dealings of Brahmans is a category primarily denoting a corpus of ritual, mythological, and normative texts composed through the *agency* of a *social group*, namely the Brahmans (although here too there is great variety),[27] asceticism and renunciation are specific modes of religious behaviour involving the adoption of particular meditational techniques, transcendental philosophies, yogic practices, etc. The creation and moreover adoption of such a life-style by an individual is not bound to a social group. In fact in many cases, it requires the abandonment of social/caste identity. Tribal religion again is more of a social rather than a religious category—although the description of tribal religion offered by Sontheimer infringes in many ways on his description of folk religion and *Bhakti*. *Bhakti* is a religious category denoting an *experiential* mode of being, and of relating to the divine.[28] Folk religion, as the term itself implies, is neither a completely religious nor a completely social category. As will be briefly discussed later, the term carries its own special conceptual problems. Furthermore, by providing descriptive definitions or criteria for the components, which in turn *define* Hinduism, Sontheimer, albeit unintentionally, moves towards a kind of essentialism.[29] Indeed, this problem would seem to face every model that attempts to be "all-encompassing", either in terms of constituent elements or in terms of organizing principles.

Folk Hinduism

The position of *folk religion* within the study of Hinduism requires a section of its own in this article, just as folk Hinduism may require a niche of its own within the discipline.—Like Sontheimer, C.J. Fuller

(1992) too argues for the autonomous status of folk or "popular" Hinduism as he calls it: "... popular Hinduism is an authentic religion, equal in standing to any other.... In particular, the view that popular Hinduism is degenerate textual Hinduism ... is completely indefensible in the light of ethnographic evidence ..." (1992: 6). Fuller further distinguishes popular Hinduism from "textual Hinduism". Following Biardeau, however, he maintains a link between "textual" and popular Hinduism: "The sacred texts of Hinduism—and the concepts, ideas, and speculations contained in them—are often vitally important to popular religion.... Nevertheless, themes central in the scriptures are not always central in ordinary people's beliefs and practices ..." (1992: 5f).[30] It is this same continuum of folk and classical/textual traditions that has concerned Sontheimer. His answer to the question "What is folk religion?" is essentially fulfilled by providing a "checklist" of empirical data or what I would call "descriptive criteria".[31] Although such an empirical checklist is certainly an important phenomenological step forward, perhaps more is required in order to establish folk religion as a discourse within the discipline. In addition, a number of recent studies tend to show that folk religion more than the other components "spills over" into or "includes" the rest of Hinduism. What then are the boundaries of folk religion? How is it to be defined as an analytic, discursive sphere within Hinduism? If folk religion is where most of the practice occurs then isn't it the "primary" feature of Hinduism?

A number of these issues were taken up exactly eight years after the IXth European Conference was held in Heidelberg. At the XIIIth European Conference on South Asia held in Toulouse in August 1994, one of the panels was entitled "Folk Religion Reconsidered"[32] in consideration of the earlier panel entitled "Hinduism Reconsidered". One of the panelists accurately states the problem of folk religion, that has long been stamped with a peripheral status as an entity lacking the qualities of "high culture", devoid of philosophy and metaphysics:

> ... in fact, folk religion occupies an eccentric status. As a latecomer in the conceptual fold of Indian religious studies it forms a kind of residual, supplementary category. It is a category of a different kind than e.g., renunciation (sanyas), bhakti or even Brahmanism (priesthood), and is still to find a secure place in the broader context of religious studies: it has to be located within a framework which it shares with those other concepts, within a common system of reference.[33]

Fourteen papers were read at this panel, presenting a wide range of materials and questions concerning folk religion.[34] Some of the issues brought up were: the relationship between oral and written literatures, the position of folk religion vis-à-vis tribal and high religion, the interface of Brahmanism, *bhakti* and folk religion, the distinction between folk religion and popular religion, folk religion as the "middle ground", and the question whether the terms, concepts and categorization adequately describe the *experience* and perspectives of individuals and groups who are the *authors* of "folk religion". Most of the field studies tended to blur distinctions between "folk", "elite", and "tribal" religion leading to a "deconstruction" of essential categories. The emphasis on religious practice called into question the validity of analytical terms for distinguishing the boundaries of the concept on the ground.

Meaning, Historicity, and Non-essentialism

In the following section I discuss the position of three scholars (G. Eichinger Ferro-Luzzi, A.K. Ramanujan, and Romila Thapar), who together represent an alternative view to those put forward by Biardeau, Smith, von Stietencron, and Sontheimer. While not denying the unity Hinduism, they emphasize historicity, and the multiplicity of meaning. The perspective offered here is non-essentialist, post-structural, and non-evolutionistic.

Eichinger Ferro-Luzzi (this volume), does not deny the existence of Hinduism as a single entity. The problem as she sees it does not lie in the nature of Hinduism but in the search for clearcut, essentialist definitions. Supporting her argument through Ludwig Wittgenstein's notion of "family resemblance", Ferro-Luzzi points out that the specific features of Hinduism are held together by "a complicated network of similarities, overlappings, and criss-crossing". To this end she introduces the concept of the "polythetic prototype" to the understanding of Hinduism. Although Ferro-Luzzi's approach is successful in its perception of abstract terms within Hinduism, it nonetheless tends to ignore the question of meaning. For example, some of the terms she discusses, such as *saṃsāra, mokṣa, yoga, karma,* etc., are strongly situated in the Sanskritic/Brahmanical tradition. Nevertheless, they too do not necessarily bear a determinate or stable meaning. The connotations of these terms fluctuate according to changing arenas of religious, social, and historical actions, and processes. The definitional problem regarding Hinduism, therefore arises not only due to the fact that it is an undefinable, non-essentialist concept, but also because of the *indeterminacy* of cultural contexts spanning the last 3,000 years.

The issue of meaning is debated by A.K. Ramanujan in two seminal essays (1989, 1990). In these essays he introduces two principles that, with utter simplicity, describe and explain the many manifestations of Hinduism. In both essays he draws our attention to the notions of "context-sensitivity" and "reflexivity". With regard to "context-sensitivity" he writes: "I think cultures (may be said to) have overall tendencies ... to idealise, and think in terms of, either the context-free or the context-sensitive kind of rules.... In cultures like India's, the context-sensitive kind of rule is the preferred formulation" (1990: 47). For example, a term central to the "Hindu world-view", namely *dharma* carries meaning only with reference to specific spatio-temporal, and social applications. This feature is in strong contrast to the ideals of western democracy, which

> express both the universal and the unique, [and] insist that any member is equal to and like any other in the group. Whatever his context—birth, class, gender, age, place, rank, etc.[35]—a man is man for all that.... Yet societies have underbellies. In predominantly 'context-free' societies, the counter-movements tend to be towards the context-sensitive.... In 'traditional' cultures like India, where context-sensitivity rules and binds, the dream is to be free of context". (1990: 54)[36]

According to Ramanujan "reflexivity" is expressed in a variety of ways:

> awareness of self and other, mirroring, distorted mirroring, parody, family resemblances and rebels, dialectic, antistructure, utopias and dystopias, the many ironies connected with these responses, and so on (1989: 189). Ramanujan emphasizes that it is not only the so-called "'Great' and 'Little' Traditions that have to be included in this network, but also Bhakti, Tantra, Buddhism, Jainism, and also Islam and Christianity".

Romila Thapar's (this volume) purpose in the essay entitled "Syndicated Hinduism" is essentially twofold. Her first aim is to bring a historical dimension to the understanding of Hinduism. Analogous to Dumont/Pockock, whose plea was for a Sociology of India based on the confluence of Indology and Anthropology, Thapar urges an analysis of the "various manifestations of Hinduism from a historical perspective". This goal is coupled with the intention to show (a) the non-linear, non-essentialist, contesting nature of pre-modern

Hinduism, and (b) the political and economic dimensions of the creation and sustenance of religious symbols, icons, institutions, sects, and territories. This is specially pertinent with regard to the many pre-modern renunciatory movements that continue to flourish today (Daśnāmis, Nāths, Rāmānandīs and so on). The second aim of Thapar's paper is to point out the factors leading to the formation of what she calls "Syndicated Hinduism". The causes are to be found in the nineteenth and twentieth century encounters with Christianity and Islam, and the resulting attempt to "semitize" and essentialize Hinduism. The overt danger of such a trend lies in the emergence of fundamentalism, which in turns supports the motivations of certain groups striving for political power. Syndicated Hinduism is a phenomenon fed by the need of the large body of the middle-class in India:

> The emergence of a powerful middle-class with urban moorings and a reach to the rural rich would find it useful to bring into politics a uniform, monolithic Hinduism created to serve its new requirements. The ideology of Syndicated Hinduism remains an ideology endorsing the status of the middle-class.

By restricting itself to certain aspects of Hindu tradition Syndicated Hinduism actually contradicts its own purpose:

> Syndicated Hinduism claims to be re-establishing the Hinduism of pre-modern times: in fact it is only establishing itself and in the process distorting the historical and cultural dimensions of the indigenous religions and divesting them of the nature and variety which were a major source of their enrichment.

Thus, the economic and political drives that went hand in hand with the establishment of distinct, and sometimes opposing sects in pre-modern India, today are rapidly blurring distinctions, layers, multi-dimensions for the sake of a static, monolithic construction of middle-class politically motivated Hinduism.[37]

III

Hinduism and Hermeneutics

Before I end, let me try to briefly state what I think the study of Hinduism is all about. What are we up to when we examine, theorize, conceptionalize Hinduism? Indologists, anthropologists, archaeologists, sociologists, historians—"South Asianists"—are, I propose, first and foremost, a breed of interpreters. By engaging in the project of "understanding" Indian history, language, art, society, religion, and culture, we are deeply involved—consciously or unconsciously—in the practice of interpretation and representation, with it social, religious, and political consequences. The study of Hinduism one could postulate is therefore primarily a *hermeneutic activity*, that initially arose as it were in the historical and societal context of "Western" science, philosophy, literature, and importantly, polity. But the western hermeneutic "project" has, no doubt—because of historical and political processes marking the last two centuries—become a shared area of reason, in which individuals belonging to the culture being "examined" also participate in the practice of interpretation. However, underlying the seemingly "global"[38] nature of "scientific" activity, certain "prejudices" of interpretation and the specific historicity of frameworks of understanding drawn from the west continue to dominate.[39] As a consequence of this, the non-Western scholar, rather than being involved in the creation of "indigenous" interpretative frameworks that contest those from the West, tends to imbibe and internalize the hermeneutic project issuing from Western scientific traditions. Ironically, it thus takes McKim Marriott (1990: 1), a scholar from Chicago, to state: "It is an anomalous fact that the social sciences used in India today have developed from thought about Western rather than Indian cultural realities." While the Western, scholar has the pivotal status of a "translator"[40] translating the "strange" signs, beliefs, customs, norms, traditions, texts, culture of the other into the language of "his/her own" culture, the non-Western scholar engages primarily in the very opposite activity of translating "his/her own" culture into the language of the other, rather than, for example, functioning as an interpreter and spokesperson for "his/her own" culture. Taken from a Western perspective, the hermeneutic project derives "authenticity" from the fact that it is rooted in that civilization's history, philosophy, science, literature, art, and so on. But what of the non-Western scholar? Where do his/her efforts derive "authenticity" from? Is it derived primarily from participating in the ongoing concerns and issues facing the so-called "global" community of scientists? Or is it derived from the continuous critical disengagement from colonial categories and thought structures, and the ever finer distinctions between "emic" and "etic" concepts?

Can a non-Western anthropology and Indology ever arrive at an "authenticity" that lies beyond taking a critical stance toward Western positions?[41] What of the "dialogic" nature of the hermeneutic endeavour? Dialogic not just in the sense of a revision and reappraisal of the interpretative "horizon" within (Western situated) disciplines, but in the sense of a dialogue between contesting hermeneutic projects, and epistemologies?[42] Is it not really the non-Western scholar who is most strongly equipped to create and engage in a dual, "dialogic" project, enmeshed as it were, in the discourses of twin cultures speaking two "mother-tongues"?[43]

Cultural and Cognitive Hegemony

However, to engage in a conversation or a dialogue between disciplines, between cultures, between self and other, is to traverse a path strewn with hindrances. While enthusiastically affirming the project of understanding and communication, we tend to forget that authentic and nurturing dialogue is grounded in that lost activity called *listening*. Since genuine listening involves laying bare the *a priori* structures, values, and perspectives that determine how one enters into a dialogue with the other, it is listening that, in the very first place, opens the forum for discovering and rediscovering oneself and the other: "listening is not simply an activity of applied thinking in which, with a minimum amount of personal involvement, one occupies oneself with an object of study; it is, on the contrary, a procedure the authentic advancement of which depends upon one's ability to re-enter one's own self ..." (Malik, S.C. 1995: 265). The commonplace alternative to the possibility of entering into a dialogue via the act of listening, is of course a monologue. The driving force behind the "monologic (and monolithic) quest" is the creation of cultural, cognitive and ideological hegemony.[44] As Ramanujan (1989: 191), points out elsewhere, "Stereotypes, foreign views, and native self-images on the part of some groups all tend to regard one part ... as the original, and the rest as variations, derivatives, aberrations, so we tend to get monolithic conceptions.... Reflexivities are crucial to the understanding of both the order and diversity, the openness and the closures, of this civilization."—One can only add that reflexivities of a critical sort are essential if an understanding is to be reached not only of *a* civilization, but *between* civilizations and people(s) as well.

IV

Yājñavalkya's Hinduism

Yājñavalkya's dialogue—as a metaphor for the dynamics of the encounter between the "one" and the "many"—profoundly symbolizes some of the significant aspects of the materials presented here. Each of the theories and approaches put up for debate have, in one way or another, attempted to grapple with the theme of "unity in diversity". Each raises different questions. And, each bears its own special problems, issues, and solutions. —Biardeau proposes a "deep" structure organized around one unifying principle. Similarly, Smith sees textual Hinduism in terms of a single, critical reference point, that is consistently redefined. Von Stietencron juxtaposes Islam, Christianity, and Hinduism, suggesting that particular Hindu traditions or religious movements correspond to the structure of "World Religions". He proposes a "oneness" that paradoxically is nevertheless "fragmentary". Sontheimer, in contrast, unifies the fragments proposed by himself, by placing them in a framework of "dynamic and fluid" interrelationships. Ferro-Luzzi persuades us to see "family resemblances" that lend coherence to the apparent disjunctures, anomalies, and "indefinables" of Hinduism. Ramanujan organizes variety and multitude, not along the lines of a single reference point found within the religion such as *Bhakti* or Veda, but around an observed principle that accounts for meaning. In a similar vein Romila Thapar urges us to pay attention to the variety, and contesting nature of pre-modern Hinduism vis-à-vis the modern expressions of a unitary, reductionist, politicized Hinduism.

Finally, all of the above needs to be situated within a larger transcultural context of interpreting, understanding, appraising, and appreciating cultural and individual selves and their counterparts. Yet, it is at this juncture that Yājñavalkya's rich construction of reality seems to falter—global in spread, the disciplines of the sciences and the humanities tend to represent a single dominant tradition. Plural words are tacitly sacrificed for the sake of a universal, inter-civilizational language and culture. Perhaps it is more than ever imperative now that the "West" and the "Rest" begin to share in a truly reflexive weave of perspectives and counter-perspectives, in which complementarities, subversions, inversions, dialectics, criticisms, revaluations, and reconsiderings all partake of a "simultaneous order"[45] across the edges of cultures.

NOTES

I would like to thank Claus Peter Zoller and Martin Fuchs for their stimulating comments on the penultimate draft of this paper. I also thank the other members of our study circle in Heidelberg for thoroughly discussing the paper with me. I'm also grateful to Anne Feldhaus for taking time to read through a very early draft. Finally, I would like to express my gratitude to Hermann Kulke for giving me the opportunity to contribute to this volume in more ways than I could have imagined as a student research assistant in 1989 while preparing the camera-ready copy of the first edition.

1. D. Lopez (ed.), 1995.
2. Davis (1995: 5) himself describes Hinduism in the following manner: "The dominant feature of South Asian religious history is a broad group of interconnected traditions that we nowadays call 'Hinduism' ... Hinduism does not share many of the integrating characteristics of other religious traditions we conventionally label the 'world religions'.... That is not to say that Hinduism, lacking these supposedly 'essential' attributes of other religions, is therefore not a religion. Rather, the historical process by which Hindus and others have come to consider Hinduism a unitary religious formation differs markedly from other traditions."
3. Here trans. by Zaehner (1982: 57).
4. If there has been any one single "school" of anthropological and Indological thought that has deeply influenced the study of Indian civilization then this has certainly stemmed from monographs written at the University of Chicago. Terms and concepts generated here during the late 50s, 60s and 70s such as "great and little tradition", "text and context", "indigenous civilization", "village India", "universalization and parochialization", "folk to urban continuum", "orthogenetic development", etc., have merged into the commonplace language of South Asianists all over the world. These trends have simultaneously been responsible for the creation of new termionologies in the ongoing project of shedding ethnocentric biases in understanding and encountering Indian culture.
5. See, for example, Shulman (1989: 7) who, in this context, wrote in his short introductory essay to the first edition of this volume: "One thinks of the strangely incompatible visions of Dumont, Biardeau, Heesterman, and more recently, Marriott and Inden."
6. Perhaps coherence and agreement are not necessarily what the discipline requires. As Douglas R. Brooks (1994: 1120f.) comparing the work of J.C. Heesterman and Brian K. Smith points out: "... both writers *working from the same example* create significantly different and yet plausible theores: they draw out radically different interpretations that compel us to think about human nature and society in strikingly different ways". The case of "working from the same example" and yet arriving at different overall conclusions on the nature of religion, ritual, and of course Hinduism, is, as Brook sees it "*...the power of theory to generate meaning from shared data and example, rather than simply reiterating the point that data demands and even presumes theory to explain it*". The point is to

engage in a "conversation" so as to "reconsider what we do in terms of why we are doing it and think it should be done".

7. My selection is bound by many horizons, both academic and personal. Ultimately, such a review can only have justification in anticipation of a future review which by virtue of its own special horizons, builds on and modifies the present one. Then again, perhaps it is only this movement—of an authentic critical dialogue—that is the "saving feature" of all academic ventures in understanding the self and its other.
8. A.K. Ramanujan (1989: 189-90) in an enlighteningly delightful essay on the dimensions of "reflexivity" in Indian textual traditions outlines three ways in which texts may relate to themselves and each other: "(1) *responsive*, where text A responds to text B in ways that both define A and B; (2) *reflexive*, where text A reflects on text B, relates itself to it directly or inversely; (3) *self-reflexive*, where a text reflects on itself or its kind. The parts or texts in relation I may be called co-text, in 2, countertexts, and in 3, metatexts." He points out further that for native commentators and readers "... texts do not come in historical stages but form a 'simultaneous order,' where every new text within a series confirms yet alters the whole order ever so slightly, and not always so slightly".
9. Future philologists may want to call this article an "interpolation" because it tends to be critical of its "parent" text! I, for one, would prefer to believe that the boundaries of even such "hard-bound" texts like *Hinduism Reconsidered* are, within certain limits, open and unbound.
10. As critical studies (Said 1978; Inden 1990) have shown, the Western interest in the "Orient" or in India has been continuously shaped by hegemonic interests whether they be of a political or of an intellectual kind.
11. By this I do not limit myself to a particular geographical location. Implied is a "modern" rationalist/substantialist way of thinking, and of constructing reality.
12. See also section III.
13. From the many significant contributions to this volume, I have chosen to focus on the essays of von Stietencron, Sontheimer, and later Ferro-Luzzi, for the reason that they provide a more a less *comprehensive* theory/approach to Hinduism. I include Thapar's essays because it places the issues surrounding Hinduism both in an historical, and more importantly, in a contemporary context. This selection of authors does not in any way detract from the importance of the other essays.
14. This specially so in the case of Sontheimer, von Stietencron, and Biardeau/ Smith. The approaches of Smith and Biardeau converge in certain important respects.
15. I do not enter into great detail here, since Biardeau's writings are generally well-known.
16. With this statement Biardeau appears to deny the possibility of individual agency, or of societal and historical variation. The authority with which she speaks and her claim to able to *know* what "every Hindu carries in his head" is one of the more peculiar aspects of Western situated "monolithic" perspectives on India. What is lacking here is the intention to enter into a dialogue with the "object" of research—a dialogue which then may undermine the "deeper" unity that is proclaimed. (Cf. also Dumont's theory of caste as the *fundamental* institution of Indian society.)

17. In terms of Sontheimer's definition of Hinduism (see later), Smith's perspective tends to deny the autonomous character of the other four components of Hinduism which are not Brahmanical. In fact Smith's thesis is not only *about* the brahmanical perspective, it also embodies it. It generates an "external" view of Hindu tradition that concurs with an indigenous one. The problem here, as with Biardeau and Dumont, lies in treating this view as the fundamental or sole perspective. [Cf. V. Das' (1995: 24-41) critique of Dumount's position on caste.]
18. See, for example, Hiltebeitel (ed.), 1990.
19. Cp. this to Davis' position (see above) that we are dealing with a "broad group of interconnected *traditions...*" (emphasis added).
20. A variant of this idea is expressed in the following humourous story which was related to the author in Hindi:
Once a Muslim, a Christian, and a Hindu began quarrelling about whose God was the greatest and most powerful. In order to prove their respective God's strength, they climbed up onto a cliff and decided to jump down one after another. Whoever's God was most powerful would save him from crashing to death against the rocks below. First, the Muslim jumped off crying: "Ya Allah!" Before he could hit the rocks, Allah saved him and he survived. Then the Christian stepped off the cliff exclaiming: "O Lord, our saviour!" He too was protected from hitting the rocks. Now it was the Hindu's turn. He uttered God's names, but no one came to his rescue and he smashed against the deadly rocks. When he ascended into heaven, he went straight to Bhagavān complaining that the Muslim and Christian had been saved, so why not him? Bhagavān replied, saying: "Well, first you took Rām's name, then Sītā's, then Mahādev's, then Bhavānīs', then Kṛṣṇa's, then Rādhā's, then Hanumān's, and after that Ganeśa's. I was so busy changing my clothes, I didn't have time to rescue you!"
21. Cf. Piatigorsky earlier.
22. To this list could be added such terms and categories as: individual, social structure, ideology, classes, oppositions, authority, value, hierarchy, kinship, etc. (see Piatigorsky above, and Marriott 1990: 2, ftn. 4). Marriott further points out the "oppositional", "dichotomic" nature of Western thought structures that pervade the social sciences: "The Reformation split 'spirit' from 'matter', 'value' from 'fact' ... the Enlightenment further split 'mind' from 'body', 'philosophy' from 'biology', 'subjective' from 'objective' and 'idealism' from 'materialism' ... the industrial and political revolution split 'urban' from 'rural', 'individual' from 'society', and 'psychology' from 'sociology'.... The separateness of the domains of the present western ethnodisciplines from each other is itself one of the most striking and troubling characteristics...."
23. Ramanujan (1990). See section on "Meaning, historicity, and non-essentialism".
24. See Marriott (1990), and section III. Getting rid of ethnocentric biases is, however, a more complex and difficult task than one would imagine. Even after Malinowski in the 1920's pointed out that "the major aim of ethnology is to understand the native from his own point of view, his relation to his world" (cited in Singer 1972: 3), the discipline continues to experience vestiges and new varieties of ethnocentricism and orientalism that slip in unnoticed. The task of entering into a dialogue between people with different cultural backgrounds, and of moving from image to reality is far from complete. As

recently as 1989 in the first edition of the present volume David Shulman urged that "at some point our understanding of Hinduism should incorporate an Indian epistemology as well—a sensitivity to the inner world of the actors viewed of course with our analytic concerns" (Shulman 1989:9). In the face of the increasing politicization of Hinduism and its accompanying "semitization" (see Thapar, below, and this volume), it is of overriding importance that scholars pursue the creation of a discourse that highlights the many contexts, layers, components, and dynamic interrelationships at the intra- and interreligious levels. As the editors of this volume note in the very last line of the introduction: "Perhaps the very strength of Hinduism lies in the fact that it cannot be forced into watertight, inflexible categories."

25. The five components are: (1) The work and teachings of Brahmans, (2) Asceticism and renunciation, (3) Tribal religion, (4) Folk religion, and (5) *Bhakti*.
26. For example, see his discussion of the Khaṇḍobā cult (this volume). Sontheimer argues for a "folk" strand of the Veda represented by Rudra and the Vrātyas, who in turn can be discerned in the mythology and rituals related to Khaṇḍobā.
27. See, for example, van der Veer (this volume). Van der Veer examines the status of present-day Brahman priests vis-à-vis Orientalist/Indologist constructions of an ideal Brahman who is conceived of as either standing at the top of the hierarhcy of ritual purity or being a renouncer who has interiorized the sacrificial process of Vedic rites. Contrary to this view propounded by Indologists and sociologists such as Heesterman and Dumont, van der Veer points out the ambivalent nature of Brahmanhood.
28. Of course *Bhakti* cannot be unitarily defined either. Thiel-Horstmann (this volume), for example, points out the discrepancies that exists between a conceptual understanding of *Bhakti* and an observation of its actual pratice. Furthermore, she draws our attention to the linkages between *Bhakti* and renunciation (*samnyās*), which Sontheimer posits as two separate components.
29. The same can be said of any kind of typologies or taxonomies of folk religion, *Bhakti*, renunciation, etc.
30. In the concluding pages of his book, Fuller states that popular Hinduism is primarily: "the religion of a multitude of gods and goddesses, whose principal attribute is their power.... Popular Hinduism is polytheistic; its numerous gods and goddesses are consistently represented as distinct beings. At the same time different deities are often seen as alternative forms of a single deity, and in some contexts every Hindu will say that ultimately all gods and goddesses are one". (Fuller 1992: 253)
31. See Sontheimer's discussion of folk religion in this volume. On problems related to "descriptive" and "analytic" criteria, see A. Malik (*draft*).
32. The questions posed in the circular for the panel were:
    "Is there something in social reality which can be identified as 'folk religion' or does the term denote primarily the perspective of the outside observer?"
    "How should we evaluate different 'components' or 'levels' of Hinduism as proposed in academic discourse?"
    "How can we conceptualize the relationship between text and practice? How do texts determine social practice and vice versa?"
33. Martin Fuchs (*draft*).

34. The proceedings of the panel are to be published in a volume tentatively entitled *Folk Religion Reconsidered* (H. Brückner and E. Schoembucher, eds.).
35. Compare the notion of "context-free", with Kant's conception of the categorical imperative.
36. If Western society tends towards the "context-free", so does Western science tend towards the search for "universal" categories, in many cases unitary theories, consistency, logical connectedness, and, alas, also reductionism.
37. In fact this is analogous to the interpretation conducted by certain historians and anthropologists/Indologists of Indian civilization. For the first time Hindus themselves are involved in an "all-encompassing" interpretation of what it means to be a Hindu.
38. As Gemma C. Fuimara (1990) points out "Western thought, and it has covered the entire globe, has failed to grasp the need to begin to understand and abide by the listening process, as a primary and indispensable requirement for coexistence. In a language which pays homage to speech one arrives at the point of concealing any culture of listening that might possibly be wedded to it". (Quoted in Malik, S.C. 1995: 247)
39. See, for example, *Thesis Eleven* (1994).
40. For the position of the scholar as "translator", see, for example, Burghart (this volume).
41. In an eye opening account of Dumont's sociology of India, V. Das (1995: 34) quotes a passage in which Dumont addresses this question in relation to the work of the Indian sociologist A.K. Saran: "But when Dr Saran deplores the fact that Indian scholars have merely 'imitated' the Westerners in the matter of sociology, the statement is ambiguous. Does he mean that Indian scholars could have made an original contribution within the framework of ('Western') sociologies and have failed to do so—that may be true—, or does he mean that they should have built up a sociology of their own, basically different from (Western) sociology, in which case he would be entirely wrong? A Hindu sociology is a contradiction in terms ... (Dumont 1966: 23)".
42. Berg and Fuchs (eds. 1993: 77-96) emphasize that a dialogue is necessary that respects distinctions and avoids a tendency towards the construction of a "global identity". What a reconsideration of Western representational modes requires then is a critique arising from non-Western epistemological and representational traditions.
43. While critically discussing some similar issues V. Das (1995: 25) directs our attention to the fact that "... there is a peculiar double bind which traps the non-Western anthropologist who wishes to relate experience and representations, gained through membership of her own society, when constructing the anthropological text ... a frank engagement with the problem is necessary if the inventories of our subject are to include modes of knowing that are different from those within classic models of studying 'other' societies".
44. See, for example, S.C. Malik (1995: 241f.) who maintains that "... non-listening has given rise to two types of conceit, one of nations and the other of scholars who believe that what they know is as old as the world. The tacit ubiquitous belief that recent Western logic represents the most reliable cognitive standpoint appears to charaterize worldwide culture."
45. See Ramanujan (1989: 190), and note 8.

REFERENCES

Berg, E. and M. Fuchs (eds.) 1993. *Kultur, Soziale Praxis, Text. Die Krise der ethnographischen Repräsentation.* Frankfurt: Suhrkamp Verlag.

Biardeau, M. 1981/1994. *Hinduism: The anthropology of a civilization.* Delhi: Oxford University Press.

Brooks, D.R. 1994. The thousand-headed person. The mystery of Hinduism and the study of religion in the AAR (American Academy of Religion). In *Journal of the American Academy of Religion.* 62, 2, 1111-26.

Brückner, H. and E. Schoembucher (eds.) *Folk Religion Reconsidered.* Proceedings of a panel of the XIIIth European Conference on Modern South Asian Studies, Toulouse, Aug. 1994 (forthcoming).

Burghart, R. (*this volume*). Something lost, something gained: Translations of Hinduism.

Das, V. 1995. *Critical events: An anthropological perspective on contemporary India.* Delhi: Oxford University Press.

Davis, R.H. 1995. Introduction to *Religions of India in practice.* Donald S. Lopez, Jr. (ed.). New Jersey: Princeton University Press.

Dumont, L. 1966. A fundamental problem in the sociology of caste. In *Contributions to Indian Sociology,* 9, 17-33.

Eichinger Ferro-Luzzi, G. (*this volume*). The polythetic-prototype approach to Hinduism.

Fuchs, M. (*draft*). Discursive practices and experiential attitudes: Difficulties in conceptualizing folk religion. Paper read at XIIIth European Conference on Modern South Asian Studies, Panel on "folk religion reconsidered". Toulouse, Aug. 1994.

Fuimara, G.C. 1990. *The other side of language—A philosophy of listenting.* London: Routledge.

Fuller, C.J. 1992. *The camphor flame: Popular religion and society in India.* New Jersey: Princeton University Press.

Hiltebeitel, A. (ed.) 1990. *Criminal gods and demon devotees.* New York: State University of New York Press.

Iden, R. 1990. *Imagining India.* Oxford: Blackwell Publishers.

Lopez, D.S. (ed.) 1995. *Religions of India in practice.* New Jersey: Princeton University Press.

Malik, A. (*draft*). Criteria for cults? Reflection on Devnārāyaṇ in Rajasthan. Paper read at XIIIth European Conference on Modern South Asian Studies, Panel on "Folk religion reconsidered". Toulouse, Aug. 1994.

Malik, S.C. 1995. *Reconceptualizing the sciences and the humanities: An integral approach.* Delhi: Manohar Publishers.

Marriott, M. 1990. Introduction to *India through Hindu categories.* M. Mariott (ed.). New Delhi: Sage Publications.

Piatigorsky, A. 1985. Some phenomenological observations on the study of Indian religion. In *Indian religion.* R. Burghart and A. Cantlie (eds.). London: Curzon Press.

Ramanujan, A.K. 1989. Where mirrors are windows: Towards an anthology of reflections. In *History of Religions.* 28/1: 187-216.

———. 1990. Is there an Indian way of thinking? An informal essay. In *India through Hindu categories.* M. Marriott (ed.). New Delhi: Sage Publications.

Said, E. 1978. *Orientalism.* New York: Pantheon.

Singer, M. 1972. *When a great tradition modernizes.* London: Pall Mall Press.

Shulman, D. 1989. Reconsidering Hinduism or: What I might have said (in part) if... In *Hinduism Reconsidered.* First edition.

Smith, B.K. 1989. *Reflections on resemblance, ritual, and religion.* New York: Oxford University Press.

———. 1994. *Classifying the universe: The ancient Indian varna system and the origins of caste.* Delhi: Oxford University Press.

Sontheimer, G.D. (*this volume*). Hinduism: The five components and their interaction.

Stietencron, H. von (*this volume*). Hinduism: On the proper use of a deceptive term.

Thapar, Romila (*this volume*). Syndicated Hinduism.

Thesis Eleven, No. 39, 1994. India and modernity: Decentring Western perspectives. Massachusetts Institute of Technology.

Thiel-Horstmann, M. (*this volume*). Bhakti and Monasticism.

van der Veer, Peter (*this volume*). The concept of ideal Brahman as an Indological construct

Zaehner, R.C. 1982. *Hindu scriptures.* London: J.M. Dent and Sons, Ltd.

HINDUISM: ON THE PROPER USE OF A DECEPTIVE TERM

Heinrich von Stietencron

I

Ever since the term "Hinduism" was introduced in the sense of "the religion of the Hindus", scholars have struggled in vain to arrive at an acceptable definition of this religion, or at least to outline the "essential core" of Hinduism. Those scholars who based their judgement on brahmanical doctrines of the Vedic, Vedāntic and Smārta traditions neglected the essentially different religious experience of a large sector of the Hindu society: those practicing the so-called "popular religion" or "folk religion" which spreads all over rural India and into the suburbs of cities and, partly through members of the serving castes and partly through personal inclination or family tradition, into many homes the high-caste Hindus. But folk religion again is not uniform. It varies from region to region, from deity to deity. Those other scholars who tried to base their judgement on *bhakti* theology of Purānas and Āgamas had access to larger sections of popular religion, but they failed to do justice to the Vedic tradition, to parts of *smārta* religion,[1] and to the numerous tribal religions which have again distinct features of their own. Still others, realizing that the religious beliefs and practices of the Hindus were too divergent to constitute a coherent religious system, believed that the social structure, the caste or *varṇa* system, was the basic unifying factor of Hinduism. This approach received widespread recognition. Yet, by relying on sociological categories alone, they ended up in making Hinduism a social system and failed to grasp, and to do justice to its religious dimension.[2] Lastly, there are those who discover basic patterns of Indian thought which create the structural unity of

"Hinduism".[3] They make an important and valid point. But such basic patterns of thought are usually common to more than one religion. They are characteristic of whole cultures and may even cross the borders of those. Christianity and Islam, for example, are both built on the same basic patterns derived from Greek and Jewish traditions of thought. And in South Asia, Jainism, Buddhism and even minor sections of Islam largely share those patterns which are supposed to constitute "Hinduism".

Why is "Hinduism" so difficult to define? It is because we always try to see it as *one* "religion". Our problems would vanish if we took "Hinduism" to denote a socio-cultural unit or civilization which contains a plurality of distinct religions.

The very term "Hindu", from which "Hinduism" is derived and which was taken over by western administrators, scholars and merchants from the Persian, caused misunderstandings in the West. The word is the Persian variant of Sanskrit *sindhu*, the Indus river, a word applied already in the Avesta both to the river and to the country through which the Indus flows. In the plural, it denotes the population living in that region: the Indus people, the Indians. This meaning is attested in Old Persian cuneiform inscriptions from the time of Darius I who expanded his realm to the Indus in 517 B.C.

For more than 1000 years the word Hindu (plural) continued to denote the Indians in general. But when, from A.D. 712 onwards, Muslims began to settle permanently in the Indus valley and to make converts among low-caste Hindus, Persian authors distinguished between Hindus and Muslims in India: Hindus were Indians other than Muslim. We know that Persian scholars were able to distinguish a number of religions among the Hindus.[4] But when Europeans started to use the term Hindoo, they applied it to the non-Muslim masses of India without those scholarly differentiations. Most people failed to realize that the term "Hindu" corresponded exactly to their own word "Indian"[5] which is derived, like the name "India", from the same Indus river, the *indos* of the Greek. The Hindu, they knew, was distinct from the Muslim, the Jew, the Christian, the Parsee and the Jain who were all present in the Indian coastal area known to western trade. Therefore, they took the term "Hindu" to designate the follower of a particular Indian religion. This was a fundamental misunderstanding of the term. And from the Hindu the term "Hinduism" was derived by way of abstraction, denoting an imagined religion of the vast majority of the population[6]—something that had never existed as a "religion" (in the Western sense) in the consciousness of the Indian people themselves.

It is worth remembering the relatively recent origin and the peculiar career of the term "Hinduism", and to have a look at the various predecessors of this term.

When medieval European writers from the twelfth century onwards became increasingly interested in fabulous India they were strongly inspired by the idea that beyond the dangerous Muslim power in the East, beyond Persia, there was another Christian community led by the legendary king John; and the early Christian merchants went East in search not only of spices, but also of fellow Christians. Some were indeed discovered on the Malabar coast (and castigated for aberration because they followed the Syrian rites). But the majority of the inhabitants of India were found to be heathens and designated by the current words for heathens: Latin *gentiles*, Portuguese *gentio*, and later by the latter's anglicised form *gentoo* (for which Hobson-Jobson cites examples from A.D. 1548 to 1837,[7] while the Dutch and German spoke of Heyden (Heiden).

The heathen, according to the dominant Christian world view in the middle ages and after, belong all to one and the same religion inspired by Satan, which raises its head in all continents in varying forms. Even as late as 1711 when Bartholomäus Ziegenbalg wrote his famous book on the religion of the Malabar heathens, he repeated the traditional view that the people of the entire earth are divided into four major religions: Jews, Christians, Mahomedans and Heathen (Caland 1926: 9). Among the heathen who are all children of the devil, the Indian heathens were considered to form one sect out of many (e.g. American, African, etc.). Ziegenbalg who studied the pagan religion on the Malabar coast, used the term "Malabarisches Heidentum" to distinguish this sect of the heathens from those in Africa and elsewhere (Caland 1926: 23 and passim).

A different early designation of the Hindus was "Banians", a name derived from the merchant community of northern India. It was sporadically used in seventeenth and eighteenth century. "A discovery of the sect of the Banians" was published by Henry Lord at London in 1630. The term was used by Dellon (1700: 94) and continued to be quoted to the end of the eighteenth century (v. Wurmb 1797: 356). But the dominant word in this period was "Gentoo" (= heathen), and it forced people to think of the differences they found among various groups of "Gentoos" in terms of *sectarian* differences. There was no other choice because heathen all over the world formed only one religion. There was no room, in this concept, for more than one religion among the heathen of India.[8]

In the eighteenth century, the term "Gentoo" was gradually replaced by the term "Hindoo". But the word simply supplanted the earlier one without changing its implications: all Hindus were thought to belong to one and the same religion. It was on the basis of this understanding that the term "Hinduism" was created in the nineteenth century in order to give a name to the religion of the Hindus.

Three different phases mark the further career of the term Hinduism. In the nineteenth century it was applied only to the living religion of the Hindus as based on the epics and Purāṇas, on the "sectarian" Āgamas and Tantras, also as regional folk traditions, and characterized largely by the devotional approach of *bhakti* and by the worship of images in daily rituals. Vedic religion, when it came to be explored with great enthusiasm, was taken to be something different, more pure, less overgrown by the jungle of superstition. And between the Vedas and Hinduism some scholars placed "Brāhmaṇism" as a religion marked by priestly speculation and priestly dominance, a religion that found expression in the Brāhmaṇas, the Upanisads, the Sūtras and Smṛtis.

Throughout the nineteenth century the term "Hinduism" was used in such restricted sense; it was applied only to a section in the historical sequence of Indian faiths. But the strong emphasis placed on the Vedic and Vedāntic heritage by the Neo-Hinduistic reform movements in the second half of the nineteenth century and in the twentieth century, as well as the growing awareness of the continuity of certain elements in the tradition, could not remain without impact on the scholarly terminology. Therefore, in the twentieth century, "Hinduism" gradually came to encompass Brāhmaṇism and Vedic religion as well.[9]

Finally, the discovery and exploration of the Indus valley civilization opened up still more remote horizons. Many speculations arose about the possible roots of Tantricism, Śāktism and Yoga in the Indus valley culture. Unfortunately, definite knowledge about the religion of the Indus civilization is rather scarce, but some continuation of elements from the Indus culture period into much later times could be shown to have existed. As a result, "Hinduism" is now often used to denote something like "the religion of the Hindus from the Vedic (and pre-Vedic) period to the present day".

II

Terms influence our thinking to no small degree. The term "Hinduism" causes us to search for, arrange, and interpret data about the religions of the Hindus in such a manner that they fit into the preconceived pattern of a coherent religious system. It is, indeed, our notion of the oneness of Hinduism which finally leads us to produce highly complex explanations or theoretical constructions (needed in no other religion with the possible exception of Daoism) in order to confirm the postulated unity in spite of so many inherent contradictions.

There is hardly a single important teaching in "Hinduism" which can be shown to be valid for all Hindus, much less a comprehensive set of teachings. What some groups of Hindus believe to be true is contradicted by statements held to be true by other groups of Hindus. Animism and polytheism, pantheism, panentheism and henotheism, dualism, monotheism and pure monism exist side by side. The elaborate ritual of the brahmanical *karmakāṇḍa,* aimed at purifying man and sacred space for communication with the divine, is drastically set off against the ritual of male or female shamans aimed also at communication with gods and suprahuman beings, but achieved through trance and possession of the expert by gods or spirits. Both these types of communication are again in essence different from the communication with God as achieved by the *bhakta,* the devotee whose essential link with the deity consists precisely in *bhakti* which is itself both a fruit of effort and a gift of god.

Other essential differences are equally striking. Continence and chastity (*brahmacarya*), rigorous asceticism, and the complete withdrawal from sense objects in meditation and yoga stand in contrast with orgiastic ecstasy as another legitimate means for god-realization. While the thick blood of cocks, goats and buffaloes continues dripping from the sacrificial altar of some Hindus, others proclaim strict non-violence and strongly denounce even ritual killing. Many believe in *karma* and reincarnation, but others are unaware of these concepts. In patent opposition to late Vedic scriptures and the *smṛtis* which justify the caste system and the exclusion of śūdras and women from sacred knowledge, some of the major *bhakti* religions fought for centuries against caste restrictions, accepted women and śūdras and even outcastes as devotees of God and rejected the validity of the Vedas.[10]

More important: the god whom one Hindu adores with full devotion as the supreme deity and as the only Lord of the universe—that same god may be considered as inferior or even totally insignificant in the eyes of another Hindu. Instead, he may either worship an altogether different god as the highest Lord, or he may reject all the gods as fictitious projections of ignorance, and therefore irreal and perishable like the world of objects around us. Moreover, the different religious groups use entirely different sets of holy scriptures said to be revealed by their highest god or foremost *ṛṣi*. They worship with different rituals and with different prayers, and they have, in some essential points, different views of cosmogony, anthropology and of the nature of salvation.

These differences have long been known. Yet the unifying term "Hinduism" and the peaceful coexistence of the Hindus jointly favoured a tendency to neglect the differences and to emphasize the common elements. The very fact that Hindus revering different gods live side by side without clashes seemed to suggest an overall polytheistic structure, combined with a partial monistic superstructure for the intellectual elite.[11] This notion seemed justified, considering that Hindus may freely choose their *iṣṭadevatā*, the deity to whom they wish to devote themselves fully. They are also free to change their favourite deity in order to find the most beneficial path for themselves. The performance of rituals for different gods is possible within the same family and even by the same person. After all, wasn't the Vedic tradition polytheistic anyway? And what do the differences between gods matter, if brahman is above and beyond all forms?

These or similar arguments contributed to support the Westerners' preconceived notion that it was *one* religion they were dealing with. Since they were used to the Christian tradition of an absolute claim for only one truth, of a powerful church dominating society, and consequently of fierce religious and social confrontation with members of other creeds, they were unable even to conceive of such religious liberality as would give members of the same society the freedom, by individual choice, to practise the religion they like.

As a result, Western students saw Hinduism as a unity. The Indians had no reason to contradict this: to them the religious and cultural unity discovered by Western scholars was highly welcome in their search for national identity in the period of struggle for national union. Moreover, translating our word "Hinduism" into their own terminology, they conceived of it as equivalent to the Hindu *dharma*, often referred to as *sanātana dharma* or eternal *dharma* in writings of the nineteenth and twentieth century. *Dharma* or *sanātana dharma* is that universal order of things, by which man is born into a certain social stratum and into one of the regional or even local religious traditions and has to behave accordingly. It is the normative basis of behaviour in consonance with cosmic order and it operates on all levels of worldly existence. Thus *dharma* may refer to the duties of caste (*varṇa*) and stage of life (*āśrama*), to the nature and tasks of male and female, or to the religious practice of various groups such as *bauddha dharma, vaiṣṇava dharma, śaiva dharma,* etc. (Note that the Indians use the same term *dharma* for all three while we use "religion" for Buddhism and "sect" for Vaiṣṇavism and Śaivism.) *Dharma* operates also in the animal and plant kingdom and in the laws of nature. It is the *dharma* of plants to grow according to their species and to serve as food for animals. Following their *dharma* the beasts of prey kill other living beings. And it is the *dharma* of fire to annihilate, to transform, and to carry oblations to the gods. Obviously, *dharma* has a much wider semantic dimension than our word "religion". Therefore the Indian acceptance of the term "Hinduism" as equal to Hindu *dharma* cannot serve to prove the existence of a "religion" called Hinduism.

In the search for the "essentials" of Hinduism at least three were considered to be universally accepted by all "sects" of Hinduism:

— the recognition of the Vedas as beginningless and authoritative Holy Scriptures,
— the belief in reincarnation and the doctrine of *karman*, by which one's own acts determine one's future life, and
— the hierarchical social structure, the *varṇa* and caste system which was sanctioned by brahmanical *smṛti* and seemed to dominate in all walks of life.

Yet none of these so-called fundamentals of Hinduism applies to all religions in Hinduism.

Major sections of the *bhakti* religions have, for many centuries, rejected the authority of the Veda. This is true for the Vaiṣṇavas and important parts of the Śaivas and Śāktas, as well as for the devotees of Kumāra and Sūrya, as is testified by numerous texts. A single song in praise of Kṛṣṇa (or Śiva, Devī, etc.) has, according to many texts, more value than hundreds of the great Vedic sacrifices, and the entire Veda cannot even compare in value with the sixteenth part of one's own sacred scriptures.[12] Of course, when an increasing number of brahmans turned to these *bhakti* faiths[13] and became devotees of Viṣṇu, Śiva, etc., they brought with them all their Vedic learning. Brahmans did play an essential role in the literary expression of *bhakti* religions. But what they introduced, in course of time, into Purāṇic and Smārta and Āgama religious literature was neither a genuine Vedic polytheism nor the Vedic sacrifice; it was mainly the *saṃskāras,* the protective and initiating sacraments of the *smṛti* tradition which accompany human life from conception to death,[14] and Vedic technical scholarship. The Veda itself had astonishingly little impact on high-class and middle-class *bhakti* religion. We should also remember that Vedic religion was—at least from the Brāhmaṇa period onwards—totally inaccessible to śūdras and outcastes who form the vast majority of the Hindus: they were, according to orthodox law, prohibited under penalty of death to hear the Veda or to take part in Vedic rituals and sacraments. It is thus obvious that at no time in history the Vedas were the sacred scripture of *all* Hindus.

Nor was the doctrine of reincarnation generally accepted. It did not yet exist, for instance, in the Veda itself, though its germinal ideas may be traced in the latest section of the Vedas and in the Brāhmaṇa literature. Certainly it did not form part of the Vedic religion proper, which was, after all, an important Hindu religion. Later, the reincarnation theory was not accepted by the materialist school of thought.[15] And since it is a doctrine for the educated rather than for the simple people, it has even today little influence on the life of a large section of the population in rural India and even less or none in semitribal and tribal areas.

As to the caste system, there were always important groups who bitterly opposed it. It was precisely the attempt to abolish caste barriers against the religious integration of śūdras, women and outcastes that attracted large masses to Viṣṇuism and Śivaism. Viṣṇuism has been open to all castes until late in the middle ages. The Liṅgāyats or Vīraśaivas abolished every caste distinction. Several Śākta and Śaiva sects with "left-handed" ritual continuously ignored caste restrictions; and the attitude of Mahātmā Gāndhī who called the outcastes *harijan* (people of Viṣṇu) and who denounced casteism corresponds entirely to the Vaiṣṇava tradition. But even without this historical evidence it would not be wise to use caste as the determining factor for Hinduism. Sociological definitions only grasp the social margins of religions. Besides, the very fact that the caste system pervades also the Christian and Muslim sectors of Indian society proves that it is no suitable criterion for identifying Hinduism as a religion.

When the search for "essentials of Hinduism" failed, and when it became obvious that it was impossible to harmonize the major conflicting elements of theory and practice, one more suggestion to explain Hinduism was advanced. It claimed that Hinduism was not a religion, but "a way of life". This solution to the problem is an ingenious effort to escape from the impossible task of grasping the "religion" Hinduism. Maybe it is not far from truth. But as a way of life, as a culture or civilization, Hinduism should not be compared with other religions, but with other ways of life and other cultures or civilizations. This solution could be improved and retain its connection with religion, if formulated thus: Hinduism is a civilization formed and enriched by a group of Hindu religions which developed a particularly liberal way of coexistence and interaction between themselves.

III

In books on Hinduism, the differences and contradictions of Hindu belief systems are generally treated as doctrinal variants of different sects, while "Hinduism" is considered to be one of the major religions of the world. It is shown by statistics to rank third in the number of its followers after Christianity and Islam.[16]

But the differences already mentioned are far too fundamental to be justly described as sectarian variants of one and the same religion. Different ritual, different theology, different holy scriptures and different highest gods: it is obvious that "Hinduism" embraces differences at least as explicitly fundamental as those between Judaism, Christianity and Islam, along with other minor religions and popular cults of the Near East. If we were to subsume all these under one umbrella term as various "sects" of one Near-Eastern religion, this would give us a proper equivalent to Hinduism. But a cry of outrage from all of these religions would stop us: they would never agree to be reduced to mere sects. They never learnt to develop that measure of tolerance which is practised and—more important—theologically or anthropologically justified in Hindu religions.[17] Therefore our choice is limited. If we accept Judaism, Christianity and Islam as "religion" and if, compelled by intellectual honesty, we want to apply the same term to comparable phenomena, we cannot avoid concluding that there are a number of different "religions" existing side by side within "Hinduism".

It could be argued that it is precisely the multiplicity of notions and of approaches to the divine, the ever-changing pattern of so many paths for the individual to choose for his progress towards prosperity and liberation, which is the characteristic feature of Hinduism and which constitutes its peculiar attractiveness. This is perfectly true. But nothing is taken away from this justified picture of interacting religious multiplicity and liberality if we conceive of "Hinduism" as a whole group of related but distinct religions.

On the contrary: While retaining all its characteristic features, Hinduism is thereby freed from the reproaches often advanced by Christian theologians who, taking it to be one single religion, accuse it of logical inconsistency, self-contradictoriness, intellectual inadequacy and sub-standard morals or social ethics.[18] All this would be true if Hinduism as a whole was to be compared with Christianity, Islam or Buddhism. But it ceases to be true as soon as Judaism, or Christianity, or Islam, or Buddhism are compared with Vaiṣṇavism, or Śaivism, or Smārta Vedāntism, or "Neo-Hinduism" and so on, and tribal religions in India with other tribal religions in predominantly Islamic or Christian or Buddhist areas of the world.

No doubt, some of the Hindu religions are closely related to each other. Some derive from the same sources, some use similar concepts, some draw on the same stock of tradition, on the same techniques of meditation, and certainly the major Hindu religions influenced each other in the evolution of their theology and religious practice. But the same close relationship, the same type of similarities derived from common origin, common stock of traditions, and common theological and ethical concepts exist between Judaism, Christianity and Islam, and yet they are different religions.

What is it that establishes difference in apparently similar forms of religion? Certainly not the individual practice, which may vary to a great extent within the same religion; nor the individual's personal set of beliefs. Rather, it is the authoritative religious tradition received and perpetuated by a wider community. Such tradition includes conception about the origin of the world and the powers at work in it, the place and duties of the human being within the world, and prescriptions for right or wrong ritual and secular behaviour: it presents a comprehensive and coherent belief system. Even in the so-called primitive or non-literate societies such a system amounts to a coherent world view, though it may not necessarily find expression in formal theological doctrine. Difference between religions is, therefore, a result of decisive variance in the authoritative traditions of belief systems. Sometimes a single disputed item in an otherwise similar set of beliefs and practices may cause one religion to be different from another—if this item is considered of extreme importance, such as, e.g. the role of Jesus in the Jewish and Christian traditions. A certain margin of tolerance usually allows for sectarian differentiation in doctrine and in practice. Yet there are limits, unseen thresholds. Overstepping them leads to segregation or expulsion and, if there are enough followers, to forming a new religious unit.[19]

In Hinduism, some important religions and some minor religions can be distinguished. In course of time, some of them became extinct, others survived, and new ones emerged. Without trying to be exhaustive, the following could be mentioned:

The originally *polytheistic* Vedic Religion is documented in the most ancient canon of holy scriptures of India and is the source of one main branch of the Indian religious tradition. In the first half of the first millennium B.C. it started excluding the low-class population from ritual for fear of impurity.[20] But gradually it also lost its hold on the majority of the upper classes. The rise of Buddhism and Jainism, and the support which these reform groups received in northern India from the merchant class and the aristocracy during the Maurya, Śuṅga and Kuṣāṇa periods, as well as the spread of the Pāñcarātra, Bhāgavata and Pāśupata cults, indicate a pronounced decline of Vedic orthodoxy in northern India from the fourth/third century B.C. onwards. In southern India this process seems to have started later, about the first century B.C. The *bhakti* religions definitely gain the upper hand throughout India in the Gupta and Vākāṭaka period. Yet Vedic religion continued to live on in the *pūrvamīmāṃsā* and in some orthodox brahman families up to the present day.

Advaita Vedānta began as a *monistic* school of thought with its roots in the Upanishads. In Śaṅkara's time it was in the process of becoming a new religion, distinct from the Veda in all its essential features, such as the concept of the divine, the concept of man, the concept of the world and of reality, and the concept of salvation. In syncretistic fusion with an eclectic Smārta tradition and, since the nineteenth century, also as an important element in the equally syncretistic "Neo-Hinduism", it has strongly influenced the educated sectors of Indian society.

A number of new religions gained prominence when *bhakti* became popular in the first centuries B.C. as a new emotional approach to salvation. Out of these, often in a process of incorporating related smaller cults into larger units, Vaiṣṇavism and Śaivism emerged in the long run as dominant religious forces. Like other *bhakti* religions they have a *monotheistic* doctrine in spite of the apparent plurality of existing gods. In each of these religions there is only one highest god, only one ultimate reality. Other gods or godlings belong to lower levels of existence, they often simply represent manifestations of different divine functions of the one deity, and they are dependent on god's will and subject to death and rebirth. This applies to the often-cited concept of the *trimūrti* also, which was sometimes adduced to prove the identity of Brahmā, Viṣṇu and Śiva, the three major Hindu gods, and therefore of the unity of Hindu religion. But the real picture as given by the texts is very different: In each of the great religions it is their own god who is the One and the Supreme, the only eternal all-powerful being. He may be called Parama Śiva by the Śaivas, Puruṣottama by the Vaiṣṇavas, etc. This one God claims the functions of creator, preserver and destroyer of the world for Himself alone.[21] It is He who manifests Himself in those three divine forms, and only in this respect they are identical in nature. But this partial manifestation of God's universal power in three functional aspects does not belong to the level of the transcendental ultimate being of the deity. It occurs only at a relatively inferior level in the creative process which leads from unity to multiplicity, a level on which the world and the living beings take already shape in final name and form. On this relatively low level the three gods Brahmā, Viṣṇu and Śiva as members of the *trimūrti* exist for a span of time and vanish again. But the Highest God (an all-pervading Viṣṇu, an all-embracing Śiva) is far beyond this functional *trimūrti*. There are many divine functions with a name given to each, but in theology monotheism remains strictly preserved. Only in Śāktism this monotheism is partly replaced by a fundamental *dualism*.

Many formerly independent cults have been absorbed into Vaiṣṇavism, Śaivism and Śāktism in course of time: The cult of Yakṣas and Nāgas (into Śaivism and, to a lesser degree, into Vaiṣṇavism), the cult of the Sun-god Sūrya (into both Vaiṣṇavism and Śaivism),[22] the cults of Nārāyaṇa and Vāsudeva (into Vaiṣṇavism), the cult of the war-god Skanda/Kumāra/Kārttikeya (into Śaivism), the cult of the elephant-headed god Gaṇeśa (also into Śaivism), the cult of the monkey god Hanumān[23] (into Vaiṣṇavism) and the cults of many goddesses (into Śāktism). The process of absorbing tribal or local rural deities continues up to the present day.

The tribal religions themselves form an important group of animist religions which scholars have treated as distinct from Hinduism. But they interact continuously with other Hindu religions in certain regions.

Several syncretistic religions have originated and grown important in India in the course of history. The *Smārtas* tried to combine some of the major *bhakti* religions with late Vedic sacraments and law as embodied in the Smṛtiṣ and with monist Vedānta. Sikhism grew out of a fusion of elements from Viṣṇuism, Advaita Vedānta, and Muslim mysticism. Finally, Neo-Hinduism presents an eclectic combination taken from various Hindu traditions and spiced with certain Christian and Muslim ideals. It must be added that, in many parts of India, popular religion in general developed a tendency towards syncretism during the long period of Muslim and Christian domination, when Hindus had to put aside religious differences and support each other in order to survive.

In spite of all mutual influence and interaction between these religions, and in spite of a common history in the same geographic area and under similar socio-economic conditions, each of the major religions retained its identity even in change. Each of the major literate Hindu religions has a history of its own, is split up in *sampradāyas*, i.e. in various confessions and denominations. But each of these religions possesses its own set of revealed holy scriptures recognized by all its members, each worships the same god as the highest deity (or reverts to an impersonal Absolute as the highest principle, or recognizes a particular pantheon). Each of the literate Hindu religions had its own clearly identifiable and often immensely extensive theological literature, each knows its great saints, its major reformers, and the founder of sects. Similarly, the non-literate religions have their own oral traditions, their own songs and rituals, their own sacred lore.

IV

Why should we take "Hinduism" as the embracing term for a group of religions rather than for a single religion containing an open variety of concepts and modes of action?

The answer is simple: Terms are intended for communication. Their purpose is to evoke in the listener a specific notion, the same notion the speaker has in mind and which should correspond to the reality which is to be conveyed. Therefore much of our intellectual and academic exchange depends on the choice of terms and on their capacity to convey specific information with a reasonable amount of clarity. If everyone can derive different sets of meaning from the terms "Hinduism" and "religion", these terms obviously fail to serve their purpose.

Our term "religion" has two different meanings: one general and one specific. Religion (singular) is a general term applied to human attempts to communicate with the divine on all levels and at all times. As a concept it presumes cross-cultural universals in human nature. Religion (plural)—and among these each single religion defined by a specifying term such as Greek religion, Roman religion, Judaism, Christianity, Islam, Shintoism, or religion of the Incas, the North American Indians, the Nuer, etc.,—are concretizations of religious systems in space and time and therefore distinct *historical* phenomena.

The term "religion" in the latter sense of a specific historical phenomenon, though able to accommodate very different forms of religious theory and practice, is subject to one characteristic condition for its use: it can only be applied to *corporately shared coherent systems* of world explanation and values; and to human actions directly related to these systems. "Corporately shared" includes—subject to historical change—a certain margin for collective (sectarian) or individual variations of interpretation and practice, but poses also limits to such variations. The individual's own conviction to belong to a given religion must, therefore, be answered by the acknowledgment of the co-religionists that he/she forms part of the religious community. Moreover, the systems must be based on a belief in the existence of superhuman beings or powers.[24] Otherwise, a distinction between religion and ideology would make no sense.

Finally, various historical religions can be grouped together according to structural similarity (polytheistic religions, monotheistic religions, prophetic religions, etc.) or according to geographical units mostly emphasizing common origin in a broad geographical region (Chinese religions, African religions, Mediterranean religions, etc.).

Now Hinduism *in toto*, with various contradicting systems and all the resulting inconsistencies, certainly does not meet the fundamental requirement for a historical religion of being a coherent system; but its distinct religious entities do. They are indeed religious, while Hinduism is not. What we call "Hinduism" is a geographically defined group of distinct but related religions, that originated in the same region, developed under similar socio-economic and political conditions, incorporated largely the same traditions, influenced each other continuously, and jointly contributed to the Hindu culture. Therefore it is only by distinguishing the various Hindu religions from "Hinduism" that comparability with other historical religions can be ensured.

A comparison with religions more intimately known to us may illustrate the consequences which result from lumping together different religions under the preconceived notion that they are one religion. Take Judaism, Christianity and Islam and which are cognate but distinct religions united by origin in the same region (Near East) and common ancestry (all stand in the Abrahamic tradition). Let us see what happens if we consider them as important sects or confessions of one single religion:

We would immediately be convinced of the correctness of this approach because of the common monotheistic concept, common prophetism, the same linear concept of history and eschatology, close similarities in religious ethics and a large number of almost literal correspondences in the statements about creation, about the patriarchs and prophets, about the nature of God and his worship, about the devil, about paradise and about man and his essential duties in life, etc.

One the other hand we would be surprised to find that this postulated religion has no common founder venerated by all, that there is no doctrine valid for all members, there is no uniform ritual nor the same religious behaviour, there is no church which organizes and guides all branches of this religion. There even is no sacred scripture common to all sects. At the most, it could be admitted that the Old Testament enjoys a certain respect with all of them, even if the Muslims think that Jews and Christians misinterpreted it, and the majority is convinced that the Old Testament has long since been superseded by new authoritative scriptures: The New Testament and the Koran. Finally and most importantly, the different sects of this religion would adore different gods with different names as their highest deity (Jahwe, Trinity, Allah).

Obviously, we would get more or less the same picture as in Hinduism, and we would certainly discover as many internal contradictions in this supposed religion as we do in Hinduism,—even more so if we add some minor popular and tribal cults of the Near East to the major literate sects (and the many sub-sects) of Judaism, Christianity and Islam.

On the other hand, if we were to distinguish the Hindu religions from each other, we would still find that each of them is divided into various confessions or *sampradāyas.* But there would be essential common features in each of these religions. Founders of Hindu religions could, in some cases, be traced. Kṛṣṇa could be regarded as such, Lakulīśa maybe,[25] and in both cases the teacher on earth is regarded as an incarnation of the highest god.

For each of the literate religions there would exist a corpus of recognized holy scriptures.[26] For the Vaiṣṇavas, e.g. we would list the *Bhagavadgītā*, the *Harivaṃśa, Viṣṇu Purāna* and *Bhāgavata Purāna* as major texts relating to Kṛṣṇa worship; the *Rāmāyaṇa* and its successors, the *Yogavāsiṣṭha-* and *Adhyātma Rāmāyaṇa* and the *Rāmcaritmānas* relating to Rāma worship; the Nārāyaṇīya Section of the *Mahabhārata*, the *Pāñcarātra Saṃhitās*,[27] the *Vaikhānasa Āgamas* and the Songs of the Ālvārs as the most important texts relating to the worship of Viṣṇu-Nārāyaṇa. It is on these and some more basic texts that Vaiṣṇava theologians have based their works. The Śaivites would have the *Śatarudrīya* and the *Śvetāśvatara Upaniṣad*, the Pāśupatasūtras, the Śaiva Āgamas,[28] some of the Tantras and the Śivasūtras, which constitute the scriptural basis for the works of their famous theologians. For the Śāktas, the corpus would be Devīmāhātmya, the Devī-, Devībhāgavata- and Kālikā Purānas and a large number of Tantras[29] (each of these communities may be said to make ancillary use of the Upaniṣads as well). Members of each religion would adore the same deity as the Highest Being and Lord of the universe. Instead of a diffuse and self-contradictory religion called "Hinduism" we would get a number of important religions which could be reasonably compared with other great religions of the world.

V

If the above argument is correct, is it necessary to abandon the term "Hinduism" altogether? I do not think so nor would it be easy to weed out a term that has been established worldwide. The term "Hinduism" can be retained, but with a shift in meaning. It is not *one* religion, but a group of distinct Indian religions. Once this connotation is accepted, we can go a step further and realize the enormous challenge which Hinduism, as a matter of fact, offers to the other world religions today. For in Hinduism it was possible to create a culture of accepted multiformity, able to develop generous liberality and tolerance between religions and ideologies to a degree which civilizations based on Judaism, Christianity and Islam were never able to achieve.

Today, the most salient feature of this liberality in matters of religion is the freedom for each individual to choose the religious path he wants to follow, and to combine different religious approaches in his personal quest for the divine, or to experiment with ritual practice and teachings of different religions in order to find the appropriate path for himself. This was not always so. The exclusiveness of the Vedic religion is a prominent example to the contrary. In other religions, too, severe testing of ability and character before initiation and the possibility of excommunication restricted the individual freedom of access to, and his acceptance in, a given religious community.

Yet there were strong factors promoting religious liberality. One was the early acceptance and affirmation of religious plurality which was brought about precisely by the exclusive character of the Vedic religion and was later reaffirmed and strengthened by the implications of the *karma* theory. Thus the "unclean" Śūdras were excluded from Vedic sacrifice, but early Sūtra literature enjoins respectful behaviour of the twice-born in front of gods and shrines of the non-Vedic population. With the evolution of the *karma* theory, all religions other than one's own received their theological raison d' être as inferior paths for people with inborn karmic pollution and reduced mental capacities. The existing plurality had an impact on the *rājadharma*, i.e. the duties of the king who was responsible for the welfare of the entire people: The king was charged with the duty to protect *all* religions in his kingdom. Other factors promoting religious liberality were the repeated influx of foreign peoples into north-western India and their assimilation; the *kṣatriya* migrations within India, caused by political upheaval in times of invasions; the missionary activities of Buddhists, Jains, various Hindu communities, Muslims and Christians; the migrations of brahmans from northern India to the south on invitation of local princes and, on a larger scale, the migration of brahmans from Muslim-controlled areas into territories still governed by Hindu rājas. Muslim and Christian dominance over large parts of India lasted for roughly 740 years (1206-1947)—a very long period during which Hindus were both influenced by the foreign religions and were forced to play down the differences among themselves and join hands in order to survive.

All these factors, with emphasis on the last mentioned, have combined to bring about that attitude of religious liberality which is truly admirable in the Hindu culture. Neither Christianity nor Islam has been exposed to similarly strong impulses from inside or to equally strong pressure from outside to develop similar religious liberality. Their insistence on the equality of man and on the exclusiveness of religious truth left little room for genuine tolerance.

Unfortunately, religious and ideological confrontations tend to become more and more dangerous in the world of today. It is time, therefore, that the Abrahamic religions as well as the dominating ideologies of East and West should start learning spiritual liberality from Hinduism.

NOTES

1. The branch of Smārtas who recognize the *smṛtis* and those systems which are directly based on them but reject the bulk of *paurāṇic* religion.
2. Books on Hinduism prior to 1965 have been listed by Norvin J. Hein (1965: 45-82, 2nd ed 1977): Since 1965, a flood of publications has appeared, dealing with Hinduism from the points of view of Indology, Sociology, Social Anthropology and History of Religions. Some are included in the second edition (1977) of Hein's bibliography; helpful is also the selective bibliography of works in French and English prepared for the library of the Centre d'Etude de l'Asie du Sud by Jean-Luc Chambard et Catherine Clémentin-Ojha. The present volume is an expression of a growing awareness that what Hinduism really is needs to be reconsidered. The tendency to view Hinduism as a category of its own still persists. But Indian religions form part of the religions of the world and Hinduism, too, has to be seen in this world-wide context.
3. One of the best examples is M. Biardeau, 1971.
4. That scholars like Abū-l Qasim, al-Masūdī, al-Idrīsī and Shahrastānī had detailed knowledge about Hindu religions was shown by Bruce B. Lawrence (1976).
5. Albrecht Weber (1899: 31) who used the term, in scholarly disoncern for the

general practice, in its literal meaning, considered the more than 30 million Indian Muslims of his time also as Hindus. Much earlier, in 1768, Alexander Dow had advocated the derivation of the word Hindoo from Sanskrit *indu* = Moon, denoting the descendants of the lunar race of kings. He rejected the derivation from the Indus river: "... and the great river Indus takes its name from the people, and not the people from the river, as has been erroneously supposed in Europe" (Marshall 1970: 114). This polemic shows that the correct derivation (from the river) was current in Europe before 1768.

6. Orientalists like William Jones, H.T. Colebrooke, H.H. Wilson and most scholars after them contributed to stabilizing this concept of Hinduism.
7. Hobson-Jobson 1886: 280f.
8. For a detailed analysis of the Western conceptual premises or preconditions of research in Hinduism see H. von Stietencron, 1988.
9. Jan Gonda (1960), in his two volumes on the religions of India, still distinguishes between the Veda, "ancient Hinduism", and "more recent Hinduism" (Veda, älterer Hinduismus and jüngerer Hinduismus).
10. Great religious poets like, e.g. Tukārām (a śūdra) or Mīrābāī (a woman) were revered as saints and greatly influenced with their songs the *bhakti* movement. In Tantrism women could act as guru. The rejection of the Vedas and of outer ritual was a necessary consequence of devotional monotheism where one's own heart was the altar, one's own emotion the gift.
11. Various forms of monism (absolute and pantheistic or pan-en-theistic) and qualified monism could provide such superstructure. Monism combines easily not only with polytheism but also with monotheism. The results differ in the degree of reality attributed to the gods and to the world; they also differ in the number of stages of reality conceived. Basically, two stages are sufficient for the monistic interpretation of polytheism: The One Being (*ekaṃ sat*) or *brahman* constitutes the full reality; the gods and the world together belong to a secondary level or a pseudo-reality (depending on the conception of *māyā* as of divine essence or illusory).

    In Monotheism, the monistic interpretation requires three stages of reality: (1) the Absolute (*param brahma*), (2) the Highest God (his name differs according to religion) and (3) the other gods (some being partial manifestations of the Highest God, others being advanced souls) and the world. Stage one and two change position in the theistic approach of the *bhakta*.
12. Statements to this effect are frequent in texts of the major *bhakti* religions. A variation of this theme is the similar relative value attributed to *bhakti* and Vedic ritual respectively. Even in minor *bhakti* religions like the cult of the Sun-god we find passages to this effect, e.g. *Bhaviṣya Purāṇa* I.23.30; *Sāmba Purāṇa* 14, 31. See also *Bhāgavata Purāṇa* 8,24.49 for the view that all other gods and gurus put together are not even able to grant a ten-thousandth part of the grace which the Lord (Viṣṇu) is offering to his devotees.
13. Brahman acceptance of Bhāgavata and early Śaiva religion is reflected in various stages of the *Mahābhārata*. The process may heve started, hesitantly, about the third century B.C. but gained momentum during the Śaka/Kuṣāṇa/Sātavāhana period. For a discussion of early conflicts arising between orthodox Vedic brahmans and those brahmans who served the new *bhakti* religions as temple priests see v. Stietenron 1977: 126-37.

14. Rosenast 1985, 193-9; Fruzetti 1982; N.N. Bhattacharyya 1968; R.B. Pandey 1949, 2nd rev ed 1969; Stevenson 1920.
15. Tucci 1923, 242-310 and 1929, 667-713. Frauwallner 1953-6, Vol. II, 295-303; Engl. transl. 1973, 215-26. Dasgupta 1940, rpt. 1961, 512-50; Basham 1951.
16. Barrett 1982, 6, global table 4, gives the following figures for 1980: Christianity 32.8 per cent, Islam 16.5 per cent, Hinduism 13.3 per cent.
17. All beings are equal in essence, but in their actual lives they are different due to the effect of *karman* acquired in former births. Consequently, their physical and mental capacities vary; and if, out of the lack of knowledge, they join inferior religious paths, this, too, is due to *karman* and adequate to their limited understanding.
18. Reproaches for moral deficiency are directed against "decadent" religious practices such as sexual promiscuity and orgiastic rites in Tantric cults; also, more generally, against religious indifference in face of acute human suffering and against religious support for the caste system which involves exploitation and inhuman treatment of the low-caste and outcaste population.
19. Jesus was firmly rooted in the religious tradition of Israel. He could have been a prophet and reformer—a role which probably corresponded to his own vision of his task. Christianity arose only because his teachings were not accepted and incorporated into the dominant tradition, and because his followers proved eventually strong enough to assert their tradition and to build a new system.
20. Vedic society had incorporated members of the ruling and priestly classes of the conquered territories in the Punjab during the early phase of Aryan immigration as can be deducted from the occurrence of non-Aryan names among the seers of Vedic hymns. The policy of strict segregation between Vedic and non-Vedic communities seems to have been a development of the Brāhmaṇa period. It is fully established in the early Sūtra period.
21. Compare, e.g. *Viṣṇu Purāṇa* 102, 66: The only Lord (bhagavān) Janārdana assumes (respectively) the designation Brahman, Viṣṇu or Śiva which effects the creation, preservation and destruction (of the world).
    sṛṣṭisthityantakāriṇīṃ brahmaviṣṇuśivātmakām
    sa saṃjñāṃ yāti bhagavān eka eva janārdanaḥ
    Also: tvaṃ kartā sarvabhūtānāṃ tvaṃ pātā tvaṃ vināśakṛt (*Viṣṇu Purāṇa* 104, 15) and many other passages in this text. Similar claims for Śiva are equally frequent. The same claim for Brahman does also occur (see, e.g. *Mārkaṇḍeya Purāṇa* 45.19 and 27-9.)
22. The interpretation of Viṣṇu as solar deity is sufficiently known. For the fusion of the Sun god with Śiva see the passage on Mārtaṇḍa Bhairava in Mallmann 1963, 8-10. Also v. Stietencron 1966, 271 and L.P. Pandey 1971, 121.
23. Or did Hanumān-worship develop from the epic Rāmāyaṇa without a monkey-worship at its basis?
24. Several attempts to define religion are discussed in Horton 1960, Goody 1961, and Spiro 1966. See also Stietencron, 1993.
25. According to Śaiva traditon Śiva-Rudra himself is the author of the Pāśupata doctrine. See *Viṣṇudharmottara Purāṇa* 3. 73. 48, *Ahirbudhnya Saṃhitā* 11. 61b-62b. *Lakulīśa*, on the other hand, is regarded as Śiva incarnate and author of the *Pāśupata Sūtras*.

26. For a more detailed account of the sacred scriptures of the Hindu religions see H. v. Stietencron 1987, 258-63.
27. Only some of the 108 canonical *Pāñcarātra Saṃhitās* are available in print. Among these, the best known today are the *Sāttvata-*, *Jayākhya-*, *Pārameśvara-*, *Pauṣkara-* and *Ahirbudhnya-Saṃhitās* and the Lakṣmī Tantra.
28. 28 Śaiva Āgamas are recognized as authoritative. Important among these are the Kiraṇa- Kāmika-, Mṛgendra- and Raurava-, Āgamas. In addition, some of the Tantras are also highly respected, notably the Svacchanda-, Mālinīvijaya-, Netra-, Mṛgendra- and Rudrayāmala-Tantras.
29. The canonical number of Tantras is 64, but there are many more in existence. The Vāmakeśvara-, Tantrarāja-, Kaulajñānanirṇaya-, Kubjikāmata-, Kulārṇava- and Rudrayāmala-Tantras are among the more famous of these.

REFERENCES

Barrett, D.B. (ed.) 1982. *World Christian Encyclopedia: A comparative study of churches and religions in the modern world A.D. 1900-2000.* Nairobi/ Oxford/New York: Oxford University Press.

Basham, A.L. 1951. *History and doctrines of the Ājīvikas.* London.

Bhattaccharyya, N.N. 1968. *Indian puberty rites.* Calcutta: R.K. Maitra. (2nd. ed. rev. and enl. New Delhi: Munshiram Manoharlal, 1980).

Biardeau, M. 1971. *L'Hinduisme, Anthropologie d' une civilisation.* Paris: Flammarion.

Caland, W. (ed.) 1926. *Ziegenbalg's Malabarisches Heidentum.* Amsterdam.

Dasgupta, S.N. 1940, rpt. 1961. *A history of Indian philosophy*, Vol. 3, Cambridge.

Dellon, Monsr. 1700. *Neue Reise-Beschreibung nach Ostindien/Darinnen die Insul Bourbon oder Madagascar, Suratte, die Küste von Malabar, Calicut, ingleichen Hanor und Goa etc. ausführlich dargestellet werden.* Dresden: Johann Jakob Wincklers.

Frauwallner, E. 1953-6. *Geschichte der indischen Philosophie.* 2 vols. Salzburg: Otto Müller Verlag. Engl. transl. by V. Bedekar: *History of Indian Philosophy*, 2 vols., Delhi 1973.

Fruzetti, L. 1982. *The gift of a virgin: women, marriage and ritual in Bengali society.* New Brunswick: Rutgers University Press.

Goody, J. 1961. Religion and ritual. In *British Journal of Sociology*, 12, 142-64.

Hein, N.J. 1965, 2nd ed. 1977. Hinduism. In *A reader's guide to the great religions* (ed.) C. J. Adams. London: Collier-Macmillan.

Hobson-Jobson 1886. *A glossary of Anglo-Indian colloquial words and phrases, and of kindred terms: etymological, historical, geographical and discursive.* By H. Yule and A.C. Burnell. London: John Murray.

Horton, R. 1960. A defintion of religion and its uses. *Journal of the Royal Anthropological Institute,* 90, 201-26.

Lawrence, B.B. 1976. *Shahrastānī on the Indian religions.* The Hague, Paris: Mouton.

Lord, H. 1630. *Two sects in the East Indies.* London.

Mallmann, M.-Th. de, 1963, *Les enseignements iconographiques de l' Agni-purāṇa.* Paris: Presses Universitaires de France.

Marshall, P.J. (ed.) 1970. *The British discovery of Hinduism in the eighteenth century.* Cambridge: University Press.

Pandey, L.P. 1971. *Sun worship in ancient India.* Delhi: Motilal Banarsidass.

Pandey, R.B. 1969. *Hindu Saṃskāras (Socio-religious study in the Hindu sacraments).* 2nd revd. ed. Delhi: Motilal Banarsidass.

Rosenast, D. 1985. Strukturen der Reproduktion im Universum des vedischen Kultes. In *Geschlechtsreife und Legitimation zur Zeugung* (ed.) E.W. Müller. (Veröffentlichungen des Instituts für Historische Anthropologie Bd. 3) Freiburg: Verlag Karl Alber.

Stevenson, M.S. 1920. *The rites of the Twice-Born.* London: Humphrey Milford, Oxford University Press.

Stietencron, H. von 1966. *Indische Sonnenpriester. Sāmba und die Śākadvīpīya Brāhmaṇa* (Schriftenreihe de Südasien-Instituts der Universität Heidelberg, 3) Wiesbaden: Otto Harrassowitz.

———. 1977. Orthodox attitudes towards temple service and image worship in ancient India. In *Central Asiatic Journal* 21/2, 126-37.

———. 1987. Heilige Schriften III: Hinduismus/Hindu-Religionen. In: Hans Waldenfels (ed.), *Lexikon der Religionen,* Freiburg, Herder Verlag 1987, pp. 258-63.

———. 1988. Voraussetzungen westlicher Hinduismusforschung und ihre Folgen. In: E. Müller (ed.), "... aus der anmuthigen Gelehrsamkeit". Tübinger Studien zum 18. Jahrhundert. Tübingen, Attempto Verlag, pp. 123-53. (German).

———. 1993. Der Begriff der Religion in der Religionswissenschaft. In: W. Kerber (ed.), *Der Begriff der Religion.* München, Kindt Verlag.

Spiro, M.E. 1966. Problems of definition and explanation. In *Anthropological approaches to the study of religion* (ed.) M. Banton, London.

Tucci, G. 1923. Linee di una storia del materialismo indiano. In *Atti della R. Accademia Nazionale dei Lincei* (Anno 320, Ser. 5, Mem.17) Roma.

———. 1929. Linee di una storia del materialismo indiano (cont.). In *Atti della R. Accademia nazionale dei Lincei* (Anno 323, Ser. 6, Mem. 2) Roma.

Weber, A. 1899. Zur indischen Religionsgeschichte. Eine kursorische Übersicht. Sonderabdruck aus "*Deutsche Revue*". Stuttgart: Deutsche Verlags-Anstalt.

Wurmb, von 1779. *Merkwürdigkeiten aus Ostindien. Die Länder-Völkerkunde und Naturgeschichte betreffend.* Gotha.

SYNDICATED HINDUISM[1]

Romila Thapar

The term Hinduism as we understand it today to describe a particular religion is modern, as also is the concept which it presupposes, both resulting from a series of choices made from a range of belief, ritual and practice which were collated into the creation of this religion. Unlike the Semitic religions, particularly Christianity and Islam (with which the comparison is often made), which began with a founder and structure at a point in time and evolved largely in relation to them, Hinduism (and I use the word here in its contemporary meaning) has been constituted largely through a range of reaction to specific historical situations. This is partly why some prefer to use the phrase Hindu religions (in the plural) rather than Hinduism. Ironically there has been little analysis of the various manifestations of Hinduism from a historical perceptive. The normative and the empirical in the analysis of Hinduism are seldom interwoven. Comparisons with Semitic religions—particularly Islam and Christianity—are not fortutious since these have been catalysts in the search for a structure among contemporary Hindus.

Whereas linear religions such as Buddhism and Jainism or Christianity and Islam can be seen to change in a historical dimension, both reacting to their original structure and the interaction with the constituents of historical circumstances, such changes are more easily seen in individual Hindu sects rather than in Hinduism as a whole. This may be a partial explanation for the general reluctance of scholars of Hinduism to relate manifestations of Hinduism to their historical context and to social change.

The study of what is regarded as Hindu philosophy and religious texts has been so emphasised as almost to ignore those who are the practitioners of these tenets, beliefs, rituals and ideas. The latter became an interest of nineteenth century ethnography but this was not generally juxtaposed with textual data. Furthermore, the view has generally been from above, since the texts were first composed in Sanskrit and their interpreters were *brāhmaṇas.* But precisely because Hinduism is not a linear religion, it becomes necessary to look at the situation further down the social scale where the majority of its practitioners are located. The religious practices of the latter may differ from those at the upper levels to a degree considerably greater than that of a uniform, centralised, monolithic religion.

Discussions on Hinduism tend to be confined to Hindu philosophy and theory. But the manifestation of a contemporary, resurgent, active movement, largely galvanised for political ends, provides a rather different focus to such discussions. It is with the projections of this form of popular Hinduism and of its past that this article forms a comment. The kind of Hinduism which is being currently propagated by the Sanghs, Parishads and Sammelans, is an attempt to restructure the indigenous religions into a monolithic, uniform religion, paralleling some of the features of Semitic religions. This seems to be a fundamental departure from the essentials of what may be called the indigenous Hindu religions. Its form is not only in many ways alien to the earlier culture of India but equally disturbing is the uniformity which it seeks to impose on the variety of Hindu religions.

My attempt here is to briefly review what might be called Hinduism through history, and observe the essentials of the earliest beginnings and the innovations introduced over time. More recent innovations of colonial times have sometimes provided the possibilities for the directions in which some segments of Hinduism are now moving. The study of Hindu philosophy and thought has its own importance but is not of central concern to this article. Religious articulation in the daily routine of life draws more heavily on social sources than on the philosophical or the theological.

Religions such as Buddhism or Islam or Christianity do diversify into sects but this diversification retains a particular reference point—that of the historical founder and the teaching embodied in a single sacred text or a group of texts regarded as the Canon. The area of discourse among the sects is tied to the dogma, tenets and theology as enunciated in the beginning. They see themselves as part of the historical process and of the unfolding of the single religion even though they may have broken away from the mainstream.

Hindu sects on the other hand generally had a distinct and independent origin related to the centrality of a particular deity and/or to a founder and to a system of beliefs. The latter could, but need not be, related to an earlier system. Only at a later stage, and if required, were attempts made to try and assimilate some of these sects into existing dominant sects through the amalgamation of new forms of recognized deities or, of new deities as the manifestations of the older ones, and by incorporating some of their mythology, ritual and custom. Subordinate sects sought to improve their status by similar incorporation from the dominant sects if they were in a position to do so.

What has survived over the centuries is not a single monolithic religion but a diversity of religious sects which we today have put together under a uniform name. The collation of these religious groups is defined as Hinduism even though the religious reference points of such groups might be quite distinct. "Hinduism" became a convenient general label for studying the different indigenous religious expressions. This was when it was claimed that anything from atheism to animism could legitimately be regarded as part of "Hinduism". Today the Hindus of the Parishads and the Sanghs would look upon atheists and animists with suspicion and contempt, for the term Hinduism is being used in a different sense.

Hinduism as defined in contemporary parlance is a bringing together of beliefs, rites and practices consciously selected from those of the past, interpreted in a contemporary idiom in the last couple of centuries and the selection conditioned by historical circumstances. This is not to suggest that religions with a linear growth are superior to what may apparently be an ahistorical religion or one with multiple historical roots, but rather to emphasise the difference between the two.

In a strict sense, a reference to Hinduism would require a more precise definition of the particular variety referred to—Brahmanism, Bhakti, Tantrism, Brahmo-Samaj, Arya-Samaj, Shaiva-Siddhanta, or whatever. These are not comparable to the sects of Christianity or Islam as they do not relate to a single sacred text and its interpretation. Many are rooted in ritual practices and beliefs rather than in texts and it has been argued that a characteristic difference relates to the orthopraxy of Hinduism rather than to an orthodoxy.[2] Present-day Hinduism therefore cannot be seen as an evolved form with a linear growth historically from Harappan through Vedic, Puranic and Bhakti forms, although it may carry elements of these. In this it differs even from Buddhism and Jainism leave alone Christianity and Islam.

Its origin has no distinct point in time (the Vedas were regarded as the foundation until the discovery of the Indus civilisation in the 1920s when the starting point was then taken back to the previous millennium), no historically attested founder, no text associated with the founder, all of which reduces its association with historicity. This of course makes it easier to reinterpret if not to recreate a religion afresh as and when required.

Many of these features, absent in the religion as a whole, do however exist among the various sects which are sought to be included under the umbrella-label of "Hinduism" which makes them historical entities. But then, not all these sects are agreed on identical rites, beliefs and practices as essential. Animal sacrifice and libations of alcohol would be essential to some but anathema to others among the sects which the Census of India labels as "Hindu". The yardstick of the Semitic religions which has been the conscious and the subconscious challenger in the modern structuring of Hinduism, would seem most inappropriate to what existed before.

We know little for certain about the Harappan religion and guesses include a possible fertility cult involving the worship of phallic symbols, a fire cult, perhaps a sacrificial ritual and rituals to legitimise rulership, some suggestive of an authoritative priesthood. The decipherment of the script will hopefully tell us more. It was earlier thought that with the ascendence of Vedic religion, the Harappan became a substratum religion, some facets of which surfaced in later periods. A different interpretation is now being put forward, and although tentative, is worth consideration. It is being suggested that some important aspects of Vedic religion may in fact have been incorporated from the earlier Harappan religion and this would include, the building of a fire-altar and even perhaps the *soma* cult.[3] The Vedic compositions even if they might incorporate elements of the earlier religion, emphasise the central role of the sacrificial ritual of the *yajña*, are suggestive of some elements of shamanism, include a gamut of deities where the *brāhmaṇa* is the intermediary to the gods and worship focuses on rituals without images. Because of the pivotal role of the *brāhmaṇa* it is sometimes referred to as the beginnings of Brahmanical Hinduism to distinguish it from other important forms of Hinduism. The Vedic compositions and the Dharmaśāstras (the codes of sacred and social duties) are said to constitute the norms for Brahmanism and the religious practices for the upper castes.

Brahmanism is differentiated from the subsequent religious groups by the use for the latter of the term Śramanism. The Buddhist and Jaina texts, the inscriptions of Aśoka, the description of India by Megasthenes and the account of the Chinese pilgrim Hsüan Tsang, covering a period of a thousand years, all refer to two main religious categories: the *brāhmaṇas* and the *śramaṇas*.[4] The identity of the former is familiar and known. The latter were those who were often in opposition to Brahmanism such as the Buddhists, Jainas and Ājīvikas and a number of other sects associated with both renunciatory orders and a lay following, who explored areas of belief and practice different from the Vedas and Dharmaśāstras. They often preached a system of universal ethics which spanned castes and communities. This differed from the tendency to segment religious practice by caste which was characteristic of Brahmanism. The segmenting of sects is of course common even among historically evolved religions, but the breaking away still retains the historical imprint of the founder, the text and the institution.

Brahmanism was free of this. The differentiating of Brahmanistic practice for a particular caste makes it an essentially different kind of segmentation. It was this segmentation which some Śramanic religions opposed in their attempt to universalise their religious teaching, as for example in the banishing of those monks and nuns thought to be creating dissension in the Buddhist *sangha*.[5] The hostility between Brahmanism and Śramanism was so acute that the grammarian Patañjali, when speaking of natural enemies and innate hostility refers to this and compares it to the hostility of the snake and the mongoose, the cat and the mouse.[6] Literature dating to after the fifth century A.D. has derogatory statements about the Jainas as heretics and Jaina literature refers to the *brāhmaṇas* as heretics and liars. This indigenous view of the dichotomous religions of India is referred to even at the beginning of the second millennium A.D. by Alberuni who writes of the Brahmanas and the Shamaniyya.[7]

Within Brahmanism there was also segmentation but seen from the outside it seemed an entity. Brahmanism did maintain its identity and survived the centuries although not unchanged, particularly after the decline of Buddhism. This was in part because it was well-endowed with grants of land and items of wealth through intensive royal patronage, which in turn reinforced its claim to social superiority and enabled it further to emphasise its distance from other castes and their practices. The extensive use of Sanskrit as the language of rituals and learning enhanced the employment of *brāhmaṇas* in work involving literacy such as the upper levels of administration and gave them access to high political office in royal courts. This again supported its exclusive status. The use of a single language—Sanskrit—gave it a pan-Indian character, the wide geographical spread of which provided both mobility as well as a strengthening of its social identity. Since it was also increasingly the language of the social elites and of administraton, the establishment of new kingdoms from the latter part of the first millennium A.D. onwards resulted in an extensive employment of literate *brāhmaṇas* and especially those proficient in the Vedas, Dharmaśāstras and Purāṇas.

The Bhakti tradition of the first millennium A.D. is sometimes traced to the message of the *Bhagavad-gītā*, which was interpolated into the *Mahābhārata*, to give the *Gītā* both antiquity and currency. The *Gītā* endorsed a radical change in that it moved away from the centrality of the sacrificial ritual and instead emphasised the individual's direct relation with the deity. An earlier formulation of a similar idea was current through the Upaniṣads where the sacrificial ritual was questioned, the centrality of rebirth was emphasised with release from rebirth being sought through meditation and *yoga* and the recognition of the *ātman-brahman* relationship. Many of the early *Śramaṇa* sects had also opposed the *yajña*. The *Gītā* did however concede that *dharma* lay in observing the rules of one's own caste, *svadharma*, and the arbiters of *dharma* remained the *brāhmaṇas*. Selfless action as projected in the *Gītā* was the need to act in accordance with one's *dharma* which now became the key concept.

This shift of emphasis provided the root in later times for the emergence of a number of Bhakti sects—Śaiva, Vaiṣṇava, Śākta and other—which provided the contours to much that is viewed as "traditional Hinduism" or Puranic Hinduism as some prefer to call it. The Pāśupatas, the Ālvars and Nāyannārs, the Śaiva-Siddhānta and the Liṅgāyats, Jñāneśvara and Tukārāma, Vallabhācarya, Mīrā, Caitanya, Śankaradeva, Basava, Lalla, Tulasīdāsa, and so on are often bunched together as part of the Bhakti stream. In fact there are variations among them which are significant and need to be pointed out. Some among these and similar teachers accepted the earlier style of worship and practice, others were hostile to the Vedic tradition: some objected to caste distinctions and untouchability, whereas for others such distinctions posed no problems. Some of the sects opposed to caste discouraged their members from worshipping in temples or going on pilgrimages and from observing the upper caste *dharma.* A few felt that asceticism and renunciation were not a path to salvation whereas others were committed to these. Kabir and Nanak for instance, infused Sufi ideas into their teaching. These major differences are rarely discussed and commented upon in modern popular writing which is anxiously searching for similarities in the tradition. Yet these dissimilarities were to be expected and were in a sense their strength.

The Bhakti sects were up to a point the inheritors of the Śramanic tradition in that some were opposed to Brahmanism and the sacrificial ritual, most were in theory open to every caste and all of them were organised along sectarian lines. They arose at various times over a span of a thousand years in different parts of the subcontinent. They were specific in time, place and teacher, and were constricted in cross-regional communication by differences of language. They did not evolve out of the same original teaching nor did they spread through conversion; they arose as and when historical conditions were conducive to their growth, often intermeshed with the need for particular castes to articulate their aspirations. Hence, the variation in belief and practice and the lack of awareness of predecessors or of an identity of religion across a subcontinental plane. Similarities were present in some cases but even these did not lead to a recognition of participation in a single religious movement. With the growth of the Bhakti sects, where many focused on a single deity, the worship of the iconic image of the deity gained popularity, or else a few sects refused to worship an image at all. Image-worship was possibly encouraged by the icons which had been used by Buddhists and Jainas from the Christian era onwards. Whereas Megasthenes visiting in the fourth century B.C. does not refer to images in discussing the religions of India, for Alberuni, writing in the eleventh century A.D., icons are a major feature of the indigenous religions.[8]

This was also the period which saw the currency of the Śākta sects and Tantric rituals. Regarded by some as the resurgence of an indigenous belief associated with subordinate social groups (gradually becoming powerful) it was, by the end of the first millennium A.D., popular at every level of society including the royal courts. The attempt in recent times to either ignore it or to give a respectable gloss to its rituals or their manifestation in the art of the period,[9] is largely because of the embarrassment these might cause to middle-class Indians heavily influenced by Christian puritanism and somewhat titillated in imagining erroneously that Tantric rituals consist essentially of pornographic performances. That there has been little effort, except in scholarly circles, to integrate such groups into the definition of Hinduism derives also from the attempt to define Hinduism as Brahmanism based on upper caste rituals and such cults were initially alien to traditional Brahmanism.

Another noticeable manifestation of non-Brahmanic religion is what has recently been euphemistically called "folk Hinduism"—the religion of the untouchables, "tribals" and other groups at the lower end of the social scale. This is characterised by a predominance of the worship of goddesses and spirits (*bhūta-preta*) represented symbolically and often aniconically and with rituals performed by non-*brāhmaṇa* priests: the later for a variety of reasons, not least among them being that since the offering and libations consist of meat and alcohol, these could be regarded as polluting by *brāhmaṇas*. Needless to say, such groups would not be able to afford the costly donations required of a brahmanical *yajña*. For the upper caste Hindus these groups were (and often still are) regarded as *mlecchas* or impure and not a part of their own religious identity. Interestingly attempts by Hindu missionaries to proselytise among such groups, lay particular emphasis on prohibitions on meat-eating and alcohol in every-day life.

The sects included in the honeycomb of what has been called Hinduism were multiple and ranged from animistic spirit cults to others based on subtle philosophic concepts. They were oriented towards the clan, the caste and the profession or else on the reversing of these identities through renunciation. The social identity of each was imprinted on its religious observances. The deities worshipped vary, the rituals differed, belief in after-life varied from the theory of *karma* and *saṃsāra* to that of *svarga* and *naraka*, heaven and hell. In the same *Mahābhārata*, where the characters of the narrative find themselves in heaven and hell at the end of the story, Kṛṣṇa preaches release from rebirth which is a very different eschatology.

This variance may in part explain why the word *dharma* became central to an understanding of religion. It referred to the duties regarded as sacred which had to be performed in accordance with one's *varṇa*, *jāti* and sect and which differed according to each of these. The constituents of *dharma* were conformity to ritual duties, social obligations and the norms of family and caste behaviour preferably as stipulated in the Dharmaśāstras or accepted as incontrovertible rules of behaviour. As has been noticed, theology although not absent, is not to the fore, nor any ecclesiastical authority, both of which again point to the difference between these religions and the Semitic. A major concern was with ritual purity. The performance of sacred duty heavily enmeshed in social obligations was so important that absolute individual freedom only lay in renunciation.[10]

But the significance of *dharma* was that it demarcated sharply between the upper castes—the *dvija* or twice-born—for whom it was the core of the religion and the rest of society whose conforming to *dharma* was left somewhat in abeyance, as long as it did not transgress the *dharma* of the upper castes. They were to that extent without *dharma* or had their own. In trying to redefine Hinduism today as a universalising religion, the implicit attempt is to try and include those without the recognised *dharma,* who have in the past been excluded; but the inclusion is not divorced from the terms of the upper caste *dharma* and this raises problems.

Hindu missionary organisations, such as those attached to the Ramakrishna Mission, the Arya Samaj, the RSS and the Vishva Hindu Parishad, taking their cue from Christian missionaries are active among the *ādivāsis,* mainly scheduled castes and tribes. They are converting these latter groups to a Hinduism as defined by the upper caste movements of the last two centuries. Not surprisingly there was a difference of opinion among some members of the upper castes in the early twentieth century on whether such groups can be counted as Hindus even prior to "conversion". The proponents of Hindutva have had contrary views about this.[11] What is important for Hindu missionaries is that these communities declare their support for the *dharma* and be ready to be labelled as Hindus in any head count of either a census or a support to a political party. That this conversion does little or nothing to change their actual status and that they continue to be looked down upon by upper caste Hindus is of course of little consequence. This is one reason why some Dalit groups have been confrontational towards caste Hindus.

The origin of the word Hindu is geographical and derives from the Sindhu river, where the Achamaenid Persians used the name Hindu with variants to refer to those that live on the cis-Indus side.[12] Later the Arabs described the area as al-Hind.[13] Initially used in a geographical and an ethnic sense, the term Hindu came subsequently to be used in a religious sense for those who lived in this area but were not Muslims or Christians. Hindus became a term of administrative convenience when the Muslim rulers had to differentiate between "the believers" and the rest. Hindu therefore referred to the rest.

The first step towards the crystallisation of what we today call Hinduism was born in the consciousness of being the amorphous, subordinate, other. In a sense this was a reversal of roles. Earlier the term *mleccha* had been used by the upper caste Hindus to refer to the impure, amorphous rest. For the upper caste Muslims and especially those not indigenous to India, were treated as *mleccha* since they did not observe the *dharma* and were debarred from entering the sanctum of the temple and the home. Indigenous converts to Islam also came under this category but their caste origins would have set them apart initially from the amorphous Muslim. Now the upper castes were clubbed together with the indigenous *mleccha* under the label of "Hindu", undoubtedly a trauma for the upper castes.

This in part accounts for the statements made by upper caste Hindus today that Hinduism in the last one thousand years has been through the most severe persecution that any religion in the world has ever undergone. The need to exaggerate the persecution at the hands of the Muslim is required to justify the inculcation of anti-Muslim sentiments among the Hindus of today. Such statements brush aside the fact that there were various expressions of religious persecution in India prior to the coming of the Muslims and particularly between the Śaiva and the Buddhist and Jaina sects and that in a sense, the persistence of untouchability was also a form of religious intolerance.[14] The authors of such statements conveniently forget that the last thousand years in the history of Hinduism, and more so the last five hundred years, have witnessed the establishment of the powerful Śankarācārya *maṭhas, āśramas,* and similar institutions attempting to provide an ecclesiastical structure to strengthen Brahmanism and conservatism; the powerful Dasanami and Bairagi religious orders of Śaiva and Vaiṣṇava origin, vying for patronage and frequently in confrontation; the popular cults of the Nāthapanthis; the significant sects of the Bhakti traditions which are to be found in every corner of the subcontinent; and more recently a number of socio-religious reform movements which have been aimed at reforming and strengthening Hinduism. It was also the period which saw the expansion of the cults of Kṛṣṇa and Rāma with their own mythologies, literatures, rituals and circuits of pilgrimage. The definition of the Hindu today has its roots more in the period of Muslim rule than in the earlier period and many of the facets which are regarded today as essential to Hinduism belong to more recent times. The establishment of the sects which accompanied these developments often derived from wealthy patronage including that of both Hindu and Muslim rulers, which accounted for the prosperity of temples and institutions associated with these sects. The more innovative sects were in part the result of extensive dialogues between *gurus, sādhus, pīrs* and Sufis, a dialogue which was sometimes confrontational and sometimes conciliatory.[15] The last thousand years have seen the most assertive thrust of many Hindu sects. If by persecution is meant the conversion of Hindus to Islam and Christianity, then it should be kept in mind that the majority of conversions were from the lower castes and this is more a reflection on Hindu society than on persecution. Upper caste conversions were more frequently activated by factors such as political alliances and marriage circuits and here the conversion was hardly due to persecution.[16] Tragically for those that converted on the assumption that there would be social equality in the new religion, this was never the case and the lower castes remained low in social ranking and carried their caste identities into the new religions.[17]

When the destroying of temples and the breaking of images by Muslim iconoclasts is mentioned—and quite correctly so—it should however at the same time be stated that there were also many Muslim rulers, not excluding Aurangzeb, who gave substantial donations to Hindu sects and to individual *brāhmaṇas.*[18] There was obviously more than just religious bigotry or religious tolerance involved in these actions. The relationship for example between the Mughal rulers and the Bundela *rājās,* which involved temple destruction among other things, and veered from close alliances to fierce hostility, was the product not merely of religious loyalties or differences, but the play of power and political negotiation. Nor should it be forgotten that the temple as a source of wealth was exploited even by Hindu rulers such as Harṣadeva of Kashmir who looted temples when he faced a fiscal crisis or the Paramāra ruler who destroyed temples in the Chalukya kingdom, or the Rāṣṭrakūṭa king who tore up the temple courtyard of the Pratihāra ruler after a victorious campaign.[19] Given the opulence of large temples, the wealth stored in them required protection, but the temple was also a statement of political authority when built by a ruler.

The European adoption of the term "Hindu" gave it further

currency as also the attempts of Catholic and Protestant Christian missionaries to convert the Gentoo/Hindu to Christianity. The pressure to convert, initially disassociated with European commercial activity, changed with the coming of British colonial power when, by the early nineteenth century, missionary activities were either surreptitiously or overtly, according to context, encouraged by the colonial authority. The impact both of missionary activity and Christian colonial power resulted in considerable soul searching on the part of those Indians who were close to this new historical experience. One result was the emergence of a number of groups such as the Brahmo Samaj, the Prarthana Samaj, the Arya Samaj, the Ramakrishna Mission, the Theosophical, Society, the Divine Life Society, the Swaminarayan movement *et al.*, which gave greater currency to the term Hinduism. There was much more dialogue of upper caste Hindus with Christians than there had been with Muslims, partly because for the coloniser power also lay in controlling knowledge about the colonised and partly because there were far fewer Hindus converting to Christianity than had converted to Islam. Some of the neo-Hindu sects as they have come to be called, were influenced by Christianity and some reacted against it; but even the latter were not immune from its imprint. This was inevitable given that it was the religion of the coloniser.

The challenge from Christian missionaries was not merely at the level of conversions and religious debates. The more subtle form was through educational institutions necessary to the emerging Indian middle class. Many who were attracted to these neo-Hindu groups had at some point of their lives experienced Christian education and were thereafter familiar with Christian ideas. The Christian missionary model played an important part, as for example in the institutions of the Arya Samaj. The Shaiva Siddhanta Samaj was inspired by Arumuga Navalar, who was roused to re-interpret Śaivism after translating the Bible into Tamil. The movement attracted middle-class Tamils seeking a cultural self-assertion. Added to this was the contribution of some Orientalist scholars who interpreted the religious texts to further their notions of how Hinduism should be constructed.[20] The impact of Orientalism in creating the image of Indian, and particularly Hindu culture, as projected in the nineteenth century, was considerable.[21]

Those among these groups influenced by Christianity, attempted to defend, redefine and create Hinduism on the model of Christianity.

They sought for the equivalent of a monotheistic God, a Book, a Prophet or a Founder and congregational worship with an institutional organisation supporting it. The implicit intention was again of defining "the Hindu" as a reaction to being "the other"; the subconscious model was the Semitic religion. The monotheistic God was sought in the abstract notion of Brahman, the Absolute of Upaniṣads with which the individual Ātman seeks unity in the process of *mokṣa*; or else with the interpretation of the term *deva* which was translated as God, suggesting a monotheistic God. The worship of a single deity among many others is not strictly speaking monotheism, although attempts have been made by modern commentators to argue this. Unlike many of the earlier sects which were associated with a particular deity, some of these groups claimed to transcend deity and reach out to the Absolute, Infinite, the Brahman. This was an attempt to transcend segmentary interests in an effort to attain a universalistic identity, but in social customs and ritual, caste identities and distinctions between high and low continued to be maintained.

The teaching of such sects drew on what they regarded as the core of the traditions, where the notion of *karma* and *saṃsāra* for instance, came to be seen as uniting all Hindus, even though in fact this was not the case. The Upaniṣadic idea of the relation between *Ātman* and *Brahman* was seen as a kind of monotheism. The need for a Book, led to one among a variety of texts being treated as such—the *Bhagavad-gītā* or the Vedas. The Prophet being an altogether alien idea, could at best be substituted by the teacher-figure of Kṛṣṇa, even though he was neither Prophet nor son of God. Congregational worship, not altogether alien to lower caste forms of worship, was systematised and became the channel for propagating these new versions of Hinduism. The singing of hymns and the common chanting of prayers became an important part of the ritual. The discarding of the icon by both the Brahmo Samaj and the Arya Samaj was like an allergic reaction. It was seen as a pollution of the original religion but, more likely it was the jibe of idol worship from the practitioners of Christianity and Islam which was a subconscious motivation. This was not a new feature, for some Bhakti teachers had earlier pointed out the incongruity of worshipping images rather than concentrating on devotion to the deity. A reaction against the icon, but a substitution virtually for the image by the Book, was and is, the centrality of the *Guru Granth Sahib* in Sikh worship.

Much of the sacred literature had been in earlier times orally preserved and served a variety of social and religious ends. The epic narratives of the *Mahābhārata* and the *Rāmāyaṇa* were converted to sacred literature by depicting Kṛṣṇa and Rāma as *avatāras* of Viṣṇu. The narration then became that of the actions of a deity. Interpolations could also be added as and when required, as for example the *Gītā*. This is a different attitude from that of the Semitic religions to the centrality of the Book, or for that mater, from that of the Sikhs to the single, sacred text. The imprint of the idea of the sacredness of the Book itself, is suggested in some late texts such as the fifteenth century *Adhyātma-Rāmāyaṇa* where it says that the reading of the text is in itself an act of worship.[22] Interestingly interpolations become far less frequent when the text is written. These new religious identities of the nineteenth and twentieth centuries were in part the inheritors of the older tradition of combining social aspirations with religious expression and establishing new sects. But at the same time they were conscious of the attempt to create a different kind of religion from the past and which gave currency to the term Hinduism.

Traditional flexibility in juxtaposing sects as an idiom of social change as well as the basic concepts of religious expression now became problematic. In the absence of a single "jealous" God, often associated with monotheism and demanding complete and undiluted loyalty from the worshipper, there were instead multiple deities, some of which were superseded over time and others which were created as and when required. Thus the major Vedic deities—Indra, Mitra, Varuna and Agni—declined with the rise of Śiva and Viṣṇu at the turn of the Christian era. The latter have remained major deities supported by sects which are not always in agreement about what the deities represent for them. This has not prevented the creation of an altogether new deity, as has been witnessed in the last half century with the very popular worship in northern India of the goddess, Santoshi Mā.

The attitude to deity would in part support the argument that it is not theology which is important in Hinduism but the mode of worship. The Vedic *yajña* has a carefully orchestrated performance of ritual with the meticulous ordering of every detail including the correct pronunciation of the words constituting the *mantra.* Worship as *bhakti* in Puranic Hinduism is more personalised and informal. The earlier emphasis on oblation and sacrificial ritual was now transformed into sharing in the grace of the deity and devotion to the deity, sometimes even taken to the extreme of ritual suicide.[23] The deity was conceptualised in a variety of ways—abstract, aniconic, an image or an image elaborately sculpted and housed in an equally elaborate temple. Devotion could also be expressed in various ways. There was no requirement of uniformity in methods of worship or in who performed the ritual. There was little ecclesiastical order involved and no centralised church. The caste of the worshipper frequently conditioned the nature of the ritual and the method of worship. This included the caste of the priest, the contents of the offering, the language and form of the prayer and even at times the particular manifestation of a deity. This was evident in even the diversity of shrines and temples in a single village.

Because worship was so closely tied to caste and recruitment to caste was by birth, the question of conversion became irrelevant. In its absence, sects emerged either independently, or through segmenting off or amalgamating with similar sects. The religious sect was also an avenue to caste mobility. Origin myths of middle and lower castes often maintain that the caste was originally of higher status but a lapse in the ritual or an unwitting act of pollution led to a loss of status.[24] Imitation of higher caste norms or the dropping of caste obligations would normally not be permitted unless justified by the creation of new religious sect. The latter would initially be regarded with hostility by the conservative but if it became socially and economically powerful it would be accommodated.[25] The absence of conversion accounted for the absence of distinction between the true follower and the infidel or pagan. Yet, distinctions of another kind were more sharply maintained, particularly among sects with a substantially upper caste following. There was an exclusion of all those who were regarded as outside the social pale and who came under the category of *mleccha*—the untouchables, some lower castes, the "tribals" and Indian Muslims and Christians. They were segregated because they performed neither the ritual duties nor the social duties required by the *dharma*. That in many cases they were prohibited from doing so, such as entering the temple for worship, did not prevent their being excluded. There was little active attempt to change this and where it was attempted, such as in the *shuddhī* movement of the Arya Samaj, the results were negligible.

It is often said that one is born a Hindu and one cannot be converted to Hinduism, for the caste identity is determined although the sectarian identity can change. The idea of conversion was much debated in the nineteenth century when various organisations wished to both reform and expand the Hindu identity as they saw it. Possibly this was also tied into the increasing consciousness of numbers with the notion of majority and minority communities being introduced into politics. Earlier it had been argued that each sect had its own regulations, obligations and duties which often drew both on religious antecedents and social requirements. Gradually if a sect acquired a large following cutting across castes, it tended to become a caste in itself. This further endorses the notion that it would perhaps be more correct to speak of the Hindu religions rather than of Hinduism. Some would argue that the correct term for the latter would be *sanatan dharma.*

There was one agency which had its roots in religious articulation and which could legitimately transgress the rules of caste and this was the range of renunciatory orders. Some of these orders restricted themselves to recruiting only *brāhmaṇas,* but in the main most of them recruited from a variety of castes. Even among the latter, although theoretically the orders were open to all, there was a tendency to prefer caste Hindus. Open recruitment was possible because renouncers were expected to discard all social obligations and caste identities, and were regarded as being outside the rules of caste and *dharma.* Joining such an order was also in some cases the only legitimate form of dissent from social obligations since it required the revoking of these obligations. The multiplicity of renouncers in India has therefore to be viewed not always as inspired by otherworldly aspirations but also by the nature of the links between the social forms and dissent.[26] The Śramanic religions were similar to these sects in that they did recruit members from a range of castes although, as was the case also with Indian Islam, Indian Christianity and Sikhism, converts often retained their original caste identity, especially in the crucial area of marriage connections.[27]

Religious sects battened on patronage, whether royal or from other members of the community. Even the renunciatory orders were not averse to accepting wealth which ensured them material comforts as is evident from the many centres of such orders scattered across the Indian landscape over the last two thousand years. The wealth ranged from small donations of labour and money to extensive grants of land. The pattern of patronage to Buddhism is repeated with other religions.[28] Renunciatory orders were dependent for alms and requirements on stable societies and had therefore to be closer to the patronage of the elite, although some did maintain a reciprocal relationship with the lower castes. The initial radical thought of some of these orders was marginalised by their need for patrons. Where such economic wealth helped these sects to build institutions, whether that of the *saṅgha*, the *maṭha*, or the *khānqah*, it provided them with access to political power with the result that politics and religion were intertwined. The real texture of Indian social history in the second millennium A.D. has been bye-passed with the obsessive concern with simplistic Hindu-Muslim relations to the exclusion of the pertinent investigation of how politics and religion at some levels were interrelated. A further aspect is that in many cases these sectarian institutions were also centres of literacy and literacy was a powerful mechanism of social control.

Caste identities, economic wealth, literacy, and access to power also contributed to providing the edge to sectarian rivalries and conflicts. Hsüan Tsang and Kalhaṇa record the persecution of Buddhists by Śaivas, and Karnataka witnessed the destruction of Jaina temples in a conflict with the Śaivas.[29] Once the Buddhists and Jainas were virtually out of the way, hostility among the Hindu sects remained, even between ascetic groups, as is evident from the pitched battles between the Dasanamis and the Bairagis over the question of precedence at the Kumbha Mela.[30] Antagonism of the latter kind was not that of the Hindu against another religion but that of particular sects hostile to each other. An assessment of the degree of tolerance and non-violence, has therefore, to take into account sectarian aggression. It is true that there were no Inquisitions. This was partly because dissent was chanelled into the creation of a separate sect which, if it became a renunciatory order, was less directly confrontational in society. Breakaway sects or new sects, even where they did not form renunciatory orders, found a rung on the social hierarchy of sects and their continuance and status was dependent on the social groups who became their patrons and supporters. Among the Hindu sects there was no centralised church whose supremacy was endangered by the emergence of new sects. However social subordination, justified by theories of impurity, replaced to some degree the inequities of an authoritarian church.

Religious violence is not alien to Hinduism despite the nineteenth century myth that the Hindus are by instinct and religion a non-violent people. The genesis of this myth was partly in the romantic image of the Indian past projected for example, by scholars such as

Max Müller.[31] Added to this were the requirements of nationalism maintaining the spiritual superiority of Indian culture of which non-violence was treated as a component. Non-violence as a central tenet of behaviour and morality was first enunciated and developed in the Śramanic tradition of Buddhism and Jainism. These were the religions which not only declined at various times in various regions of India, but were persecuted in some parts of the sub-continent. One is often struck by how different the message of the *Gītā* would have been and how very much closer to non-violence if Gautama Buddha had been the charioteer of Arjuna instead of Kṛṣṇa. Gandhiji's concern with *ahimsā* is more correctly traced to the Jaina imprint on the culture of Kathiawar. Not that the Śramanic tradition prevented violence, but at least it was a central issue early on in the ethics of Buddhism and Jainism and only later enters the discussion of some Hindu sects.[32]

Sectarian institutions acted as networks across geographical areas, but their reach was limited except among some renunciatory orders. *Bhakti* as a religious manifestation was predominant throughout the subcontinent by the seventeenth century; yet curiously there was little attempt to link these regional movements to forge a single religious identity. Each tradition used a different language and there was no ecclesiastical organisation to integrate the development. There was however the gradual building up of network around Kṛṣṇa worship at Brindavana and later Rāma worship at Ayodhya which incorporated teacher and disciples from eastern and southern India, with new foci of worship and the demarcating of a sacred topography associated with the life-cycle of the deity incarnate and a renewed emphasis on the benefits of pilgrimage. One of the side effects of pilgrimage is that it can increase the catchment area of worshippers. Nevertheless even pilgrimage tended to remain largely regional, as for instance in the pilgrimage to Paṇḍharapura in the worship of Viṣṇu as Viṭṭhala which followed a well-defined circuit relevant only to Maharashtrian worshippers. The limitations to pilgrimage lay both in the nature of the cult and also in problems of distance and easy transportation. The Bhakti sects saw themselves as self-sufficient, with religious forms closely tied to local requirements. The closest to ecclesiastical organisation were the *maṭhas* associated with Śankarācārya, but these had a limited religious and social jurisdiction.

A suggested historical explanation for the spread of Bhakti sects links them to the feudalising tendencies of the period after A.D. 500 and parallels have been drawn between the loyalty of the peasant to the feudal lord being comparable to the devotion of the worshipper for the deity.[33] The Bhakti emphasis on *mokṣa* through devotion to a deity and through the belief in *karma* and *saṃsāra* was a convenient ideology for keeping subordinate groups under control. It was argued that they might suffer in this life, but by observing the *dharma* they would benefit in their next birth. The onus of responsibility for an unhappy condition was therefore on the individual and not on society. This gave the individual an importance which was absent in real life and therefore served to keep him/her quiescent. An explanation which requires lower castes to admit to misdemeanors even in a previous life, would hardly be widely acceptable. Common as was the belief in *karma* and *saṃsāra* it did not preclude the growth at a popular level of the concepts of heaven and hell. The multiplicity of memorials to the dead hero—the hero-stones—which increase in number after A.D. 500, and are found scattered in many parts of India, make it evident by symbol if not by inscription that the hero on dying a hero's death, was taken up to eternal life in heaven.[34]

The segregation of social communities in worship and religious belief and the absence of an over-arching ecclesiastical structure demanding conformity, was characteristic of the Hindu religions. Attempts at introducing an authority were made on a small scale, such as the Śankarācārya *maṭhas,* doubtless influenced by the model of the Buddhist *saṅgha.* These did eventually become centres of pilgrimage, particularly among caste Hindus who could afford to make the journey and among renouncers. But the important source of funds and concerns related to the upper castes. The segregation led to the possibility of each group leading a comparatively separate existence. The clash could come in the competition for support and patronage. This might partially explain the notion of tolerance with which the nineteenth century invested indigenous Indian religions. However, sectarian rivalries existed, sometimes taking a violent form and the coming of Islam added to the number of competing sects.

It was however within the broad spectrum of what has been called Puranic religion and that of the Bhakti sects that there was a dialogue between these and Islam resulting in some mutual borrowing. Curiously there was little overt interest in Islamic theology among learned *brāhmaṇas.* There are hardly any major studies of Islam in Sanskrit whereas the regional languages do provide evidence of a lively interest, either directly or indirectly, in the religious interface between Hindu and Islamic religions.[35] Interestingly, Muslims were referred to not as such but as either Turuṣka/Turk, Śaka, Yavana or *mleccha.* The first three have a historical ancestry and were used for people coming from central Asia or west Asia and the last referred to social distance. It is strange that what we today see as an essentially religious difference does not get projected in these terms although it was evidently present.

The more learned among Muslim authors such as Abu'l Fazl merely give resumés of Brahmanism when it comes to details about the indigenous religions, presumably because this was the most prestigious. There is much less detail of the other sects except in a generalised way. Abu'l Fazl refers to the strife among the various indigenous religions which he attributes to diversity in language as well as the resistance of Hindus to discuss their religions with foreigners.[36] He lists four kinds of worship among Hindus: the pre-eminent is the pūjā of the image, the second is the *yajña* or sacrificial ritual, the third is *dāna* or gift-giving and the fourth is *śrāddha* offered in honour of the ancestors.

Islam and Hinduism are generally projected as two monolithic, antagonistic religions, face-to-face. For the conservative in Islam the Indian experience must have been bewildering since there was no recognizable ecclesiastical authority to which it could address itself. It faced a large variety of belief systems of which the most noticeable common feature was idol-worship—but even this was by no means uniform. This may also partially account for the success of the Sufis as agencies of conversion to Islam, their beliefs and religious practices sometimes being more flexible and varying as compared to the Islam of the theologians.

It is often said that the Hindus must have been upset at seeing Turkish and Mongol soldiers in their heavy boots trampling the floors of the temples. This would certainly have been traumatic. But the question arises as to which Hindus were thus traumatized? For the same temple now entered by *mleccha* soldiers was in any case open only to the caste Hindus and its sanctum would have been barred to the larger population consisting of the indigenous *mleccha.* The feelings of the latter were of little concern to the caste Hindus who had worshipped at these temples. The trauma was therefore more in the nature of the polluting of the temple rather than the confrontation on any substantial scale with another religion.

Brāhmaṇa-Śramaṇa hostility did not disappear over time. It kept cropping up and books authored by *brāhmaṇas* in the first millennium

A.D. often refer to Buddhists and Jainas as heretics—*pakhaṇḍa*—and the same word is used in some Jaina texts for *brāhmaṇas*.[37] Brahmanism was also distanced from certain Bhakti sects and some Śākta groups, since the latter in particular had rituals offensive to Brahmanism. Inevitably however with the increasing incorporation of Tantric ideas into the religion especially of the elite groups, one expression of the claim to legitimacy was the "Sanskritisation", literally, of the texts of such sects. This required both the accommodation of some categories of *brāhmaṇa* priests in the performance of the ritual, when with decline of Vedic ritual by this time other forms of ritual held out a more promising patronage for the *brāhmaṇas*; as well as a process of "brahmanisation" of the priests who had earlier performed the rituals. The separateness of such sects was forced to narrow though not to amalgamate, when they were all, *brāhmaṇas, śramaṇas* and the rest, forced to come under the single label of Hindu. A formal closeness was imposed on them by the coming of Islam and the categorisation for the first time of all indigenous cults as "Hindu" where the term carried the connotation of "the Other".

A further crisis came with the arrival of Christianity riding on the powerful wave of colonialism. This experience of both Roman Catholic and Protestant Christianity was very different from the much earlier arrival of Syrian Christianity which came in the wake of traders and had a limited geographical reach. In the projected superiority of Semitic religions, it was once again the Hindus who were regarded as "the Other" and this again included both the Brahmanic and Śramanic religions. This time the Christian dialogue was with Brahmanism and this was not altogether unexpected considering that the Indian middle class was to emerge from the ranks of the upper castes, and among these, initially, the *brāhmaṇas,* were the more significant.

Inevitably the Brahmanical base of what was seen as the new or neo-Hinduism was unavoidable. But merged into it were also various practices of upper caste worship and of course the subconscious model of Christianity and Islam. Its close links with certain nationalist opinion gave to many of these neo-Hindu movements a political edge which remains recongnisable even today. It is this development which was the parent to what I should like to call Syndicated Hinduism and which is being projected by some vocal and politically powerful segments of what is referred to as the Hindu community,[38] as the sole claimant to the inheritance of indigenous Indian religion.

It goes without saying that if Indian society is changing then its religious expressions must also undergo change. But the direction of this change is perhaps alarming. The emergence of the powerful middle-class with urban moorings and a reach to the rural rich would find it useful to bring into politics a uniform, monolithic, Hinduism created to serve its new requirements. Under the guise of such a Hinduism, claiming to be the revival of an ancient, traditional form, but in effect being a new creation, an effort is made to draw a large clientele and to speak with the voice of numbers. This voice has been created to support claims of majoritarianism based on a religious identity in the functioning of democracy.

The appeal of such a Hinduism to the middle-class is obvious since it becomes a mechanism for forging a new identity aimed at protecting the interests of the middle-class, even if this is not made widely apparent. To those lower down in society there would be the attraction of upward mobility through a new religious movement. Such groups having forsaken some of their ideologies of non-caste religious sects, as from the Bhakti tradition, would have to accept the *dharma* of the powerful but remain subordinate. A change in this direction has introduced new problems. In wishing away the weaknesses of the old, one does not want to bring in the predictable disasters of the new.

Perhaps the major asset of what we call Hinduism of the premodern period was that it was not a uniform, monolithic religion, but a flexible juxtaposition of religious sects. This flexibility was its strength and its distinguishing feature, allowing the inclusion even of groups questioning the Vedas, disavowing caste and the injunctions of the Dharmaśāstras. The weakening or disappearance of such dissenting groups within the framework even of religious expression would be a considerable loss. If Syndicated Hinduism could simultaneously do away with social hierarchies, this might mitigate its lack of flexibility. But the scramble to use it politically merely results in realignments within the hierarchy.

Syndicated Hinduism draws largely on reinterpreting Brahmanical texts of which the *Gītā* is an obvious choice, defends the Dharmaśāstras and underlines a brand of conservatism in the guise of a modern, reformed religion. The model is in fact that of Islam and Christianity. There is a search for a central book and recently, on the wave of the Ramjanmabhoomi agitation, there has been a focus on the *Rāmāyaṇa* with the insistence on the historicity of Rāma which makes him into a founder. Ecclesiastical authority is sought for in requesting the Śankarācāryas to pronounce upon all matters religious, social and political. Meetings of the *dharmasansads* call upon *dharmācāryas*, *sādhus* and *sants* to give opinions on any matter of importance, which is then said to be binding even if opposed to the Constitution or the rulings of the Supreme Court of India. This is described as the Hindu Vatican. That these persons may be self-appointed *sants* and *sādhus* is of no consequence. Worship is increasingly congregational and the introduction of sermon-style homilies on the definition of a good Hindu and Hindu belief and behaviour, are becoming common at marriages and funerals and register a distinct change from earlier practice.[39] This form of Hinduism ends up inevitably as an over-simplified Brahmanism with garbled versions of elements of Bhakti and Puranic forms of belief and practice, largely to draw in increasing numbers of supporters.

The call to unite under Hinduism as a political identity is if anything, anachronistic. Social and economic inequality, whether one disapproves of it or condones it, was foundational to Brahmanism. To propagate the texts associated with this view and yet insist that it is an egalitarian philosophy is hardly acceptable. Some religions such as Islam are, in theory, egalitarian. Others such as Buddhism restrict equality to the moral and ethical spheres of life. The major religions arose and evolved in societies and in periods when inequality was not only a fact of life but was not questioned as a matter of right. The social function of these religions was not to change this but to ameliorate the reality for those who found it harsh and abrasive. Further, as a proselytising religion, Syndicated Hinduism cannot accept a multiplicity of religious statements as being equally important. Clearly some beliefs, rituals and practices will have to be selected from among an extensive range, and be regarded as essential and therefore more significant. Such an essentialising of scripture invests it with the potentialities of fundamentalism. This is a substantial departure from the traditional position. Who does the selecting and from what sources and to what purpose, also becomes a matter of considerable significance. In the absence of a single, authoritative scripture, those who make this selection will be questioned by others, unless they can back up their selection with the threat of force or control over power. This assertion is also encouraged by the success of comparable organisations in various parts of the world, based on a sharply contoured body of belief and practice backed by scripture emanating from a religious tradition.

Equally important to Syndicated Hinduism is the means of its propagation. It uses a variety of existing organisations from the erstwhile rather secretive RSS to the strident Bajrang Dal. The thrust is aggressive and categorical rather than persuasive. There is an impressive exploitation of modern communication media—audio-visual and print—with a substantial dose of spectacle, drama and hysteria. Television serials on Doordarshan, such as the *Rāmāyaṇa* and the *Mahābhārata* present what is intended to be the received version of these texts and others such as *Chanakya* are an evident underlining of Hindu nationalism with the pretext of using history. Received versions are an attempt to erode variants. Television serials have accelerated the pace of propaganda from the more slow-moving, "mythological" films of earlier decades. The resort to media presentations gives it a veneer of modernisation, but the essential message remains conservative.

Another factor of increasing importance to this Syndicated Hinduism is the trans-national dimension in what might be called the Hindu diaspora—the dispersal of Hindus in various parts of the globe. In the pre-modern period there were Indians settled mainly as traders in many parts of Asia, but these were small settlements. The large colonies of present times are related to colonial needs. These are the result either of migrations in the nineteenth century when immigrant labour was moved by the colonisers to other parts of the British empire such as to Guyana, Surinam, Trinidad, Malaysia and Fiji, or of traders being inducted into east and south Africa, or of the arrival of workers and/or professionals in the United Kingdom, North America, Saudi Arabia and the Gulf, after 1947, in search of better job opportunities. Such communities settled outside India, experience a sense of cultural insecurity since they are minority communities, frequently in a largely Christian or Islamic society. Their search is for a form of Hinduism parallel to Christianity or Islam and with an idiom comprehensible to these other two which they can teach their children (preferably we are told, through the equivalent of Hindu "Sunday" schools and video films). These communities with their particular requirements and their not inconsequential financial support also provide the basis for the institutions and propaganda for, Syndicated Hinduism.[40]

The importance of this diaspora is reflected not only in the social links between those in India and those abroad supporting this new form of Hinduism, but also in the growing frequency with which the Sanghs and Parishads hold their meeting abroad and seek the support and conversion of the affluent.[41] Conversion often takes the form of re-establishing faith in this new Hinduism and creating a demand for the overt expression of this loyalty as a form of identity. This is not to be confused with the guru-cult in affluent societies where there is little attempt to convert people to Hinduism, but rather to suggest to them methods of "self-realisation" irrespective of their religious affiliations.

The creation of this Syndicated Hinduism for purposes more political than religious and mainly supportive of the ambitions of an emerging social class, has been a long process during this century and has now come more clearly into focus. Whatever political justification it might have claimed in the past as a form of nationalist assertion against British rule, no longer exists. Its growing strength relates to a number of features which have come to dominate the contours more particularly of urban middle class Indian society today. Changing social mores result in a sense of insecurity, particularly as the move towards a consumer oriented society is now on the increase and keeping up with the consumer market is seen as a necessity. The change in the economy brings in greater scope for individual enterprise, witnessed in the phenomenal expansion of the Indian middle-class, not just since 1947 but more so in the last two decades. But the required competition implicit in a liberalised, marked economy also increases the sense of insecurity. The injection of egalitarian ideas into a hitherto hierarchical society creates its own forms of social disequilibrium. The solution is sought in the search for a scape-goat or an enemy within and here the politics of the partition of India in 1947 return forcefully in the building up of hostility against the Muslims, hostility which can easily be extended to Christians and when occasion demands, to Sikhs. This hostility further feeds the insecurity and sense of powerlessness of those communities which are smaller in numbers and often disadvantaged. There is also the tacit recognition that the lower castes cannot be subordinated for long given the use of the ballot and the concession to reservations in the struggle for a place in the corridors of power. But the concern for the lower castes and Dalits is essentially a form of tokenism. The ideology of Syndicated Hinduism remains an ideology endorsing the status of the middle-class.[42]

Social groups in the past have expressed their aspirations in part by creating new religious sects. We are now witnessing a movement that seeks to go beyond sectarian appeal and claims to represent "the Hindus" and insists on a particular identity for all those who are technically called Hindus, irrespective of whether they wish it or not. In a sense the notion of "the Hindu" as it evolved in Islamic writing has now come to fruition in this claim. The emergence of Syndicated Hinduism is different both in scale and scope and is not restricted to the creation of a new sect but a new religious form seeking to encapsulate all the earlier sects. The extensive use of the media is a paradigm change in communication and permits of the possibility of reaching an all-India audience. The sheer scale as well as motivation, call for concern. Syndicated Hinduism claims to be re-establishing the Hinduism of pre-modern times: in fact it is only establishing itself and in the process distorting the historical and cultural dimensions of the indigenous religions and divesting them of the nuances and variety which were major sources of their enrichment. The survival and continuation through history of many such religious manifestations was not only through power and dominance but also in many instances through the sense of security that their presence and existence would not be prohibited. There is something to be said for attempting to comprehend the real religious expression of Indian civilisation before it is crushed beneath the wheels of the Toyota-*rathas.*

NOTES

1. This article was first published under the title of "Syndicated Moksa?", in *Seminar*, September 1985, No. 313 and intended for the general reader. It remains substantially the same except for some up-dating and the addition of a few references. I would like to thank Kunal Chakravarty for his comments on the earlier article.

   Reference is made in this article to "the Semitic religions", a term used for Judaism, Christianity and Islam. It refers primarily to the fact that their scriptures were written in the Semitic languages, such as Hebrew and Arabic, and to the similarities in their religious tradition. The term is not intended to mean the Semitic race, since this would exclude the major point under discussion which is their structure of belief and practice, very different from that of Hinduism.
2. F. Staal, *Exploring Mysticism*, Berkeley 1975, 65, 173.
3. F. Staal, *Agni*, Vol. I, Berkeley 1982, 27-166; H. Converse, "The Agnicayana Rite: Indigenous Origin?", *History of Religion*, 1974, 14, 81-95; I. Mahadevan, "The Cult Object on Unicorn Seals : a sacred filter?", *Purātattva*, 1981-3, 13-14, 165-86.
4. Strabo 15.1.39; Arrian 11; J.Bloch, *Les Inscriptions d'Asoka,* Paris 1950, 97, 99, 112; S. Beal, *Si-yu-ki*, Delhi 1969 (reprint).
5. This is clear from the well-known Schism Edict of Aśoka. Bloch, op. cit., 152-3.

6. S.D. Joshi (ed.), *Patañjali Vyākarana Mahābhāṣyam*, Poona 1968, 2.4.9; 1.4.76.
7. E. Sachau, *Alberuni's India*, Delhi 1964 (reprint), 21.
8. J.W. McCrindle, *Ancient India as Described by Megasthenes and Arrian*, London 1877, 98; Strabo, 15.1.59. Sachau, op. cit. 111ff.
9. For a sober interpretation see the discussion in Devanagana Desai, *Erotic Sculpture of India*, New Delhi 1975.
10. Romila Thapar, "Renunciation: The making of a Counter-Culture?", in *Ancient Indian Social History: some Interpretations*, Delhi 1978, 63-104; "Householders and Renouncers in the Brahmanical and Buddhist Traditions", in T.N. Madan (ed.), *Way of Life*, Delhi 1982, 273-99.
11. Gyan Pande, "Which of us are Hindus" in G. Pande (ed.), *Hindus and Others*, Delhi 1993, 238-72.
12. R.G. Kent, *Old Persian*, New Haven 1950, 170ff.
13. A. Wink, *Al-Hind*, Delhi 1990, 10ff.
14. Romila Thapar, *Cultural Transaction and Early India*, New Delhi 1993.
15. Ashim Roy, *The Islamic Syncretistic Tradition in Bengal*, New Jersey 1983; H. van Skyhawk, "Vaishnava perceptions of Muslims in eighteenth century Maharashtra", in A.L. Dallapicola and S. Zingel-Avelallemant (eds.), *Islam and Indian Religions*, Stuttgart.
16. S.I. Zaidi and S. Zaidi, "Conversion to Islam and Formation of Castes in Rajasthan," in A.J. Baisar and S.P. Verma (eds.), *Art and Culture*, Delhi 1992.
17. For example, R. Eaton, *Sufis of Bijapur*, New Jersey 1978, 310ff.
18. As for example, K.K. Datta (ed.), *Some Firmans, Sanads and Parwanas* (1578-1802), Patna 1962; B.N. Goswamy and J.S. Grewal, *The Mughal and Sikh Rulers and the Vaishnavas of Pindori*, Simla 1969.
19. Kalhana, *Rājataraṅginī*, 7.1081-95; P. Bhatia, *The Paramaras*, Delhi 1970, 140ff., 269. *Epigraphia Indica*, VI, 38 v. 19.
20. D. Knopf, "Hermeneutics versus History", *Journal of Asian Studies*, 1980, 39, 3, 495-505.
21. Romila Thapar, *Interpreting Early India*, Delhi 1993.
22. Romila Thapar, "A Historical Perspective on the Story of Rama", in S. Gopal (ed.), *Anatomy of Confrontation*, Delhi 1991, 153ff.
23. This is occasionally illustrated in memorial stones dedicated to a person who has committed ritual suicide with a depiction of the act. N.K.L. Murthy, "Memorial Stones in Andhra Pradesh", in S. Settar and G.D. Sontheimer (eds.), *Memorial Stones*, Dharwad 1982, 212ff.
24. For example, V. Das, "A Sociologial Approach to the Caste Puranas of Gujerat: A Case Study", *Sociological Bulletin*, 1968, 17, 141-64.
25. An interesting case in point is the history of the Liṅgāyat sect in Karnataka, originally a religious sectarian movement but today a powerful caste as well.
26. Romila Thapar, "Dissent and Protest in the Early Indian Tradition", *Diogenes*, 1981, 113-14, 31-54.
27. For example, Imtiaz Ahmed, *Caste and Social Stratification Among the Muslims*, Delhi 1973.
28. Buddhist sects initially began with small gifts of cells, cisterns and assistance with building a *stupa*, or royal investments with guilds of which the interest was donated; and later, as at Nalanda, received the revenue of a hundred or even two hundred villages. Romila Thapar, "Patronage and Community", in B.

Stoler Miller (ed.), *The Powers of Art*, Delhi 1992, 19-34. Nasik Cave Inscription No. 10, *Epigraphia Indica*, 8.78ff. S. Beal, *Life of Hiuen-Tsiang*, Delhi 1973 (reprint), 112.

29. Romila Thapar, *Cultural Transaction and Early India*, 19ff.
30. These were so endemic that there are miniature paintings of the Mughal period depicting such battles.
31. M. Müller, *India What Can it Teach Us?* London 1983, 101ff.
32. Sporadic killing apart, even the violence involved in the regular burning of Hindu brides, does not elicit any threat against the perpetrators of such violence from the spokesmen of Hinduism. Feminist groups are the main agitators against such acts.
33. M.G.S. Narayanan and Kesavan Veluthat, "Bhakti Movement in South India", in D. Jha (ed.), *Feudal Social Formation in Early India*, Delhi 1987, 348-75.
34. S. Settar and G.-D. Sontheimer (eds.), *Memorial Stones*, Dharwad 1982; Romila Thapar, "Death and the Hero", in S.C. Humphreys and H. King (eds.), *Mortality and Immortality: The Anthropology and Archaeology of Death*, London 1981, 293-316.
35. For example, N. Wagle, "Hindu-Muslim interactions in medieval Maharashtra", in G.-D. Sontheimer and H. Kulke (eds.), *Hinduism Reconsidered*, Delhi 1997, 134-52.
36. Abu'l Fazl, *Ain-i-Akbari*, III, trans. H.S. Jarret, Delhi 1978 (reprint).
37. For example, Kṛṣṇa Misra, *Prabodhacandrodaya*, ed. V.L. Pansikar, Bombay 1916; Vimalasūri, *Paumacariyam*, ed. H. Jacobi, Varanasi 1962.
38. The Rāṣṭra Svāyamasevaka Saṅgha and the Vishva Hindu Parishad in particular, as is evident from a reading of their periodicals and literature.
39. Given today's centrality of the notion of profit and the market and the message of the media, the sale of cassettes and tapes with pre-recorded hymns and sermons in support of uniform practice and belief, are often on sale where there are large gatherings, such as at funerals.
40. According to *Fortune International*, Indians in the USA are the richest foreign born group, in Britain they own 60 per cent of all retail stores, and in Hongkong, control a tenth of its exports.
41. The most recent example of this was the convention organised by the Vishva Hindu Parishad in Washington in 1993 to commemorate the anniversary of Vivekananda's visit to America. Where, a century ago, Vivekananda was virtually introducing Hinduism to an international audience as a religion given to tolerance and religious laissez-faire, what was now being commemorated in his name was an aggressive, assertive, outgoing drive for a religious identity with strong political aspirations for Hindus both in the United States and in India.
42. This was demonstrated for example in the anti-reservation movement by members of the middle-class taking to the streets and to self-immolation, when the V.P. Singh government announced the implementation of the Mandal Commission Report.

THE EMERGENCE OF MODERN 'HINDUISM' AS A CONCEPT AND AS AN INSTITUTION: A REAPPRAISAL WITH SPECIAL REFERENCE TO SOUTH INDIA[1]

Robert Eric Frykenberg

The central argument of this essay is that, unless by "Hindu" one means nothing more, nor less, than "Indian" (something native to, pertaining to, or found within the continent of India), there has never been any such a thing as a single "Hinduism" or any single "Hindu community" for all of India. Nor, for that matter, can one find any such thing as a single "Hinduism" or "Hindu community" even for any one socio-cultural region of the continent. Furthermore, there has never been any one religion[2]—nor even one system of religions—to which the term "Hindu" can accurately be applied. No one so-called religion, moreover, can lay exclusive claim to or be defined by the term "Hinduism".[3] The very notion of the existence of any single religious community by this name, one may further argue, has been falsely conceived. A continued and blind acceptance of this concept—not to mention an uncritical but all too common holding of many underlying assumptions about it during the past century—is not only erroneous, but, I would argue, it is dangerous.

Indeed, to take this thesis further, the concept of "Hinduism" as denoting a single religious community has already done enormous, even incalculable, damage to structures undergirding the peace, security, and unity of the whole Indian political system. What's more, continued popular use of this concept and popular belief in the existence of a monolithic "Hinduism"—in short, fervent adherence to any doctrine which assumes that there is one single religion embraced by the "majority" of all peoples in India—can still do even greater damage. If such usages and beliefs continue to be dogmatically and persistently maintained, there is no telling how much more harm such a notion may yet do to the wellbeing of India's peoples.

For this reason, both the origins of the term "Hinduism" and its application as a metaphysical instrument for conceptualizing socio-religious realities in India need to be better understood. But, without appreciating the actual historical contexts of events in which the term has been used, and misused (whether during the past two centuries or during the past eight decades of this century), better understanding is not possible. The very exercise of dealing with details of hard data and with documents describing past influences upon current historiography, requires us to begin, first of all, with definitions. By attempting to distinguish between past and current meaning of the words "Hindu" and "Hinduism", one can hope that some critical misperceptions and problems surrounding these concepts may be brought to light.

I

It is well known that the term "Hindu," as a general label for things of India or things from India, can be traced back into remote antiquity. Earliest references, according to the latest edition of *Oxford English Dictionary* (1971)[4], go back to the Achaemenian "Zend" (or "Zendu"); and were taken from the Sanskrit name "Sindhu" (for the river Indus). In the words of W.C. Smith:

> The term *Hindu* and its dialectical alternative *sindhu,* are the Indo-Aryan word for 'river', and, as a proper noun, for the great river of the northwest of the subcontinent, still known locally as the Sindh and in the West through the Greek transliteration as 'Indus'. As a designation for the territory around that river (that is meaning roughly, 'India') the word was used by foreigners but not internally, and indeed it (and the Persian counterpart 'Hinduism', introduced and used by Muslims) is still primarily an outsiders name for the country (the Indian name for India is *Bhārat*). 'India' (*Hindu'ush*) is first found in two monument inscriptions of Darius in Iran.[5]

Half a century later Herodotus brought the term into Greek (*History,* iii, 98). By then, it was also found in Aramaic where, in the Book of Esther, we read that "Ahasuerus reigned from India even to Ethiopia" [1: 1] and that the Persian empire consisted of "the provinces which are from India to Ethiopia" [8: 9].

So used, "Hindu" also referred to the natives of northern India or anything that was native thereto. So used, it was also later adopted by Al Biruni who, in his great treatise on India produced during the reign of Mahmud of Ghazni, mentions "theories of the Hindus" being similar to "theories of the Greeks".[6] So used, the term came into later Persian and Urdu usage as applying to anything non-Muslim or native to "Hindustan".

As also shown in the work of Joseph T. O'Connell, the word "Hindu" appeared in *Gauḍīya Vaiṣṇava* texts of the sixteenth century (1973: 340-3). But here also it appears only in texts describing episodes of strained relationships between Hindus as natives and Muslims as foreigners ("Yavanas" or "Mlecchas"). The term, we are told, was never used by Hindus among themselves to describe themselves; moreover, the term "Hindu dharma" which occurs seven times, four times in Bengali texts, was only used in the same way and never with any explicit definition or discussion of what "Hindu" or "Hindu dharma" itself meant. "Hindu dharma", therefore, is the closest resemblance to the term "Hinduism" which can be found to have arisen out of indigenous sources within India.

The term "Hinduism", on the other hand, is truly modern. As such, it may be seen as a relatively recent invention. Its very first use, as far as can be known, may not altogether be certain; and it remains somewhat debatable. Yet, when the terms "Hindu" and "Hinduism" first began to come into vogue in modern times, these were simply convenient labels for describing *all* things in India , *all* things Indian, and *any* form of culture or system of religion arising within or uniquely peculiar to the continent. Moreover, whether understood as a concept of doctrinal or religious (philosophical/theological) identification or as a category of social and political analysis, the word was certainly not indigenous to India.[7] Consequently, however one looks at it—and especially whenever the concept is used to designate a particular and reified "religion"—the concept has always remained so slippery and soft that, to this very day, no one has ever been able to give us a crisp or precise or satisfactory definition. Indeed, except by reference to clear geophysical limits to the subcontinent itself, no one can readily show us exactly what boundaries circumscribe the cultural or religious phenomena which the concept purportedly attempts to describe or represent[8].

Definitions, therefore, remain our first and most profound problem. The terms "Hindu" and "Hinduism" have always been used—and are still being used—to cover a wide-ranging multitude of meanings. Thus, as already indicated, during the late eighteenth century when the concept first began to be used, the term "Hindu" was applied to anything which was of India, anything "Native" or "Indian". As such, as a socio-political concept, it related especially to things pertaining to the cultures and peoples of Hinduism proper, or even to the same in South India. In this sense, references to "Hindoo" Christians or "Hindoo" Muslims—namely, references to Christians and Muslims, etc., of India who were characteristically and distinctively "Hindoo" or Indian in their culture and style of life—are not uncommon.

In a related sense, "Hindu" was also a negative term. It was the term used, in negative ways, to characterize *all things in India* (especially elements and features found in the cultures and religions of India) which were *not* Muslim, *not* Christian, *not* Jewish, or, hence, *not* Western. "Hindu", in this sense, was a term of exclusion. As such, the term came into style and eventually supplanted the word "Gentoo".[9] The word "Gentoo" had also, until then, been applied mainly to Telugu-speaking peoples and to their culture (as distinct from Tamil-speaking peoples, who were designate as speaking "Malabar").[10] These earlier expressions were used by Europeans long before the word "Hindu" or "Hinduism" had been properly discovered or, in the latter case, invented. Conversely, these other terms were being used when the word "Hindu" was still being used to refer, more strictly, to something which could be *found in* Hindustan, something which *represented* Hindustan, or something which was *characteristic of* inhabitants of Hindustan.

In still a narrower sense, however, "Hindu" and "Hinduism" were the terms which were later applied to all high culture and religion in India, but especially to that which was of Aryan, Brahmanical or Vedic origin. This is the definition which many still use. This, indeed, is what is often meant nowadays when these terms are casually employed.[11] But the properly indigenous term for *that* particular high culture and religion, as more correctly designated in its own sacred (and Sanskritic) terminology, should perhaps really have been "Dharma", or "Sanatana Dharma" or "Arya Dharma".[12] The expression Hindu Dharma was certainly never used in this way; nor could it be equated with the term "Hinduism," except as it might have been used to designate all others who were *adharma* and *mleccha*, or beyond the pale and polluting. Moreover, adoption of this "classical" or "high" definition required, at the very least, acceptance of a whole system of Brahmanical doctrines, as especially arising out of or embodied within the *Catur-Veda* ("Four Vedas" as the ageless the beginningless source of all knowledge), as rooted in the *Catur-Varṇya* ("Four Varṇa System" as a foundation logic for the hierarchical ranking of all forms of mankind), and as ultimately resting upon the absolute law of *dharma/karma* (leading to the incarnate migration and transmigration of beings). In a "classical" sense, therefore, the term "Hinduism" was made to embody and to embrace *varṇāśramadharma.*

Varṇāśramadharma—the ontology which describes the pure reality of a segmented and separated social existence, the epistemology which posits a stratified and structured system for the colour-coding for all mankind into ethnic elements, and the ethnical system which prescribes strict adherence to pollution rules, carefully discriminating between things "clean" and "unclean"—was (and is) thus perceived as having always been part of the very essence of this high tradition. *Varṇāśramadharma,* as a concept, has also been made to encompass everything from the philosophical and the ritual features of cosmic order in all its highest sophistication to the bloodiest, crudest meanest, and most savage practices of the most primitive of people (including all other life-forms). Vacant from this sense of Hinduism was any room for a concept of common humanity.[13]

It is within the framework of this more "Brahmanical" or "classical" meaning of the term, moreover, that most of the early nationalist leaders of India, almost from the time of (proto-nationalist) Rammohun Roy all the way down to Gandhi and Nehru, learned to use the terms "Hindu" and "Hinduism". However these "national" leaders were first captured or enthralled, and whatever may have been the vision which this newly-coined concept of Hinduism inspired in them, it is ironic that the enthrallers were themselves none other than European Orientalists. It was from such scholars in the Enlightenment, from Nathaniel Brassey Halhed and William Jones and right down to Max Müller (if not down to our day), that this coin was first minted and then brought into such wide circulation. Few of the early Orientalists, or their Brahman pandits , would themselves have necessarily used the term "Hinduism" certainly not as a gloss to describe any single classical culture or any single high religion arising out of ancient India. Interesting and ironic also is the fact that the linguistic medium of this nationalistic enthrallment with India's ancient heritage was English. Initially at least, it was not by means of the Sanskrit texts which the Orientalists used but by means of translation from Sanskrit texts that use of this cover word evolved. English—albeit English in its "Hinduized", Indianized, Sanskritized, "Prakritized" (or "Indish") form (in Roman script)—became a vehicle for its transmission.[14] The use of the word "Hinduism" in this context was as a conceptual device, a tool for the handling of certain philosophical, religious, and theological ideas.

Yet, in still other senses—in what is now often referred to as "popular Hinduism"; what is called "temple Hinduism"; what is called "bhakti Hinduism", what is called "village Hinduism" and what is sometimes even called "tribal Hinduism"; not to mention other localistic forms of Indian culture and religion which some think of as being quintessentially "Hindu"—the term "Hinduism" has been and still is often compounded and confused with any or all of the above usages. The result has been a jumbling and scrambling of signals. Vagueness of usage had led this concept into trackless deserts of nonsense. And, indeed, if all of the various forms of localisms and local forms of Animism were also loaded into this concept, as so often also seems to happen, nonsense would be, and indeed, often has been, but further compounded. Finally, to the degree that all of these definitions have been incorporated into one grand definition, sometimes under the name of "Puranic Hinduism", to that degree the term itself has also begun to acquire cosmic properties, insomuch that it has been made to pertain, once again, to almost anything and everything which exists anywhere in India—or anywhere else, for that matter.[15] This final kind of omnibus definition of the concept of "Hinduism" results, by *reductio ad absurdum,* in bringing us full circle back to where we began—or to nowhere.[16]

For all that, even this rather quick listing of variant definitions is hardly sufficient. It leaves out the crucial roles played by modern conversionist and revivalist movements, of various kinds (these movements, so important to any contemporary understanding of "Hinduism" are treated below). Yet, however far from exhaustive and however far from sophisticated or thorough these definitions may be, they at least serve to emphasize the assertion that "Hinduism" (if not the word "Hindu") is a concept so *soft* and *slippery,* so opaque and vague, that its use all but brings critical analysis to a halt and intellectual discourse to the verge of paralysis (if not futility).

But for us merely to struggle with the conceptual and definitional problems is not enough. Abstract models of what constitutes "Hinduism" or "Hindu" culture and religion have been favourite preoccupations among scholars for two centuries. From Abbé Dubois to Louis Dumont, Cartesian constructions of truly wondrous artistry and symmetry have been built. Like intricate mobiles dangling from the sky, these metaphysical contraptions, with all their intricately moving parts, have bedazzled and fascinated us. Yet, when set against the hard details of descriptive date and when applied to historical circumstances on the ground, empirical findings have never quite matched these models. Data seems never to have been sufficient to give these metaphysical formulations consistency to match their creativity. Evidences of actual events, taken out of actual space and time and possessing actual locality and temporality, seem always to have been riddled with so many exceptions that they could never quite fit the conceptual fabric which has been especially constructed for them. This certainly seems to be true when one looks for some sort of consistent and monolithic "Hinduism" in South India. *Modern* "Hinduism" as it has actually grown up since the eighteenth century is something else, something quite different. One can find no single, all-embracing religion which can be traced all the way back to the Vedas. Rather, what one discovers is something which is the product of a socio-political process—a process of reification which has evolved during the past two centuries. It is thus that "Hinduism" has evolved.

II

How does one isolate and measure hard elements which indicate the emergence of *modern* Hinduism in south India? If One seeks to answer this question by trying to distinguish "modern Hinduism" from all forms of indigenous religion which might, at some hazard, be designated as "premodern" or "traditional" but which for want of any other single omnibus concept to cover all such institutions, might also have previously been called "Hinduism", then one must find ways to separate and trace those elements which are modern from all the rest. But, in order to do this, one must have some criteria of deciding what is modern, some further means of deciding how data can be selected. And, since this too is a problem which is fraught with slippery difficulties, and since virtually no criteria can be fully defended or be found wholly free from bias and inconsistency, one might just as well leave this problem alone and take an entirely different approach. One might approach this problem from the opposite end—that is, empirically and historically—from events. One can begin by making some arbitrary choices and decisions, and by simply describing some of the things which actually happened in south India.

For purposes of this analysis, therefore, "modern Hinduism" is seen as that form of corporate and organized and 'syndicated' religion which arose in south India and by which highly placed and influential groups of Brahmans, supported by Brahmanized Non Brahmans, did most of the defining, the manipulating, and the organizing of the essential elements of what gradually became, for practical purposes, a dynamic new religion. Moreover, this process of reification, this defining and organizing of elements which they did, occurred with the collaboration, whether witting or unwitting, with those who governed the land. What was produced was a centralization, rationalization, and bureaucratization of information (Dykes 1854: 232).

Brahmans have always controlled information. That was their boast.[17] It was they who had provided information on indigenous institutions. It was they who had provided this on a scale so unprecedented that, at least at the level of All-India consciousness, a new religion emerged the likes of which India had perhaps never known before. In other words, those who ruled over the country—those who presided over the executive, judicial, and legislative functions of the state and who exercised authority in the administration of state decision—were influenced by the hosts of officials who worked with them every day. The hosts handled most of the paperwork. They had done this before, for previous rulers. Now they did this again and did this in such a way that the rulers themselves became instruments of local and indigenous influences. Local officials, either Brahmans or Non-Brahmans who were of "high" *varṇa* and ritually "clean" by local standards, exercised a crucial, if not determining, role. In course of time, these very ingredients of the state rulership, both European and Native, served to bring modern Hinduism into being.

How this came about can perhaps best be understood visualizing a kind of dialectical tension—or, a sort of oscillating interplay between countervailing forces or between two parallel processes, both of which contributed to the rise of modern Hinduism. Within both of these processes, influential Brahman or Brahmanized Non-Brahman notables who came from the same gentry of Madras or, to lesser extent, from agrarian elites in the countryside (*mufassal* districts), played a crucial and ever increasing role. The first of these two processes occurred within the matrix of the political structures of the imperial State itself. The second of these two parallel but intermingling lines of development grew up alongside but outside the State structures. It was a process which was at once social and political, cultural as well as religious. This process can be shown to have periodically been in dialectical opposition to structures of the political Establishment. What was produced, as a consequence, was an organized or "syndicated" religion,[18] a "Hinduism" which could attempt to vie with major world religions—especially with the religions of Semitic origin—for equal recognition and standing.

III

Let us, then, look first at the development of modern Hinduism *within* the Raj. In previous studies, I have argued that the Company's Raj was actually, for most intents and purposes, a *de facto* "Hindu Raj" (Frykenberg 1982a: 21-42). By this, I meant several things: that the Raj, as an imperial system of rule, was a genuinely indigenous rather than simply a foreign (or "colonial") construct; that, hence, it was more Indian than British in inner logic, regardless of external interferences and violations of that logic by Britain (especially during the Crown period of this Raj); that, in terms of religious institutions, indigenous elites and local forces of all kinds were able to receive recognition and protection, as well as special concessions, from the State; and moreover, that they had been able to do this in direct proportion to their ability—whether by power of information control, numbers, noise, skill, or wealth—to influence local governments.

It is in the sphere of religious establishments, however, that the Raj became especially "Hindu". It is this sphere that, by yielding to special interests, the Government of Madras itself became instrumental in facilitating the rise of a centralizing and modern and syndicated Hinduism. Yet, it must be emphasized that this modern Hinduism was never the vehicle of more than a few tiny elites. It was never, as such, representative of any "majority community" in south

India (except in its own later, often self-serving, claims).

The roots of this modern symbiosis between government and local elites can be found in seventeenth century Madras. According to locally composed Sanskrit manuscript, entitled *Sarva-Deva-Vilāsa.*[19] Madras became the centre of an affluent and efflorescent cultural and religious awakening. In consequence there was a "celebration of the gods (and goddesses)". Whether presiding in stone or in flesh, local deities received all sorts of wealth. Their dwelling places were enlarged and enriched and multiplied. Their service establishments increased in size. Their festivals attracted even larger numbers of celebrants and devotees and pilgrims. And their patronage provided permanent hospitality and residence for more and more artists, dancers, musicians, poets, and scholars. The political significance of such developments was not overlooked by the rulers. Europeans (Farangis) though they were, they too provided suitable tokens of propitiation, sometimes making endowments. Certain rulers themselves, but more often their Baniya agents (Dubashis) made appropriate gestures of support. In short, under the Raj, alien rulers and influential elites worked closely together in their own mutual self-interests and benefit to do what was politic. Their mercantile-cum-military efforts, whatever their private or personal motives, were seen to have been blessed by local deities. As the economy flourished and brought wealth to the city, the gods smiled and danced.

No single process perhaps better highlights the growth of the "modern Hindu" establishment in south India than the successive stages of policy taken with respect to temples and temple endowments. While the immediate motives for Regulation VII of 1817 have yet to be fully fathomed and while direct reasons for that action have, in consequence, yet to be fully explored, plausible explanations are possible. The "takeover" of direct responsibility for the administration, building, upkeep, and general maintenance of temples and their functions seems to have been inspired by what can only be described as essentially "conservative" impulses—as profoundly socio-political and socio-economic but also, incidentally, as antiquarian and conservationist.

Some of the roots of these impulses would seem to lie in the nascent "Orientalism" of the late eighteenth century. Epitomized in the north by the vision of Warren Hastings and his scholarly proteges (Halhed, Jones, Wilkins, etc.), in the south this seem originally to have come out of the efforts of Colin Mackenzie and his Brahman entourage. It was through their initial efforts, followed by those of Brahmans who surrounded Thomas Munro, Walter Elliot and other successors of the Scottish Enlightenment in Madras, that a colossal campaign in the collection of information (artistic, antiquarian, and historical) occurred. Few countries in the world have ever had the benefit of such enlightened, if also exceedingly canny, concern and curiosity. Moreover such early efforts to discover and preserve the exotic remains of an entire past civilization were anything but impractical. Survey of antiquities, of archaeological remains and objects, of epigraphic and numismatic sources, and of any and all grand legacies from previous centuries, were conducted on a hitherto unprecedented scale. The information about materials so sought out and acquired was then catalogued and preservation efforts initiated. All of these efforts were begun *before* the State took formal responsibility for the running and care of temples. But, in the end, what was initiated and eventually achieved was control. This control was more comprehensive and more integrative than anything previously known or even thought possible.[20]

From 1817 onwards, consequently, the Government of Madras took direct responsibility for the daily exercises of "Hinduism". All ceremonies being conducted within all the temples under its sway, from the largest and oldest institutions of Kanchipuram, Madurai, Srirangam and Tirupati (to name but a few of the most prominent places) to the newest and tiniest *koils* which sprang up, whether by a busy roadside or in some remote village, came under direct management of the imperial State. Not only did the State take control over temple revenues and supervise temple repairs; but it also enforced entrenched local customs and practices in which it might otherwise have never been involved. By such control, the State acquired the proceeds of taxes upon pilgrims and the surpluses gained at fairs and festivals, as well as similar benefits from all places where large numbers of people came together—from temples, *tīrthas*, and *melā* grounds.[21] For such control, the State also required its personnel, both military and civilian, including those who were Muslim and Christian (and European), to attend festivals and celebrations (*melās, tīrthas*, etc.), regardless of protests or qualms of conscience at blood sacrifices. It saw to it that prescribed numbers of labourers were commandeered for the pulling of the many enormous temple cars which had to be ceremonially moved in every locality of the Madras Presidency (such number of coolies coming to many hundreds of thousands a year). It either turned a blind eye to institutionalized local blood rituals and temple prostitution (involving hundreds of thousands of *devadāsīs*) or, as sometimes happened, it stood silently by while some of its own servants, both Native and European, propitiated such institutions. In the remotest *mufassal kachcheri,* its twice-born (*dvija*) officials sat like deities and would not allow themselves to be approached by *mleccha* petitioners from menial and polluting communities (Frykenberg 1979: 311-21; 1982b: 34-52).

Yet, at the same time, in order to collect and refine the accuracy of its own information resources and its information networks, the State also supported special schools and employed batteries of those same *dvija* officials. These served as its authorities—*munshis, pundits, shastris, vakils,* translators and such (in such places as the courts and *kachcheries,* in the Sadr Adalat, in the College of Fort St. George, in the Oriental Manuscripts Library, and in the University). These pandits, along with many local European authorities (such as C.P. Brown, Walter Elliot, J.H. Nelson, Robert Caldwell, Robert Sewell, Thurston, and many others)[22] established a tradition of learning, research, and scholarship which could provide the State with reliable information on each and every religious traditions found within the authority of Madras Presidency.

Eventually, when this policy of "Hinduization" was discovered for what it truly was, it provoked a profound shock. The policy was deemed by opponents, both in India and Britain, to be inherently "heathen" if not "anti-Christian". When those who were pious in Britain fully realized what their avowedly Christian nation was actually allowing to happen in India—that an agency of Light was truly in alliance with forces of Darkness and Evil—their reaction was predictable. This discovery led to the formation of the Anti-Idolatry Connexion League, a lobby specifically organized to produce evidence and to fight against the State's violation of "religious neutrality". At the same time, on the other side, the Company's governments in India were attacked by those who saw that, at the very least, this policy constituted a gross "interference" with Native customs and institutions. Such was the storm of outrage that the Government of Madras eventually found itself gradually forced to retreat. Nevertheless, the Government managed to drag its feet and managed to prevent any actual reversal of its operations. It continued to do this for more than thirty years (from 1833 to 1863).

It is also interesting to note, on the other side, that this policy was never attacked by Brahmans, nor by the newly forming Madras Hindoo Association (forerunner of the Madras Native Association and the Madras Mahajana Sabha), nor by the governing Board of the Pachaiyappa Charities. In short, those who were supposedly being interfered with were not only remarkably silent and submissive, they were also eventually aroused and only goaded into counteracting efforts by the virulently anti-Hindu rhetoric of the attacks upon the Government's policy. Such attacks served to awaken a public "Hindu" consciousness which had never before existed.

Nevertheless, after thirty years of agitation and controversy, a new policy of supposedly enshrining the principles of "Non-Interference" by Government became law and eventually came into force. But, by the time Act XX of 1863 was passed, an entirely new "Hindu" public had already begun to arise in Madras. This new non-official, professional elite was able to effectively use litigation and court decrees to bring about a further consolidation of modern Hinduism. Brahman lawyers of Mylapore and Egmore, Chettiyar mercantile and banking families in the cities, and Zamindari magnates of the *mufassal*, effectively fought for control of various temple endowments. In the process, by using the entire legal apparatus of the State as their battleground for the settlement of disputes and for the handling of local resources to engage in various local struggles, these forces were able, whether inadvertently or not, to gradually build a structure of legal precedents for the rise of an entirely new religion (Price 1979: 226-34).

All sort of issues pertaining to "*the* Hindu" religion or "Hinduism", as this now became known and ever more reified, were settled in this manner. The structure of precedent law which now emerged served as the foundation for a new kind of court enforced "corporate Hinduism" the likes of which had never been seen before (Sontheimer 1964: 45-100). By the time the Madras Legislative Assembly finally passed Act II of 1927, again effectively reversing the legislation of 1863 and, for all practical purposes, reinstating Regulation VII of 1817, the structures of this new kind of state-supported "corporate Hinduism" were already in place. By its provisions, Act XX of 1927 formally created the Hindu Religious and Charitable Endowments Board and (Administrative) Department. With subsequent modifications (in 1952 and later), this institution has remained in force ever since (Mudaliar 1974; Beckenridge 1976; Appadurai 1981: Chaps. 3, 4, and 5).

By this time, from 1927 onwards, there could be little doubt that a new kind of religious system, a kind of unofficial, state-sponsored "Hinduism" which was predominantly if not overwhelmingly Brahmanic and Sanskritic, with Shramanic overtones, had come into being. All that was needed thereafter was for a new concept of "majority" and of "majority community" to arise and for the myth of "Hindu majority" to become consolidated in the popular mind (Frykenberg 1987: 267-74). That task was easily accomplished by the public media. This vehicle, already epitomized by such papers as *The Hindu* and *Kalki,* was itself largely in the hands of the rising establishment of a newly "syndicated Hinduism" which was itself heavily Brahman dominated and *dvija* in character (V.T. Rajshekar 1985: 41).

IV

This, then, brings us to the second major process which, in dialectical opposition to the power Establishment of the imperial State, served to bring modern Hinduism into being. This process, being at once socio-political and "representational", consisted of movements and pressure groups which grew up *outside* the structures of the State. These groups, lobbying for special constituencies, sought to modify those structures. They did this in order to suit particular aspirations or needs at points where these came into conflict or impinged upon those of the State. Organized agitation, petition, and other pressure and tactics became the *modus operandi* of various groups which became part of this process.

Here we must turn to another thread in this already snarled and tangled web. This has to do with the radical conversion movements which have occurred in modern times. All too often, for want of alternatives, such movements have been labelled "Hindu"; and , all too conveniently and closely, they have also been identified with and lumped into a common "Hinduism". Such movements in varying degrees, have all blended various elements found in other forms of Hinduism (as defined earlier), and then added some particular kinds of revivalistic, fundamentalistic, or nationalistic fervour and flavour which were distinctive. As first seen in south India, such movements made their earliest appearance in the 1820s, 1830s, and 1840s. All such movements seem to have been reactions to other radical conversion movements which had previously disturbed the *status quo* of social institutions in some locality and which, if traced far enough, can be found to have originated in Europe. Moreover, while previously there had been missionary movements which had attempted to bring about radical conversions within local societies of south India, none of these earlier movements had provoked the same kinds or intensities of reaction as those which were provoked during the nineteenth century. One form of pietistic Protestant Christainity from Northern Europe had brought a contagious virus of radical conversion to the Tamil coast and to Tanjore at the beginning of the eighteenth century. But not until this movement had become profoundly indigenized and taken to villages of the Tirunelveli countryside by radical Vallalar preachers had mass conversions brought about any seriously violent counter-actions from local gentry. And again, only when newly radical conversion movements were being brought about by fresh waves of European missionaries who were now of the same nationality as the ruling power and who began to agitate for special kinds of favourite treatment under law while, at the same time, they were attacking the Government for its "satanic" role in the process of Hinduization (by aiding and abetting the efforts of the Anti-Idolatry Connexion League, as indicated above) does one begin to see a rise of serious reactions from "Hindu" gentry both in Madras and throughout those parts of the Presidency where local institutions began to feel the impact of missionary agitations. These local Hindu reactions did not really begin until the 1820s and 1830s.

Interestingly, and ironically, it is only when Christian missionary activities became tainted by a new and rising ethos of "colonialism" and by undue (if not, as seen by some, to be an "unfair" and/or, at least, an unpolitic) reliance upon raw political power that such activities were either endangered or irretrievably damaged. Indeed, perhaps no single set of movements did more to further the growth of modern Hinduism in its "corporate" and its "revivalistic" forms than missionary institutions which were of this alien or colonialistic character. Both in the radical reactions which they provoked within local societies and in the educational institutions which were resisted, infiltrated, utilized, and ultimately copied by these same local elite societies did the rise of "Hinduism" in its modern manifestations probably owe more to certain missionary institutions than to anything else.

In south India, the first organized effort to raise a standard of resistance against radical conversion and against "colonialistic" missionary activity was the Vibuthi Sangam (or "Sacred Ashes Society"). Little is known about this shadowy organization, except that it first appeared in the 1820s in reaction to what was happening in Tirunelveli and that it advocated forcible reconversion and subordination of radicalized Shanar Christians to the agrarian order from which they were seeking to extricate themselves. The banners of the Dharma Sabha and of the Chatur Veda Sidhanatha Sabha (also known in Madras as the "Salay Street Society"), in contrast, were raised within the city of Madras during the 1830s and 1840s.[23] As with the Vibuthi Sangam, we do not know who led these early groups, how they were organized, or from what parts of local society they gained membership.

A second wave of such organizations, much more moderate in tone and more clearly focused upon specific educational, social, and political issues also began to come into being during the 1830s and 1840s. The Hindu Literary Society, Pachaiyappa's Charities, and the Madras Hindu Association were followed a decade later, in the late 1850s, by the Madras Native Association and, still later, by the Madras Mahajana Sabha. These organizations, clearly led by the Brahman and other highborn notables of Madras, were joined and strongly supported by a number of prominent Europeans, especially those who were incensed by the aggressiveness, insensitivity, and crude self-righteousness of some missionaries.[24] When efforts to bring reforms in Government policy were heeded, first in London and Calcutta and then in Madras itself, high caste communities soon found more than enough outlets for the fulfilment of their ambitions. The development of an elitist system of modern education (Frykenberg 1986: 37-65), as seen in the foundation of Madras University and the establishment of the Department of Public Instruction, and the rise of the other profession, especially in law and journalism, provided plenty of grounds for satisfaction. Some of these elitist "Hindu" moderates were among those who would later constitute a core of Madras delegates at early sessions of the Indian National Congress. Some, whether from Mylapore or Egmore, were founding members of the Madras Vakils Association.[25] Some more were to become acolytes of Annie Besant and the Theosophical Society in Adyar.

Still others, even at the risk of being "excommunicated" by the Shankaracharya at Kanchi, strove for "Hindu reform". Attempts to abolish such customs as female infanticide, child marriage, dowries, and temple prostitution (*devadāsis*), to allow widow remarriage, or to deal with many other "evils", however, seem to have been aimed more at the moral self-strengthening of the high-born elites in south India than at an ameliorating of dire conditions and degradation within backward elements of the entire society.[26] From the time of Vennelacunty Soob Row in the 1820s to that of the Veerasalingam a century later and from the rise of Sir T. Madhava Rao to that of Sir N. Madhava Rao, Sir C.P. Ramaswamy Aiyer and C. Rajagopalachari, there were dedicated and high-minded notables who tirelessly devoted themselves to what they saw as the eradication of social evils in their day.

But the extremist movements which began in south India with the Vibuthi Sangam and the Dharma Sabha—with their conservative resistance to change, with their rigid adherence to *varṇāśramadharma*, and with their caste exclusiveness—served to raise the alarm. It was this kind of reaction to perceptions of danger and threats to the social order which, ever since, has brought various forms of "Hindu" revivalism and fundamentalism into existence. These south Indian movements can be seen merely as forerunners, in turn, of later movements which grew up in the north and west of India and which since the turn of this century, have returned to the south. Movements such as the Arya Samaj,[27] the Nagari Pracharini Sabha,[28] the Hindu Mahasabha, and the Rashtriya Swayamsevak Sangh (RSS) have themselves been radical reactions to what were perceived as threats to the status quo. More recently, movements which seem to be even more extremist and revivalistic have arisen. Chief among the most recent of these are such militant and revivalist *jagarans* as the Vishwa Hindu Parishad (with its Dharma Sansad and Bajrang Dal, or youth wing),[29] the Virat Hindu Sammelan, Hindu Samajotsav, and the Shiv Sena.[30] These and other radical movements have recently generated other features in what may now be called "corporate", "modern", "organized" or "syndicated Hinduism".[31]

This process of reification has served to give modern Hinduism the character of a simulated "world-religion"—a character which is all too easily swallowed and then certified by naive and uncritical savants of oriental religion in the West. It has even provided the new religion with discrete form of denominationalism and certain "ecclesiastical" features which would have been quite out of character with the older sectarian institutions (*maṭhas*, *sampradāyas*, etc.) of

India's past. A new kind of "Hinduism" has arisen, "Hinduism" which not only resorts to "evangelizing" or "proselytizing", which not only has spawned a wide variety of "missions" and free-wheeling but profitable mercantile and entrepreneurial enterprises (e.g. Maharishi Rajneesh, Satya Sai Baba, Anand Marg and much more), but some of whose advocates are chauvinistic and fundamentalistic, even imperialistic in their demands. In claim to "represent" *all* the "pure" peoples (and, by inference, authority also over all other peoples, if not over *all* forms of life), protagonists of "Hinduism" in this sense have now given the term all sorts of new meanings. Advocates for this kind of "Hinduism" can now insist that they speak for "*the Hindu majority*" and that this is a majority which they alone *represent* (whether by divine fiat, by fiat of nature, by Tantric power, by some other kind of mandate). It is this Hinduism which, they insist, must have complete socio-political dominance over all peoples of India.

V

Since the thinking about this essay was begun, nearly two years ago, a new recognition of modern Hinduism has been begun to surface, both in scholarly as well as in journalistic circles. In September 1985, the results of "a symposium on some of the complexities of a dominant religion" which was directly concerned with "the Hindus and their isms" appeared in *Seminar.* Perhaps the most noteworthy single essay in this collection is that by Romila Thapar, sister of Romesh Thapar, the then (1985) editor of *Seminar,* and a professor of history at Jawaharlal Nehru University. Her essay raises many of the same points and, indeed, argues a thesis which is similar to that which has been presented here.

Declaring that "the term Hinduism as we understand it today to describe a *particular religion* is modern", she goes on to consider its creation:

> Inevitably, the Brahmanical base of what was seen as the new Hinduism was unavoidable. But merged into it were various bits and pieces of upper caste belief and ritual with one eye on the Christian and Islamic models. Its close links with certain nationalist opinions gave to many of these neo-Hindu movements a political edge that remains recognizable even today. It is this development which was the present-day *Syndicated Hinduism* [italics added] which is being pushed forward as the sole claimant to the inheritance of indigenous Indian religion (Thapar 1985: 21).

If there is one word which most come to mind and which seems most to epitomize the character of cultures and religions in south India since the eighteenth century, it is the word "*discontinuities*".[32] Discontinuities between different groups of people and between different cultures are among some of the most fascinating and attractive features of life in peninsular parts of the continent. Variety and disjunction is so endlessly fascinating and so kaleidoscopic that boredom seems impossible. Hundreds of ethnically and ideologically and ritually distinct communities, none of which will interdine nor intermarry, are a living mosaic of *discontinuities*. Either all of them are "Hindu"—by which one means that all of them live within same areas, localities, and regions and are thus commonly "indigenous" or "native" and thus commonly "Indian"—or none of them are.

Examples of common participation in certain kinds of activities or of contractual obligations which have for centuries provided linkages between communities—across the barriers and boundaries of discontinuity—cannot simply be seen as exceptions which prove a rule. Rather, such examples give us clues for understanding how, despite discontinuities, it has been possible for a commonality of things *Indian*, as distinct from *Hindu* culture, to emerge. Does the fact that an Untouchable Madiga or Chakriyar leatherworker makes and beats the drums for a civic ceremonial or a common festival make him or his community Hindu? Does the fact that a Muslim mahout cares for and rides the elephant of a large temple make him a Hindu? Does the participation of Parava or Nadar or other Christian communities in ceremonies connected to major or minor local (temple) deities make them Hindu? Does an endowment by a European to a temple ritual make that European Hindu? If Christian doctors and nurses work in a local hospital which is maintained by temple endowments, are they thereby Hindu? What is it that an image-maker when he uses the same molds to produce plaster or clay or even metal (*pañcaloha*) figurines both of a Blessed Virgin Mary and of a Mariamman? Are we to characterize him and his work as being both Catholic and Śaiva Siddhānta? Is he Hindu or Catholic? And, if one or other or both, how is this so?

There was a time, not long ago, if not still, when any and all Untouchables—all *mlecchas*, whether lowly local outcastes or barbarian aliens from overseas—were prohibited from entering any proper temple. Being *adharma* and beyond the pale of *dvija* purity, local pollution rules almost invariably forbade them from being considered "Hindu" in any participatory or respectable manner. There are still many places in south India—*agrahāra* villages or Brahman quarter, etc.—where the "unclean" may *never* enter, or may enter by accident at the peril of their lives. By the 1931 Census, the list of "Scheduled Castes and Tribes" who were officially classified as "untouchable" or "criminal" or "aboriginal" contained 117 names.[33] Did these communities not share enough of a common culture or a common religion for them to be considered Hindu? How then are we to interpret the words of protest which the Adi Dravida Jana Sabha recorded a dozen years earlier: "We would fight to the last drop of our blood any attempt to transfer the seat of authority in this country from British hands to the so-called high caste Hindus"?[34] What did they mean? What fear did they articulate?

The point at issue, therefore, is whether there is any scientific or systematic way to determine who was or who is or who is not a Hindu. However much the Registrar General of the Census or however much contemporary politicians may insist upon lumping nearly 80 per cent of the peoples of India under this categorical designation, it is almost impossible to determine how many of peoples so categorized would identify themselves as "Hindus" and, moreover, what such a self-identity would mean in a religious, as distinct from a cultural or geographical or national or political context. Context, indeed, may be seen as making all the difference.

G.P. Deshpande, in suggesting that this "majority community" could well be the creation of journalistic parlance, has recently asked: "Is it a case of simulated identity which over the years has been accepted as true identity?" Perhaps the answer to this question, he suggests, is that such terms as "Hindu" and "majority community" are merely "pop talk" survivals which would not exist were it not that "minority" communities are relatively easy to define and describe. In other words, "the majority community syndrome is also a way of looking at people. There are Hindus in the sense that there has developed in this country a way of looking at people or the so-called 'majority community' as the Hindus. This was perhaps not the case before colonialism came to this country. It is doubtful if the people talked of themselves as Hindus before the colonial phase in our history" (Deshpande 1985: 23-5).

NOTES

1. Since earlier drafts of this essay were written, work done by Wilfred Cantwell Smith, Heinrich von Stietencron, Romila Thapar, and Peter van der Veer have come to light. These serve, in different ways to reinforce my central argument. I must also acknowledge, with gratitude, my debt to Günther Sontheimer and Hermann Kulke both for providing the occasion and, by their own work, the inspiration for this study.
2. Wilfred Cantwell Smith 1964, argues that the very term "religion" is itself no less erroneous or dangerous. It is the invention of modern times, arising and being applied, for the most part, in the nineteenth and twentieth centuries.
3. W.C. Smith (1964: 61): "The term 'Hinduism' is, in my judgement, a particularly false conceptualization, one that is conspicuously incompatible with any adequate understanding of the religious outlook of the Hindus. Even the term 'Hindu' [an Indian or non-Muslim inhabitant of India] was unknown to the classical Hindus. 'Hinduism' as a concept they certainly did not have."
4. Oxford, 1971: OUP. Vol. H, 293-4 (*OED*).
5. W.C. Smith [1964: 249 (note 46)]. In so saying, Smith relied upon the scholarship in Fr. Spiegel, *Die altpersischen Keilinschriften, im Grundtext mut Übersetzung, Grammatik und Glossar.* Leipzig: 2nd ed. 1881, Vol. I (lines 17-18, A, line 25), 50, 54, 246.
6. Edward C. Sachau (transl. and ed.), *Alberuni's India.* London: Routledge & Kegan Paul, 1888, Preface, x-xlvi, 4. In this regard, it should be noted that while Sachau himself referred to Abū Al-Raihān Muhammad Ibn 'Ahmad Al Biruni's great work by the Greek term "Indika", its proper title may perhaps more appropriately be "*Tarīkh al-Hind*".
7. While exact instances of early usage may be uncertain, and hence debatable, sample early usages are found in the *OED.* This (Vol. H, 294) traces "Hindooism" back to a 1829 reference in the *Bengalee,* 45; and then cites an 1858 instance by Max Müller in *Chips* (1880, II, xxvii, 304: "Hinduism is a decrepit religion and has not many years to live". Modern English use of such terms as "Hindoo" and "Hindooism" probably began to become current by the end of the eighteenth century. For early usages see: Peter Marshall (ed.), *The British discovery of Hinduism in the eighteenth century.* Cambridge: CUP, 1970: Introduction, 1-44; Dow, 114; Halhed, 149-50; Jones, "On the Hindus', 246-61. Also see: Rosanne Rocher 1983.
8. *Webster's New Collegiate Dictionary,* 7th ed., 1961, informs us that Hinduism is: (1) "a body of social, cultural and religious beliefs and practices native to the Indian subcontinent"; (2) "the dominant cultic religions of India marked by participation in one of the devotional sects"; (3) "a religious philosophy based on Hinduism—e.g. *karma*". None of these definitions is satisfactory, the last being nothing more than a circular tautology: i.e. "Hinduism is a philosophy based on Hinduism."
9. John Zephaniah Holwell, in his *The religious tenets of the Gentoos* (1767), deals with this term; and Nathaniel Brassey Halhed, in his *A code of Gentoo laws* (1776), alludes to the term as one "affixed by Europeans" and, possibly, by the Portugese on their first arrival in India who heard it "applied to mankind in

general"; and adds that "perhaps also their bigotry might force from the word Gentoo a fanciful allusion to gentile or Pagan." (Marshall 1983: 150), op. cit., 150.

10. One must recall, in this connection, that earlier European (or Farangi) contacts with India—whether first through Portugese channels which were mainly Roman Catholic or, later, through Dutch or English (if not also French) channels which were predominantly Protestant and secular—had mainly taken place in south India, insomuch that there had been relatively little occasion for referene to the things of Hindustan (or Indostan).
11. Sometimes the term "High" or "Philosophical Hinduism" is also used to designate this particular variant of Indian cultures and religions. Again, as has been pointed out to me by Peter van der Veer, there is a distinction which is commonly made, both between and within different traditions found in India, between traditions which are "shastric" and traditions which are "pramanic" in character; moreover, this seems to have been, since ancient times, dealing with "discontinuties" between different beliefs, communities, and practice. Furthermore, such distinctions are exemplified, if not illuminated, by the way in which all parties within the great Minakshi-Sundaresvarar abode (temple) in Madurai refer to "the idea of *the* Agamas". Fuller (1984) and Parry (1985).
12. "Dharma" means "Proper or Rightful Order" of all things, or "Correct System," or even "Rightfulness" (vs. Righteousness), hence "Sacred" or "Duty" or "Religion"; "Sanatana" means "Old" and hence "Sacred" or "Traditional"; and finally, "Arya Dharm" means "Order or Religion or System of the Aryans". The knowledge which describes this system, both as science and as an ideology, was "Vedic" knowledge.
13. V.T. Rajshekar (1985: 41-7) gives one of the latest recognitions of this perspective. The classic positions were those taken up by such leaders as Ambedkar and Azariah. In doing so they antagonized Gandhi. Indeed, it may well have been their successful mass movements among Untouchables, especially during the 1920s and 1930s, which promted Gandhi to "annex" or "co-opt" Untouchables into the "Hindu" nationalist fold by the simple device of calling them *harijans* by advocating their admission to temples and other symbolic bastions of "clean" caste dominance.
14. *Saturday Review* (London 1857), 460-61, refers to Europeans who became "Hindooised". *Memorials of the life and letters of major-general Sir Herbert B. Edwardes by his wife*, London, 1886, II, 296, refers to the "Hindooized" Mohammedans in India. For further references, see *OED*, 294.
15. *The Sphinx speaks,* New Delhi: Sadgyan Sadan, 1963, by J.P. Singhal, for example, would want us to believe that when protoplasm first oozed from the primordial slime, 960,000 years ago, this must have happened in the Indo-Gangetic Plain and that the first noteworthy sound to come therefrom must have been "Om"! By such logic, an evolving chauvinism reaches a new peak of cosmological claims.
16. Heinrich von Stietencron, "Hinduism: On the proper use of a deceptive term", (p. 6 in MS.), writes: "As far as religion is concerned, we are left, not with solutions, but with *continuing contradictions*" (Italics mine). (Editors' note: The referred sentence is not in the present version of H. von Stietencron's contribution.)

17. "What we ought to have is *information*. The first, the seocnd and the third thing a government ought always to have is *information*", Lord Ellenborough had written to Sir John Malcolm, in another context. (Ingram 1979: 156).
18. For this new conceptualization, I am indebted to Romila Thapar (1985: 14-22).
19. Translated and edited, with a critical historical analysis, by the late V. Raghavan, and published in *The Adyar Library Bulletin*, 21, 3, 4 and 22, 1, 2 (n. d.: 1956?), this is a unique palm-leaf manuscript in the Grantha script.
20. In this respect, one must remember that repairs to temples and sponsorship of public fairs and festivals had always been among the duties of indigenous rulers, both small and great. Thus, by stepping into the shoes of these previous rulers, the Company not only took a poweful set of instruments into its own hands, but it made itself acceptable to local Brahman elites. The radical difference, of course, lay in the fact that the Company integrated all such local institutions into one, huge, over-arching system of legitimization and control. What began in 1639, when the Company itself became an indigenous ruler in one locality, ended by its integrating all of south India. Arjun Appadurai, *Worship and conflict under colonial rule: A South Indian case*, Cambridge: CUP, 1981, brings this out in detail.
21. After all, as Heinrich von Stietencron has so acutely reminded me, such places had for centuries been the nerve centre of an All-India communication network. Moreover, they still served as important nodes for opinion-generating and opinion-disseminating throughout India, something which accelerated with the increasing use of new road (and rail) facilities.
22. See G.D. Reddy and Bangorey [pen name of B.G. Reddy] (eds.) *Literary Autobiography of C.P. Brown*. Tirupati: SVU, 1978; Robbert Sewell, *Sir Walter Elliot of Wolfelee: A sketch of his life and a few extracts from his note books*. Edinburgh, 1896; J.H. Nelson, *Madura Country: A Manual*, Madras, 1886, etc.
23. Less strident, more eclectic and inclusivist, if not irenic, in nationalistic fervour, and more open to Christian, European and Muslim members of society, on the other hand, were the Hindu Literary Society, the Madras Hindoo Association, the Madras Native Association, and even the Madras Mahajana Sabha, in its earlier stages. These were groups in south India which might be compared, in their openness, with such Bengal institutions as the Hindu College of Calcutta or Brahmo Samaj or Raja Rammohun Roy.
24. Following in the spirit of Sir Thomas Munro, the Madras Governor who died of Cholera while on tour in Cuddapah and whose Brahman and British acolytes fought to preserve his policies in subsequent decades, were many local European residents of Madras. George Norton (Advocate General), Malcolm Lewin (a staunch Unitarian), John Bruce Norton (practicing barrister), C.D. Powell (professor of Fort St. George College; first principal of Pachaiyappa's School), Peter Pope [secretary of Madras University (High School)], William Taylor (renegade missionary, orientalist, author of *Madrasiana*), Eardley Norton (barrister), and many more.
25. John J. Paul has just completed a Ph.D. dissertation on this at the University of Wisconsin, Madison.
26. Veerasalingam became one of the most prominent of the *mufassal* reformers of the early twentieth century. The lists of reformers, of their more conservative opponents, are long. *An Indian view of Hindu customs: Lectures by Rao Bahadur*

Kandukuri Viresalingam Pantulu. Translated by E.E. Silliman (manuscript copy in possession of the author).

27. See Kenneth W. Jones, *Arya Dharm: Hindu Consciousness in 19th Century Punjab.* Berkeley: UC Press, 1976, many articles and papers on this.
28. *The Nagari Pracharini Sabha (Society for the Promotion of the Nagari Language and Script) of Benares, 1893-1950: A Study in the Social and Political History of the Hindi Language* (Madison: University of Wisconsin, Ph.D. Dissertation, unpublished, 1974).
29. I am indebted to Peter van der Veer who, both in private comment and in his article "God must be liberated! A Hindu Liberation Movement in Ayodhya". *Modern Asian Studies* 21, 2, (1987), 283-301, emphasizes the point that religious identity is never a "primordial attachment" but that it is always an option open to the soical actor who may articulate, underplay or stress this identity, depending on the situation in which he finds himself. It may be an identity forced upon him from without or from within, and therefore always the result of a political process.
30. *India Today* (May 11, 1990), 30-9 (cover story).
31. "Syndicated Hinduism", already alluded to on page 95, is a concept recently developed by Romila Thapar, in her article "Syndicated moksha" (1985: 14-22), now part of this volume, pp. 54-81
32. I am indebted to James Manor for this concept. His insightful comments and discussions have been invaluable to me in my work on this theme.
33. *Census of India* (1931), Vol. XIV, 339-46. G.O. [Government Order] 227 (27 June 1930), Public (Services); G.O. 719 (2 July 1931), Public (Services), App. III.
34. *Reports of the Franchise Committee.* New Delhi: GOI, 1918-19, 19f.

REFERENCES

Appadurai, A. 1981. *Worship and conflict under Colonial rule: A South Indian case.* Cambridge: CUP

Beckenridge, C.A. 1976. *The Sri Minaksi Sundaresvarar temple: A study of worship and endowments in south India. 1800-1975.* Ph.D. diss., University of Wisconsin.

Deshpande, G.P. 1985. The plural tradition. In *Seminar* 313 (September), 23-25.

Dykes, J.B.W. 1854. *Salem, an Indian collectorate.* Madras.

Frykenberg, R.E. 1979. Conversion and crisis of conscience under company Raj in south India. In *Asie du Sud, tradition et changements: VIIth European Conference on South Asian Studies,* Sevres 8-13 juillet 1978 (*Colloques Internationaux du Center National de la Recherche Scientifique*), Paris, 311-21.

———. 1982a. The socio-political morphology of Madras: An historical interpretation. In *South Asia: City and Culture* (ed.) K.A. Ballhatchet and David Taylor. London: Center of South Asian Studies, SOAS, University of London/Hong Kong: Asian Research Service (Papers of the Seventh European Conference on Modern South Asian Studies (published under UNESCO auspices), 21-42.

———. 1982b. On roads and riots in Tinnevelly: radical change and ideology in Madras Presidency during the nineteenth century. In *South Asia IV*, 2 (December), 34-52.

———. 1986. Modern education in south India, 1784-1854: Its roots and its role as a vehicle of integration under Company Raj. In *The American Historical Review* 91, I (February) 37-65.

———. 1987. The concept of "Majority" as a devilish force in the politics of modern India: A historiographic comment. In *Journal of the Commonwealth History and Comparative Politics* 25, 3 (November), 267-74.

———. 1993a. "Constructions of Hinduism at the nexus of history and religion", In *Journal of Interdisciplinary History*, 23, 523-50.

———. 1993b. Religion, nationalism and Hindu fundamentalism: The challenge to Indian unity. In *Ethnic Studies Report* (Kandy) 11, 2, 125-42. (ICES Annual Lecture, 20 August 1993, published as a separate pamphlet).

———. 1994. Fundamentalism in South Asia: Ideologies and institutions in historical perspective. In *Accounting for fundamentalisms: The dynamic character of movements*. Chicago: University of Chicago Press, 1994. (*The Fundamentalism Project: Volume VI*. Edited by Martin Marty and R. Scott Appleby.)

Fuller, C.J. 1984. *Servants of the goddess: The priests of south Indian temple.* Cambridge: CUP.

Ingram, K. 1979. *The beginning of the Great Game in Asia, 1828-1849.* Oxford.

Jones, W.J. 1976. *Arya Dharm: Hindu consciousness in 19th century Punjab.* Berkeley: UC Press.

Marshall, P. (ed.) 1983. *The British discovery of Hinduism in the eighteenth century.* Cambridge: CUP.

Mudaliar, C.Y. 1974. *The secular state and religious institutions in India: A study of the administration of Hindu public religious trusts in Madras.* Wiesbaden.

Nelson, J.H. 1886. *Madras country: A manual.* Madras.

O'Connell, J.T. 1973. Gauḍiya Vaiṣṇava symbolism of deliverence from evil. In *Journal of the American Oriental Society* 93, 3, 340-43.

Parry, Jonathan P. 1985. The Brahmanical tradition and the technology of the intellect. In *Reason and morality* (ed.) J. Overting (ASA Monograph) London: Academic Press.

Price, P.G. 1979. Raja-dharma in nineteenth century South India: Land, litigation and largess. In *Contributions to Indian Sociology* 13, 2 (NS), 226-34.

Rajshekar, V.T. 1985. Anti-human. In *Seminar* 313 (September), 41-47.

Reddy, G.D. 1978. ...and Bangorey [pen name of B.G. Reddy] (eds.) *Literary autobiography of C.P. Brown.* Tirupati: SVU.

Rocher, S. 1983. *Orientalism, poetry, and the millennium: The checkered life of Nathaniel Brassey Halhed.* Columbia MO: South Asia Books; New Delhi: Motilal Banarsidass.

Sachau, E.C. 1888. Transl. and ed. *Alberuni's India.* London: Routledge and Kegan Paul.

Sewell, R. 1896. *Sir Walter Elliot of Wolfelee: A sketch of his life and a few extracts from his note books.* Edinburg.

Singhal, J.P. 1963. *The Sphinx speaks.* New Delhi: Sadgyan Sadan.

Smith, W.C. 1964. *The meaning and end of religion: A new approach to the religious traditions of mankind.* New York: Macmillan 1962, 1963; Mentor; 1964.

Sontheimer, G.-D. 1964. Religious endowments in India: The juristic personality of Hindu deities. In *Zeitschrift für vergleichende Rechtswissenschaft.* 67, 45-100.

Spiegel, Fr. 1881. *Die altpersischen Keilschriftinschriften, im Grundtext mit Übersetzung, Grammatik und Glossar.* Leipzig, 2nd ed.

Thapar, Romila 1985. Syndicated moksha. In *Seminar* 313 (September), 14-22. (Reprinted in this volume).

Veer, P. van der 1987. God must be liberated! A Hindu liberation movement in Ayodhya. In *Modern Asian Studies* 21, 2, 283-301.

RELIGION, REACTION AND CHANGE: THE ROLE OF SECTS IN HINDUISM[1]

Anncharlott Eschmann

Every religion knows different "sects" or "schools". By introducing changes and thereby provoking reactions they usually play an important role in the development of the religions. Though this may be—roughly speaking—the role of sects in all religions, there are considerable differences in the way changes are introduced in different religions and in the way reactions are taking place. Particularly in Hinduism the very specific and vital role of sects in the process of continuous formation and reshaping of tradition is often underestimated as one is often inclined to look at Hinduism as a closed, somehow static system, unsympathetic to change and developments.

The term "sect" is a Christian one. Although applied to other religions, it tends to retain still some of its original meaning. It therefore seems advisable to start with a short explanation of what sect means within Christianity, especially as the Christian concept of sect influenced the modern development of Hinduism. Sect is the Latin translation of the Greek term "*hairesis*", the literary meaning being "choice". In the Greek context the term originally denoted any philosophical school or religious community one might choose to belong to. Being used by Jews and Christians the term acquired a definite negative connotation, designating opinions, schools or communities whose tenets were not only considered to be deviating, but to be altogether wrong. With the development of the Latin and Byzantine churches and their growing power, the notion of heresy became more important. Not only was a false doctrine resented and fought as such, it was moreover considered as a sinful contradiction against the established dogma and confession of the orthodox church, which claimed to be the only steward of the means of redemption. The term "sect" thus acquired a thoroughly negative meaning, a community which sticks to heretical tenets condemned by the orthodox church, having thereby "cut off" itself from orthodoxy. It was because of this meaning that the etymology of the word "sect" was reinterpreted: being originally derived from the Latin verb *sequi* ("to follow") it was later on considered to be a form of *secare* ("to cut"). This connotation of the word "sect" was also adopted by Protestantism, being itself a sect in the view of Catholicism, a church in its own view.

The very brief survey shows that, within Christianity, "sect" is always both an offspring of the church and opposed to the "church". It was the great theologist and historian Ernst Troeltsch (1865-1923) who, being influenced by Max Weber, took up a systematic study of the various concepts of sects. He considered the ideas of church, sect, and mysticism as the three constituent elements of Christianity, which determined its development. He defined "church" as the broad institution administrating the means of grace and redemption. Relying on the objective character of these means rather than on the subjective sanctification of the individual, the church is able to admit masses as well as adapt itself to the world and its mundane affairs. The sect is exactly the opposite. According to Troeltsch it is based on a free union of deeply religious and most conscious Christians, separating themselves from the world and usually remaining confined to small following. They stress the commandment instead of the grace and try to establish the Christian regimen more or less radically whilst waiting for the coming Kingdom of God. Troeltsch's definitions are like those of Max Weber ideal types which define conceptual ideals rather than actual structures.[2]

One has to distinguish between the "ideal" concept of sect and church as defined by Troeltsch,[3] and the "pragmatic types", i.e. the historically grown actual churches and sects. Within the "pragmatic" Protestant Churches the sects had a new and slightly different meaning. Setting out on educational, social and missionary activities, Pietism and other movements developed special forms of subsidiary organizations which bridged in a way different needs of church and sect. Amongst these religious societies the Society for the Propagation of Christian Knowledge, the Young Men's Christian Association (YMCA) and the Salvation Army are particularly well-known. Their aim is to penetrate the church from within by creating specific organizations for different purposes and for different classes, age groups and ranges of people. These organizations bear several typical features of a sect. They consist of comparatively small congregations, and emphasize ethical strictness. Membership is attained by choice and mostly conveys the feeling of belonging to an elite. They show even features of a typical antagonism between sect and church, but as they mostly do not aim at introducing doctrinal changes, usually no segregation occurs. The subsidiary organizations played and still play a considerable role in development of Christianity. Most activities towards social welfare and general education in the last two centuries were accomplished through this type of religious institutions. It is therefore not astonishing that their organization and activities deeply influenced the various forms of "modernism" of other religions.

The fundamental role of Christian sects, as dissenting separately organized communities, is obvious. By protesting against the prevalent tradition, and going back to the "original sources" which they set out to reinterpret, the sects are continuously introducing elements of reform and, through the means of interpreting the scriptures anew, sometimes even radical changes. The very formation of a sect—i.e. the partial segregation from the main church—is the reaction of the main tradition against the changes introduced by the sect. Though officially rejected at first, on the long run the changes advocated by the sect influence the main stream of tradition. The church has to adapt itself to the claims advocated by the sect and has to remedy the abuses criticised by the sect, etc.

Modern Sociology of Religion has tried to define the term "sect" in such a way as to be more easily applied to the "pragmatic" types within Christianity as well as to similar institutions in other religions. Whereas "church" is understood to be the broader organization, converting a wider region, "sect" is determined as a relatively small community being only a rather isolated section of a broader religious institution. Its characteristics are a spirit of protest and criticism against the institutional means of redemption, voluntary joining, ethical strictness and a feeling of being an elite.[4] This definition clearly reflects the Christian origin of the term and its indebtedness to Troeltsch and Max Weber. All its characteristics can only be understood out of the basic confrontation with the Christian concept of church, and will hardly apply to religions where there is no church-like organization.

II

In Hinduism the term "sect" was introduced by analogy. Western scholars of the nineteenth century as for instance H.H. Wilson,[5] named the various religious Hindu communities accordingly as sects which were distinguished by traditions and scriptures and rituals of their own and by worship of certain gods and often their founder as well. These names have persisted ever since.

But the similarity between Hindu and Christian sects is merely a superficial one. In Hinduism these groups have a very different function and position. As a matter of fact there exists practically no Sanskrit word meaning "sect" in the sense of a heterodox community. On the contrary, the term usually translated as sect, *sampradāya*, has instead a connotation of orthodoxy! It literally means "what is handed over", i.e. "tradition", and in modern Indian languages has also become an equivalent of "religion" (Hindu-*sampradāya* for instance). What constitutes a so called Hindu sect is not the fact of being rejected by a central authoritative institution. It is the tradition founded by a "sage" or "saint" (*ācārya, guru*). For instance, the school founded by Śaṅkarācārya, generally considered to be one of the most venerable and orthodox manifestations of Hinduism, is called *sampradāya*. But the same term is used to denote dissenting and protesting communities like for instance *Vīraśaivism*. These "radical *sampradāyas*", as one might call them, introduced not only doctrinal changes, but in many cases also were advocates of radical social change. They challenged orthodoxy by, for instance, not admitting image worship or by not recognizing and even deliberately trespassing caste barriers.

It was probably the German scholar Joachim Wach who first pointed out the unique character of the *sampradāya* in the context of comparative sociology of religion.[6] Unlike a Christian sect, it does not primarily rely on a close community of lay men. Instead, the very core of their religious activities are the centres where the tradition is handed down, namely the *āśramas* and *maṭhas* and in general the monastic orders initiated by the founder. The lay community is in most cases not strictly defined, only very few groups, like *Vīraśaivism* or the *Manbhaus* do have a special initiation ceremony for lay members, too.

The extraordinary position of the *sampradāya* emerges from the three special features which are characteristic of Hinduism. The first and perhaps most striking of these features is the absence of any centralized institution which could control orthodoxy. There are institutions defining and supervising orthodoxy, but, and this makes all the difference, they are of consequence only within a certain place or region and are usually linked with a certain caste. Moreover, the object of their definitions is mostly not doctrinal. It is mainly in the realm of ritual and social behaviour that orthodoxy has to be proved, an orthodoxy not generally defined but qualified by caste and by region.

The concept of "qualified orthodoxy" allows Hindu tradition its tolerance and openness. This concept also explains, why Hinduism never developed any church-like institution. The exception is, of course, the well-known attempt to invest the *maṭhas* allegedly founded by Śaṅkara with a sort of pontifical dignity, which in practice however never acquired an unchallenged authority. A church-like institution was, so to speak, apparently not necessary because of the very existence of the caste system. Castes were able to perform many of the functions usually assigned to churches. For instance the selection and training of priests—one of the most important prerogative of churches—could be left to the family tradition of the Brahmins. Accordingly there was no need for the political authority to establish an unified state church: the installation of Brahmanical state cult at the royal court would be sufficient. Caste and church as defined by Troeltsch have striking similarities: the power to excommunicate or outcast rebels—the trusteeship of "sacraments" like marriage, admission by birth and the connection with political authority. Caste being to a certain degree the equivalent of a church, it is natural that it should also be the counterpart of the sect. But whereas the Christian churches have tried to reject the sects and their attempts to introduce changes, thereby causing segregations, caste and *sampradāya* are basically supplementary. These links between caste and *sampradāya* are strengthened by the second special feature of Hinduism, the institution of the guru.

The words of a spiritual teacher, or guru, are considered as direct revelations. His teachings may be questioned by other schools but can never completely be ruled out because of the lack of a central institution. Moreover, a guru is considered by his disciples as a god incarnate. It is said to be easier to obtain the forgiveness of a god than of one's guru. In spite of this exalted position, neither to become nor to follow a certain guru is in any way limited to certain castes or persons. Everybody can become an ascetic, a *yogī* or *saṃnyāsī*, and potentially a guru thereby overcoming the barriers of caste. Everybody is equally free to follow whatever school or guru he likes, as long as he fulfils the basic ritual and social requirements of his caste. In traditional Hinduism redemption is considered to be an individual affair. Although socially determined by birth, spiritually the individual is free to choose his own way of redemption, the guru to be followed and even the god to be worshipped.

Even if, like in the case of radical *sampradāyas*, the new elements introduced by a guru strongly oppose the caste system, they may yet be assimilated by this very system. What happens, if a new school arises and declares for instance the non-validity of caste, and in practice tries to overcome it? Up to the present day there is more or less the same variety of possibilities: The members of the new sect may be outcasted and, being subject to social and economic boycott, eventually give up their new creed. On the other hand this is by no means bound to happen. The newly established sect can also, in spite of its doctrines, not really touch the caste organization. Its members may for instance once a year dine together, but nevertheless continue to marry within their own castes. Examples of both these possible reactions against the introduction of changes can for instance be observed in the history of the Mahimā Dharma movement in Orissa.[7] But a radical *sampradāya* can also—in the long run—develop into a newly recognized caste which may or may not remain "open", i.e. accept members from all castes, and may even, as has happened in *Vīraśaivism*, develop subcastes of its own. The historical role of *sampradāyas* in traditional Hinduism is to keep continually in motion the doctrinal as well as the social and, to a lesser degree, the ritual tradition. They may not attempt to change fundamentally the traditional system but they are guarantees that Hinduism never becomes a completely closed system.

The sociology of religion has, since Max Weber, acknowledged the role of sects and thus of radical *sampradāyas*, too, as agents of social mobility.[8] What is seldom appreciated in the general doctrinal development enforced by them, a development which often leads to renewed attempts to initiate also social change. This is possible because of the third peculiar feature of Hinduism, i.e. the nature of its holy scriptures. We have seen that in Christianity the first reason for the formation of sects was the definition of the canon. The general acceptance of a canon, as we find it in most religions with holy scriptures, limits considerably the possibilities of change. Changes can only be introduced by the means of translating and interpreting already existing scriptures.

The Hindu "canon" of holy scripture consists of two *parts* the second of which—astonishing enough—still remains unfinished. *Śruti,* literally "what is heard", is considered to be the immediate, literal revelation and contains the Vedas, Brahmanas and Upanishads. "*Smṛti*", literally "what is remembered", is considered to be the revelation not literally taken down but only "remembered" by the rishis. *Smṛti* includes the two great epics *Rāmāyaṇa* and *Mahābhārata,* the Purāṇas, the law books, etc. Some of these texts like for example the *Bhagavadgītā,* have become much more important for the actual practice of Hinduism than the Vedic ones. In theory *smṛti* must go back to some element of the *śruti.* So the orthodoxy or validity of some *smṛti* text can be questioned and opposed. But, as already noted in connection with the teachings of a guru, such an objection may be raised by other groups, but can never be generally enforced by them due to the lack of a church-like central institution in Hinduism. On the contrary, the contents of the *smṛti* not being strictly defined, new texts may arise. It is stated for instance in the *Mahābhārata* that the question of *dharma* and *adharma,* i.e. religion and non-religion, or right and non-right, "are both subject to the limitations of country and time".[9] It is therefore not astonishing, that the religious texts written in the regional languages have as a matter of fact become the medium of an evergrowing extension of the *smṛti.* This gives to Hindu tradition an enormous freedom. Commenting on recognized sacred texts and translating them into regional languages is the only traditionally sanctioned way of introducing new elements and thoughts, which may lead to the composition of new texts and the establishment of new *sampradāyas.*

One of the most important texts of the *smṛti* literature, the *Bhāgavata Purāṇa,* for instance, is in itself a product of such a process of change and reaction. It contains a criticism of the position of Brahmans and the efficiency of their rituals. Instead, *bhakti,* the pure devotion, poverty and low birth are considered to be more helpful for attaining salvation. As van Buitenen has shown, the literary expression of such views raised strong reactions from the side of the *smārta* Brahmins. Texts like *Yāmuna's Āgamapramāṅya* show how strongly Brahmins opposed the recognition of Bhāgavata priests[10] and criticised the *Bhāgavata* as corresponding neither to the *śruti* nor to *smṛti*. But their struggle had no lasting effect. On the contrary, the importance of the *Bhāgavata*, obviously being the expression of a large popular movement, increased tremendously. Its importance reached a new stage when it was translated into regional languages and became the most venerated holy text of the respective region. In Orissa, for instance, the translation into Oriya was done by a member of the *Pañcasakhā* School in the sixteenth century. This movement propagated very unorthodox views. It denounced the position of the Brahmans, was against idolatry, temple cult, pilgrimage, etc. True worship is only found within one's own soul, true pilgrimage is the *yoga* which reaches the *tīrthas* (sacred places) within one's own body.

What is important in regard to our argumentation is the fact that the *Pañcasakhās* based their radical views on the *Bhāgavata Purāṇa*, a text which had been recognized in the meantime. By being able to do so they could now even go one step further. In their own scriptures they announced the imminent victory of this true worship over the current Brahmanical one. Of course, there was again a strong reaction from the side of the Brahmanical orthodoxy, but nevertheless the writings of the *Pañcasakhā* spread all over Orissa and were, in the long run, accepted nearly by everybody. These scriptures, once having themselves been the expression of a new movement, are now considered as traditional proof (*pramāṇa*) by another, later, and even more radical movement. The Mahimā Dharma, founded in the nineteenth century, claims to be the fulfillment of the prophecies (*mālikās*) of the *Pañcasakhā*, and again radicalizes its quest for change. What originally was considered to be a secret doctrine became converted by them into rules and regulations. For instance, the mere questioning of the superiority of the Brahmans in Mahimā Dharma developed into the strict prohibition to enter their houses or to eat their food. The condemnation of image worship initially also a secret doctrine of the *Pañcasakhā*, was externalized and radicalized to the extent that in the late nineteenth century members of the Mahimā Dharma attempted to burn the famous wooden image of Lord Jagannātha in Puri.

Coming back to the conventional definitions of sects, I think it is obvious that they do not apply to traditional Hindu *sampradāyas*. As "opposition church", sects don't exist in Hinduism. The main features of more recent definitions, i.e. the spirit of protest and the consciousness of being an elite are also rather irrelevant for the *sampradāya*. The spirit of protest will soon be assimilated and the feeling of being the "chosen people" never developed strongly in Hinduism as redemption is considered to be an individual affair.

Thinking along the lines of Troeltsch, the *sampradāya* has elements of a mysticism-type of religious congregation, especially as it is linked to the institution of monastic orders. But the *sampradāya* is more, for it develops definite doctrinal as well as ritual traditions. It is a structure of its own, where the institution of an ascetic order becomes the centre of a ritual, doctrinal and even social tradition which is clearly distinct and yet stays within the main stream of orthodox tradition. This tradition is caused by a process whereby originally new and unorthodox changes can be assimilated and integrated more easily than in other religions. In the process of integration the originally heterodox, "revolutionary" movements and tenets undergo two opposite developments. They become more and more generally respected and respectable on the one side and, at the same time, may become more and more radical. This ambivalence may lead or at least support new movements or even radical changes.

III

Within the framework of the present paper one may ask which role "sects" in traditional Hinduism played in the confrontation between Hinduism and modernity. It is an astonishing fact that initially radical *sampradāyas* did not play a significant role in Hindu modernism and its attempt to reconcile tradition with the modern materialistic and rationalist "*Weltanschaüüng*". All modernistic movements have tried to introduce social consciousness and social reforms in the religious programme. Social claims and the quest for social changes, advocated by the radical *sampradāyas*, would have served the purpose very well. But curiously enough such references occurred rather late.

Rammohun Roy, the founder of modern Hinduism in theory rejected nearly everything that was essential in Hinduism. His was a deistic concept of a "natural religion" completely in accordance with reason. As Voltaire, he saw this natural religion as the true source and basis of humanity to which an enlightened mankind must return. In the historical manifestations of the different religions he saw nothing but depravations of an originally pure idea. A similar static conception of religion was present with Dayananda Sarasvati, the founder of the

Arya Samaj, who tried to restore what he believed to be the original teaching of the Veda and at the same time the foundation of all religions.

Both the great movements of Brahma Samaj and Arya Samaj were fundamentally opposed to the living Hindu tradition, and wanted to replace it. They took over, to a considerable degree, all the Christian misunderstandings and prejudices of the time, and therefore, tried to abolish all that seemed obsolete to them. The scriptures to be read or accepted were strictly limited, new forms of ritual and cult with only some Hindu elements in it were introduced and there were attempts to overcome the caste system. In spite of the deep differences between Arya and Brahma Samaj they are quite similar in structure: they both tried to establish Hindu churches according to the model of the Protestant churches of the time. Like Protestant churches the *samajs* organized themselves as broad institutions relying on laymen and on specially selected, trained and supported "ministers".

Hindu modernism also took over the forms of subsidiary organizations developed by Protestantism. The *samajs* had their own Young Men's Associations, their tract societies, medical missions, educational societies, etc. A great deal of admirable social work especially amongst the tribes and scheduled castes was accomplished through these organizations. Brahma and Arya Samaj both had been founded to become Hindu churches, embracing and unifying the whole of the Indian nation. Although of considerable success for certain times and regions, these movements could not accomplish such a large task. What happened to them was the opposite of what has happened in Europe and America, where sects had become churches. What was meant in the case of the Brahma and the Arya Samaj to be a church became most definitely a sect in its above defined "Christian" definition. Criticism of the institutional means of salvation namely the cult, ethical strictness and the feeling of being an elite is present in the *samajs* as well as an usually strong reaction and repulsion of the orthodoxy. For, to counteract modernism some parts of Hinduism while consciously remaining in their traditional tenets, emphasized caste and image worship, adopted modern organizational structures which considerably reinforced the strength of their anti-modernistic struggle. Especially the different forms of subsidiary organizations of anti-modernistic leagues like Bharata Mahamandala and Rashtriya Svayamsevak Sangh, took over ideas connected with these Christian sects, for instance missionary elan and social commitment.

But the development of Hindu modernism and the interactions with Christianity do not end here. Evidently, the current of modernization could not, in the long run, leave aside the living Hindu tradition. It was extensively taken up in two different ways. One was by means of literary work and literary movements. The starting point of this literary modernism was the first modern comment on the *Bhagavadgītā*, written in 1866 by Bankim Chandra Chattopadhyaya. Modern interpretations of Hindu scriptures, especially the *Bhagavadgītā*, proved to be of considerable influence by giving to the English educated people a new and acceptable approach to their own tradition. These interpretations as given for instance in the works of S. Radhakrishnan, became widely recognized in post-independence India being even quoted by the Supreme Court of India, and seem to signalize the development of a new concept of orthodoxy in Hinduism no longer qualified by caste and region.

While referring more and more to its own tradition, modern Hinduism also rediscovered the *sampradāya*. It was Swami Vivekananda who first took it up again in organizing the Ramakrishna Mission. This movement no longer tried to replace Hinduism by a new type of organization, as the *samajs* had done, but set out to spread the teachings of their guru Ramakrishna and the school founded by his disciple Vivekananda. Exactly like a traditional *sampradāya* the movement does not primarily rely on a congregation of laymen, but on a monastic order. All subsequent modern Hindu movements, the Aurobindo as well as the Gandhian movement, were organized in the same way: a relatively small centre, an ashram, a monastic order or a community of very devoted persons around which different classes and types of men can gather in different ways and without the necessity of any formal initiation. Also the more recent movements like the Society for Krishna Consciousness, which are no longer concerned with social or national problems, and have an increasing success in the West are organized along these lines. It is striking to see how, after the Christian concept of Church and sect had been introduced into Hinduism in the nineteenth century, it is now the Hindu *sampradāya*, which spreads into the realm of Christianity.

The organizational structure of the *sampradāya* proved to be equally fitted for the purpose of mission abroad as for the purpose of spreading Hindu modernism in India. The reason is, that it allows everybody an access of his own; the individual may adopt a new way of life, but he may as well continue his traditional way of life, taking up only new interpretations. It was therefore this form of institution which, along with the literary movements, succeeded best in creating a new and modernized religious identity and thereby laid the foundations to the national identity of independent India. The attempt to build Hindu churches could not fulfil that task and was therefore given up. But the forms of subsidiary organizations taken over from Protestantism persisted, being adopted also by later modern movements like the Ramakrishna Mission, and introduced into Hinduism a specific type of missionary and social work.

Contemporary Hinduism still contains all the different forms of change and reaction dealt with in this survey. Traditional forms of radical *sampradāyas* still continue to exist. They nowadays meet not only with an orthodox reaction of the traditional type, but also with the different types of modernization—the *samajs*, the various modern *sampradāyas* and the general orthodoxy of modern interpretations, thereby creating new complexes of change and reaction.

NOTES

1. Reprinted from *Religion and development in Asian societies*, Colombo: Marga Publications 1974, pp. 143-57 (the text has been slightly revised by H.K.).
2. Max Weber, "Politische und hierokratische Herrschaft", in: ibid., *Wirtschaft und Gesellschaft*, ed. by J. Winkelmann, Cologne 1956, pp. 916ff.
3. Ernst Troeltsch, *Die Soziallehren der christlichen Kirchen und Gruppen*, Tübingen 1912, p. 967.
4. These characteristics are given by G. Mensching, *Soziologie der Religion*, Bonn 1968, pp. 240-4. It is interesting how, in order to be able to apply the term sect to Hinduism, Mensching tries to somehow reinterpret the element of splitting typical of the Christian sect: "Das kann sowohl bedeuten, dass die Sekte sich aus einer grösseren organisatorischen Einheit absplittert und dabei zugleich aus dem Abstammungskomplex dieser Grossgemeinschaft einzelne Elemente heraushebt und einseitig in den Mittelpunkt stellt, als auch, dass die einzelne Sekte mit anderen Sekten ein Ganzes bildet, während es keinen eigentlichen Religionsorganismus gibt, von dem sie sich gelöst hatte" (p. 238).
5. H.H. Wilson, *A sketch of the religious sects of the Hindus*, London 1861, Reprint under the title: *Religious sects of the Hindus*, Calcutta 1958.
6. Joachim Wach, *Religionssoziologie*, Tübingen 1951, pp. 143ff.
7. A. Eschmann, Mahimā Dharma: An Antochthonous Hindu Reform Movement, In *The Cult of Jagannath and the regional tradition of Orissa*, ed. by A. Eschmann, H. Kulke, G.C. Tripathi, New Delhi 1978, pp. 375-410.

8. For instance David G. Mandelbaum, *Society in India*, Vol. II "*Change and continuity*", Berkeley 1970, pp. 543f. "Jati mobility has been one adaptive process in this social system, the rise of sectarian groups may be another. Once a sectarian rise had been accomplished, the new group continued in the common pattern of jati mobility."
9. P.V. Kane, *History of Dharmaśāstras*, Vol. V, Part II, Poona 1962, pp. 1629f.
10. J.A.B. van Buitenen, On the Archaism of the *Bhāgavata Purāṇa*, In *Kṛṣṇa: myths, rites and attitudes*, ed. by Milton Singer, Chicago, pp. 31ff.

HINDUISM THROUGH WESTERN GLASSES A CRITIQUE OF SOME WESTERN VIEWS ON HINDUISM

Gaya Charan Tripathi

'*ātmaupamyena puruṣaḥ pramāṇam adhigacchati*'
"That which is termed as 'valid knowledge' is often nothing else but a subjective assessment of the things."

Vālmīki in *Rāmāyaṇa*

The Western Perspective

I still remember very vividly an interview of a famous French author taken by some German journalist and broadcast in the evening programme of German Television in Summer 1972. The occasion was the award of Nobel Prize for literature of that year. What shocked me was the ignorance of that great French literary figure about the literature written in Asian languages. Upon the question of the journalist as to why the Nobel Prize for literature is awarded almost exclusively to the works composed in European languages and not in Asian languages, the French author replied that the literature produced in Asian and African languages was a sort of "Folk literature of traditional character" which did not deserve any serious consideration as a piece of Literature or Art!

I felt sorry for the ignorance of that prominent literary figure of France who obviously did not have any idea of the richness, the literary value and human qualities of the vast literature produced, for example, in Indian languages. Those who have first-hand access to any one of the modern Indian languages, know well that the literary beauty and thought-content of the novels, short stories, epics or poems produced in Indian languages are not inferior in any way to the works produced in Europe or America. Yet the literary critics in other parts of the world do not seem to have a correct idea or impression of the Indian literary productions and are guided mostly by their preconceived notions. They hold their views, based mostly on incomplete information and biased opinions as absolute truth and the pity is that if anyone tries to correct their vision (especially if this 'anyone' happens to be from one of those 'developing nations' in Asia or Africa), they react very sharply, sometimes even aggressively, to his statements accusing him of partisan attitude. However, it is interesting to note that in the West the faith, philosophy and literature of an Asian or African country undergoes gradual upvaluation with the enhancement of the economic and political importance of that country. The case of Japan and Korea may be cited as an example.

The easiest and the most common way in the West to deny a non-European people an achievement or a phenomenon which the Europeans are proud of calling as their own and which they wish to lay their exclusive claim on, is to *define* it in such a way and so narrowly that only the Western pattern of this phenomenon would fit into it. How many times have I heard in the university circles of the West from the learned professors that true philosophy is a prerogative of the ancient Greece and the modern West, and that India has not given rise to any philosophy because the definition of the philosophy is ... this this this ... and the Indian philosophy obviously does not fall within this definition! 'India does not have any true religion because the religion, in the true sense of the term, should be defined as ... such such such ... and these characteristics do not apply to Hinduism nor, for that matter, to Buddhism or Jainism.' As an illustration to this mentality the reader is referred to the book *Hinduism and Buddhism* by Monier Williams in which he denies the status of "true religion" to Buddhism because according to his self-invented definition, a "true' religion must necessarily have a belief in one single personal God which Buddhism does not have".[1]

Such definitions which are the outcome of narrow outlook assume sometimes ridiculous proportions. An Indological colleague of mine in the West once denied the existence of cows in India. "You do not have real '*cows*' in India", he remarked, "these animals are in fact called *zebus* ; the term 'cow' is a misnomer for them". Now Indians will have to learn from the Europeans how to call and designate the animals which have been a part of the fauna of this country since ages. It were the British who taught us that these bovine creatures are to be called by the name 'cow' in their language (i.e. English) which we readily learnt and accepted since it was akin to the word *go/gauḥ* in Sanskrit or *gāya* in Hindi. But no, we were mistaken! There may be an Indo-European affinity between the two words, there may be an ancient definition saying that 'the animal with a hump on the back and a dewlap under the neck is called '*gauḥ*' (*kakutsāsnâdimattvam gotvam*), but the Indian cows still would not qualify for the title of 'cow' since that is reserved only for the cows found and bred on Jersey Island or in Friesenland!

Some Commonly Held Views of the West on Hinduism

Let us now examine some of the most common misconceptions of the Western scholars about Hinduism. What I propose to review in the following are mostly the views prevalent among a large number of moderately learned people of the Western society which have been gathered by me during my own interactions with the people at the university and the common level. They represent a sort of *communis opinio,* general opinion of the people at large, who may or may not have had the occasion to come into direct contact with Hinduism. It is obvious that these views have been generated and propagated in the West basically and in the first instance through the writings on Hinduism by the Indologists and the Historians of Religion.

A. The caste system

Let us start with the notorious caste system of India about which every Westerner believes to know something or the other. It is not unusual with the Western scholars to see the caste system of Indian society in direct relationship with Hinduism and to treat it more or less as an outcome of it. Those who wish to criticise Hinduism hardly ever fail to highlight the point that Hinduism breeds social inequality and tries to justify it with its religious code.

I do not think that it is proper to see and evaluate the caste system exclusively in terms of social inequality or social injustice. The system is so complex and multifaceted that it usually defies its comprehension in totality to an outsider. No social system, especially a system which is based on or which aims at exploitation of a group of its members can last so long and be so firmly rooted in the psyche and behaviour of the people as the Indian caste system has been, withstanding all historical changes and strong social upheavals; nor can it be said to be only negative and disadvantageous to the society. Its rôle in preserving age-old social and cultural traditions, in acting as a care-taking organisation in case of need to poors and destitutes, in preserving the social and ethnic identity of a group, in building resistance against foreign religious and cultural influences has also to be taken into account.

It is also not widely known that a sort of strong "family relationship" transcending the caste barriers existed and still exists among the members belonging to different castes and different social groups in the village society where the persons belonging to different castes are "brothers", "sisters", "maternal and paternal aunts", "uncles", "nephews", "nieces", etc., to each other and this relationship is zealously maintained in personal behaviour and in social inter-actions.

The origin and the exact process of the growth of the caste system shall perhaps always remain shrouded in mystery. But that *varṇa* system is of Indo-European origin, which has later been superimposed on the previously existing "*jāti*" system of India cannot be doubted since not only are there cognate words corresponding to *brahman, kṣatra* and *viś* in a number of Indo-European languages (for which the reader is referred to the *Etymological Dictionary of Sanskrit* by M. Mayrhofer) but the system of the threefold division of the societies in priests, nobility and common-folk can be shown to have existed elsewhere, too. The system was perhaps an effort to re-form and re-structure the multi-tribal society of Madhyadeśa by giving the people a new identity cutting across the tribal barriers.

B. The myths of the "other-worldly" character of a Hindu

Following the views of certain Indologists of the earlier generations, it is very common with the Western scholars (e.g. Albert Schweitzer) to stress the "world-fiendly" ("weltfeindlich" = hostile or inimical to the world) character of Indian religions, especially of Hinduism. According to the opinion of these scholars Hinduism is "Welt-abgeneigt", i.e. averse to the worldly affairs and is primarily and mainly concerned with the problem of salvation or getting rid of the cycle of life and death since it considers the human life on this earth as burdensome and the material world as an illusion. Now, this is an over-exaggeration of the Hindu view of life and does not represent the true nature of Hinduism.

A normal Hindu is as much concerned with the world and its affairs as his Western counterpart. He is in no way less practical and in no way less involved in the material world than the follower of any other religion. We should not forget that besides *mokṣa*, to a Hindu, there are two other very important *puruṣārthas* ("arms of life") to be achieved in this life namely *artha* (wealth) and *kāma* (fulfilment of desires) which have precedence over the final *puruṣārtha* which is *mokṣa*. The illusory nature of the World and the idea of *mokṣa* may be of relevance to a handful of *saṃnyāsins* who live away from the society, much like the Christian monks in the monasteries of medieval Europe, but when a common Hindu thinks about the life after death, he thinks of and aims rather at going to 'heaven' and does not strive towards ultimate salvation leading to the complete dissolution of his personality. He is, in fact, in no hurry to attain the *mokṣa* because he has a long chain of innumerable future existences before him in which he has sufficient time and scope to work for it!

The picture of a Hindu as of a person averse to the pleasures of life and as the one who does not accept the realities of this world has been generated by overemphasizing (or should we say: "misinterpreting"?) the Advaita branch of Vedānta Philosophy which is but one school of Vedānta beside at least five others. The Advaita Vedānta has been projected as the "cream" of Indian philosophy, the ultimate culmination of Hinduism, by the Theosophists and the preachers like Vivekānanda towards the end of the nineteenth and the earlier part of the twentieth century. Ramakrishna Missions all over the world have now taken upon themselves the task of propagating these views and have propagated them with such a vehemence that the fact that only a very insignificant minority of Hinduism subscribe today, or did it in the past at any given time, to the views of the Advaitism regarding the unreal character of the world, has actually been lost sight of. The followers of this view are mostly the monks living in the *maṭhas* belonging to the Śaṅkarācārya school of thought. Śaṅkara has hardly any following among the *gṛhasthas* or householders who belong mostly to other schools of Vedānta like Rāmānuja (Tamilnadu), Vallabha (Gujarat), Nimbārka (Andhra, Rajasthan), Madhva (Karnataka) or Chaitanya (Bengal) which are termed as "Vaiṣṇava" *sampradāyas* (= schools, "sects"). These Vaiṣṇavas follow the path of devotion to a personal God which can best be pursued living within the society by showering love and affection on all living beings.

C. Lack of charitable activities and social responsibility

Some Western critics of Hinduism, especially those inspired by missionary spirit, highlight the charitable activities of Christianity and point towards its absence in Hinduism. To my mind this is neither kind nor fair to a people whose kings (e.g. Harṣavardhana of Kanauj, 606-47 A.C.) are known to have distributed the entire collections of their treasury to the poor and needy every five years at Prayaga as attested by Xuanzang (Hsüan-tsang) in his memoirs (cf. also *Raghuvaṃśa* of Kālidāsa, Canto 5.1-5). Charitable activities are parts of every high religion because they constitute the core of their social philosophy. In India, too, charity or *dānam* has been praised directly and through a number of myths and legends right since the time of *Ṛgveda* through the Upaniṣads, to the *Mahābhārata*, Purāṇas and Dharmaśāstras. The story of gods, human beings and demons approaching Prajāpati for receiving a discourse in ethics (cf. *Bṛhad Ā. Up.*, V.2) and Prajāpati teaching the importance of "*da*" to each of them (*dama* or "restrain" for the gods, *dāna* or "charity" for human beings and *dayā* or "compassion" for the demons) is a nice example of the importance attached to this principle in Indian religion. The *smṛtis* enumerate *dāna* as one of the 10 cardinal virtues or the core tenets of the *dharma*.[2]

A number of social and private organisations as well as numerous persons in their individual capacity have all along been engaged in charitable activities in Hindu society and the stress on such activities by Buddhism and Jainism is too well-known to be mentioned here. In fact, the system of *varṇāśrama*—which foresees that at any given time some three-fourth of the total male population, i.e. the *brahmacārins*, the *vānaprasthins* and the *saṃnyāsins*, as well as a sizable population of monks have to live upon the alms (*bhikṣā*) received from the householders (*gṛhasthas*)—could not have developed or sustained itself, had there been no charitable activities in the society and no munificence among its people, whereas it looks like that the much publicised caritative activities carried out by an organized Church, especially in Asian and African countries, with the money received from its Western followers as church tax, revolve round the idea of presenting a superior picture of Christianity and ultimately aim at luring the "heathens" to the Christian fold.

D. The polytheism of Hinduism

The tendency to see and judge all Indian religious, cultural and philosophical phenomena in the light of Western ideology is also seen in the strong condemnation of the Hinduistic polytheism by Christian writers, especially missionaries of the nineteenth century. The presence of a large number of gods and temples dedicated to them in India annoyed them and the belief in many gods instead of a single, the most exalted one, was depicted as something primitive, a stage preceding the emergence of a high religion. It was neither properly understood nor properly represented that the existence of myriads of temple as well as faith in and worship of a multitude of gods for various worldly purposes does not affect or impair the belief of a Hindu in the Highest Divine Substance, which is but one and which alone is the creator, sustainer and destroyer of the universe.

Further, to regard polytheism as something inferior to monotheism is an undue imposition of a semitic ideology on Indian culture. Why should monotheism be regarded as a sort of philosophical advancement over the polytheism? There are equally strong arguments to support the contrary. Polytheism is not necessarily an earlier stage of development in the human thought and belief, nor to my mind Christianity is a monotheistic religion in the strict sense of the term with its belief not only in the Trinity but also in a number of tutelary deities and saints, etc.

E. The monistic/monotheistic character of Hinduism is of late origin

Europeans often take pride in contending that the Jewish folk was the first to resort to monotheism and feel proud that the religion which they follow and which believes in one single God has its origin in the cultural background of Judaism. First of all it is not a historical fact that the Jews were first with a religion with a monistic system of thought. A number of references may be cited right from the *Ṛgveda* through the pages of the Upaniṣads to show that in spite of directing their prayers to a multitude of gods, the Vedic Aryans basically believed that there is one single abstract source for the origin of this world which is beyond the categories of *sat* (existent) and *asat* (non-existent). This one substance holds the world, destroys it in the end and is the only one which/who is to be worshipped and admired.[3] The Upaniṣads even went to the extent of describing their Brahman as and equating it with *śūnya* (0) because that is the only perfect number immutable and unchangeable, as all numbers—positive or negative—emerge from the zero and get merged into it.[4] Even if anything is subtracted from it or if it is divided, it remains the same zero. It is neither a positive number nor negative and yet, at the same time, it transcends the both. In the same way Brahman is perfect in itself, is beyond positive and negative characteristics and transcends this world. It is unchangeable and immutable. Its quantity or quality does not undergo any change even if the universe comes out of it or gets dissolved into it. For the number one (1), it has to be explained how and when it has come into existence, but for zero it is not required. It is always there even when noting is there, and so is God.

If one were to postulate that the reduction of the number of gods from "many" into "one" is an intellectual advancement, we must also admit that the concept of moving from one to zero is a further, much more sophisticated a philosophical advancement. That the concept of the Highest and the Absolute substance of this world as a Zero finds its further development in the Śūnyavāda of Buddhism, ought to be well-known.

F. Hindus to not have a uniform concept of God

I have met many a Westerner who, after having visited a series of temples in India, is led to believe that Indians do not have any concept of an *abstract God* or even one single personal God. Some even believe that just as there are two main sects in Christianity in the form of Catholics and Protestants, in the same way the Hinduism is divided into many sects: the two most prominent of them being the Śaivism and Vaiṣṇavism. They also believe that the concept of *Personal God* for the follower of these sects is identical with the personal appearance of Viṣṇu or Śiva; in other words, the Hindus visualize their highest personal God as having the traits and characteristics of their *iṣṭadevatā*, i.e. Śiva, Viṣṇu, Devī, Gaṇeśa and Sūrya, etc.. This is simply not true.

To an outsider it may apparently seem to be so, but in reality the fact is otherwise. Śiva, Devī (Mother Goddess) or Sūrya (Sun god) may be the most favourite deities of a certain group of people who venerate them, offer them worship and request them to grant their wishes, but even the devotees of these gods do not consider them to be the highest and the absolute God who creates this world, who is permeated through the whole universe, who is the one who sustains and destroys the universe, the one who is omniscient and omnipresent. The *iṣṭadevatās* are there to be approached with reverence and humility. They are to be worshipped and propitiated for the attainment of worldly or trans-worldly desires but they are never granted the status of the highest Divine Principle which lies beyond this creation and which governs this universe. It will thus be a folly to believe that for the followers of the various religious sects of Hindus, the concept of the highest Personal God is identical with the concept of their *iṣṭadevatā*. Even while worshipping his *iṣṭadevatā* or a deity for a certain specific purpose or on a certain occasion and even while showering upon him the highest possible praise and honour, the worshipper is very well aware of his or her relative status in comparison to the absolute, personal or impersonal (attributeless) God who is always present in the mind of the people as the Absolute Principle behind all deities and gods and who alone is imperishable, immutable and omnipotent. The worship of the Divine—commonly called the *Bhagavān* or *Īśvara* by the Hindus and mostly conceived of as having a qualified (*saguṇa*) nature and a quasi-personal character—through its various desirable manifestations or *iṣṭadevatās* is a common and easy way of approaching and communicating with the Divine because the absolute Principle otherwise appears too subtle to be approached.

What I want to say, is, that behind all these phenomena of polytheism, a strong undercurrent of monotheism is clearly available and also discernible in the minds and the hearts of the adherents of Hinduism and it will thus be totally wrong to contend that Hindus are divided as worshippers of this or that particular *Devatā*, that these *Devatās* have nothing in common with each other and that their followers and worshippers have various concepts of divinity absolutely divergent from each other.

G. The "idolatry" of Hinduism

For its practice of so-called "idolatry", too, Hinduism came under heavy attack in the tracts of many western writers of the nineteenth and the early twentieth century. In the first instance it would look rather strange because Christianity all along its long and glorious tradition has been excessively friendly and favourable to the "cult of images" and has produced some of the best religious art of the world in all possible mediums. And when we add to this the fact that the Catholic churches in a number of South-European countries have the same type of cult images in their sanctum and the ritual of offering worship to them consisting of sprinkling of holy water, offering of flowers and lamps and distribution of "*prasāda*" (in the form of wheat wafers) is not much different from the ritual practised in Indian temples, the strong condemnation of Hindu "idolatry" by some Western writers seems neither logical nor reasonable.

In spite of this, some western scholars, driven by the Anglican-Protestant ideology whetted by missionary zeal launched a scathing attack against the "monstrous" cult images of Hinduism—especially those having semi-anthropomorphic features—ignoring their subtle symbolism. It was strongly projected that the practice of having images as cult-objects and of worshipping them, represents the beliefs and practices of culturally backward and unadvanced social groups and those who worship abstract symbols are religiously far more advanced.

Western scholars also miserably failed to appreciate the aesthetics of Indian art. Biased in their opinion by the aesthetics of Greek and Christian art and basing their opinion on the canons derived therefrom, they could never come to terms with the Indian deities having some unanthromorphic features like multiple arms and multiple or animal faces. They either remained blissfully ignorant about the deep symbolism of these images or deliberately ignored it. They also failed to properly understand the subtle ritual of the ceremony of *pūjā* underlying the worship of these images.

As I have shown elsewhere in detail,[5] the ritual of *pūjā* is a very subtle and spiritual phenomenon which seeks a communion with the Divine through the image. It is not the image *per se* to which, in fact, worship is accorded but to the "splendour" (*tejas*) or the light of the deity which has been transferred temporarily from the heart of the worshipper into the heart of the image.

The worshipper first undergoes a strict ritual of purification of Self. He, thereafter, in the course of meditation, destroys his present mundane body and creates an entirely new body for himself which is free from pollution and sin. After an elaborate ritual of the purification of Self and after having assumed a body equivalent in characteristics and nature to the body of his *iṣṭadevatā,* he meditates intensely and in a concentrated manner on the meaning of the *mantra* to be used in the worship. This deep meditation on the sense of the *mantra* gives rise to the emergence of the splendour or the *tejas* of the deity in the heart of the worshipper. With the help of a handful of flowers held under the nostrils of the worshipper on which this *tejas* is made to descend and which are later placed on the head of the image, the *tejas* of the deity is transferred into the heart of the worshipable image. The *tejas* of the deity remains in the image till the ceremony of *pūjā* continues. Thereafter it is again taken out of the image and inhaled back into the heart of the worshipper. The image is thus only a frame, a structure for the deity to be invoked into it. It is not an object of worship and veneration by itself as alleged by the unknowledgeable critics of 'idolatry' or casual visitors to a temple. It serves as an instrument through which that particular deity may be visualized in the mind of the viewer. It helps the worshipper create his own image of the deity in his heart.

Uniconic images having no particular shape or form and representing almost all important deities of Hinduism are also commonly found all over India. These are only symbols associated with a particular god or goddess. A number of examples may be cited from all over India where the image is a piece of unhewn stone devoid of any shape or form, having either a 'pre-Hinduistic' or a 'non-Hinduistic' origin, which has been identified with and worshipped as a particular deity. The most commonly known example of this phenomenon in Jammu-Kashmir region are perhaps the three uniconic images worshipped as Lakṣmī, Durgā and Sarasvatī in the famous Vaiṣṇava Devī temple at Jammu. Śiva of the famous Liṅgarāja temple at Bhubaneswar and Mahabaleshwar (Dist. Satara), Gaṇapati at Mahāvināyaka in Orissa and Varāha-Narasiṃha in Simhāchalam (Andhra) are other examples of the phenomenon. The black *śālagrāmas* (basically ammonites) from the river Gaṇḍakī are worshipped all over the country as Viṣṇu-Vāsudeva. Some of these uniconic symbols placed now comfortably in a nicely built temple, may originally have been tribal cult-objects representing some tribal deity (cf. the four wooden figures in the Jagannātha temple). But Hinduism took them over and assimilating them in its cult, adopted them to its ideology and identified them with one of its significant gods thus completely changing or transforming their nature and identity, though the figures remained the same. The figure of Jagannātha serves as a good example of this phenomenon which has first been identified with Narasiṃha, then with Puruṣottama-Viṣṇu (though it has iconographically nothing in common with the images of Viṣṇu) and or Kṛṣṇa and elevated finally to the highest personal as well as impersonal or absolute Divine Principle of the universe.[6] The magnanimity and flexibility of Hinduism with which it accepts the symbols and beliefs of the people which originally stood outside its pale and the facility with which it incorporates them into its system ought to be stressed and highlighted more strongly than it has been done till now.

The deity may be invoked in Hindu religious practices into almost any conceivable object; into an iconic or uniconic form of an image, into a piece of wood or stone, into a painting or even water. In fact the most common form of Hindu *pūjā* in ancient times seems to have consisted in invoking the deity to be worshipped into a pitcher full of water in which certain auspicious articles like a piece of gold, a few precious stones and herbs, etc., have been dropped and which has been covered with a lid containing cereals like unhusked paddy, rice or barley. Though later the worship of the deity in a pitcher was replaced by the worship in an image, yet the rite of *kalaśa-sthāpanā* still plays an important rôle in the worship of, for example, the Mother Goddess. During her festival lasting for nine days in spring and during the autumn Navarātra, the Goddess, in the household ritual of worship, is invoked in a pitcher containing water in which she is believed to be present for full nine days till a *visarjana* is made towards the end of the ritual bidding her farewell. The ritual of preparing *arghya* water for the deity with which the pūjā is carried out is a remnant of this old practice. The practice of invoking the deity into waters for the purpose of worship, still forms the most important aspect of Hindu pūjā on the Island of Bali which is why the Hindu religion of Bali is known as *Āgama Tīrtha* or the "religion of holy water".

The Hindu also does not find any problem in invoking the deity on to a geometrical diagram known as *yantra* where she (the deity) is accorded worship in the centre of the diagram. A *yantra* is obviously an intricate system of geometrical figures, designed, conceived and evolved by the learned where each figure has its own symbolic meaning. But as far as the common and simple people of India are concerned, any symbol or visible sign can serve as a seat for the deity. Whenever a deity is to be offered worship and his or her image is not available, the womenfolk of Indian villages print a mark of their palm on the wall of a room and worship this *pañcāṅguli* mark (palm-impression with all five fingers visible) as the desired god or goddess. Flowers, lamps, incense and *naivedya* (food), etc., are offered to this *pañcāṅguli* mark in the same manner as if it be an iconic image of the deity concerned. The worship of the goddess Ṣaṣṭhī (the goddess of child-birth) is carried out in this very fashion even to this day in all Hindu households on the sixth day after the birth of a child.

Monotheism and polytheism, personal and impersonal, abstract and concrete, image and symbols are so intricately interwoven with each other in the Hinduism that it is impossible to tell them apart. Hinduism is not exclusive, it is all pervading and all-inclusive. This multi-directional openness in the sphere of faith and practice makes Hinduism enormously rich which satisfies the needs and religious sentiments of all temperaments and all strata of society. It is, however, also the reason which makes Hinduism almost incomprehensible for an outside observer who has a set pattern of thought and a fixed concept of religion in his mind and who wants to comprehend this religion in its diversity, variety and uniqueness through the traditional definitions or his own preconceived notions.

NOTES

1. It was perhaps incumbent upon Monier Williams to express such views because he was the occupant of the Boden Chair of Sanskrit at Oxford which had been founded for the 'special object' of promoting the translation of scriptures into Sanskrit so as to enable his (i.e. Boden's) countrymen to proceed in the conversion of the natives of India to the Christian religion (cf. Preface to his *Sanskrit English Dictionary,* 1899, p. IX). Compare also his remarks in *Modern India and the Indians,* p. 262: "When the walls of the mighty fortress of Brahmanism are encircled, undermined and finally stormed by the soldiers of the cross, the victory of Christianity must be signal and complete."
2. Cf. *Yājñavalkya Smṛti,* I.122: ...*dānam damo dayā kṣāntiḥ, sarveṣām dharmasādhanam;* see also I. 90-7.
3. Cf. *Ṛgveda.* I. 164.46 (*ekaṃ sad viprāḥ bahudhā vadani*...); X. 129.6 (*yo asyādhyakṣaḥ parame vyoman*); VS, 32.1 (*tad evāgnis tad ādityaḥ tad vāyus tad u candramāḥ*); cf. also VS, 17.19 (*viśvataḥ cakṣuḥ ...deva ekaḥ*).
4. *Bṛhad Ār. Up.*, V. 1.1. (*khaṃ brahma*), *Gaṇapati Pūravatāpanī Up.*, III.1 (*śūnyam vai paraṃ brahma*); *Nirvāṇopaniṣad* (*śūnyam na saṅketaḥ parameśvarasattā*); *Tejobindu Up.* (*śūnyātmā sūkṣmarūpātmā viśvātmā*...), etc.
5. Cf. A. Eschmann, H. Kulke, G.C. Tripathi (eds.), *The Cult of Jagannath and the Regional Tradition of Orissa,* Delhi 1978 (2nd ed. 1986), pp. 285-308 and G.C. Tripathi, in: *Journal of the Asiatic Society of Bengal,* 29.2 (1987), pp. 83-93.
6. Cf. A. Eschmann, H. Kulke, G.C. Tripathi, "The Formation of the Jagannātha Triad", in: A. Eschmann etc., *The Cult of Jagannath and the Regional Tradition of Orissa,* pp. 169ff and G.C. Tripathi, "The Evolution of the Concept of Jagannātha as a Deity", in: *Journal of the Oriental Institute,* Baroda, 25 (March-June 1976), pp. 272-85 (also included with minor changes in A. Eschmann etc., ibid. pp. 477-90 under the title "Jagannātha: The Ageless Deity of the Hindus"). Further G.C. Tripathi, Mahāpuruṣavidya: An Unknown Text on the Glorification of Puruṣottamakṣetra, in: *Journal of Ganganatha Jha Kendriya Sanskrit Vidypeetha,* Allahabad, 38-9 (1982-3), pp. 35ff. (esp. pp. 39-50).

HINDU-MUSLIM INTERACTIONS IN MEDIEVAL MAHARASHTRA

N.K. Wagle

Shāh-Munī, the eighteenth century Muslim bhakti poet, in his Marathi work, *Siddhānta Bodha*, observes:

> The *avindhas* (Muslims) consider the ways of the Maharashtra *dharma* as being twisted and upside down. And these people abhor the doings of the Yavanas (Muslims). *Avindhas* say, "The Maharashtra *dharma* is false." The Maharashtras say, "The *avindhas*' way is upside down." There is a rift between the two. No one knows whose *dharma* is better. Some say that the ways of both are identical. Īśvara and Allāh are one and the same. But due to ignorance they (Hindus and Muslims) do not understand the meaning [of this statement]. (Phaḍke 1972: ch. 18, 13-17)

Allauddin Khalji's conquest of the Yādavas of Devagirī (1296) signalled the entry of Muslims into Maharashtra. The Muslim rulers dominated that area continuously from the fourteenth century until the end of the seventeenth century. Over the centuries of co-existence, the two communities had to make adaptive compromises to co-exist. While doing so they seem to have entered into a symbiotic relationship by coming to terms with the mores and norms of each other. This symbiotic relationship, however, does not preclude social tensions. In medieval Maharashtra, the underlying theme in Hindu-Muslim relations does not seem to be one of "secularism" or "peaceful co-existence".[1] Neither is the period characterised by constant clashes of totally disparate ideologies making their co-existence a historically painful experience.[2] The present paper deals with the dynamics of this symbiosis. Illustrative examples are drawn from the historical-biographical literature (*caritra-bakhar*), the writings of the three Marathi bhakti poets, Eknāth, Shekh Mahammad and

Shāh-Munī, the eighteenth century legal documents and the modern *pīr* worship in Maharashtra. Through focusing on Hindu-Muslim symbiosis, certain "inclusive" strategies of Hindus, hopefully, would become apparent.

HISTORY AND HISTORIOGRAPHY: MUSLIMS IN THE HINDU SCHEME OF HISTORY

The writing of the *caritra-bakhars* (historical biographies) began with the advent of Maratha rule under Śivājī (Rājvāḍe 1929: 348f; Hervāḍkar 1957: 8f). However, such writings were not unknown earlier in Maharashtra. An example is the *Mahikāvatīcī bakhar*, an early seventeenth century work (Rājvāḍe 1924). The re-writing of history in Maharashtra started earnestly in the third quarter of the eighteenth century when the Maratha hegemony had become secure, not only in Maharashtra but also in large areas of Gujarat, Malwa, Karnataka and Rajputana. There was a need felt by the Maratha historians to relate their history to other glorious periods of Indian history. It was the age of Maratha "imperial" history. The Marathas had succeeded the Mughal rule. We find, therefore, the Maratha historians consciously trying to accommodate and legitimize the Muslim rule and the Muslim presence in their history. In other words, they felt that it was necessary to legitimize the Muslim rule so that the subsequent Maratha rule would not be compromised. There is thus a deliberate move to accommodate Muslims in their scheme of history.

Many *caritra-bakhars* include a dynastic list of the rulers.[3] In some instances, the list begins with the traditional golden age (*kṛta yuga*), and through the *kali yuga* (the dark age), it covers ancient and medieval "Hindu" dynasties. The list of Muslim rulers follows next. But the transition to the Muslim rulers proved to be a difficult proposition and had to be explained. The *Cāryugācī bakhar* (the history of the four *yugas*), an unpublished MS dated 1795, mentions the *Ramala śāstra* as the authority of the Yavanas (Muslims) which describes their origin and the dynastic rule. The *Ramala śāstra*, according to the *Cāryugācī bakhar*, originated with God Śiva. In a Sanskrit *śloka* in that *bakhar*, which is in Marathi *moḍī* script, to underline the importance of the event the author states:

Śrī Īśvara Śiva told Pārvatī (his wife) the *Ramala śāstra*. Pārvatī told this to

Skanda. Skanda told this to Nārada *munī*. Nārada told this to Bhṛgu *ṛṣi*, who, in turn told this to his son (Śukra). Śukra told this to the Yavanas. Therefore, the *Ramala śāstra* is held in esteem as a great *śāstra*.[4]

The origin of the Yavanas is explained through Paigaṃbar (the Marathi term for Prophet Muhammad) by the same *Ramala śāstra* in a Sanskrit *śloka*.[5]

Once residing on Mount Kailās in the Himalayas, Śiva felt sad and forlorn because his wife Pārvatī and son Gaṇeśa were not beside him. As he was contemplating their absence, Paigaṃbar *munī* manifested before Śiva. Śiva said to him, "I have invited you to search for my son and wife." Paigaṃbar brought Pārvatī and Gaṇeśa over to him at a moment's notice. Pleased, Śiva gave him a boon, saying, "you will appear on this earth in human form." By the grace of Śiva's boon seven Paigaṃbars appeared on earth. They are Ādam, Ayedarī, Bhyah, Kukuma, Rahimān, Aserdya, Danu Asuyara. The *Ramala śāstra* states that seven Paigaṃbars were the wisest and the most honoured of the Yavanas. They descended to earth in the *Kaliyuga*. They started the *san* (Muslim era). Hastināpur was renamed as Dillī and that was the beginning of the *yavanī Pātshāī* (Muslim empire).[6]

The message of this *bakhar* writer is clear: the Paigaṃbar and the Yavanas emerged on this planet because of the divine grace of Śiva. The *Ramala śāstra* of the Yavanas is known to Śiva first. The Yavana dynastic rule and the subsequent list of their kings is thus blessed by Śiva. In another place the *Cāryugācī bakhar* narrates the rise of the Muslim rule in prosaic manner:

On account of Śiva's boon, Paigaṃbar reincarnated as a human being on this earth. And because of the blessings of that Paigaṃbar, the Yavanas obtained the kingdom of Dillī.[7]

Ciṭṇīs' *Sapta prakarṇātmaka caritra* gives a rather elaborate explanation of the rise of the Yavana dynasty:

Paigaṃbar became overcome by the display of a fervent form of devotion on the part of Rukhnuddin (Mohammad Ghur). Paigaṃbar flogged him with an iron chain (*laṅgār*), twelve times. Rukhnuddin bore with the pains and said, "enough". Paigaṃbar than gave a boon to him that he and his descendants would rule the kingdom of Dillī for 1200 years.

The Piṭhor Rājā Chauhāṇ in spite of his brave efforts, could not defeat the enemy. Piṭhor Rājā realised that he would have no hope of winning the battle that was to ensue between him and Rukhnuddin, because God had bestowed the kingdom to Rukhnuddin. The Rājā killed all his women and children (*kabile pure karun*), wore the ocre coloured robes (*keśri pośākh*) [of a martyr] and died in the battlefield. The Kingdom was lost. Indraprastha was named Dillī. (Hervāḍkar 1967: 5)

The emergence of Muslim rule in India was an event of great magnitude and the historians of Maharashtra had to explain it to their readers in order to make it relevant to them. The notion of divine intervention is a well tried purāṇic device used in Maharashtra. Divine intervention was the cause of the rise of Śivājī, an incarnation of the God Śiva himself. The Brahman Peshwas were the *aṃśadhāris* ("essence-holders") of Paraśurāma, the sixth incarnation of Viṣṇu (Wagle and Kulkarni 1976: 14). It is thus God's will, through Paigaṃbar, according to the Hindu historians of Maharashtra, that assured the emergence of Muslim rule in India. Thus, in dealing with the formal Muslim dynastic list, there is no recrimination found against them. The spirit of accommodation is the historians' guideline.

The *Paraśurāma caritra*, a history of the Brahman Peshwa dynasty was composed by a Brahman author in 1773. While describing the dynasty, it accommodates the Muslim rule by way of dynastic list and attendant comments that appear in the *caritra*. The author of the *caritra*, however, uses the Kali motif. Kalī in the *caritra* is the personification of the evil *Kaliyuga*. It is the central motif of the *caritra*. All the discomfitures of Peshwa family and all the calamitous events are attributed to Kalī. The evil Kalī is always contrasted with the goodness of the Peshwas, the *aṃśadhāris* of Paraśurāma, the *avatāra* of Viṣṇu. As in the *Cāryugācī bakhar* there are genealogies (*vaṃśavaḷis*) of both Muslim and Hindu rulers. Concerning the beginning of the Muslim rule in India, it is said:

Kalī established the *san* (Muslim era) in the Yavana *deśa* (country) and then brought it over to *svadeśa* (one's own country). Kalī, hoping to destroy *dharma*, and to usher in great prosperity for the Mlecchas (Muslims), himself went to their country to bring them. (Wagle and Kulkarni 1976: 33, 156f)

There are no other comments about the origin of the Yavanas in the text. But the origin of the *pīr* (Muslim holy men) is interestingly and fancifully told in the *Paraśurāma caritra*:

Mahamad had two brave sons, Hasan and Husen. Both brothers, Hasan and Husen, were the Shāhs of their *deśas* and were of demonic disposition. Because of Kalī's influence, their minds became afflicted and they began hating all Hindus and fought with them. The Hindus emerged the stronger (of the two) and Hasan died in the battlefield. Hasan died in the 7th night of the *moharum.* Husen became frightened after his brother's death. For two or three days he tried several battle tactics but he was killed. The Yavanas still mourn his death and wail on that day. Because of Kalī's powers they became *pīravallīs* (saints) and gave rewards to their people.

It became widely known that the *pīrs,* the creation of Kalī, assumed the shape of wind. On their locations, the Yavanas celebrated their *urs* every year. This practice spread to the East, West and to Draviḍa and Karnāṭaka countries. The image worshippers (*devatānukula*), too, celebrated annually that which was dear to the Mlecchas. The people of Sindh, Lāhor and Kāśmir *deśa,* the Yavanas and worshippers of Kalī, all of them celebrated the *urs.* Yavanas thus rose to prominence and they did not care for the authority of the kings of *svadeśa.*[18]

The authors of the *Paraśurāma caritra, Cāryugācī bakhar* and *Sapta prakarṇātmaka caritra* are obviously distorting Islamic history and mythology. Hasan and Husen fighting the Hindus, Śiva giving a boon to Paigaṃbar and Paigaṃbar flogging Rukhnuddin are cases in point. But the author's aim is to accommodate Muslims and Muslim history through the medium of myths and legends, thereby making the events meaningful to their readers. Asim Roy's recent study[19] of the Bengali Muslim "cultural mediators", who were engaged in making Islam more acceptable to new and potential Hindu converts in Bengal, offers a striking parallel to the above cases. But it was easier for Hindu writers to use the *avatāra* theme of Paigaṃbar, since it is a part of their established purāṇic tradition. Roy's study gives us a viable alternative to the "assimilative pull" concept of Hinduism. As Roy succintly states: "The most significant part of the attempt to reduce the polarity between the endogenous (Hindu) and exogenous (Muslim) tradition relates to the anxiety of the mediators to bring the prophet himself in line with comparable symbols of the Hindu tradition" (Roy 1984: 95). The "Hindu" historiography, however, is an "endogenous" tradition and could, therefore, easily accommodate Islamic rule.

Muslim rule was acceptable as long as it sustained the *dharma* of the Hindus. In the middle of the description of the Muslim dynastic list, the *Paraśarāma caritra* observes:

The King of the Yavanas protected this earth with justice (*jagatī jñyārjite rakṣitī*). The four *varṇas* which had accepted the Pāṇḍavas (the rulers of Hastinapur in the *Mahābhārata*) as their chiefs accepted these (Muslims) as their own. The Yavanas reciprocated this honour and protected the tributary chiefs (*saṃsthānikas*). They treated the Brāhmaṇas, Kṣatriyas, Vaiśyas and

Śūdras, each according to their merits. They did not violate the *tīrthas* and *kṣetras* (religious centres) and they showed great consideration in maintaining them. They listened with great respect (*atyādare aikitī*) to the debates of the *śāstras* and the stories of the *Mahābhārata*. However, some Muslims found such activities objectionable and contrary to their tenets and contemplated the dissolution of this amity. (Wagle and Kulkarni 1976: 35f)

EKNĀTH AND HIS HINDU-TURK DEBATE (SAṂVĀD)

Eknāth (1553-99), one of the most famous Marathi bhakti poets, illustrates in his Hindu-Turk (Muslim) debate the intensity of religious tensions and polemics between the two communities in sixteenth century Maharashtra.[10] The debate is full of recrimination. Consisting of 66 stanzas, it subsumes the issue arising out of *dharmaśāstric* rules of purity and worship, the theology of the epics, Purāṇas and Vedas.[11] The justification and rebuttal of image worship appear as a key point of the debate. The Korāṇic rituals, *hadith* and *Sharia*, are incorporated as points of the debate. The debate ends significantly on a note of mutual accord and harmony of thought, kind of idealised version of the symbiosis the two communities would achieve.

HINDU: Really, you and I are of one mind. The dispute became aggravated over the question of the norms of social order (*jātī dharma*) (lit. caste-*dharma*) in the realm of God these do no apply. (vs. 60, 414)

TURK: What you say is true. For God, caste does not exist. There is no separateness between God and his devotees (*bande*), even though Hazrat Rasul (Prophet) has spoken that God is unapproachable. (vs. 61, 414)

EKNĀTH: They (Hindu-Turk) greeted each other and with respect they embraced.... The dispute resulted in a settlement. From differing views, a consensus was achieved. (vs. 62, 64, 414)

The actual dabate (only a few excerpts are given below) was full of hostile exchanges of views.

EKNĀTH: The Turk says to the Hindu that he is a "kāfar" (*Hinduku Turak kahe kāfar*). The Hindu answers, "I will be contaminated (*viṭāḷ*), stay away from me."

A quarrel started between the two. And it was the start of a great debate. (vs. 2, 412)

TURK: Listen to what I say, Brahman your *śāstra* (*śāstar*) is useless. You affirm that God has hands and feet. What a stupendous thing to say. (vs. 3, 412)

HINDU: Listen, Turk, you great idiot (*mahāmūrkha*), ignoring the truth that God is in all living things, you have become an atheist (*śunyavādaka*). (vs. 4, 412)

TURK: You Hindus are really bad (*tumhī Hindu assal bure*). The stone statue governs your lives. You make that into God. With an *ektārī* (one string instrument) you draw his attention. In its presence you read the *purāṇ*. Men and women, all stand in front of it. You bow down and fall flat on the ground. Is it not the case, you great idiot (*baḍe nādān*)? Dressed in *nimb* leaves, the (half) naked (*sādhus*) congregate, and young women follow them about. Your Vedas are a poor show. All their sayings are useless. You make such a noise. Your God must be lying unconscious. (vs. 30-3, 413)

HINDU: God is in all places: in water, in wood and stone. This is the essential import of your book. Look, you yourself are unaware of it. The Turk is totally ignorant. Even as the *ghee*, melted or solid, is one material, God is one, with attribute or without (*saguṇa, nirguṇa*). You abhor images. You are an utterly senseless idiot. God fulfils the wishes of his devotees (*bande*). This is the doctrine of your book. Why don't you grasp it? I have pointed out your shortcomings to you.

God is near you, yet you shout at him from a distance "*ek bār Allhā, ek bār Allhā*" (one time Allāh, one time Allāh"—obviously a pun on "Allahu Akbar", the Muslim prayer call). The rest of the time is whiled away. He has not met you yet. You hail people at a distance; to those who are near you, you whisper. You should meet Him at a close range (fig. you should worship the image). By shouting you merely wake the children.

You consider God is towards the west (Mecca). Are all directions empty? You say God is everywhere, yet you cannot comprehend this, you idiot.

Five times a day are devoted to God. Are other times lost? You have cheated your own *śāstra*. For you, God is in only one direction. You tell us, we worship stones. Why do you place stones over the dead? You worship the Haji (spirit) of the stone. You believe the tomb to be the true *pīr*. Why do you conserve the bones of those who are only corpses? You cover the stones (tomb of the *pīr*) with flowers and cloth and burn incense before it. (vs. 34-42, 413)

TURK: You say God resides in all living beings. Tell me the place where you people all eat together. They do not touch each other and stay apart from one another. There is cleavage between every two castes (*jamāt*). If so much as a grain of other's food falls on you while you eat, you will be at his throat. (vs. 44, 45, 413)

HINDU: You Turks are total idiots (*param mūrkha*). You cannot distinguish between faultless and faulty. When one starts administering pain to another, how can he reach heaven? Because of God (i.e. by natural cause), the animal dies, it becomes carrion. When you dispose of an animal, that is holy and pure, you have indeed, become more pure than God! The Yavanas are full of deceit and guilt. When you sacrifice a chicken, it flutters (in pain) in front of you. What do you gain from this. The sacrificed goat reaches heaven. Then what use is your praying and fasting. Why don't you kill yourself to attain heaven.

Both Hindu and Muslim (Musalmān) are God's creation, brother. (But) observe the determination of the Turk; he has to catch a Hindu and make him a Muslim. (vs. 50-5, 413)

Shekh Mahammad: A Muslim Perception of Hindus

When Rāmdās, an activist, and, supposedly, anti-Muslim *sant* of Maharashtra praises Sayyad Shaikh Mahammad Qādiri (Shekh Mahammad in Marathi) as a great *sant,* his character assumes a special status. Moropant, yet another well known Marathi poet of the eighteenth century, too, admires the spiritual greatness of Shekh Mahammad and asserts that "even the Brahmans praise him with great enthusiasm as a great Musalmān" (Quoted in Ḍhere 1967: 85).

Shekh Mahammad's Muslim identity is beyond compromise. Most scholars of Marathi bhakti literature assume that Shekh's Guru was a Hindu Brahman, Cānd Bodhale.[12] Bodhale, himself was a *murid* (disciple) of Rāje Muhamad, Shekh's father. In the world of the sadhus and the *sants,* symbiosis was a working proposition. The above information indicates that it was possible for a Brahman to accept as a *cela* (disciple) a Muslim and that a Muslim could be accepted as Guru for a Brahman. This happened without a formal requirement to change one's religion. Cross-fertilization of this type of interaction surely led to a better understanding of the mores of the two communities. Judging by Eknāth's Hindu-Turk debate, discussed earlier, knowledge of Islam was readily available to Hindus without joining the Muslim rank as a member of that community.

Shekh Mahammad is best known for his *Yogasaṃgrāma,* a philosophical work dealing with the theme of the soul's struggle to realize and experience God. The *Yogasaṃgrāma*[13] is an unusually frank critique of Hindu ritualist Brahmanism and the *śāstras* on the one hand. On the other hand, it is an attack on the popular folk-gods. The work denounces, in no uncertain terms, such practices as smoking tobacco, prostitution, animal sacrifices offered to the local folk-gods and goddesses and self-induced tortures like hook-swinging. For example, commenting on the shrines of the mother goddess as found along the roads and amidst the fields, Shekh Mahammad says, "If the deities were all that powerful, how come the dogs urinate on them?" (*devatā aste samarth paṇa tar toṇḍāvar kā mutate śvān*) (*Yog.* 14, 70).

In the *Yogasaṃgrāma*, Shekh Mahammad freely accepts Hindu Gods like Rāma, Kṛṣṇa, Śiva and Viṣṇu. He illustrates his ideas with example from the Purāṇas and philosophical texts. Each of the eighteen chapters of the *Yogasaṃgrāma* begins with an invocation to God Gaṇeśa. But his writings reveal him as monotheist. He describes his God as formless (*nirākārī*) indistinct (*avyakta*) without attributes (*nirguṇa*) and invisible (*alakṣa*). The structure of Islamic belief in one God is still with him.

In fiftysix languages one God is exalted with different words (*chappana bhaṣā vacan prakāra karatī ek Allākī jikir*). Cleavages arise because of harangues in different tongues (*Yog.* 17.4). I salute the sacred *Om* by which the God creator (*Nārāyaṇ*) is known. Muslim salute him as *yā Allāh* (*śrī karī om namojī Nārāyaṇa yā Allā mhaṇti yavana*). (*Yog.* 1, 52)

In a lighter vain, he comments that if there were (two gods) (Hindu) Hari and (Muslim) Allāh, they would have perished fighting each other (*Harī Allā jarī donaste tarī te bhāṇḍa bhāṇḍon marate*) (*Yog.* 1, 95). The syncretistic ideas of Shekh Muhammad are revealed further when he tells people, in a true *sūfi* way, to trust their religious mentors:

While Muslims call him *saccā pīr* (the true *pīr*) the Marāṭhās call him *sadguru* (the true *guru*). The is no difference between these two. Brothers open your eyes (*saccā pīr kahe Musalmān Marhāṭe mhaṇavitī sadguru pūrṇa parī donhit nāhī bhinnatvapaṇa ākhī khol dekho bhāī*). (*Yog.* 17, 3)

Among the Marāṭhās it is the *sadguru*. For the Muslims it is the *saccāpīr*, who enables one to cross the ocean of existence. The others will sink in it and pull others with them (*Yog.* 16, 57). Ignoring the attestations of good people and those found in the great Purāṇas, the people worship the demonic gods (*bhute pujītī*). But how will that [god] who has assumed the shape of a stone cross the ocean of existence with a devotee. If one were to be hit by a stone on the head, blood would gush forth out of the wound. For fulfilling a vow, fools fashion gods out of gold and silver and kill living creatures to appease them. (*Yog.* 16, 59-61)

Shekh Mahammad's Muslim identity surfaces in a candid statement he makes to smooth the anxiety felt by Hindus of his times. The area around Ahmadnagar in Maharashtra was then under control of Muslim rulers. His statement also reflects the points of frictions between the two communities:

People say of me, he is of a *mleccha jāti* (Muslim). That is why he reviles our gods. We cannot trust him. We see Musalmāns smashing the images and destroying our temples. He is surely one of them. The images have been turned to dust. What is there left to worship now. The tradition (*paramparā*) of the Yavanas is to destroy our gods. He is of their lineage (*hā tyāṃcyācā gotyā*). We shall not, therefore, listen to what he says. Shekh Mahammad says, Musalmāns are also created by God. Born as a Musalmān, he is well versed in Qurāṇ and Purāṇ. For his own welfare he listens to the perfected holy ones (*siddha sādhakās mānalo*). One should not search for the origin of a person who exalts God (*jyālā nuvujlta Īśvara tyācā śodhu naye kulācāru*). (*Yog.* 16, 02-67)

Shāh-Munī and Hindu-Muslim Interactions

Shāh-Munī emerged in the third quarter of the eighteenth century, a period of Maratha history that saw Maratha Hindu rule well established in Maharashtra and beyond. Deeply rooted in Hindu scriptures as found in the Veda, Purāṇa and Dharmaśāstra, he writes with knowledgeable insights into Hindu popular and high religion. Although he was an expert in Hindu ideologies, his own bent was towards Mahānubhāv doctrines (Ḍhere 1976: 127-9). Shāh-Munī is best known for his monumental work *Siddhanta Bodha* (which is in 50 chapters with 9858 verses, and was composed in 1778, Phaḍke 1972). In a purāṇic fashion, Shāh-Munī explains the origin of the "fifty-two *varṇas* and eighteen *jātis*". This was a standard expression for describing the entire caste-class structure of Maharashtra as found in the late eighteenth century documents and literary works:

Mahāviṣṇu (God creator) explained the division of the *varṇas* (*varṇa bhed*) to God Brahmā. I have told you the ways of the Yavanas before, I shall now add to it. Dilva was a great *riṣi* (sage). Yavanas called him Ādam. Dilva worshipped Mahāviṣṇu (God in the Muslim sense) and hated Śiva. Kārfava worshipped Śiva constantly and ridiculed Mahāviṣṇu. Their enmity grew day by day. Kārfava built a Śiva temple (*śivālaya*) and propitiated [the image] with regular rituals. Dilva built a *Maśid* (mosque) and started praying in it (*karitā jahālā nimāj*). One day Kārfav's cow, entering Dilva's abode, stood in his *Maśid*: Diva said to himself, "this cow is standing in the centre of my house of worship." With anger, he ran to beat her with a stick. The cow counter-attacked and gored him to death with her horns. His hotheaded son, Musal, became extremely furious and with a weapon killed the cow and avenged his father's death by eating her flesh. The sons born in his lineage became like him and started killing cows and eating them. Dilva's house is called *din* (a Marathi term used for the Muslim religion) and Musal's descendants are known as Musalmāns. The enmity against Kārfav was maintained [in Musal's lineage], hence Maharashtra is called Kāfar (infidel). They [Musalmāns], therefore, break the images and Śiva temples and hate the gods. This is the origin of the *yavana jāti.* (*S.B.* 23, 196-210)

Shāh-Munī is using a purāṇic style myth to explain the origin of the Muslims. Shāh-Munī's "*purāṇa*" (the fifth Veda) gives, or rather rubber-stamps the certificate of genuine local roots of the community of Islam. Thus both Hindus and Muslims have roots in Vedic ṛṣidom. However, Shāh-Munī's Dilva *ṛṣi* worships Mahāviṣṇu, the attributeless God. Kārfava's God is Śiva in the form of a *liṅga* worshipped in the temple. Shāh-Munī seems to be giving a local colouring to a conflict between the two communities by making it a sectarian Viṣṇu-Śiva conflict. Sectarian conflicts between Śaivites and Viṣṇuites were a recurring feature of medieval Hinduism in Maharashtra and south India, although the bhakti tradition of both regions had tried to overreach it. Shāh-Munī thus makes the conflict indigenous to the soil. The fanciful etymologies, of the words, *Musalmān* and *Kāfar*, are in line with the methods of the traditional Hindu pandits and *paurāṇikas* in Maharashtra and elsewhere in India. Shāh-Munī appears to be more sensitive to Hindu-Muslim tensions than Shekh Mahammad. The latter lived essentially in an area under Muslim political control in the late sixteenth and early seventeenth centuries. Shāh-Munī lived under the Brahman Peshwa's rule in the late eighteenth century.

Shāh-Munī is far more generous in his use of Hindu imagery in the *Siddhānta Bodha.* But he appears to be very consistent throughout in pointing out his preference for an attributeless God. In other words his God is within the framework of the monotheistic conception of god in Islam. He articulates his faith in no uncertain terms in the *Siddhānta Bodha.* He describes the origin of the Muslims:

Mahāviṣṇu, the Īśvara, is the supreme ruler of this world. His rule stretches from this land (*karmabhūmī*, India) to the milky primeval ocean of Mahāviṣṇu who rests there on the eternal serpent. From Mahāviṣṇu sprang Paigaṃbar (*tyāpāsun pīr Paigaṃbar*) who descended to earth. From Paigaṃbar we find the spreading of Yavanas (*yavana yāticā vistār*) throughout the world. Out of the millions of gods (*daivat*) a select 80 thousand became wise Paigaṃbars and established the *mleccha dharma* (Islam). That sustainer of the world Nārāyaṇa created the four *śāstras* which the Yavanas call the Qurāṇ. The Yavanas read the Qurāṇ which is the word of God (Nārāyaṇa). Believing in Paigaṃbar, the Yavanas worship God. The Yavanas call Nārāyaṇa the great Allāh (*Nārāyaṇālā yavana mhaṇatī thor Allā*). They worship Mahāviṣṇu with great devotion. Mahāviṣṇu declared the truth in the Qurāṇ: "That there is no one greater than I. I am Brahmā, Viṣṇu and Harīhar. I am the originator of Nature. I am the controller of the Universe. Besides me there is no one who punishes and saves". (*SB*. 18, 97-117)

The *Siddhānta Bodha* is not without its share of criticism of the social mores of the late eighteenth century Maharashtra. Shāh points out social hypocrisy and ills. He dislikes the divisive forces of the *jāti* system. Scornfully he asks:

Cokhāmeḷā (the untouchable Mahār bhakti sant of Maharashtra) worshipped God and people kept their distance from him. Will there be a separate Mahār quarter in heaven for Cokhāmeḷā to reside in? The low-born and high-born enter the river, fill their pots with water and come out. The high-born say, "Don't touch us. Keep away from us." A little while before they were standing in the same water. Shāh-Munī knows that it is a futile exercise to uphold a distinction between one's own *jāti* and another's. For him the distinction does not exist. (*SB*. 50: 400-2)

Law and Hindu-Muslim Interaction

A good illustration of Hindu-Muslim symbiotic relations is to be found in the sphere of law in Maharashtrian society. The properly tried law cases before a formal court convened by the government would depict social reality at a given point more accurately than that which can be gleaned from religious literature, with its biases and prejudices. The adjudicative rules in a court are geared to sustaining equity in law. Both the parties in the case have the opportunity to express their views and a review is made by the adjudicators. In relation to the paper's theme, I have singled out two Maratha law cases, one adjucated in 1701 and the other in 1742.[14] The 1701 case was fought during Aurangzeb's time when the region, where the case was fought, was under his jurisdiction. The 1742 case was settled during Shāhū's regime when the Marathas controlled that region. Both cases involved judgement by ordeal in a mosque.

In 1742, the legal dispute was between two Muslims, Bāvākhān bin Ismāil Ghorī and Polādshāh Sayyad (both *ashraf* Muslims)[15], over the right of ownership to the headship of a village in Maharashtra. The case was tried by Hindu administrators. The dispute was not resolved in the regular judicial trial, with witnesses and documents produced as evidence. In order to break the legal deadlock, with the consent of both parties, a trial by ordeal in a *maśid* (mosque) was agreed upon. The parties went to the mosque of Rānjaṇgāv near Pune. They began the divine ordeal of the mosque, as it is called in the legal document (*maśidīcī kriyā*), by placing ashes of burnt frankincense on each other's hand as an act of affirmation of the truth of their statements. In this case they asserted their version of the claims to the rights of ownership. As agreed upon previously, they encamped in the mosque for fifteen nights watched over by the *mujāvar*, the keeper of the mosque and the government people. The *mujāvar* gave a written testimony about the events which took place in the mosque:

> On the first day Polādshāh's hand quivered at the time of receiving the ashes. On the third day the lamp lighted by Polādshāh would not burn; the oil overflowed. Attempts were made to light the lamp twice, but it only fluttered intermittently. For eight consecutive days the lamp lighted by Bāvākhān burnt with great consistency. On the fourteenth and fifteenth day he [Polādshāh] became ill.

The *mujāvar* declared that Polādshāh was overcome by the manifestation of divine greatness (*śrī devācī ajmat ghaḍlī*). Bāvākhān won the trial by ordeal in the mosque. Rājā Shāhū restored the rights of ownership to Bāvākhān based on the ordeal.

The other trial in the mosque of Rānjaṇgāv took place in 1701.[16] Both the disputants were Hindus in this case and the dispute was in connection with the headship of a merchant guild. A Hindu chief ordered the trial because of a legal deadlock. In this case too, the *mujāvar* was the key witness of the events which took place in the mosque during the fifteen nights trial period. The *mujāvar* reported that on the fifth day about midnight, Mānāji, one of the disputants, made an awful sound as if he were suffering from acute pain and said thrice, "get off my chest", as if possessed by evil spirits. Mānāji lost the case.

Ordeals in the mosque are referred to as *maśidīcī kriyā.* The mosque is referred to in the two Marathi documents as *śri devul* (temple), *śrī devāce ghar* (house of God). The honorific *śrī* is indicative of the sanctity of the place. *Maśidīcī kriyā* (ordeal in the mosque) is equated with *śrī divya* (ordeal of God). For legal purpose the mosque and God of Muslims had the same standing as the Hindu temple and God of the Hindus.[17] The use of language here is indicative of the willingness of each community (more particularly Hindus) to accept a common sacral denominator. Islamic law, in theory at least, prohibits resorting to trial by ordeal. Hindus are not expected to hold a mosque as a place of veneration. It is evident from these cases that the parties, Hindus and Muslims were willing to accommodate each other's religious sensibilities in the pursuit of justice.

Pīr Worship and Hindus: A Case of Dāvalmalak

Pīr worship of Hindus could be construed as a good example of Hindu accommodation of an essentially Muslim practice of India. A case of Hindu worship of Dāvalmalak is a case in point. According to *sūfī* hagiographical literature, Abu-Masud better known as Dāvalmalak, was a *pīr* of the Chisti order and a *murid* of Shāh Alam of Gujarat. Within a century of his death in 1484, his fame had spread throughout Maharashtra. Presently most of the memorial shrines of Dāvalmalak are located in the Marathwada and Vidarbha regions of Maharashtra (Piṭake 1914: 35-7; Pohanarkar 160: 14-70; see also Ḍhere 1967: 161-4). The worship of Dāvalmalak was in vogue in Eknāth's time (1523-99). In his *johār,* Eknāth remarks:

> The people worship the begging bowl of Dāvalmalak.
> They become *fakirs* ((Muslim mendicants) once a year.
> Having cured their eyes of their disease, they eat
> *malidā* (a milk-based sweet offered at the shrine of
> the *pīr*) from the hand of a Turk. (cit. in Ḍhere 1967: 162-3)

Rāmdās, the mid-seventeenth century Marathi *sant,* in the course of lamenting the demoralization of the Brahmans in the Maharashtra says:

> Some go on pilgrimage to Dāvalmalak.
> Some worship the *pīr* and some on their own embrace Islam
> *kityek turuk hotī āple īcchene* (Ḍhere 1967: ibid.).

Shāh-Munī also observes that the "Brahmans go to Dāvalmalak". Even today in Maharashtra, according to R.C. Ḍhere, the tradition of pilgrimage to Dāvalmalak is followed by such castes as Dhangars, Tiḷole, Kuṇbī, Telī, Bhuī, Mahār and Māṅg, and, of course, Muslims. A number of Marathas and Brahmans are believers in Dāvalmalak. There are Brahmans in Maharashtra whose family name is Dāvalbhakta (Dāval-devotees). At the present time in the Marathwada area on the onset of eye trouble a Hindu believer in Dāvalmalak makes a pilgrimage to Dāvalmalak shrine. He is prepared with a blue cloth for begging and a wooden hoe. He is accompanied by a group of companions. He shouts, "Dom Dom Dāvalmalak", and begs for food. For he must subsist only on food obtained by begging. At the end of the journey, he places the begging cloth and hoe on a triangular stand. He gives gifts to the *mujāvar,* the keeper of the shrine. Through him he offers homage to the shrine. In turn the *mujāvar* gives him as the '*prasād*' of the Dāvalmalak, *malidā.*[18] Then he gives a feast (*bhaṇḍāra*) with the grain remaining from his begging. Then he waits to receive in dream a message from the spirit of Dāvalmalak that his eyes will be cured and that he may return home.

In the Vidarbha area of Maharashtra, Dāvalmalak is known to cure the eye diseases of both men and cattle. There are two modes of worship. One is known as *baiṭhi kundarī* (to give a feast in one's house) or *phirtī kundarī* (to travel to Dāvalmalak's shrine and give a feast). The pilgrims carry a coloured cloth for begging, a small stick, a wooden hoe and half of a dried white gourd called *pātār.* On their way many people feed them and the act of feeding is called the worship of *pātār.* It is the same as the *gadā pujatī* referred to by Eknāth. In Vidarbha, the *kundarī* feast may consist of a chicken and goat dinner (Ḍhere 1976: 164).

Concluding Remarks

Shāh-Munī and Shekh Mahammad refer to non-Muslims of Maharashtra as *Marhāṭa* and *Maharashtra.* For themselves they use terms such as *avindha,* Yavana, *mleccha* and, the preferred expression, Musalmān. The expression *Maharashtra Dharma* is used by Shāh-Munī as a comprehensive term of reference for brahmanical and folk practices, theology from the Vedas, Purāṇas, *Mahābhārata* and *Rāmāyaṇa,* dharmaśāstra and *dvaita* and *advaita* philosopical tenets.

In Eknāth's Hindu-Muslim debate the issues singled out as being specifically Hindu are a belief in the Veda and Purāṇa, image worship and *jāti* rules. The juxtaposition of traditions of Muslims with Hindus in the debate, thus, exposes the distinctiveness and general characteristics of Hinduism. It also tells us about the dynamics of adoptive compromises needed to lead a relatively unfettered life for the two communities.

In the historical and biographical literature in the eighteenth century Maharashra, when the Muslims had lost political control of that region, Maharashtra's historians are seen as accepting Muslims as legitimate past rulers of India and Maharashtra, and as a community anchored to the soil. The acceptance of the Muslim rulers is accomplished through a purāṇic style myth of origin in the *Ramulu śāstra*. Whatever is stated in the *śāstra* must be true—it does not matter whether it is Hindu *śāstra* or "Muslim *śāstra*"—and lends authenticity to the myth.

Muslim poet-saints like Shekh Mahammad and Shāh-Munī were canonized as great saints by Hindus on account of their contributions to the bhakti tradition of Maharashtra. While staying within the framework of the monotheistic concepts of Islam, they were willing to accommodate gods of the Hindu pantheon as long as those gods conformed to their conception of God as devoid of definable attributes, indistinct and being one entity. Shāh-Munī uses a purāṇic device to explain the origin of Islam through Mahāviṣṇu, his version of Allāh; the Hindu-Muslim differences are explained away by another origin myth. By describing Dilva "the founder of the Muslim community", as a Vedic seer, he is, like the Hindu historians of Maharashtra, making the Muslims acceptable members, rooted in the tradition of Maharashtra. Shāh-Munī and Shekh Mahammad struck at the bases of brahmanical rituals and caste divisions. Both were aware of the antipathy between Hindus and Muslims. They hoped that this would be melted away through belief in God.

The popular *pīr* worship was nearer to the Hindu beliefs in terms of the perceived efficacy (*karāmat* in *Sūfi* terms) of their gods and deities to bestow pragmatic rewards. Hindu believers in Dāvalmalak without giving up their own Hindu identity, were willing to assume temporarily the Muslim identity of a fakir, if this would help them to alleviate physical deformities and pains. Muslims, Brahmans, Mahārs and others through centuries have been worshipping Davālmalak.

In the law cases examined above one finds to what extent the two communities were willing to share each other's institutional mores in the pursuit of a just settlement.

NOTES

1. For the "peaceful coexistence" and "secularism" approach, see Chand (1936); Mujeeb (1967); and Kabir (1955).
2. For the classic exponent of the theory of Hindu-Muslim incompatibility and distrust, see Ahmad 1964.
3. Rājvāḍe 1924: 60-8. For the list of Muslim kings; see N.K. Wagle and A.R. Kulkarni 1976: 32-9; Nandurbārkar and Dāṇḍekar (eds.) 1895: 1-33.
4. *Cāryugācī Bakhar* (unpubl. MS.), pp. 9-10. The MS. is without the author's name but was most probably written in 1795 from the internal evidence.
5. A part of the *śloka* in four lines, written in Sanskrit, appears in Nandurbārkar and Dāṇḍekar: 1-33, but the details of the seven *paigaṃbars* (prophets) are missing in the *Digvijaya.* The subtitle of the *śloka* is "*vacana of the Ramala śāstra* (the sayings of the *Ramala śāstra*)". Nandurbārkar, the editor of the *Digvijaya,* says (p. 25, footnote) that he found the *śloka* in Ciṭṇīs' *Sapta prakarṇātmaka caritra.* However, it is not found in R.V. Hervāḍkar's edition of *Sapta prakarṇātmaka caritra* (Hervāḍkar: 1967).
6. *Cāryugācī Bakhar,* p. 10.
7. Ibid.
8. Wagle and Kulkarni 1976: 33, 156; *Mahikāvatīcī Bakhar* (Rājvāḍe 1924: 83-8). According to the *Mahikāvatīcī Bakhar,* Allauddin Khalji with his two sons, Hasan and Husen, attacked the king Rāmdevrāv of Devagiri. One of the ministers of Rāmdev killed Hasan, the son of Allauddin. Husen was killed by Chitragupta, another of his ministers. Allaudin killed Rāmdevrāv in revenge according to this *bakhar.* The advent of Islam in Maharashtra is thus associated with Allauddin's victory.
9. See Roy 1984. For the function of mythology as a model for human behaviour, see Eliade 1965: 1-10.
10. For social and political background of Eknāth's period which saw the domination of Muslim Sultans over much of Maharashtra, see, N.R. Phāṭak, *Śrī Eknāth* (Phāṭak 1950: 33-50). Phāṭak has also critically analysed the Hindu-Turk *Saṃvād* in the context of Eknāth's period (ibid.). See also Soṇavaṇe 1907: 1-14. Soṇavaṇe (p. 10) narrates an hagiographical account of an encounter between Eknāth and a Muslim. The incidence is given by Soṇavaṇe as an example of Eknāth's forbearance and determination (*sahanśilatā*) when he was confronted with an hostile and humiliating situation:

    > Nāth was on his way home after taking a bath in the Gaṅgā (Godāvarī river). A Muslim after chewing a *pān* spat on him. Nath without uttering a word went back to the river and took his bath. He again encountered the Muslim who, it seems, was waiting for the freshly bathed Eknāth's arrival only to spit on him. These acts of spitting and bathing went on for a while. A crowd gathered to see who would win this 'contest'. In the end the Muslim gave up spitting and withdrew shamefacedly.

11. Sākhare 1952. The references are to the verse and page numbers of that

edition. For another English rendering of the Hindu-Turk debate see Zelliot 1982: 171-95. Zelliot also has provided a picture of the political and social environment of Eknāth's times in the article. Cf. N.R. Phāṭak's contribution mentioned earlier.

12. See R.C. Ḍhere, 1967: 89. Ḍhere is of the opinion that Cānd Bodhale, who according to him was a Brahman, adopted Muslim *sūfi* practices and the *sūfi* dress. Because of such a behaviour, Muslims adopted him as their own. His *samādhī* has now become a Muslim *dargāh*. In effect, Bodhale became a Muslim *pīr*. The official record of the Qādiri Sūfī order *Sijrā-i-Qadirī*, Cānd is referred to as Sayyad Cāndsāheb Qādri. Janārdan Swāmī, a Hindu and *guru* of Eknāth was a disciple of Cāndsāheb (Ḍhere 1967: 88-9).
13. See Ḍhere 1967: 12, 26-100. Although Shekh's critique of Hindu rituals and practices are scattered through his 18 chapters of the book, it is particularly intense in the above section. The *Yogasaṃgrāma* references mentioned in this paper are from Ḍhere's edition.
14. For a detailed analysis and translation of the two law cases see N.K. Wagle 1983: 314-34.
15. See Bāvākhān Gori v. Polādshāh Said, 12 August 1742 in Vad (ed.) 1900: 36-41. For translation and analysis of the case see Wagle 1983: 320-6.
16. See Gāvarseṭī v. Mānāji Bandh (AD 1700), in Rājvāḍe (ed.) 1914: 61-6; see for translation Wagle 183: 326.
17. The Hindu members of the tribunals were sometimes sent to the Muslim *dargāh* (the tomb of a *pīr*) and, once there, were made to take an oath that they would abide by the truth of the case. See Narsiṅgrāv Ṭhākur v. Marāḷ, 30 November 1726, *Shāhū Daftar Rumāl* No. 6, cited in Gune, 1953: 292.
18. Piṭake (1914: 37) finds the role of the *mujāvar* and the act of receiving the food from a Muslim, very instructive. He says that normally if a Hindu Maratha peasant (Kuṇbī) were to receive food from the hands of a Qāzi (Muslim theologian-jurist), he would be instantly excommunicated from his community. But in the case of Dāvalmalak's worship a Muslim's food becomes acceptable because it is *kuḷācār*, an acceptable norm. Piṭake observes that such acts at the religious level went a long way in establishing amicable relationships between Hindus and Muslims.

REFERENCES

Ahmad, A. 1964. *Studies in Islamic culture in the Indian environment*. London: Oxford University Press.

Chand, T. 1936. *Influence of Islam on Indian Culture*. Allahabad: Indian Law Press.

Ḍhere, R.C. 1967. *Musalmān Marāṭhī Saṃta kavi*. Pune: Jñānarāj Prakāśan.

———. 1976 (ed.) *Śekh Mahaṃmad, Yoga Saṃgrāma*. Pune: Abhirūcī Prakāśan.

Eliade, M. 1965. *Myth and reality*. New York: Harper and Row.

Gune, V.T. 1953. The judicial system of the Marathas. Diss. Series 13; Poona: Deccan College.

Hervāḍkar, R.V. 1957. *Marāṭhī bakhar*. Pune: Venus Prakāśan.

———. 1967. *Malhār Ramrāv Ciṭṇīs, Sapta prakarṇātmaka caritra.* Pune: Venus Prakāśan.

Kabir, H. 1955. *The Indian heritage.* Bombay: Asia Publishing House.

Mujeeb, M. 1967. *The Indian Muslims.* London: George Allen and Unwin.

Nandurbārkar, N.K. and Dāṇḍekar, L.K. (eds.) 1985. *Khaṇḍo Ballāḷa, Śrī Śivājī digvijaya: Śrī Mahārājāṃcī bakhar.* Baroda.

Phāḍke, V.K. (ed.). 1972. *Śrī Santa Śahāmunī kṛta Śrī siddhānta bodha.* Pune: Yasvant Prakāśan.

Phāṭak, N.R. 1950. *Śrī Eknāth.* Bombay: Mauj Prakāśan.

Piṭake, H.R. 1914. 'Shāh Dāvalmalak'. In *Vividhajñāvistāra* 45, (January), 35-7.

Pohanarkar, N.S. 1960. 'Dāvalmalak'. In *Pratiṣṭhāna,* (February), 14-17.

Rājvāḍe, V.K. 1914. (ed.) *Maraṭhyāṃcyā itihāsācī sādhane,* vol. 18, Bombay.

———. 1924. (ed.) *Keśavācārya, mahikavitācī urf māhiṃci bakhar.* Pune: Citraśāḷā Press.

———. 1929. *Aitihāsik prasthāvanā Rājvāḍe lekhasaṃgraha.* Part I, Pune: Citraśāḷā Press.

Roy, Asim 1984. *The Islamic syncretistic tradition in Bengal.* Princeton: Princeton University Press.

Sākhare, B.S. 1952. (ed.) *Śrī Eknāth Mahārāj yāṃcyā abhaṃgācī gāthā.* Pune: Indirā Prakāśan.

Soṇavaṇe, B.S. 1907. *Eknāth ani Tukārām.* Pune: Bandhusamāj.

Wagle, N.K. and Kulkarni, A.R. 1976. *Vallabha's Paraśarāma caritra.* Bombay: Popular Prakashan.

———. 1983. 'The ordeal in the mosque of Rānjaṇgāv: An aspect of dispute resolution in eighteenth century Maharashtra'. In *Islamic culture and society* (eds.) Milton Israel and N.K. Wagle. New Delhi: Manohar.

Zelliot, E. 1982. A medieval encounter between Hindu and Muslim: Eknāth's drama-poem Hindu Turku Samvad. In *Images of man: religion and historical process in South Asia* (ed.) Fred W. Clothey. Madras: New Era Publications.

THE CONCEPT OF THE IDEAL BRAHMAN AS AN INDOLOGICAL CONSTRUCT

Peter van der Veer

1 Introduction

Anthropologists often fail to relate the study of meaning to that of social action. However, when they concern themselves with civilizations, frequently qualified by adjectives such as "high", "great" and "ancient", the problem becomes acute. Renouncing the study of this connection is a form of abdication for an anthropologist. I wish to submit that this withdrawal is caused by a feeling on the part of the anthropological community that they are "outsiders" and "intruders" in a field which has been dominated for so long by disciplines like islamology, indology, in short by oriental studies. In what might be an attempt at gaining respectability the anthropological upstart seems to be inclined to perpetuate the static and harmonious image of a "Hochkultur" that he encountered in the works of the textual scholars.

The orientalist perspective in the study of Hinduism has above all resulted in a picture of Indian society as static, timeless and spaceless, and dominated by the Brahmans as guardians of the sacred order of society (Cohn 1968: 7).[1] There can be no doubt that this picture has haunted anthropological research on Hinduism. This is especially clear in the attempts to combine, in one way or another, the approaches of textual scholars and anthropologists. The most influential of those attempts has, of course, been that of Louis Dumont and David Pocock who declared that "a Sociology of India lies at the point of confluence of sociology and indology" (1957; see Dumont 1970: 2). Their programme was to develop a sociology of values and ideas, for which they relied upon the indological interpretation of those (Sanskrit) texts in which the Hindu "system of meaning" was laid down. In Dumont's work this leads to an orientalist perspective which coincides, at least partly, with the perspective of the learned Brahmans who were the authors of these texts. The ambiguity and confusion inherent in religious beliefs and actions, as found by the anthropologist in his field, are simplified by reducing them to a unifying ideology. Moreover, change and history also disappear from the scope of interest of the anthropologist, since the ideology is derived from texts belonging to the classical period of Hindu civilization, before the Muslim invasions. History itself, these authors assert, can only be understood in terms of Hindu ideology (cf. Dumont 1970: 147; Biardeau 1981: 9).

There are several objections to be raised against this orientalist perspective, but we will limit ourselves to two major ones. The first is that the structures of power and changing power relations are separated from the production and management of meaning. In fact, one of the major problems in the anthropological study of religion is the tendency to divorce it from the study of economics and politics. This implies the relative neglect both of the politics of religious organization and the relation between on the one hand changing religious orientations and experiences and on the other hand economic and political processes (cf. Van der Veer 1987). The question of how power creates religion or what the historical conditions necessary for the existence of particular religious practices or discourses are (Asad 1983: 252), is evaded. The orientalist perspective is a theological rather than an anthropological or historical one.

The other major objection concerns the use of an ideological model derived from the indological interpretation of Sanskrit text. Reference to the textual tradition raises many problems. In the first place texts are generally taken from the Vedic and Classical periods of Hindu Civilization, i.e. texts dating from about 1000 B.C. to A.D. 1200. The idea that a model derived from these texts can be applied to Indian civilization and society of all times and places is based upon the assumption that "traditional" Hindu society was and is a kind of 'frozen' social reality. This assumption is clearly mistaken. The study of the textual traditions after A.D. 1200 shows significant changes in beliefs and practices as well as considerable ideological debate. Already in the sixties the Indologist van Buitenen (1966: 40) observed that anthropologists who wished to collaborate with textual scholars in their endeavour to understand modern Hinduism, should take the study of much more recent (vernacular) texts as their starting point.

Secondly, those who want to have recourse to indological materials should pay more attention to the nature of these materials. A text is always a social text, written from a certain point of view which pertains to certain social group. By selecting texts one may obtain a partial view on the social and historical situation. Dumont, for example, is often accused of presenting the Brahmanical ideology without paying attention to other ideologies in, what Edmund Leach has called, "his mixture of Vedic ideas and contemporary facts". A solution to this specific problem would be the construction of more cultural models, deriving from several native ideologies, as found in the texts. Such a proposal has been made by Richard Burghart (1983), who argues that we should study the intra-cultural debate of the ideological representations of Brahmans, kings and ascetics whom he regards as the major actors in Hindu society.

This solution, however, does not account for what I am tempted to see as the most important problem that arises when anthropologists refer to the textual tradition. The social significance of texts in contemporary India seems to be too easily assumed. Those texts which are designated by Indologists as important are often disregarded or are insufficiently known by the contemporary actors (cf. Fuller 1984). Moreover, texts do not lay down anything at all, and certainly not beliefs which are very diverse and are only exceptionally the subject of debate among theologians in such places as Benares. Most remarkable is the plasticity of the past in a literate society such as India. In India one finds a mixture of oral and textual traditions which might be even more variable than the oral history of some African societies. "Ancient" texts can be made by the day as I actually observed in Ayodhya (cf. Parry 1985b), while tradition can be transformed in accordance with changing social configurations. To adopt the "emic" view that there is an unchanging, scriptural source for all actual practices in Hinduism is a methodological fallacy.

Nevertheless, the orientalist perspective, developed by anthropologists and Indologists in the fifties and sixties, still dominates the study of contemporary Hinduism. As far as I see it, the central task facing the anthropological study of Hinduism is to break away from the orientalist perspective and the intellectualist and theological overtones that have dominated it from the start. In the rest of this paper I will attempt to show that this perspective is misleading where one should expect it to be most fruitful: the interpretation of values and behaviour of the Brahman priests in Hinduism. First, I will introduce the two major arguments concerning the social position of the Brahman priest which are both ultimately based on indological models, before turning to a discussion of field data collected among pilgrimage priests in north India.

A God on Earth

According to an ancient cosmological myth the social organism was the body of Purusha, the primeval man. This original body was cut up to form four specialized *varṇas* or social categories. The Brahman *varṇa* was born from the mouth of the Purusha and had the duty of teaching and studying the Vedas, performing sacrifices for two of the lower *varṇas*, and accepting gifts in exchange. The Kshatriya *varṇa* was born from the arms of Purusha and had the duty of fighting enemies, protecting the other *varṇas* and offering gifts to the Brahmans. The Vaishya *varṇa* sprang from the thighs of Purusha and had the duty of producing the things to be sacrificed by means of herding cattle and tilling the soil. Finally, the Shudra *varṇa*, born of the feet of Purusha, had the duty of serving the other *varṇas* which were engaged in the sacrifice. The first three *varṇas* were called "twice-born" or *dvija*, since they underwent a second ritual birth which enabled them to learn from their Brahman teachers (*guru*) the divine sounds of the Veda. The Shudra *varṇa*, however, was forbidden to hear the sacred Veda. In a way, the Shudra had to worship the "twice-born" just as the "twice-born" had to worship the gods.

In this Vedic myth the central position in the sacrifice, and by consequence in society, was taken by the Brahman priest who was like a god on earth and acted as an intermediary between the gods and the other two *varṇas* partaking in the sacrifice. In post-Vedic society the Brahman retained his elevated position at the summit of the social hierarchy. Most authors on Hinduism concur in this opinion. Dumont (1972: 84) writes that "the Brahmans being in principle priests, occupy the supreme rank with respect to the whole set of castes". Moreover, the Brahmanical view of society, its scale of value, is often seen as the ideal model of Hindu society as a whole (cf. Biardeau 1981: 9; Obeyesekere 1984: 429; Burghart 1985: 9). Some even go so far as to argue that Hindu society is based upon the Brahmanical value system.

This opinion is, for example, advanced by Edward Harper in an influential article on ritual observances and beliefs concerning pollution among the Havik Brahmans of south India. Harper's argument is that Hindu society "is organized around the task of caring for its gods, and a division of labour among the castes is necessary to attain this end" (1964: 196). Since gods can only be worshipped by mortals of high ritual purity (i.e. Brahmans), this inherent purity must be preserved by lower castes who remove impurity by taking up defiling activities. Thanks to this social organization all members of the community derive benefit from the worship given by the Brahmans to the gods. A fundamental Hindu idea, according to Harper, is that "respect-pollution" provides a link between gods and Brahmans, and between Brahmans and other men. In Hindu worship (*pūjā*) the devotee's acceptance of the left over food of the gods indicates a hierarchical distance between the divine and the human as well as between the Brahmans and other men. This line of interpretation is followed by more recent authors like Babb (1975) and Marriott and Inden. The latter write that the codes of Hindu worship require the existence of complex local communities of caste and that "the priest must be a male of the highest, most godlike caste available—ideally a Brahman skilled by heredity in the maintenance of ritual boundaries between substances and empowered to transform them" (1975: 985).

This might be said to be the first set of opinions, in which the Brahman, as priest, holds the supreme rank in Hindu society. The notion that the exchange between men and gods in Hindu worship establish a hierarchical society, in which the Brahman is the purest being on earth, a kind of demi-god between men and gods, is in fact on several points at odds with observed reality and even with part of the Brahmanical tradition itself. In a clear exposition of the Hindu theory of gift (*dānadharma*) Marcel Mauss argues that the position of the Brahman is ambiguous, because the gift creates a bond between the donor and the recipient: "The gift is thus something that must be given, that must be received and that is, at the same time, dangerous to accept. The gift itself constitutes an irrevocable link especially when it is a gift of food. The recipient depends on the temper of the donor, in fact each depends upon the other" (1974: 58). The ambivalence of the god on earth is therefore that, ideologically, he is presented as superior to every other human being, but that, materially, he is completely dependent on the gifts of his fellow men for his livelihood. Mauss adds that the Brahman's obligations to receive threatens his superiority a fortiori in the relation with the traditional sacrificer (*jajman*), the Hindu king.

The Indologist Heesterman (1985: 26-44) argues that in the Vedic ritual texts an original pattern of the sacrifice can be discerned in which two parties exchanged life and death. The sacrificer is charged with the evil of death and, by means of the various offerings and the gifts (*dakṣiṇā*) which represent the parts of his body, he disposes of his impure self. Thus he is reborn as pure, while it is the function of the Brahman officiant to take over the death impurity of the patron by eating from the offerings and accepting the *dakṣiṇās*. In the later, classical, pattern of the ritual the Brahman has to safeguard his purity by keeping aloof from others and their gifts. The highest Brahman is the Shrotiya, one learned in the Veda, who does not accept gifts. According to Heesterman, the development of Brahmanical theory also led to an interiorization and individualization of the ritual which culminated in the institution of renunciation.

These arguments lead to a second set of opinions, in which the ideal Brahman is said to be a renouncer, not a priest. There seem to be two things involved here. First, the material dependence of the Brahman priest on the gifts of the king, which results in the Brahman loosing "the transcendant status that formed his literally priceless value" (Heesterman 1971: 46) and, second, there is the transference of evil that makes the Brahman a recipient and remover of evil from the world, which seems even more to threaten his social position as the acme of purity. Heesterman's solution is that "as the representative of transcendence, the ideal Brahman can logically only be a renouncer, as indeed he is in the classical texts" (loc. cit.). Dumont (1971: 74f) offers a different explanation, namely that the Brahman who accepts the gifts of the king only faces a fall within the social category of Brahmans , which is different from a fall from or of the category as a whole. This suggestion has been followed by Fuller (1984), who also focuses on the relative inferiority of the Brahman priest vis-a-vis other non-priestly Brahmans. According to Fuller, the priests' relative inferiority can be defined in terms of the lack of ideal qualities. This general explanation can be differentiated in relation to the different configurations in which priestly groups are operating in India. In the north the acceptance of gifts, especially in the context of inauspicious rituals, endangers the status of the Brahman priest. This point is illustrated by the material collected by Parry (1980; 1985a) on the Mahabrahmans of Benares. The Brahman priest is here presented as a kind of sacrificial vessel (*pātra*) into which gifts and food are put in order to get rid of evil (*doṣ*) and sin (*pāp*). In the south the priest's status is endangered by his lack of Brahmanical learning, when compared with ascetic Brahmans such as the Shankaracharyas.

In an earlier paper (Van der Veer 1985) I have already tried to show that priesthood is an optional occupational identity for Brahmans. This does certainly not imply that it is a free option, since there are several social (political and economical) constraints on the their choice. It should be emphasized that the status of the profession does not entirely depend on ideological factors, such as its relative purity or impurity, but also on economical considerations, such as the income one derives from it. Much of the discussion reviewed so far, however, asks attention for a specific issue: the position of the Brahman priest at the receiving end of the gift-ritual. In this paper I would therefore like to focus on the social implications of the acceptance of gifts by Brahmans. My material derives from fieldwork among the Pandas of the north Indian pilgrimage centre of Ayodhya.

2. The Pandas of Ayodhya

2.1 Introduction

Ayodhya is a pilgrimage centre or *tīrtha* in the north Indian state Uttar Pradesh. In accordance with its literal meaning in Sanskrit of "ford", the term *tīrtha* is used for places where a river can be crossed. Ayodhya is situated on the bank of a sacred river, the Sarayu, which has descended from heaven. Sarayu is a goddess, just like Ganga and many other great rivers in India. The river, then, is connected with heaven and the pilgrim crosses over to heaven at the *tīrtha* by, for example, making contact with the world of the ancestors. Besides being situated on the bank of the river Sarayu, Ayodhya is the birthplace of the Hindu god Ram.

The Brahman specialists of the pilgrimage centre are called *tīrth purohits* or Pandas. The functional title *tīrth purohit* simply means 'priest of the pilgrimage centre' as distinct from *kul purohit* which means "priest of the family". Panda (*pāṇḍā*) derives from the Sanskrit word *paṇḍita* which means "who has knowledge" and which is commonly used in north India to address Brahmans. Many of the north Indian pilgrimage centres have Panda communities. In Ayodhya there are two rival communities, called Bhareriya and Gangaputra respectively. They are in constant conflict over the right to practise the Panda profession. Both communities claim to be ancient endogamous castes of Brahman stock which have been exclusively devoted to the Panda profession from the times of Lord Ram in a different world period (*yug*).

The pilgrim visits Ayodhya for a number of reasons, not all of them made explicit. The purpose which was most often mentioned to me was to acquire merit (*puṇya* or *kalyāṇ*), but an often more implicit purpose was to get rid of impurity (*aśauca*), sin (*pāp*), or illness (*rog*). In general, the pilgrim will not make a clear distinction between the worship of Ram in the Ramanandi temples and the worship of Brahmans, gods and ancestors on the bank of the Sarayu. To some extent, however, an analytic distinction can be made between on the one hand a spiritual complex, in which the devotion to Ram is central and which is dominated by Ramanandi *sādhūs* who are specialized in a specific theology and worship of Ram, and on the other hand a ritual complex, which is dominated by Brahman Pandas who are specialized in those rituals of Brahmanism for which *tīrthas* are appropriate places. In fact, this is largely an organizational distinction, which is of greater significance to the specialists themselves than to the average pilgrim, to whom all the ritual acts he performs in Ayodhya have an interconnected meaning. When he wants to worship Lord Ram in a temple he needs the assistance of a Ramanandi *sādhū* who acts as an officiating priest in the worship (*pūjā*) of Ram. When he wants to worship the river Sarayu on the religious area (*kṣetra*) of Ayodhya, or to perform an ancestor-ritual or take a ritual bath in the Sarayu, he needs the assistance of a Panda.

Most of the rituals, in which the Pandas are specialized are performed on the bank of the river Sarayu. The riverbank is parcelled out by the Pandas into a large number of plots on which they have erected their stalls (*chowkees*), often not more than a couple of wooden fourposters placed along the riverside in rectangular formation. The riverside is further divided in bathing-areas (*ghāṭs*) which sometimes have stone steps (*pakka*) or are simply the sandy bank of the river (*kaccha*). The Pandas, when they are not engaged in performing rituals, sit at their stalls and wait for pilgrims to come. Their agents (*gomastha*) are posted at the bus and railway stations to welcome pilgrims and conduct them to these stalls which bear symbols such as an elephant or bicycle, so that the illiterate pilgrim will also be able to recognize the stall of his Panda. Some of the rituals, however, are performed in the Pandas' houses. Often pilgrims stay in houses or lodges (*dharmśālas*) belonging to Pandas. Certainly the central ritual in which the Ayodhya Pandas are specialized is that of the gift (*dān*). The nature and the implications of this ritual will be the subject of the rest of this section.

2.2 The nature of the gift-ritual

There can be no doubt about the importance of the gift (*dān*) to the Brahman in the Hindu ritual system. In ideological terms the Brahman could perhaps best be compared with the sacrificial fire, and indeed this comparison is often made by my informants: "Brahma (who stands for the supernatural world) has two mouths: Agni (the sacrificial fire) and the Brahman". In this way fire sacrifice and gift-giving to a Brahman are equal Moreover, inside the Brahman—as in other beings—Agni is present in the form of the digestive fire. The analogy with the fire-sacrifice is of course clearest in rituals in which the Brahman eats what is given to him, but more generally people tend to conceive of the Brahman's acceptance of even inedible gifts in terms of digestion (cf. Parry 1985a). Like Agni the Brahman seems a god in his own right as well as intermediary between the supernatural and society. The sacrificial fire has to be worshipped as a physical presence of Agni, who is the same as Brahma, and in the same way also the Brahman has to be worshipped. These ideas—and I want to emphasize this point—are not just part of an ancient ideology to be found in Sanskrit texts, but are also part of the ideology and practices of my informants in present-day Ayodhya. Besides being equated with the sacrificial fire, the Brahman is seen as a sacrificial vessel (*pātra*). The word pātra is used for the Brahman priest. A modern comparison is made by equating the Brahman with the mailbox: "You give something to it and it is brought to its destination." It implies that everything given to a Brahman is brought, unseen, to its destination.

Jonathan Parry has been working on the symbolical interpretation of gift-giving to Brahmans. In his ethnographical descriptions he presents two diametrically opposed views on the gift. In his book on the caste and kinship in Kangra (1979) the gift to the priest (*kul-purohit*) is interpreted as having "the character of a charitable donation humbly offered to someone of superior status, whose condescension in accepting the gift allows the donor to acquire merit" (op. cit., 65f). In a later article, based upon fieldwork among the Mahabrahmans of Benares, he presents a quite different view of the gift by observing that "as all the Brahman specialists see it, *dān* is bad not just because it subverts their ideal ascetic independence, but more importantly because the acceptance of *dāṇ* involves the acceptance of the sins of the donor" (1980: 103). One could argue that only the perspective has changed from that of the donor who acquires merit to the recipient who receives sins, but it seems that there is more involved. In fact, it is a shift away from the point of view, developed by Dumont and several American anthropologists, that the Brahman as priest holds the foremost rank in Hindu society and that he exchanges material goods for spiritual merit to the view, developed by Heesterman, that with gifts evils and sins are transferred to the recipient and that a Brahman must therefore avoid gift relations. In the first interpretation social hierarchy is established by reciprocal exchange, while in the second the gift is unreciprocal. The Brahman is called a cesspit which absorbs, but gives nothing in return.[2]

I would propose to consider the gift in its context: the relation between patron and priest and the nature of the thing given (cf. Mauss 1974: 58). We may begin with the relation between patron and priest, which is of course an example of what is often called the jajmāni-system. This system, being the "traditional" or "natural" economy of Hindu India, has been discussed in a great number of anthropological publications and I do not intend to cover the same ground yet again.[3] As Commander (1983: 296-8) points out, the locus of the system is the possession of land: "For it is land or its produce that provides the crucial 'good' disbursed, upwards or downwards, by the jajman." It is important to note that the Brahman priest stands somewhat apart from the other service groups which are tied to a caste of patrons (*jajmāns*). The service castes (*kāmins*) depend economically on the caste(s) of landholders, and this dependence implies an inferior status. It is, however, a meritorious act to give a Brahman rent-free land (*saṅkalp, birt* or *dharmārth*) and by the acceptance of such a donation a Brahman family may become economically independent. The balance of power between patron and Purohit changes decidedly in favour of the Purohit, when he becomes economically independent. Miller (1975: 131f) argues that the pandit who is a free agent, receiving payment for specific performances, should be distinguished from the Purohit, who is tied to particular Jajmans in a hereditary relationship. The independence is seen as degrading and so it is better for a Brahman to have land than to be involved in a somewhat degrading dependence on patron.

In the case of pilgrimage priests we should, however, add another observation. A central feature of the jajmani-system as described in the historical and anthropological literature seems to be that it operates in a kind of autarchic village economy in "a miniaturized economic universe" and that it falls apart when labour becomes mobile (Commander 1983: 286, 309). The Pandas have, however, always been working in a political and economic universe as large, in principle, as the Indian subcontinent itself. A *tīrtha* like Ayodhya is a "centre out there", to use Victor Turner's phrase, and its catchment area, though expanding in the last two centuries, has always been regional. Conclusions drawn from the general discussion of the jajmani-system cannot therefore be easily applied to the field of pilgrimage. There is, for example, a great increase in the number of pilgrims contracting jajmani relations with Pandas of Ayodhya in the nineteenth century, while the general picture is that the system lost its importance in the same period. On the other hand, given that jajmani relations have become less important in the same age during the course of this century, the implications are rather similar to what has been observed in general: money becomes more important than wage-in-kind, agents who act as middlemen between pilgrims and priests attain a dominant position in the new system, the relative security of the jajmani-system is replaced by the impoverishment of many priests and the relative success of a few.

This is also no doubt significant for the relation between Jajman and priest, which is at least much less of a face-to-face relationship, in which consideration of relative status play an important role, than it is the case in a village setting. In a small-scale village economy with little occupational mobility a priest will feel his dependence on landholding patrons repeatedly in subtle ways. In the large-scale economy of the pilgrimage system jajmani relations are much more impersonal. The names of the Jajmans are entered into registers and the priest may see his Jajman only once a year, or even once in a lifetime.

Parry (1979: 80) points out that the Purohit's service is essential to the patron's status, so that the Purohit-Jajman relationship tends to be more perdurable than that between the patron and the service castes. Pilgrimage is clearly a status ritual which in the eighteenth and nineteenth century spread from "old elites" to "new elites". On the other hand, the status of the patron is clearly of importance for that of the Panda. In this connection it is enlightening to see the Pandas' view of their relation with the most important patrons, the rajas. They describe most eloquently their connection with the rajas of all parts of India who gave them huge gifts. These are clearly matters of great pride and it is with bitterness that they recall how they attempted to continue these relations after India's independence, but were rebuffed by the impoverished ex-royal families. Certain relations seem to confer status on the priests as well as the other way around.

Finally, dependence might be to some extent degrading, but it also confers economic security. Patronage means obligations and rights. The priest is tied to the patron, but the patron also to the priest. Jajmani relations are therefore ambiguous. They offer protection and a secure income, but on the other hand they are often felt to be the cause of inferiority because they imply a certain dependence on the resources of the patron. In the large-scale economy of pilgrimage it seems that the element of economic security is of greater importance to the Pandas than the element of inferiority which would be his daily experience in a village owned by his jajmans. In fact, jajmani relations are highly valued among Pandas at present. This can be explained by referring to the changing organization of pilgrimage. The established Pandas with their fixed constituency of patrons are losing ground to entrepreneurs who make a better use of agents in directing new pilgrims to their houses and riverside-stalls. New jajmani relations are still contracted, but the majority of the pilgrims only comes to Ayodhya for a short visit and does not want to be involved with long-standing hereditary obligations to Pandas. Nowadays most pilgrims only give a fee (*dakṣiṇā*) to the priest for performing some ritual on their behalf without becoming his regular Jajman. Money is also more often used instead of the customary wage-in-kind. In these circumstances one can easily understand those established Pandas who idealize the past in which their jajmani relations implied a secure source of income.

When considering the gift in its context, we should not only pay attention to relation between patron (the donor) and priest (the recipient), but also to the nature of the thing given. First of all, it may be useful to point out the difference between three presentations in the chain of ritual acts. First, we have the gift proper (*dān*) which, as we have seen, is considered to be equal to the sacrifice, secondly, we have the so-called *saṅgitā*, a small gift which is said to make up for a possible deficiency in the central gift, and finally, we have the *dakṣiṇā*, a gift which my informants interpret as a remuneration, a fee for the priest's service so that he may be free for the priest's services. The idea is that the priest has to be paid for his services so that he may be free to accept the gift as a sacrificial vessel. The Brahman priest has therefore two separate functions in the gift ritual: to act as a vessel and to officiate as a priest. In the first function he has to digest a gift on behalf of a supernatural being or on his own behalf as a god on earth, while in the other he presides over the ritual. This is, of course, a rather abstract distinction, but it has important social implications, since some Brahmans may act as ritual specialists (*karmakāṇḍin*) in the ritual and accept a fee (*dakṣiṇā*) for that, while refusing to accept the *dān*. Moreover, *dakṣiṇā* or fees are not only given for priestly services, but also as a payment for the service of a Brahman teacher (*guru-dakṣiṇā*).

The gift-ritual starts, like every sacrifice and like the pilgrimage as such, with the explicit pronouncement of the intention (*saṅkalp*) of the donor. The donor takes some unhusked rice in his hand, prays to the god he wants to worship, then announces the intention of his ritual and the name and the clan of the Brahman who will accept it. When pronouncing the intention the donor of course says what result (*phal*) he desires. The Brahman who officiates in the ritual has finally to declare that the ritual has been performed properly and thus "bear fruit" (*saphal*). It is therefore always perfectly clear with what purpose a ritual is performed.

There are different supernatural beings to be worshipped and propitiated as well as different intentions with which one undertakes a ritual. There is, in short, a differentiation in gifts which corresponds, to some extent, with a differentiation among the Brahman priests. The Pandas of Ayodhya make a distinction between two types of gift: auspicious (*maṅgal* or *vicārini*) and inauspicious (*amaṅgal* or *avicārni*). Auspicious are those addressed to gods, ancestors and Brahmans (as Brahmans) with the intention of acquiring merit (*puṇya*), a better *karma*, well-being, health, prosperity and all the good things of this life and the next. Inauspicious ones are those addressed to the ghost of a deceased person (*pret*), to the inauspicious planets or to the gods or Brahmans with the intention of warding off evil (*doṣ*) or getting rid of sin (*pāp*) or illness (*rog*).

The most unambiguously ominous gifts are accepted by special groups of Brahmans. The gifts for the deceased's ghost (*pret*) are accepted by the funeral priests, the Mahabrahmans, who are avoided by every other Hindu like death itself, which is probably not much dissimilar from the attitudes people in Western society have towards undertakers. The Mahabrahmans of Ayodhya form an endogamous priestly group with seemingly clearly defined caste boundaries. It seems that they do not have jajmani relations which are comparable to those of the family priest or the Panda. Reciprocity with Brahmans who impersonate the deceased's ghost seems undesirable.

Gifts to inauspicious planets are given to Bhareriyas who are a much less clearly bounded "caste" than the Mahabrahmans (van der Veer 1988). In Ayodhya they clearly aspire to the profession of Panda with his jajmani relations, but my impression is that as long as they accept gifts for ominous planets (*grah-dān*) they cannot have hereditary ties with patrons. The Bhareriyas appear to be caught in a poverty-trap (cf. Parry 1979: 66). They seem to be impoverished Brahmans who are forced to accept for their livelihood gifts no other Brahman would care to accept.

The Pandas of Ayodhya declare themselves to be (mainly) involved with auspicious gifts. They receive gifts on behalf of Ram, Shiv or the river Sarayu. More generally, the Ayodhya Panda is regarded as the human embodiment of Shri Ayodhyaji, the sacred centre itself. The pilgrim makes offerings to the total sacred field (*kṣetra*) which he visits: the object of pilgrimage is the object of giving or sacrifice. The supernatural beings as well as the whole area where they are thought to reside are powerful, have an influence on our mortal well-being and the pilgrims pray that this influence may be auspicious (*maṅgal*). Nevertheless, the Pandas do accept some inauspicious gifts in the context of such rites as *prāyaścitt-dān* and *tuladān*. The general idea in an expiation ritual (*prāyaścitt*) is that if the sins involved are very serious, the gift has to be given to any Brahman who is willing to accept them. When no one can be found, the gift is given in a symbolic way to sacred grass (*kuśa*) which in such cases is said to represent a Brahman recipient. Some Pandas deny that they accept such gifts, while they accuse others of doing so. Other Pandas argue that it is not they who accept this kind of gift, but that it is the river Sarayu which absorbs all sins. It is clear, however, that this kind of gift is not easily accepted and that when it is accepted the Pandas will not give much publicity to it. In the *tuladān* ritual a patron (*jajmān*) is weighed against a counterweight of gifts. The counterweight is given to the Panda with the idea that he absorbs the patron's illnesses. All Pandas I have interviewed made it clear that they would refuse such a gift, but outsiders told me that in the time of the rajas this ritual was sometimes staged. There can, however, be no doubt that in less conspicuous rituals pilgrims try to get rid of their illness by giving donations to Pandas and, since this intention has to be expressed, the Pandas cannot be taken unawares.

However, the commercialization of the pilgrimage system puts matters in a different light. According to my informants what was most important in the aforementioned expiation ritual was for the "sinner" to get a certificate from the Pandas declaring that the ritual had been properly conducted. This certificate can be taken to the caste council (*pañcāyat*) which had imposed the punishment, so that the "sinner" could be readmitted into the network of commensality, marriage and other relations in his caste. The interesting thing is that nowadays it is not only Pandas who issue these certificates, but also some abbots of Ramanandi temples. They are newcomers to this market and have managed to create a situation in which they receive pilgrims in their temples in almost the same way as it is done by the Pandas. This fact throws a curious light on an aspect of the theories we have discussed earlier. The Pandas do actually not appear to be interested in renouncing their priestly profession, but on the contrary, the so-called renouncers want to intrude on the pilgrimage market in the garb of Pandas.

Having discussed the gift in its context, we may take the following observations on the social implications of the gift-ritual. First of all, it seems to be clear that it is better to be a landholding Brahman who can—if he wishes—act as a free religious agent than to be a priest who is dependent on the material resources of his patrons. Such an independent Brahman can, without much difficulty, accept food when he is fed as Brahman (*brahmbhoj*) and accept a fee (*dakṣiṇā*) for priestly services. He is, however, also in a position to decline certain gifts which he finds threatening. The ideal Brahman is therefore economically independent. The impoverished Brahman is in a difficult position. His material needs can force him to accept gifts which are dangerous. However, it is interesting to note that it is the most ominous gifts which are given as totally unreciprocated ones. The Bhareriyas do have a constituency in which they go from door to door, but they do not have specific families as their hereditary patrons. The same seems to be true for the Mahabrahmans who divide their shares in the funeral business according to days in the year.

A second observation is that the scale of transactions in a pilgrimage system is of a totally different order from that of the transactions in a village setting. The dependence on jajmans who only come once in their lifetime to Ayodhya is felt to be rather less important than the income they bring to their Pandas. This may explain the real struggle to contract jajmani relations in the nineteenth and twentieth century among Ayodhya Pandas. It is especially those families which had established positions in the system on the basis of their jajmani relations that deplore the present decline of such relations, instead of being glad to find themselves at least in a position to follow the injunctions of Brahmanical literature. In Ayodhya, jajmani relations which are at present in jeopardy are highly valued by the Pandas.

The nature of the gift-ritual has also changed. The great patrons of the Pandas were the rajas who gave huge gifts as a conspicuous ritual. The new elites, such as the Marwaris for example, are not interested in this kind of conspicuous status ritual, with the result that the scale of gift-ritual has declined and there has been an increase in simple rituals in which the Panda is given some fee (*dakṣiṇā*). Moreover, the complexity of the pilgrimage system has created a situation in which the agents of the Panda are a kind of buffer between him and the donor. Only in a few cases will a big Panda receive gifts personally. In most cases the agents will do it on his behalf. The greatest Panda of Ayodhya, Gangaram, demands fifty per cent of all the offerings given by "his" pilgrims to whatever agent or Panda. His only concern is income, not the "danger of accepting gifts". This might be seen as the cynical attitude of a non-believer, but this is not the case. Gangaram is in fact a very strict Brahman who regards himself as a "good vessel" (*supātra*) despite his murderous reputation. Finally, as we have seen, others try to intrude into this economic field by performing expiation rituals, though they are not Pandas but renouncers.

3. Conclusion

"If we concern ourselves with activities as well as with values, with what men do as well as what they think, there are certain advantages to be gained." This simple statement was part of F.G. Bailey's polemical reaction to the position taken by Dumont and Pocock in their editorial in the first issue of *Contributions to Indian Sociology* (Bailey 1959: 90). It is surprising that a statement of such simplicity can still be quoted with some benefit, more than twenty years later. We have seen that there are two sets of interpretations of the position of the Brahman priest in Hindu society. The first is that the Brahman priest has the highest rank in the caste hierarchy, since he is the intermediary between the supernatural powers and the world. His purity and his position in the exchange system make him a god on earth. This interpretation is, however, easily contradicted, when we consider the function and activities of Brahman priests like the Mahabrahmans and Bhareriyas. Moreover, the relation of a Brahman Purohit, family priest or pilgrimage priest, with particular Jajmans who support him does not make him superior, but rather inferior.

Should we then follow the second set of interpretations which stress that the god on earth is not the priest, but the learned Brahman renouncer who refuses to accept gifts? To put it differently: Do the Pandas of Ayodhya actually model themselves on the ideal Brahman, the world renouncer, and do they see renunciation of the priesthood as the highest goal in life? Is the acceptance of gifts the cause of the relative inferiority of Brahman priests in Ayodhya? From interviews and participant observation I have never been able to discern anything having the faintest connection with the cultural model of the "ideal Brahman". The Pandas are engaged in a daily struggle for livelihood and their actions and orientations are connected with that struggle. Moreover, this is not a modern phenomenon resulting from a process of secularization, but it was already existent in the nineteenth century. When the pilgrimage market expanded and the British started to define the rights of participants in the system, the actions of the Pandas were directed at getting as large a share as possible. It was the positive right to practise the Panda profession which was highly valued among Pandas in that period. Its attraction grew with its increasing market-value.

Pandaship is a profession. The conditions in which this profession has to be practised have changed drastically in the course of the last century and a half. The acceptance of gifts is clearly an important aspect of this profession, but the sheer multi-faceted complexity of the gift as a ritual practice makes it impossible to give a general interpretation of its social implications in terms of Brahmanical ideology. We have to consider the gift-ritual in its context. All the elements of the practice have changed in the above-mentioned period: donors, recipients, things given and relations between donors and recipients. We should therefore not be surprised to find for example that the vanishing jajmani relations with kings are highly valued among the Ayodhya Pandas, although this seems to be in opposition with parts of the "Brahmanical ideology".

As a conclusion, we should be wary of applying static orientalist models to the interpretation of the values and behaviour.[4] Instead we may pay more attention to what Brahman priests actually "do" in ritual practices and the way in which these practices like the rest of their activities change in "history".

NOTES

This paper draws from my monograph on Ayodhya (Van der Veer 1988). Fieldwork for it was carried out at intervals between 1978 and 1984 with the financial help of the Netherlands Foundation for the Advancement of Tropical Research. Earlier versions of the paper were presented at seminars of the London School of Economics and the Oriental Institute, University of Oxford. I want to thank late Ram Raksha Tripathi for his generous help during my fieldwork and Andre Beteille, late Alan Entwistle, Bob Frykenberg, Chris Fuller, Richard Gombrich, Jonathan Parry, Arie de Ruijer and Bonno Thoden van Velzen for their helpful comments. I would also like to take the opportunity to express my thanks to Hermann Kulke and late Günther Sontheimer for providing the occasion to reconsider these matters again with the participants of the "Hinduism Reconsidered" panel in Heidelberg in 1986.

1. In the paper the term "orientalist perspective" is used to refer to the way anthropological interpretations make use of indological constructions of Indian reality.
2. Parry (1986) has argued that this unreciprocated or "pure" gift pertains to a specific kind of society, namely state societies with an advanced division of labour and a significant commercial setcor as well as, most importantly, the belief system of a world religion. This is an important attempt to relate society with ritual practice.
3. It should be clear that the concept of the "jajmani-system" as a system is largely a colonial and anthropological construct. I use it here only to contrast the position of the family priest in the village with that the pilgrimage of priest. Jajmani relations in the religious context refer to the hereditary relations between patrons and priests.
4. This does not mean that much of what has been discussed above in relations to actual ritual practices could not be found in one or another way in the

Brahmanical literature, as in fact is shown by Trautmann's discussion of this literature (1981: 277-93). It should, however, be clear that to find some idea in the Sanskrit literature which is similar to what is found in actual practice is altogether different from explaining the actual practice.

REFERENCES

Asad, T. 1983. Anthropological conceptions of religion: Reflections on Geertz. In *Man* (NS) 18, 237-59.

Babb, L. 1975. *The divine hierarchy; Popular Hinduism in Central India.* New York.

Bailey, F.G. 1959. For a Sociology of India? *Contributions to Indian Sociology* 3, 88-101.

Biardeau, M. 1981. *L' Hindouisme. Anthropologie d'une Civilisation.* Paris.

Burghart, R. 1983. For a sociology of India: an intral-cultural approach to the study of "Hindu Society". In *Contributions to Indian Sociology* (NS) 17, 2, 275-99.

———. 1985. Introdution: Theoretical approaches in the anthropology of South Asia. In *Indian religion* (eds.) R. Burghart and A. Cantile. London.

Cohn, B.S. 1968. Notes on the history of the study of Indian society and culture. In *Structure and change in Indian society* (eds.) M. Singer and B. Cohn. Chicago.

Commander, S. 1983. The jajmāni system in north India. An examination of its logic and status across two centuries. In *Modern Asian Studies* 17, 2, 283-311.

Dumont, L. 1970. *Religion, politics and history in India.* The Hague.

———. 1971. On putative hierarchy and some allergies to it. In *Contributions to Indian Sociology* (NS) 5, 58-81.

———. 1972. *Homo Hierarchicus.* London.

Fuller, C.J. 1984. *Servants of the Goddess.* Cambridge.

Harper, E. 1964. Ritual pollution as an integrator of caste and religion. In *Journal of Asian Studies* 23, 151-97.

Heesterman, J.C. 1971. Priesthood and the Brahmin. In *Contributions to Indian Sociology* (NS) 10, 265-93.

———. 1985. *The inner conflict of tradition.* Chicago.

Marriott, McKim and Inden, R. 1975. Caste systems. In *Encyclopaedia Britannica,* Vol. 3, 982-91.

Mauss, M. 1974. *The gift.* London.

Miller, D.B. 1975. *From hierarchy to stratification.* Delhi.

Obeyesekere, G. 1983. *The cult of Pattini.* Chicago.

Parry, J.P. 1979. *Caste and kinship in Kangra.* London.

———. 1980. Ghosts, greed and sin: the occupational identity of the Benares funeral priests. In *Man* (NS) 15, 88-111.

———. 1985a. Death and digestion: the symbolism of food and eating in north Indian mortuary rites. In *Man* (NS) 20, 612-30.

———. 1985b. The Brahmanical tradition and the technology of the intellect. In *Reason and morality* (ed.) J. Overing. London.

———. 1986. The gift, the Indian gift and the 'Indian Gift'. In *Malinowski Memorial Lecture.* In *Man* (NS) 21, 453-74.

Trautmann, T.R. 1981. *Dravidian kinship.* Cambridge.

Van Buitenen, J.A.B. 1966. On the archaism of the Bhagavata Purana. In *Krishna: Myths, rites and attitudes* (ed.) M. Singer. Honolulu.

Van der Veer, P.T. 1985. Brahmans: their purity and their poverty. On changing values of Brahman priest in Ayodhya. In *Contributions to Indian Sociology* (NS) 19, 2, 303-21.

———. 1988. *Gods on Earth. The management of religious meaning and identity in a North Indian pilgrimage centre.* London and Delhi.

———. 1987. God must be liberated. A Hindu liberation movement in Ayodhya. In *Modern Asian Studies* 21, 2, 283-301.

HINDUISM AND NATIONAL LIBERATION MOVEMENT IN INDIA

Horst Krüger

The irregular, contradictory, inhibited and deformed development of the socio-economic structure in colonial India had a sustained effect on the sphere of ideology. The existence and the continuity of pre-capitalist production relations accounts for the tenancy of life shown by traditional institutions and structures with their pertaining patterns of thought and behaviour.

In India the concept of pre-capitalist production relations is simultaneously related to the notion of caste. The far-reaching overlapping between caste and social structure notably in the rural areas caused the consolidation of the caste-like stratification by the social strata, and vice versa. The resulting traditionally religiously sanctioned miserable situation of the lowest strata beyond economic dependence made it possible, for the landlords to exploit their tenants to the utmost.

Another outcome of the caste system was that there was not only a gap between the exploiting, ruling higher and oppressed lower castes, but equally between the lower castes themselves with each of them thinking to be higher- or lower-ranking against the other.

Affiliation to caste played also an important role in the embittered clashes between the various groups of intellectuals waged for access to the different levels of administrative apparatus. There was a new type of caste-oriented and religiously substantiated consciousness emerging from the struggle of competition for education and jobs.

The diversified caste-orientated composition obstructed the emergence of unified class-consciousness of the Indian workers. Many of them belonged to the lowest castes; the share of "untouchables" was especially high.

Although industrialization and other factors tended to bring about structural changes in Indian society, certain castes dominated (and continue to dominate down to this day) certain callings and professions while other castes were, in practice, excluded from them. This is generally true of industry, trade, government services, white-collar professions, and also in manual occupations. In Bombay, for instance, which was the main centre of Indian textile industry, "untouchable" workers were kept out of the weaving section of textile mills. And touchable and "untouchable" workers continue to live in separate blocks of chawls in Bombay, now as in the past (Sardesai 1979: 12). From the very beginning it was evident that caste cuts through class, just as class cuts through caste.

It is applicable to all social classes and strata in India prior to the First World War that they were directly or indirectly related to the backward, pre-capitalist agrarian situation. This meant that there was a continuous flow and influx of traditional ideas from this side. They did not only prevent the impoverished peasantry from becoming fully aware of their own social situation, but also had an inhibiting effect on the formation of consciousness of the emerging working class recruited primarily from peasantry refreshing and consolidating its ranks again and again from there.

The close correlation between large sections of the Indian bourgeoisie and the rural area determined its attitude towards the agrarian issue and it was afraid of a democratic solution of this issue. The underdeveloped social structure and the close links to the rural area influenced the intelligentsia, too. Its still existing commitments to the feudal and semi-feudal agrarian relations prevented the ideologists of the national liberation movement in India from drawing up a revolutionary agrarian programme. As a result they were unable to bridge the gap between them and the broad masses of peasants and to mobilize the popular masses for the national liberation struggle. Instead, they developed concepts of nationalism where utopian ideas of a harmony of classes played a great role together with the idealization of the pre-colonial past of India.

Indian industrial workers resorted to strikes when exploitation and oppression became unbearable. This tendency was quite early recognized by Indian industrialists like J.N. Tata who wrote already in 1888 that the employers should take precautions against strikes as far as possible. Trade-Unions and high wages would be the hurdle which should be avoided (Wacha 1915: 83ff). And when the Fabian

Society of Bombay had organized a series of open lectures on socialism in October-November 1890 which sparked off the first public discussion on aspects of socialism in India, the representatives of the vested interests became immediately alarmed. After claiming that the dissemination of socialist ideas in Europe had encouraged dissatisfaction and tumult among the poorer classes and had raised hindrances in the way of prosperity the newspaper *Bombay Samachar* taking sides with the industrialists said: "For centuries together the Indian labouring classes have been free from any such doctrine as Socialism and have been working with peace and contentedness, contributing their mite to the general prosperity of the country. Nobody ought, therefore, to desire disturbing these classes by spreading Socialism among them" (*Bombay Samachar* 7.11.1890).

Indian intellectuals became more and more aware of the social problems produced by the capitalist large-scale industry in hitherto unknown dimensions in Europe and in USA—wealth and poverty class-struggle and the erosion of traditional concepts of moral and ethical values. And, as noted by S. Sarkar, "a search had begun for a peculiarly 'Indian' (or 'Asian') path which could preserve the virtues of traditional society even while solving the economic problems of the country" (Sarkar 1973: 104f).

This ideological trend was represented by the monthly *The Dawn* which was published by Satish Chandra Mukherjee in Calcutta since 1897. In addition to this journal he founded the Dawn Society in 1902 intending to give a small elite of students in Calcutta a systematic religious, moral and intellectual education. In his younger days Mukherjee had been influenced by positivism but was increasingly attracted later by Ramakrishna and his disciples, most of all by Swami Vivekananda. At the beginning of the nineties he finally turned to orthodox Hinduism. He took the vow of celibacy and decided to devote his life to educating the youth (Mukherjee, H. and U. 1957: 181ff).

From 1898 onwards, the "Dawn" repeatedly warned against the uncritical transplantation of industrial capitalism from the West to India. Mukherjee has based his essays on careful studies of the economic history of the West leading him to very clear and perspective conclusions. He says: "Modern Industry as it obtains in the West, means a clear grasp, in the first instance, of the fundamental fact of the perpetual conflict of interest between the rent-receiving land-owner, the wage-earning labourer, and the profit-earning capitalist."

He warned that those who would seek to introduce the industrial system from the West must not do so in a light-hearted or in an ignorant fashion. They must not be confused by "a bewildering notion of magnitude, vigour, and substantiality" and they must not be impressed by the "spectacular show" of the English manufacturing towns. An Indian student of economic history cannot rest satisfied with suggestions of an untutored intellect. And "when the question arises of transplanting silently but nevertheless surely, a whole body of ideas and institutions which are admittedly tainted at the root, he would pause and analyse in order to discover if the industrial problem of India cannot be solved in any other way than by a wholesale incorporation, the good with the bad, the bad with the good" (Mukherjee 1898: 182f).

Contrary to the majority of his Indian contemporaries Mukherjee is aware of the problems resulting from the conflict between labour and capital as well as from the struggle of the organized working-class movement. According to his opinion the introduction of the capitalist industrial system from the West to India would create "a small highly organized minority of capitalist class, foreign or native, the growth of whose power and influence would not mean the growth of happiness of the masses" (1898: 231). Together with his further comments on this subject it is obvious that he is taking sides with the exploited masses (1898: 232). But nevertheless he regards with apprehension "the other danger, the political danger of gigantic labour-organizations pitted against capitalist organization". Mukherjee understands that the workers must organise themselves and form trade-unions in order to withstand capitalist exploitation, for "if such labour-organizations are never formed all the worse (relatively speaking) for India. For the unchecked growth of a highly organized capitalistic class would ultimately mean only *industrial serfdom* the labouring population would, in fact, be reduced to the level of slaves (not physically, of course, but worse from the economic point of view)" 1898: 232).

Which way out does Mukherjee recommend? He visualizes the Indian "industrial salvation ... in the direction of a wider application of the principle of individual family organizations of workers, craftsmen and agriculturists supplemented (but never displaced) by capitalist organizations...". In this manner the individual workers would be given the needed independence and competence as well as a place in a progressive social economy. Besides that this would mean "to lay the axe at the root of all industrial warfare ...." (1988: 232).

To transform this social conception into reality, Mukherjee asked for a scheme of national education, "that would fix appropriate duties and appropriate work for classes of individuals in the evolving social system; that would recognize, indeed the law of special functions or specialised structures ..." (1898: 232). Orthodox Hinduism as the ideological basis of national education had been clear in 'Dawn' already in 1897 saying "while remaining fully alive to the usefulness and the necessity" of other systems of culture, "Western or Eastern", "as Hindus we propose to make a special study of Hindu life, thought and faith, in a spirit of appreciation..." (quoted after Sarkar 1973: 156).

Mukherjee wanted to reorganize the economic problem in such a manner that the "competitive principle would give way to one based on a higher ethical basis" (Sarkar 1973: 156). Within the social structure envisaged by him, material progress should be given a place "but only a subordinate, though recognized, place in a progressive Hindu social organization". As Bipan Chandra has pointed out Mukherjee was led to recommend as early as 1900 a corporate society primarily based on small scale individualistic organization (1966: 393). "My idea, then, is to help on the work of national development by putting before us the ideal of a higher culture for all workers, in all the various department of activity, spiritual, intellectual, military, commercial and wage earning; by giving to each class a fixed, recognized and independent place in the social organization..." (1900: 265). And this caste-ridden conception of a stratified society made explicitly provision for the "maintenance or support of higher classes or workers developed to the discovery or spread of truths" (1900: 264).

Mukherjee's ideas about the organization of industry mainly based on small-scale production were in their combination with conceptions of the traditional Hindu social structure economically reactionary. Although they contained correct observations on the negative social consequences of industrial capitalism they refer to petty-bourgeois conceptions of a corporative society with a "Brahmin aristocracy of the intellect" (Sarkar: 107f) on the top far away from the toiling masses. Progressive, revolutionary social ideas from the West were to be prevented access to Indian society. Instead of them traditional Hindu thinking was to provide the dominating ideology.

Mukherjee's remark "that India, with her memories of a higher civilization and with the instincts of higher culture *still* intact", will establish the conceived social order faster than other nations (1900: 297f), facilitated that integration of his ideas into the general current of Hindu revivalism and promoted their spreading after 1905.

The interaction of important internal and external factors had prepared the soil since 1905 for public discussions on progressive ideas in India. It was not at all coincidental that the intensive discussion of socialist ideas began in India in 1905. In the preceding years an essential prerequisite had been created to enable leading representatives of the national liberation movement to orientate deliberately towards the international working-class movement by increasingly overcoming the illusion so far harboured even with the radical wing that the British Liberals would respect the right of self-determination of the Indian people and would advocate the elimination of colonial rule. At the same time the contacts and commitments to the socialist working-class movement undergoing a tremendous upswing on the international level of those years became closer and more numerous (Krüger 1984: 46ff) A Socialist League was founded in Calcutta in 1907 (Krüger 1985: 340ff).

The parallelity between the discussion of socialist ideas and the revolutionary upswing of the national liberation movement was apparent. At the same time this fact pointed to an important aspect that essentially influenced the process of uptake and propagation of socialist ideas in India prior to 1917. The contact with socialist thoughts and the establishment of contacts with the international working-class movement were effected from the Indian side from the standpoint of nationalism. This applied both to leading representatives of the liberation movement in India and to members of Indian national-revolutionary groups abroad. It was them who expected above all aid and support in the national struggle of liberation to be supplied by the international working-class movement. On the objectively conditioned basis of the anti-imperialist front of social and national movements of emancipation the first germinating forms of the alliance emerged between both the revolutionary forces.

The Indian patriots came into contact with various ideological currents within and outside the working-class movement. They in part took over their views without being aware of the differences existing in principle between these views and scientific socialism. From the position of nationalism the colonially oppressed Indian people made use of substantial elements of traditional thinking. This version of Hindu revivalism spread in India. It included a downright anti-Western tendency. The utility and usefulness of these new ideas were tested and decided to its use. This was not at all an unconditional, mechanical transfer of progressive ideas from the West, but rather a process of conflict and demarcation, selection and readaptation of progressive ideas to the Indian situation in line with the social character and the political-ideological attitude of the social forces that were confronted with these new ideas. The thoughts absorbed from the West were frequently mixed up with nationalistic, traditional and utopian, mostly religiously coloured ideas. In this way the specific aspects of the ideology emerged which had been acquired by the most progressive forces of the Indian liberation movement of that time.

Although it was possible in the cities and towns to incorporate more strata of the population into the national liberation movement the social basis of the movement was broadened only insufficiently, whereas its major weakness, i.e. the isolation of the national leadership forces from the popular masses, was retained (Sarkar: 78).

British colonial oppression and exploitation of India had led to despondency, loss of self-confidence, and even to an inferiority complex in the whole country. To regenerate self-confidence among the people Hinduism was adopted in certain aspects to the requirements of the political-ideological struggle against British rule.

The upswing of the national liberation movement was accompanied by an increase in revivalist ideas which vindicated ideologically the activities of radical and national-revolutionary forces and served as an instrument of contact towards the masses as well as strengthened even the nationalistically motivated declining attitude towards all western influences within the radical wing of the national liberation movement. It was proclaimed, therefore, that the ancient Indian "spiritual" civilization was superior to the "materialist" West.

It must be remembered, however, that critical and warning voices were already raised against this development at least from 1905 onward. The most outspoken criticism came from the well-known leader of the Sadharan Brahmo Samaj, Sivnath Sastri, who represented throughout several decades a modernist, progressive trend of thinking in Bengal. He had inspired already in the mid-70s of nineteenth century Bipin Chandra Pal and a few others to take a remarkable pledge which included among others the point never to serve the foreign government because it did not have any moral right over its subjects and was not sanctioned by God. Another point was: "We shall not build up nor protect private property; all shall have equal rights to whatever we earn and each one of us will take from the common pool according to our needs and dedicate our lives to the service of our motherland" (quoted after Sehanavis 1976: 16f). This pledge was a combination of Brahmo ideals and urge for freedom as pointed out by M. Chattopadhyay. The last point contained egalitarian and elements of vague socialist ideas (1981: 295).

In this connection a poem should be mentioned which was written and published by Sivnath Sastri in the first issue of *Bharat Sramajibi* (Indian Workers) in 1873. It was entitled "Sramajibi" and in it S. Sastri makes a rousing call to the Indian toilers to wake up and assert their own rights.[1] This poem is an indication of the fact that Sivnath Sastri together with others represented a radical trend with pro-working class bias among the Brahmo Samaj (Chattopadhyay: 296).

In June 1888 Sastri attended a meeting of socialists at Annie Besant's house in London when visiting Great Britain.[2] Before returning to India he decided to buy socialist literature writing in his diary, for "such literature is essential to aquire necessary knowledge about the tasks facing the new society that we are going to build" (quoted after Sehanavis 1976: 18f). And he further noted down: "Socialist society is in favour of Communism. In such a society all men are to have equal rights in social, economic and political spheres" (quoted after Chattopadhyay: 296). This long process of ideological development finally led S. Sastri to the conclusion in the Swadeshi period when he became witness to strikes and the first efforts of founding trade unions: "The working class has realized that unless they stand united, they cannot stand up to the owners. That is why strike has now become widespread. Workers have become united and set up trade unions and they are en masse becoming its members. The aim of such trade union is to defend the interests of the working class" (quoted after Das 1975: 25).

It was that progressive outlook which enabled Sivnath Sastri to strike a first note of warning in the article "Swadeshi Craze—Respect for the past laudable, but not worship of the past" (quoted after

Sarkar: 60). In another article "National Unity" he warned against the danger which newly-revived provincial, religious and caste sentiments could pose to the unity of India (ibid.). Finally, in 1906, in the article entitled "The Ills of Patriotism", he emphatically turned against the hatred of everything foreign, the uncritical defence of the present way of life, the revivalist glorification of the past, and without mincing words he declared: "The patriotism which glorifies our past as ideal and beyond improvement and which rejects the need for further progress is a disease" (ibid.). However, such a forward looking attitude was rare in those days.

Along with emerging revivalism went a reinterpretation of the *Bhagavad Gita* proving that the holy scripture did not teach passivity, but action without fearing physical consequences, for *atma* was imperishable, immortal.

Also some elements from the fund of experiences stored by the European working-class and certain, selected socialist ideas were taken up and incorporated into ideological conceptions which, however, retained their nationalist character. Very often a blending with traditional, mostly Hindu (very rarely Islamic) conceptions took place.

There was a broad spectrum of ways and methods using religious-orthodox thinking and caste mentality in the political and social struggles in those years.

Traditional thinking could be used—at least temporarily—for progressive aims, for instance, to mobilize industrial or railway workers to participate in the anti-colonial struggle. Intellectuals who were members of the radical wing of the national liberation movement in Bombay-Maharashtra led by B.G. Tilak used the traditional caste hierarchy to mobilize the textile workers for the political general strike in 1908. The workers hailing from Maharashtra belonged to the lowest castes or were untouchables. They had profound respect for and were ideologically dependent on the upper castes. This fact was used by leaders of the radical wing who were Brahmans. The majority of the Indian clerks working in the textile mills belonged to the caste of Chitpavan Brahmans; they exercised a strong influence on the jobbers in the factories. The jobbers were more or less depending on these clerks but had the workers well in hand. In this way using the caste hierarchy "seditious" ideas could be spread among the workers.

The agitators who worked directly among the masses also used caste susceptibilities in combination with religious feelings. For instance, notices were posted at places frequented by workers in Bombay. One such notice said that any man going to work after the midday interval would be regarded as the son of a sweeper or of an European. Both were outcastes. The strikebreaker was threatened with the loss of his caste. Another notice stated that men who continued to work would be thought guilty of killing kin (*Times* 19.8.1908).

Religious sanctions were also used in the successful strike of the workers at Bengal-Nagpur Railway Workshop of Kharagpur in September 1906. In the official report on strike it is said that "the ringleaders influenced a sufficient number of workmen to support their declaration that no one was to attend work the following day under the penalty, in the case of Hinduism, of being made to eat cow's meat and, in the case of Muhammedans, pig's flesh". Bones and flesh of cows were collected at roadsides to be pelt at willing workers (quoted after Sarkar: 223).

These methods of agitation show that the radical agitators worked among the masses more on the basis of religious sentiments than on class issues. But their appeals greatly helped to stiffen the resistance of the working class and promoted the unity of all the anti-imperialist forces.

In the Swadeshi period when trade-unions began to appear in India also Tilak's *Kesari* strongly advocated this new trend. Under the caption "Railway Union" Tilak took up this issue. Referring to the forming of a railway union in Calcutta he emphasized the necessity to follow this example in Bombay as well: "It is extremely necessary in the modern period of struggle for living to take up the work of organising unions of the western type and run them without break." After discussing this question in detail Tilak finally brought forward the argument based on Hindu tradition: "In the Kali age, the spiritual, supernatural or physical strength does not reside in each individual separately, but according, as the saying goes, in Kali age power resides in the collective organization, it will reside only in the organization (union). It is needless to say that this principle, embodied in the Puranic dictum, is very valuable" (quoted after Dange 1973: LIVf).

Strikes and trade-unions were enthusiastically welcomed by Indian nationalists, if these new forms and methods of struggle could be directed against the colonial administration and against foreign, i.e.

British undertakings. But along with it the warning voices raised against an industrialization according to European pattern did not cease to be heard, because they referred especially to the emerging "antagonism between wage-earner and capitalists" (*Bengalee* 19.10.1905). At that time an ideological current came up which was outcome of the attempt to create a synthesis between socialist ideas and extremely nationalist, strongly Hindu-revivalist thoughts. Its most prominent representative was Aurobindo Ghosh.

Aurobindo Ghosh had become acquainted with Socialism during his long stay in Great Britain. Soon after his return to India he began to voice his views on topical political questions. In November 1893 he declared that "with the whole trend of humanity shaping towards democracy and socialism, on the calibre and civilization of the lower class depends the future of the entire race" (quoted after Mukherjee, H. and U. 1958: 100).

Aurobindo also made the next move by applying his knowledge on the decisive relevance of the working strata to the situation in India when writing that with the "proletariate resides, whether we like it or not, our sole assurance of hope, our sole chance in the future" (quoted after Mukherjee: 108). And he called the "proletariate" the "real key of the situation". Ghosh was the first in India who used the term "proletariat", but not in a Marxist sense, but rather in a much wider and general sense. His concept was reminiscent of Vivekananda's ideas of the shudras, the working people and working masses. Ghosh recognized the "very great potential force" of the "proletariate" and called upon the bourgeois forces "to understand and elicit his strength" to be in this way the "master of the future" and the "crown of the nation and its head" (quoted after Mukherjee: 120). His call on the citizenry to elucidate the working masses and to liberate them from their ignorance was meant first of all to overcome the isolation of the Indian National Congress from the masses. At the same time his conceptions were influenced by experiences made in Great Britain where the socio-economic and political conditions were much more advanced than in colonial India.

In the years up to the Swadeshi period Aurobindo's views underwent certain modifications. He continued to express his opinion about the future of socialism writing, for instance in 1907 that "socialistic democracy is undoubtedly the next stage in the human march" (Ghosh 21.11.1907). But contrary to those first years after his return from England he did not resume his former statements on the importance of the "proletariate" although he himself as well as the daily and weekly *Bande Mataram* edited by him gave detailed reports on the strike actions of the Indian workers. However, neither the bourgeoisie nor the proletariate are mentioned in this connection, but a pointed class-indifferent point of view is taken there. The article "Liberty and Our Social Laws" is of relevance in this context. Recognizing that strikes had become very common in India, Ghosh takes this phenomenon as the expression of the fact that the people were realizing the "supreme necessity of freedom for the well-being of a nation". In this way the basis of the national movement will be broadened, for the "struggle for freedom will cease to be sectional and isolated". He calls, therefore, upon the "Nationalists to take up the strikes in hand, and turn them to account". The "poor people" striking against British undertaking, Government establishments and the British-Indian railway authorities should be supported in their struggles, for "to help the poor in the assertion of their rights serves the cause of freedom, and also establishes the *bona fides* of our intentions". To avoid any misunderstanding Ghosh explicitly declares that the nationalists "are fighting for no class superiority, to win political power for any section or class is not our object; but we want the general elevation of the people..." (Ghosh 17.9.1907).

There is a certain anti-capitalist tendency in the writings of Aurobindo Ghosh at that time. He warns the intellectuals, "the over-intellectualized", against their belief in salvation by industrialism. To go abroad, study industries and return to enrich themselves and their country he calls a necessary part of the national "*yajña*" but it is only a part and not even the chief part, for according to Ghosh commercial and industrial expansion are often accompaniments and results of political liberty and greatness—"never their cause" (Ghosh 5.4. 1907). He tells his countrymen that nothing more easily leads to national death and decay than a prosperous servitude. Again, this does not mean to dispense with industrialization. Not at all, he says: "We must strive indeed for economic independence", for only by hitting British despotism economically it will be possible to remove half the inducement (the other half being military) England now has for keeping India in absolute subjection. "But", Aurobindo declares, "we should never forget that politics is a work for the kshatriya and it is not by the virtues and methods of the vaishya that we shall finally win our independence" (Ghosh 5.4.1907).

According to Aurobindo Ghosh there are two political forces

opposed to each other which cannot co-exist in the modern political world. The first is the "force of socialist democracy which tries more and more to recognise man as a divine being full of infinite possibilities and refuses to permit any class or individual to degrade him by using him as a convenience, tool, slave or drudge". The other force is the "recrudescence of the old savage element which tries to enjoy the world by enslaving mankind" (Ghosh 21.11.1907). However, Ghosh does not attempt to give a historical or economic explanation for this. Far away from this, he declares that the latter force is a result of modern science, for it "banishes God from the world" making men animals of tremendous power whose sole aim is to perfect their material and intellectual strength. From this tendency of science Ghosh deduces the worship of the "strong man" or "superior man" whom he sees at the bottom of capitalism, imperialism and all the other reactionary forces of the day He enumerates their different forms (ibid.). Ghosh certainly touches upon problems existing in the social and political reality of his time. But his basic attitude is determined by religion and a general want of scientific approach prevents him from fully understanding the "manifestations" criticized by him.

It is of interest how Ghosh explains the difference between caste and class. According to his definition these two social categories are the result of the basically different social development in India and Europe: "The civilization of Europe has always been preponderatingly material and the division of classes was material in its principles and material in its objects...." And further: "The division of classes in Europe had its roots in a distribution of powers and rights and developed and still develops through struggle of conflicting interests; its aim was merely the organization of society for its own sake and mainly indeed for its economic convenience" (Ghosh 21.9.1907). The classes are not traced back to production relations, but as in the case of Swami Vivekananda (1950: 172) and B.G. Tilak (Shay 1956: 64f) to "Western materialism".

In contrast to this the Indian "civilization has been preponderatingly spiritual with a moral basis.... The division of castes in India was conceived as a distribution of duties" (Ghosh 21.9.1907). "Western materialism" is countered here by "spiritualism" of the East. It should be remembered that not only Aurobindo Ghosh (12.10.1907) but also Swami Vivekananda (148: 19) and B.C. Pal (1958: 152) use the existence of class contradiction and social inequalities in Europe in order to justify the Indian caste system.

When Ghosh was criticized for intending to introduce "the European idea of socialism", he answered his critics: "Socialism is not an European idea, it is essentially Asiatic and especially Indian." And he continued: "What is called Socialism in Europe is the old Asiatic attempt to effect a permanent solution of the economic problem of society which will give man leisure and peace to develop undisturbed his higher self." The necessity of the application of socialist principles he justifies saying that without Socialism democracy would remain a tendency that never reached its fulfilment: "Socialistic democracy is the only true democracy, for without it we cannot get the equalised and harmonised distribution of functions" (Ghosh 21.9.1907).

The revivalist attitude underlying Ghosh's writings becomes very transparent when he continues arguing that the aims of "Socialist democracy" are "also the aim of Hindu civilization and the original intention of caste" (17.9.1907). For him the fulfilment of Hinduism is the fulfilment of the highest tendencies of human civilization and it must include in its sweep the most vital impulses of modern life. This means in the words of Aurobindo that Hinduism will not only include democracy and Socialism, but will "purify" and "raise" them "above the excessive stress on the economic adjustments" and will teach the people "to fix their eyes more constantly and clearly on the moral, intellectual and spiritual perfection of mankind which is the end" (21.9.1907).

Another aspect worth mentioning here is that Aurobindo Ghosh and others were anxious to bypass and to exclude the issue of social antagonisms and class-struggle in India. While in the past the Hindu teaching *karma* served to justify social differences not infrequently, now the approach to the social question was modified in a way. With the advent of a more progressive historical situation now the "Vedantic message of equality" was more intensively advanced (Ghosh 22.9.1907), where the allegedly egalitarian rationale of Hinduism found its expression. This approach served to mask social contradiction. In this way it had become possible to stand up for reforms in the Hindu society and at the same time to praise the traditional system as exemplary for the world. This trend became especially visible at the example of the caste system that was possible to be criticized in its present-day degenerate form, while at the same time the restoration to its original, allegedly ideal state was propagated in the form of the varna-system.

The idealization of the caste system was primarily done in averting the criticism from the colonialist side. But at the same time it was largely a kind of ideological conflict and a defence against those ideas that pointed to the existence of social contradictions and propagated their revolutionary conquest.

At that time, Ghosh was convinced of the victory of Socialism. His anti-imperialist attitude was clear. He turned against the monopolies and voiced criticism on the greed for profit by the capitalists. For this reason the ideological platform maintained by him up to 1908 contains progressive elements which under the conditions of the national liberation struggle had assumed a positive function. But simultaneously he was proponent of Hindu revivalism with all its social, political and ideological implications. His progressive views were loaded with the heavy burden of outdated traditional Hindu views and thus were widely devalued and even converted into the opposite. Objectively this road after a short term intensification of the national liberation struggle did not result in a continued progressive ideological development, but rather obstructed this development.

NOTES

1. "Wake up, brother workman!
   A new era has come,
   Men and women are on the move.
   The time to sleep is no more,
   Wake up..." (Chattopadhyay, K.: 161)
2. Annie Besant was a member of the socialist movement in England for some time. In the 80s she was a member of the Fabian Society and of the Social-Democratic Federation and participated in founding trade unions of unskilled workers. In 1889 she became a theosophist.

REFERENCES

The Bengalee. Calcutta, 19.10.1905.

The Bombay Samachar. Bombay, 7.11.1890. In *Report on Native Papers Bombay*, week ending 8.11.1890.

Chandra, B. 1966. *The rise and growth of economic nationalism in India*. New Delhi: People's Publishing House.

Chattopadhyay, K. n.d. *Bharat Sramajibi*. Calcutta.

Chattopadhyay, M. 1981. *Society and politics in Bengal* (1857-1885). Calcutta University: M.A. Thesis.

Dange S.A. (ed.) 1973. *AITUC. Fifty years*, Documents. Vol. 1. New Delhi: People's Publishing House.

Das, P.K. 1975. *Sivanath Sastrir Aprakasita Baktrita O Smarek Lipi*. Calcutta.

Ghosh, A. 5.4.1907. Many delusions. In *Bande Mataram*, Calcutta.

———. 17.9.1907. Liberty and our social laws. In *Bande Mataram*, Calcutta.

———. 21.9.1907. Caste and democracy. In *Bande Mataram*, Calcutta.

———. 12.10.1907. British blindness, In *Bande Mataram*, Calcutta.

———. 21.11.1907. The tragedy in Lisbon. In *Bande Mataram*, Calutta.

———. 22.9.1907. The unhindoo spirit of caste rigidity. In *Bande Mataram*, Calcutta.

Krüger, H. Die internationale Arbeiterbewegung und die indische nationale Befreiungsbewegung. 1984. Band 1: *Indische Nationalisten und Weltproletariat. Der nationale Befreiungskampf in Indien und die internationale Arbeiterbewegung vor 1914*. Berlin: Akademie-Verlag. 1985. Band 2: *Anfänge sozialistischen Denkens in Indien. Der Beginn der Rezeption sozialistischer Ideen in Indien vor 1914*. Berlin: Akademie-Velag.

Mukherjee, H. and U. Mukherjee. 1957. *The origins of the national education movement* (1905-10). Calcutta: Firma K.L. Mukhopadhyay.

———. 1958. *Sri Aurobindo's political thought (1893-1908)*. Calcutta: Firma K.L. Mukhopadhyay.

Mukherjee, S.C. 1898. Aspects of economic life in India. In *The Dawn* 5, 6, Calcutta, pp. 150-4, 179-83.

———. 1900. Advanced economic thought in the West: How to solve the labour-capital problem. In *The Dawn* 6, Calcutta, pp. 161-7.

———. 1900. The Indian economic problem. In *The Dawn* 8, 9, 10, 11.

Pal, B.C. 1958. *Writings and speeches*. Vol. 1. Calcutta: Yugayatri Prakashak Ltd.

Sardesai, S.D. 1979. *Class struggle and caste conflict in rural areas*. New Delhi: People's Publishing House.

Sarkar, S. 1983. *Modern India 1885-1947*, Delhi.

Sastri, S. 1864. *Englander diary*. Calcutta: Bengal Publishing Pvt. Ltd.

Sehanavis, C. 1976. *Socialism in India 1832-1917*. New Delhi: Shaheed Prakashan Pvt. Ltd.

Shay, T.L. 1956. *The legacy of the Lokamanya*. London: Oxford University Press.

The Times. London, 19.8.1908.

Vivekananda, S. 1948. *The complete works*. Vol. 3. Almora: Mayavati-Almora-Himalayas.

Wacha, D.E. 1915. *The life and work of J.N. Tata*. Madras.

HINDUISM AS SEEN BY THE NIZĀRĪ ISMĀ'ĪLĪ MISSIONARIES OF WESTERN INDIA: THE EVIDENCE OF THE GINĀN

Françoise Mallison

As a student of the medieval Hindu Gujarātī devotional literature I happened to chance upon the texts of some *ginān*, sacred songs of the Ismā'īlī Khojā, edited in the Gujarātī script and language at Bombay. I had the revelation of a religious tradition very much akin to the non-sectarian Vaishnavism of the fifteenth-sixteenth century in Gujarāt and it took me some time, not being a specialist of Islam, to secure copies of the collections of these devotional songs as they are now edited for religious purposes in Bombay,[1] and to realize that these present collections were a result of both a very ancient tradition and some more recent events.[2]

Ismā'īlism

The Islamic sect of the Sevener Shī'a or Imā'īliya is a branch of the Shī'a, with numerous subsects and a chequered history. It traces its origins back to the succession of the sixth Imām Ja'far al-Ṣādiq in A.D. 765. His son and successor Ismā'īl had died before him, and Ismā'īl's partisans claimed his son Muḥammad as the seventh Imām, while the main branch of the Shī'a claims the Imām for Ismā'īl's brother Mūsā al-Kāẓim.

The propagators or missionaries (*dā'ī*) of the Ismā'īlī movement developed an intense activity everywhere in the Islamic world either as builders of political power leading to the establishment of the Fāṭimid dynasty at Cairo (909-1171) or as the instruments of the Ismā'īlī thought which provides an esoteric interpretation of Islam based on cosmogonic myths and builds up the concept of the Imām with the help of various philosophical systems mainly gnostic, neoplatonic and Zoroastrian. Ismā'īlism always proved its flexibility by being able to adapt itself to the various political and cultural environments it encountered, by means of attracting brilliant minds to secure success. It weakened, however, its political claims by a series of schisms, one of the most important of which sealed the decline of the Fāṭimid in 1094 when the partisans of the Imām Nizār who separated from the Fāṭimid and took refuge in the north-west of Iran at the fortress of Alamūt, were confronted with those of his brother Musta'lī. And from the branch of the Musta'lī resulted the Tayyībiya in the Yemen who in 1539 emigrated to Gujarāt where they constituted the Bohrā community, whereas the conversions produced by the Nizārī branch missionaries in western India, in Gujarāt and around Bombay, in Kutch and in Sind, are known under the name of Satpanthī or Khojā. The *ginān* were composed for the sake of the Satpanthīs or Khojās by the Nizārī missionaries. The Nizārī destiny experienced many upheavals, but the most important event concerns the doctrine: in 1164 the Imām Ḥasan'alā dhikrihi al-Salām proclaimed the *Qiyāma* (resurrection), i.e. the completion of the world, the end of the primacy of the *Sharī'a,* the initiation of a new era in which priority is given to the spiritual life of the soul. Thus the Imām is consecrated as the epiphany of the creative word itself, and the goal of the believer becomes the "knowledge" of the Imām, being equivalent to the knowledge of God. The Nizārī Ismā'īlīs are the only Shī'ite sect to have a living and physically present Imām: the Āgā Khān, who is regarded as the perfect incarnation of God, being the "Imām of the time".

In 1256 the Mongols conquered Alamūt and the Nizārī communities were dispersed. Persecuted as heterodox and divided by a schism in the fourteenth century, they had to move several times. The Qāsimshāhi branch stayed at Anjudān and Kirmān from the eighteenth century onwards. Their Imām obtained the title of Āgā Khān just before emigrating to Sind in 1840 and then onwards to Bombay where the privileges of the Āgā Khān over the Khojā community were officially recognized in 1866 by means of a court case. The search for historical evidence required for the trial enabled to prove that the Khojās were an offshoot of the Nizārī Ismā'īlī sect (with followers in India and elsewhere). The trial was instrumental in stimulating scholarly research among the Ismā'īlī themselves as well as in the West. The open-mindedness of the third Āgā Khān, Sultān Muḥammad Shāh, transformed his followers into one of the most progressive bodies of the Muslim world who felt free from the threat of the so-called orthodox Muslims who until then had compelled the Ismā'īlī to hide their convictions. The manuscripts of the *ginān* could then surface, be copied and published openly, not any longer in the secret *khojkī* alphabet but in the Gujarātī script, the headquarters of the community being located in Bombay and the majority of the faithful being Gujarātīs.

Nizārī Preaching in India

The origin and development of the conversion movements (*da'wā*) are difficult to define due to the lack of precise sources other than the *ginan*, the apologetic nature of which confined them to relate the miracles accomplished by the main missionaries who had arrived from Iran. As such they are the only local sources of information (Nanji 1978: 7). It seems normal that the Imām of Alamūt had remembered the provinces of Sind and Multān which had already come into contact with the Ismā'īlism of the Qarmatian and Fāṭimid times, for, in spite of Maḥmud of Ghazna having destroyed their traces in 1006-25, some groups of believers had continued to exist there incognito. The first Nizārī missionary or Pīr (tenth-twelfth century?) to reach Gujarāt or Sind is a legendary hero: Satgur Nūr, said to have converted the king of Gujarāt, Siddharāj Jaysiṃha (1094-1143). Satgur Nūr's mausoleum can be seen at Navasārī, south Gujarāt. Among the following dā'ī, three are traditionally associated with the corpus of the *ginān*. Pīr Shams, the twentieth in the list of envoys, is said to have reached India during the fourteenth century and to have been active at Ucch and Multān where he was buried. The actual organizer of the community was Pīr Ṣadruddīn (A.D. 1400). He founded the *jamā'at-khāna* (places of prayer and worship) and gave the name of *Khawāja* (Lord) to his converts belonging to the Lohaṇa caste in Kutch. And as Khojās, the Nizārī Ismā'īlī were known in the subcontinent. Pīr Ṣadruddīn was succeeded by his son Ḥasan Kabīr al-Dīn at whose death (at the end of the fifteenth century) the community was unable to agree on a successor and the followers of his eighteenth and youngest son, Imām Shāh, declared themselves independent and founded with Nar Muḥammad Shāh, son of Imām Shāh, the new sect of the Imām-Shāhī (Iwanow

1936). This schism marked the end of the important conversion movements, the community being later on re-organized from Iran on an administrative rather than a missionary basis.

The duty of the *dā'ī* implied that they were fully conversant with the local conditions and the language of the area in which they operated. The *ginān* reveal a pedagogic method by means of which the *dā'ī*, without acculturizing their faithful, were able to lead them to the "true path" (*satpanth*) consisting in nothing more than the fulfilment of their former beliefs. This method of conversion adopted the images and concepts familiar to the Hindu population re-explaining their hidden meaning and actual purport within the Ismā'īlī doctrine. The Hindu myths take an Islamic shape: Brahmā becomes the prophet Muḥammad whose daughter is equalled with Śakti or Sarasvatī. But the most prominent is the use made of the doctrine of the *avatār* of Viṣṇu. As framework of a cyclic temporality (i.e. the Hindu *yug* and *kalpa*, and the Ismā'īlī seven cycles) requires a saviour for each era, the saviour of our present *kali yug*, that is the Kalki of the Vaiṣṇavas, necessarily was Hazrat Ali and continues to be his successor, the presently living Imām, the Pīr having assumed the role of guides towards this long expected saviour. The utilization of Hinduism is not limited to points of doctrine but includes the borrowing of metaphors, literary forms and all the ritual and cultural practices, to such an extent that the content of the *ginān* becomes a witness of contemporary Hindu practices and beliefs.

THE *GINĀN*

The word "*ginān*" is derived from the Sanskrit *jñāna*, i.e. knowledge acquired through meditation, and denotes various compositions by the *dā'ī* in the vernaculars of the their converts in order to provide them with a sacred literature. There would be about 800 *ginān*, of various length, composed from the thirteenth century until the beginning of the twentieth century, the date at which the corpus ceased to increase (Nanji 1978: 10). Many of their features, their origin, the mode of transmission, the literary form and their actual use, remind of those of the *pad* and *bhajan* of the medieval Vaiṣṇav bhakti of northern India (Nanji 1978: 14 et Schimmel 1980: 73).

The *ginān* were first transmitted orally, which implied a want of stability of the texts. The earliest available manuscript is dated A.D. 1736 but manuscripts are quoted to have existed as early as in the sixteenth century (Nanji 1978: 10-13). These manuscripts were written in the *khojkī* script in order to assure their secrecy; the script is said to be a proto-nāgarī and one of the oldest written forms of Sindhī (Nanji 1978: 8-9). The *ginān* exist in six languages: Multānī, Panjābī, Sindhī, Kacchī, and above all Gujarātī, not to speak of the jargon of the *sādhu* the *sādhukkaṛī bolī* (Nanji 1978: 9), and sometimes in several of these languages at the same time, this fact pointing to the possibility of translation. Since the beginning of the twentieth century, the lithographed and printed texts use the Gujarātī (or even the Latin) alphabet, and in the process the language sometimes took a Gujarāt shape.

The *ginān* are usually in verse, adopting the *chaupāī* and *dohā* forms.[3] The length varies much, the shortest count four to five stanzas. The lengthier *ginān* usually have an abridged version (*nāno* or *ninḍho*), and some popular *ginān*—so it seems— were provided with a longer version (*moṭo* or *vaḍho*). Each *ginān* contains the signature of its author (or *bhaṇitā*), they are supposed to be sung or recited, each has its *rāg* transmitted orally from generation to generation. The use of the musical element is essential to the transmission of the sacred message, as in Hindu devotional poetry. Certain *ginān* are called *garbī* (they are attributed to Pīr Shams), they were not danced but sung (Mallison 1991). The oldest manuscripts classify the *ginān* according to their ritual function in the religious ceremonies,[4] and not according to the *rāg*, whereas the printed texts regroup them according to their presumed author, the Pīr, not avoiding multiple attributions, thus pointing to an uncertain transmission. According to A. Nanji, the decision was taken in the sixteenth century to put the text into writing and to attribute each *ginān* to one of the three great Pīrs (Pīr shams, Pīr Ṣadruddīn, and Pir Ḥasan Kabīr al-Dīn), the founding fathers of the community. Later compositions repeat the same themes, and the inspiration seems to dwindle (Nanji 1978: 16-17). Ali Asani groups the texts of 200 representative *ginān* published in popular collections according to their themes (Asani 1977: 14-19):

1. the missionary *ginān*: (a) portraying Islam and Ismā'īlism as the completion of the Vaiṣṇav tradition, especially the *Dasa avatāra gināno*, (b) taking stock of the traditional heroes of Hindu mythology (Hariścandra, Draupadī; the Pāṇḍav), (c) providing with the hagiography of the Pīr;

2. the *ginān* dealing 'with a variety of eschatological and cosmological themes';

3. the *ginān* telling how to achieve an unblemished moral conduct;

4. the *ginān* necessary for certain holidays and ceremonies;

5. the *ginān* dealing with the mysticism of the Indian Ismā'īlī. These are certainly the most interesting of the corpus, they describe the path towards the ultimate experience of spiritual unity of the interior reality of the believer on one side and the interior reality of the Imām on the other, i.e. they strive to describe the union with God. They either give an account of this very experience, or they are petitions (*venti*) for the vision of—or union with—the Imām. These *venti* are usually recited at dawn before the early morning meditation at the *jamā'at-khāna*. The *ginān* belonging to the fifth group are popular because of their emotional character, one finds them in almost all modern collections. These *ginān* mirror the devotional poetry of medieval bhakti in Northern India and reflect on the popular mystic Hinduism of the fourteenth, fifteenth and sixteenth centuries.

HINDUISM MIRRORED BY THE *GINĀN*[5]

The *dā'īs* took for a starting point the themes of the Hinduism observed among the population they intended to convert: i.e. merchants and peasants, not belonging to the higher castes. The language of the *ginān* is meant for this non-Sanskritized population. The brand of Hinduism developed in the *ginān* literature appears in fact endowed with all the characteristics of the religion of the Vaiṣṇav Sants of northern India. For instance, cult of the divine Name, so dear to the Sants, is highly recommended. We find terms almost equivalent in some *ginān* and in some *pad* of the first poet of Vaiṣṇav bhakti in Gujarāt: Narasiṃha Mahetā (fifteenth century):

- *ginān*:

Śloka Nindho (or *Śloka Nāno*) attributed to Pīr Ṣadr al-Dīn, v. 19 (Nanji 1978: 124)

'Build your boat in the name of the Lord
and fill it with the load of truth
If the wind that blows is one of love and devotion,
then the Lord will certainly guide you ashore.'

venti of Pīr Ḥasan Kabīr al-Dīn, v. 38[6]
'Lord, with the aid of your Name, the great oceans give way.'

- Narasiṃha Mahetā: *Bhakti-jñāna pada* 47, v. I[7]
'Embark on the vessel of the Name of Nārāyaṇa,
if you want to defy the terrible dangers of the ocean of existence
against the waves and tides of this dreadful ocean
let [your boat] sail in the breeze of His grace.'

and again

- *ginān*: *Brahma prakāśa* of Pīr Shams, v. 2[8]
Sata śabda kā karo vicārā,
Pīra śāha kahojī vārama vārā.

- Narasiṃha Mahetā: *Bhakti-jñāna pada* 18, v.1., and 20, v.1.[9]
Kṛṣṇa kaho, kṛṣṇa kaho vaḷi vaḷi kṛṣṇa kaho!

and

Hari hari raṭaṇa karo, kaṭhaṇa kaḷi kāḷamāṃ.

The divine Name to be repeated is sometimes termed *Sat śabda* (cf. *Brahma prakāśa*, v.1: *Sata śabda hai gurū hamārā* "the word of truth is our *guru*") and, then it means the meditative support entrusted secretly to each believer by the Imām. It is commonly called *bol* and it works as the *mantra* given by the *guru* to their disciples. As in the case of the Sants, the authors of the *ginān* used the symbolic language and the tantric practices of the Nāth-yogīs.[10] For instance, the repetition of the *bol*, and *jap*, can be *ajap* ('mental, meditative').[11] The liquor of immortality (*amī, amṛta*)[12] which is sometimes simply called *prem* (for *prem ras* 'the elixir of love')[13] appears always at the time of illumination or of the experience of union with God. A *bhakta* poet such as Narasiṃha Mahetā also makes use of these symbols.[14]

In this *ginān* of Pīr Shams one also finds the exaltation of the interior religion:

'My mind is my prayer mat, Allāh is my Qāḍi
and my body is my mosque.'[15]

All exterior manifestations of the religion, be it in Hinduism or in Islam, are mocked at. Kabīr himself could have composed the lines contained in the following *ginān*:[16]

'...Who in this world is a Hindu
and who a Musalman?
The Hindu goes to the sixty-eight
places of pilgrimage, while the
Muslim goes to the mosque.
Yet neither the Hindu nor the
Muslim knows my Lord, who sits—Pure'.[17]

God is the interior *guru*, sat *guru*[18] or *guru nar*[19] who summons the faithful to become awake to the true path (*satpanth*),[20] the exclusive domain of heroic souls (śūro).

It is not the purpose of the *ginān* to elucidate the complexities of Ismā'īlī philosophy but in their own way they preach one of its essential tenets: the uniqueness of the divine entity who created the manifold world for his own enjoyment,[21] and the *ginān* try to make the believer realize this uniqueness within himself (Nanji 1978: 114). Narasiṃha uses the same type of phraseology to convey in his so-called philosophic *pad* the pure monism (*śuddhādvaita*) of the nature of God (Mallison 1986: 138-55, *pad* XL-XLVII).

Unlike the Pīr, the Vaiṣṇav Sants never had a special devotion for the totality of the *avatār* of Viṣṇu, and they were not concerned, so it seems, by the *avatār* to come, Kalki, but a fair number of them made use of the symbol of the *virah bhakti* to convey their longing for the divine love and they often gave Vaiṣṇav names to the Supreme Being. This is also done by the composers of the *ginān*. One of the recently discovered *pad*[22] of Narasiṃha Mahetā describes the pangs of separation (*virah*) and shows word-to-word similarities with the *venti* of Ḥasan Kabīr al-Dīn:[23]

venti, v. 20	*Ejī bhara jobana māro āvīyo*
	Lord, the bloom of youth is upon me,
Narsī, v. 2	*Bhare re jovaṃna māṃhāṃ nahī malo to;*
venti, v. 21	*Huṃ chauṃ tamārī nāra*
	I am your devoted spouse,
Narsī, v. 3	*Huṃ chuṃ nārī nātha tamārī;*
venti, v. 29	*Ejī sāmī lāja amārī tame rākhajo*
	Lord, preserve my honour,
Narsī, v. 5	*Lāja rākhī amārī.*

The stylistic similitude maybe points to some common folklore pattern, but it is nonetheless striking. We find in the *ginān* and in the *pad* of Narasiṃha Maheta (who comes closer to the authors of the *ginān* than the other Vaiṣṇav Sants, because of the Gujarātī language) the same partiality of alliterations and assonances,[24] they also sometimes use identical formulas. For instance, the emotion which grasps the seeker at the advent of the ultimate experience leaves him wordless with a tight throat: *gada gada kaṃṭhe.*[25] The same words are there to describe the condition of Narasiṃha Maheta when a vision of Śiva converts him to the bhakti of Kṛṣṇa.[26]

A survey of names given to God in the *ginān* illustrates the attitude of their authors towards Hinduism. They are indebted to the bhakti of the Sants, in as far as they are *nirguṇi*, adepts of the formless all-pervading Godhead, but like also some of the Sants, they are turned towards a kind of devotion where the absolute Reality can be embodied in Viṣṇu-Hari or in one of his *avatār* and ultimately in the Imām. As for the first tendency, we find the names of *Nirīṃjana,*[27] *Alakha,*[28] *Gura,*[29] *Gura Nara,*[30] *Sāmī* (for *Svāmī*),[31] *Nāthajī,*[32] *Purṇa Paribrahma.*[33] For the second tendency there are *Tribhovara Śāma,*[34] *Tribhovara Rāya,*[35] *Jadurāya,*[36] *Śrīvara,*[37] *Raṃgi Rāya,*[38] *Harajī.*[39]

The borrowings from mystical Hinduism by the *ginān* in their present form are not always visible at first sight. The meaning was lost among the followers who need no more the support of their ancestral Hinduism to understand their present faith, as had been necessary for the first converts.[40] But, meanwhile, the obscurities of the texts were never removed because their totality was considered sacred and because they belong to a strongly esoteric movement.

The interest of the *ginān* is not restricted to their links with Hinduism. They are permeated with Sufi concepts and symbols and Islamic thought. But the features of Hinduism revealed by them are of some bearing for the history of the origin of the Vaiṣṇav bhakti, especially in Gujarāt where the position and dates of Narasiṃha Maheta are still under discussion.[41] Finally, the evidence of the *ginān* draws the attention to the fact that the Ismā'īlī *dā'ī* were not the only ones to tap the surrounding Hinduism of the time. The Jain, in their own right, drew on the wealth of Kṛṣṇa bhakti either to retell the Kṛṣṇa legend with a hurriedly concocted Jain conclusion or even simply to take pleasure in exposing the feats of Kṛṣṇa.[42] Conversely there is at least one example of Vaiṣṇav borrowing from Jainism[43] and we can imagine the possibility of borrowing from Ismā'īlism.

The popular revival of medieval mystical Hinduism from the fourteenth to sixteenth century, as transmitted by the vernacular texts, appears in manifold variegated manifestations as an open culture on which outside religious movements could draw and inside which they could feel at ease.

NOTES

1. Three books were collected:
   (1) *Mahāna isamāīlī santa Pīra Śāmsa racita gīnāno saṃgraha* (106 *gināna* out of which 28 *garabī*), neither place and date of publication nor the name of the editor are given.
   (2) *Mahāna isamāīlī santa Pīra Sadaradīna racita gīnānono saṃgraha*, 1 (217 *gināna*), Bombay, 1969, no name of the editor.
   (3) *Mahāna isamāīlī santa Pīra Hasana Kabīradīna ane bījā sattādhārī pīro racita gīnāno no saṃgraha* (79 and 23 *gināna*), no place, no date, no name of an editor.
2. On the history of Ismā'īlīsm in the Indian subcontinent and of its Nizārī branch see: W. Ivanow 1948; A. Asani 1977; S.C. Misra 1964; A. Nanji 1978; A. Schimmel 1980; F. Daftary 1990. For a most up to date survey and thorough study of *ginān* see: Ch. Shackle, and Z. Moir 1992.
3. These are the most common meters. The *dohā* is a verse of two lines each of 24 instants. Each line is divided into two *caraṇ* and six feet 6+4+3, 6+4+1; the *caupāī* is a verse of four lines of 16 instants each: 6+4+4+2.
4. One finds the same type of classification of the Braj *pad* sung during the Krishnaite Vallabhan cult.
5. In order to protect themselves from the persecutions by orthodox Muslims, the Khojā Ismā'īlī observed Hindu practices: burning of the dead, ceremony of the *janoi*, observance of the "Hindu code of Law" (*Mitākṣara* law as administered in the law courts) and even intermarriages with Hindus. These practices were not interfering with their faith. What we try to decipher in the *ginān* is not a simple Hindu external appearance, but real elements of Hindu doctrine.
6. *Pīra Hasana Kabīradīna gīnānono saṃgraha*, no. 3, p. 17, translated by A. Asani (1977: Appendix, 56).
7. I.S. Desai (ed.), 1913. *Narasiṃha Mahetākṛta Kāvyasaṃgraha*. Bombay: Gujarātī Printing Press: 488.
8. The *Brahma prakāśa* is a long *ginān* which describes the mystical stages and the way to reach them. It is not edited in the *Pīra Śāmsa racita gīnānono saṃgraha*. The reference is to a personal typed copy.
9. I.S. Desai (ed.), 1913: 476.
10. In the hagiographical acounts, the Nāth-yogīs appear to be rather the challengers of the *Pīr*, as to which of them would be able to perform the most extraordinary miracles! Cf. A. Nanji (1978: 51-2): the story of Satgur Nūr who having defeated the yogīs was presented with their earrings, the weight of which amounted to five maunds!
11. Pīr Shams: *Prema pāṭaṇa rājā mana sudha* (*moṭuṃ gināna*), v. 73 *satapaṃtha*

paramaṇe cālīyā japīyā ajampīyā jāpa (*Pīra Śāmsa racita gīnānono saṃgraha*, no. 28; 31).

12. Pīr Shams: *Prema pāṭaṇa rājā mana sudha* (*nānuṃ ginā̄na*), v. 12 *uṭho radīyāde rāṇī amī pīyo.* (*Pīra Śāmsa...*, no. 9; 8).
13. Pīr Shams: *Brahma prakāśa*, v. 9 *pīvata prema hovata matavālā* (Cf. note 8).
14. Cf. *Bhakti jñāna pada* no. 24, Desai (ed.) 1913: 478, and also *Bhakti jñāna vairāgya pada* no. 58, Sh. Jesalpura (ed.) 1981. *Narasiṃha Mahetānī kāvyakṛtio.* Ahmedabad: Sh. Jesalpura, 388.
15. This verse is from a famous *ginān* of Pīr Shams, quoted by A. Nanji 1978: 121.
16. Ibid.
17. Cf. the lines of a *pad* of Kabīr (quoted by Vaudeville, Ch. 1974: 88):
    The Hindu invokes the name of Rām,
    the Musalmān cries: 'Khudā is One!'
    But the Lord of Kabīr pervades all.
18. Cf. *venti* of Pīr Ḥasan Kabīr al-Dīn, v. 37 (*Pīra Hasana Kabīradīna gīnānono saṃgraha*, no. 3; 17).
19. Ibid., v. 46; 18.
20. Cf. *ginān* of Pīr Shams: *Uṃcathī āyo baṃde* (*Pīra Śāmsa racita gīnānono saṃgraha*, no. 44; 49-50).
21. Cf. the *venti* of Ḥasan Kabīr al-Dīn, v. 26
    Ejī Sāmī puraṇa parībrahma tame alakha rūpī,
    jugatī śuṃ vakhānuṃ tamārī.
    (*Pīra Hasana Kabīradīna gīnānono saṃgraha*, no. 3; 16).
22. U. Desai 1983. Narasiṃha Mahetānāṃ be apragaṭa pado. *Sambodhi* 11 (Ahmedabad, L.D. Institute of Indology), 2nd part: 102-3.
23. *Pīra Hasana Kabīradīna gīnānono saṃgraha*, no. 3 (*venti*) 16, transl. by A. Asani 1977: Appendix 55.
24. For instance: *halatra-palatra* (*Pīra Śāmsa racita gīnānono saṃgraha*, no. 44, v. 2; 49) or *duhāga-suhāga* (*Pīra Hasana Kabīradīna gīnānono saṃgraha*, no. 3 *venti*, v. 12; 15).
25. Pīr Shams: *Brahma Prakāśa*, v. 7 (cf. note 8); Pīr Ḥasan Kabīr al-Dīn: *venti*, v. 39 (*gīnānono saṃgraha* 17).
26. Narasiṃha Mahetā: *Putrano vivāha* I, 3: K.K. Shastri (ed.) 1969. *Narasiṃha Mahetā kṛta ātmacaritanāṃ, kāvyo*, Junagadh; Narasiṃha Mahetā corā samiti; 6.
27. *Pīra Hasana Kabīradīna gīnānono saṃgraha*, no. 3 (*venti*), v. 1, v. 3; 14.
28. Ibid., v. 6.
29. Pīr Shams: *Prema pāṭaṇa rājā mana sudha* (*nānuṃ ginā̄na*, v. 3, *gīnānono saṃgraha*, no. 9; 7; *moṭuṃ ginā̄na*, v. 6. no. 28; 27).
30. *Pīra Hasana Kabīradīna gīnānono saṃgraha*, no. 3 (*venti*), v. 46; 18.
31. *Sāmī* is one of the most quoted names of God. See for instance *Pīra Hasana Kabīradīna...*, no. 3, v. 4; 14.
32. Ibid., v. 11; 15.
33. Ibid., v. 26.16.
34. Most probably for *Tribhuvana Śyāma* (Pīr Shams, *Prema pāṭaṇa rājā mana sudha*, v. 11, *gīnānono saṃgraha*, no. 9; 8).
35. *Pīra Hasana Kabīradīna...*, no. 3 (*venti*), v. 7 and 10. The "King of the three worlds" may be a name for Śiv as well as for Viṣṇu. But when *rāya* is replaced by *śāma* (see the preceding note), it points to Viṣṇu. A. Nanji (1978: 151) tells

how Satgur Nūr was understood to be the "Master of the three worlds" by the king Jaysiṃha, this name being according to A. Nanji, in his note 97 (1978: 164), "an epithet for a deity in Hinduism". The epithet might not be there without a purpose, as, in a yogī context—and this was the case in the episode reported—the "Master of the three worlds" would be Śiv, the Lord of the yogīs. In the case of *Tribhovana Śāma*, the epithet seems to point to Viṣṇu's *avatār Trivikrama*. *Trivikrama* is of special relevance in Gujarāt as the divinity of Dvārkā: *Trivikrama-Raṇchoḍ* (see F. Mallison, 1983: 245-55).

36. *Pīra Hasana Kabīradīna...*, no. 3 (*venti*), v. 11; 15.
37. Ibid., v. 50; 18.
38. Ibid., v. 32; 17.
39. Pīr Shams: *Prema pāṭaṇa rājā mana sudha* (*moṭuṃ gināna*), v. 7 *gīnānono saṃgraha* no. 28: 28.
40. There is a tendency nowadays to forsake the too striking Hindu appearances of Ismā'īlī ways and to revert to the Arab garb of Islam. For instance, since 1957, by a decision of the Imām, the daily prayer is recited in Arabic and not any longer in the vernacular of the *ginān*, and in the more recent editions of the *ginān*, the word *Sāmī* (*Svāmī*) is sytematically replaced by *Maulā*.
41. The tradition assigns to Narasiṃha Mahetā the dates AD 1414-80. They have been challenged on the basis of the external influences on his *pad* by the Kṛṣṇa bhakti prevalent in the sixteenth century (see F. Mallison, 1974: 189-201).
42. Cf. The introduction of H. Bhayani to his edition of the *Harivilāsa* [S. 2021 (1964). Harivilasa—eka madhyakālīna jainetera phāga—kāvya. *Svādhyāya* 2,3 (Baroda, Oriental Institute), 286-90]. And also: H.S. Bhayani, 2026 (1969) Jaḷakamaḷa prabhātiyānī prācīnatā ane kartṛtva. *Svādhyāya* 7, 4, 398-412, reprinted in 1972. *Anusaṃdhāna*. Ahmedabad: Sarasvati Pustak Bhandar; 55-78, dealing with the story of the *Nāgadamana* episode. Again M.R. Majumdar, 1922. *Sudāmācaritra*. Baroda: M.R. Majumdar: 205-9: the *Somakṛta Sudāmāsāra* which is an account of the story of Sudāmā, the friend of Kṛṣṇa by a Jaina author (F. Mallison, 1979. Saint Sudāmā of Gujarāt: should the holy be wealthy? *Journal of the Oriental Institute*, Baroda, 29, 95-6.).
43. A fifteenth century description of the 'perfect Vaiṣṇav' includes Jain prescriptions in his patterns of good conduct, see A.M. Bhojak, 1978. Kavi Māvā-Māvajī racita vaiṣṇavabhaktaprabaṃdhacopāī.; *Sambodhi* 6, 34 (Ahmedabad, L.D. Institute of Indology) 2nd part, 1-5.

REFERENCES

Asani, A. 1977. *The Ismā'īlī Ginān literature: Its structure and love symolism*. Harvard (undergraduate thesis, to be published).

Daftary, F. 1990. *The Ismā'īlīs: their history and doctrines*. Cambridge: CUP and Delhi: Munshiram Manoharlal.

Ivanow, W. 1936. The sect of Imam Shah in Gujarāt. In *Journal of the Bombay Branch of the Royal Asiatic Society*, NS., 12, 19-70.

———. 1948. Satpanth. In *Collectanea* (ed.) Ismaili Society. Leiden: EJ. Brill, vol. I, 1-54.

Kassam, T.R. 1995. *Songs of wisdom and circles of dance. Songs of the Satpanth Ismā'īlī Muslim saint, Pīr Shams.* Albany: State University of New York Press (McGill Studies in the History of Religion).

Mallison, F. 1974. Notes on the biography of Narasiṃha Maheta. In *Annals of the Bhandarkar Oriental Research Institute* 55, 189-201.

———. 1979. Saint Sudāmā of Gujarāt: Should the holy be wealthy. In *Journal of the Oriental Institute*, Baroda, 2990-9.

———. 1983. Development of early Krishnaism in Gujarāt: Viṣṇu-Raṇchoḍ-Kṛṣṇa. In *Bhakti in currrent research* 1979-82. (ed.) M. Thiel-Horstmann, Berlin: Dietrich Rainer Verlag; 245-55.

———. 1986. *Au point du jour, les prabhātiyāṃ de Narasiṃha Mahetā.* Paris: Ecole Française d'Extrême-Orient.

———. 1991. Les chants *Garabī* de Pīr Shams. In *Litteratures mèdièvales de l'Inde du Nord,* (ed.) F. Mallison, Paris: Ecole Française d'Extrême-Orient, 115-38.

Misra, S.C. 1964. *Muslim communities in Gujarat.* London: Asia Publishing House.

Nanji, A. 1978. *The Nizārī Ismā'īlī tradition in the Indo-Pakistani subcontinent.* New York: Caravan Books.

Schimmel, A. 1980. *Islam in the Indian subcontinent.* Leiden-Köln: E.J. Brill.

Shackle, Ch. and Z. Moir, 1992. *Ismaili hymns from South Asia. An introduction to the Ginans.* London: SOAS South Asia Texts, no 3.

Vaudeville, Ch. 1974. *Kabīr,* Oxford: Oxford University Press.

MULTIPLE APPROACHES TO A LIVING HINDU MYTH: THE LORD OF THE GOVARDHAN HILL

Charlotte Vaudeville

1. "Govardhan", a Mountain Deity

Mountains and Nāgas, divine cobras, both connected with forest termite mounds, appear as the oldest objects of cult in the Indian folk tradition.

Among divine mountains, the "Govardhan"[1] hillock situated in the Braj area, west of Mathura, is celebrated as a sacred locus as well as the seat of a powerful deity. The Govardhan deity is either identified with the hill itself, which he pervades, or conceived as residing within a rocky cave at the bottom of the hill. The sacred hill itself is said to assume the shape either of a bull or of a snake, the latter having its mouth at the "Mānasī Gaṅgā" and its tail at "Puñchri".[2] For the people of Braj, Govardhan is both the hill and the Lord of the Hill. The former may be directly worshipped under its rocky form, whereas the latter may manifest Himself whenever and wherever He chooses, in an anthropomorphic or non-anthropomorphic form.

As a mountain deity, Govardhan is not isolated. It belongs to a group of ancient folk deities, such as Murukaṉ of Tamilnadu, Khaṇḍobā of Maharashtra, Mailāra of Karnataka and the ubiquitous Bhairava. Sontheimer remarks that "the predominant element in the origin of Murukaṉ and Khaṇḍobā is the worship of the mountain in the forested tracks by hill tribes and pastoralists". [...] "The origins of the god [Khaṇḍobā] may also be found in the worship of the anthill, the seat of snakes in which form the god may also appear. The anthill is characteristic of the forest. It should be ploughed by farmers lest they would suffer great harm. For the forest tribes and the pastoral communities, it was not only the seat of snakes but the seat of wealth and thus the origin of sheep" (Sontheimer 1979: 2).

The close connection between divinities belonging to the forest and pastoral background is demonstrated by the recurrent legends about the divine presence being revealed to cowherds by cows spending milk into the holes of a hill or an anthill. God Mailār at Ādimailār had his origins in an anthill inhabited by snakes. The cows of a certain Gomuni used to spend milk into the holes of that anthill. Kapila Muni advised Gomuni, who changed the hill into a form of Mārtaṇḍa Bhairava.[3]

A similar legend is found in Tamilnadu concerning Lord Venkaṭeśvara of Tirupati, another famous hill deity; as to the Lord of the Govardhan Hill, the discovery of his divine presence by a cow (supposed to be descended from one of Lord Kṛṣṇa's own cows) is narrated at length in the Braj *vārtā* known as *Śrī Nathjī prākatya kī vārtā* (Vaudeville 1980: 19-20).

Popular belief about the deity of the Govardhan hill is closely linked to the old *govardhana-dharaṇa* myth, a myth well attested in ancient iconography, from the Kuṣāṇa period (According to Goetz: second-third century A.D.) onwards. In all ancient *govardhana-dharaṇa* icons, the Lord of the Hill, in the form of a young man, effortlessly lifts the top of the rocky hill and holds it over his head with his risen left arm: so doing, the Dweller of the Hill manifests Himself as a divine hero of unbounded strength, a *vīra*. Within the rocky cave itself, cows and cowherds are represented, suggesting that the cave itself is a cow-pen and that the *vīra* Himself is the protector of the cows and the cowherd tribes as well.

Besides the hero's posture, another characteristic of the *govardhana-dharaṇa* icons is the very long and thick "garland" falling from the hero's lifted left arms to his knees and passing behind his right shoulder: though usually mentioned as a "garland", the object very much resembles a large snake. No snake mouth or hood however is visible; the hill—or rather the hill-top[4]—rests flat over the hero's upturned hand with its five visible fingers.

In the Kuṣāṇa icon mentioned earlier, the hill-top is figured by a row of five conical stones—a design suggestive of the *tāla* (Borassus tree), well-known as the standard of the Nāga deity Balarāma or Saṅkarṣaṇa.[5] In later iconography, however, the five conical stones are not apparent, though the *tribhaṅga* posture assumed by the hero remains the same. In all ancient *govardhana-dharaṇa* icons, it is only the hand which emerges from the hill. In medieval legend, the mysterious hand emerging from the hill and suggesting a *nāga* hood, assumes much importance. As we shall try to show later, the Govardhan myth as a whole and the Govardhan folk-cult and folk-ritual, as preserved in Braj today, can hardly be understood without taking into account the lingering presence of god Baladeva-Saṅkarṣaṇa the original Nāga within the sacred hill, "shaped like an anthill".

Old icons are not explicit about the signification to be given to the hero's gesture—apart from a manifestation of the infinite power attributed to the Lord of the Hill, who might just as well be *yakṣa.* In the Hindu medieval tradition, however, from the *Harivaṃśa* downwards, the hero is identified with Kṛṣṇa-Gopāl, and the *govardhana-dharaṇa* episode is interpreted both as a gesture of defiance and as an act of compassion: the lifting of the hill is meant to protect the Gopās and their cattle from god Indra's anger. According to the *Harivaṃśa,* Indra's anger is supposed to have been aroused by Kṛṣṇa's daring challenge when he exhorted the Gopās to give up Indra's worship and to present the food offerings to the divine hill and to Himself, as the true Lord of both Gopās and cattle.[6] God Indra then retaliated with a terrible storm and downpour, unleashed by his armies of blue rain-clouds. In the *Harivaṃśa* and the Vaiṣṇava *Purāṇas* as a whole, Kṛṣṇa's exhortation to the tribe to give up Indra's worship clearly amounts to a repudiation of the Vedic-Brahmanical tradition and to an enforcement of the validity of the archaic folk tradition.

Actually, no ancient *govardhana-dharaṇa* icon represents Indra, Kṛṣṇa-Gopāl's putative enemy, and his army of clouds. The deity's appearance is benign and peaceful, suggesting a divine manifestation granted to the faithful cowherd tribe rather than a challenge or a threat. This manifestation is said to have taken place on the very day on which the cowherd tribe celebrated its great annual feast known as *Annakūṭ* or *Govardhanapūjā.* This festival, which is celebrated on Kārttikka *śukla* 1, is clearly an autumnal festival, in which blue rain-clouds would seem out of place.

The Puranic legends about the conflict between the Vedic god Indra and the cowherd tribal god Kṛṣṇa-Gopāl—a conflict in which the former is defeated and humbled—find their origin in cowherd lore: as champion of the cowherd tribe, Kṛṣṇa is set against Brahmanical gods in general and their king Indra in particular. Every year, when the autumnal session sets in, Indra and his blue clouds depart, leaving behind an abundant food-crop. This is interpreted as a "victory" which is celebrated with an enormous meal offered to the divine hill, as well as to the Lord of the Hill, who is also the Lord and protector of the Gopās. In the *Govardhanapūjā* or *Annakūṭ* festival, Kṛṣṇa-Gopāl and the Lord of the Hill are but one. As leader of the cowherd-folk, Kṛṣṇa-Gopāl vindicates the independence of the tribe and its attachment to its own un-Aryan tradition and un-Aryan ways of worship.

2. Aniconic Shrines on the Govardhan Hill

Characteristically, the most archaic Govardhan shrines are situated on the southern part of the hill.[7] They are mostly aniconic, open-air shrines, in which god Baladeva (in Braj "Baldev") is conspicuously worshipped under the fond name of "Dāūjī", "the Elder Brother"; "Mukhārvind", the "Sun-Face" or "Lotus-Face" of the Govardhan deity, popularly called "Girirāj", lit "King of Hills", usually refers to his younger brother, Kṛṣṇa-Gopāl.

2.1. Old Dāūjī

The dilapidated "Old Dāūjī" shrine is situated atop the southern part of the hill, between the Anyor and the Jatipurā villages, respectively located on the south-eastern and the south-western borders of the hill (see map). Though now generally ignored by the Vallabhite and Gauḍīya Vaiṣṇavas, the old Dāūjī shrine is still visited by local Brajvāsīs. "Old Dāūjī" is an aniconic shrine, in which the abiding presence of god Baldev or Dāūjī is symbolically represented by five lying Govardhan stones arranged in a semi-circle, canopy-like, on the floor.

2.2. Ḍhunkā Dāūjī or Luk-luk Dāūjī and the Chappan Bhog

"Ḍhunkā Dāūjī" or "Luk-luk Dāūjī", lit. "spying" or "peeping" Dāūjī, is an open-air shrine situated on the top of the hill, south of Jatipurā village, above the *parikrama* road. Opposite the road stands a large kitchen, used every year by the Vallabhites engaged in cooking the huge amount of food necessary for the so-called *Chappan Bhog* (lit. "fifty-six dishes" festival), a celebration which is one of the highlights of the autumnal pilgrimage (*Braj-yātra*). The various kinds of food are displayed under a large *paṇḍal*, down the hill slope. Meanwhile, "Ḍhunkā Dāūjī" is supposed to be peeping from his den above, eager to catch a view of the food display below, a display to which he is apparently denied access. In the hands of the Vallabhite priests, the presiding deity within the *paṇḍal* takes on the form of "Śrī Nāthjī" (i.e. Śrī Govardhannāthjī), the Lord of the Govardhan Hill. The deity is dressed like the Jatipurā "Mukhārvind";[8] like the latter, it is fitted with a stuffed cotton black arm—the *left* arm, instead of the right arm, as in all proper Baldev icons all over Braj—a characteristic which makes it an ambiguous figure.

Curiously in the matter of food, the Baldev ritual is maintained: the *Chappan Bhog* display includes only *pakka* food, which represent god Baldev's regular diet.[9] The Vallabhite priests change the deity, but not the food ritual.

The Ḍhunkā Dāūjī shrine itself is a curiously crumbled rock, showing a depression in the middle and surrounded by large Govardhan stones standing in a row over the depression, all of them daubed with *sindūr*. The highest stone, which stands in the middle may be interpreted as a *svayaṃbhū śivaliṅga*—or as god Dāūjī Himself. The other stones probably represent associated folk-deities.

2.3. The Jatipurā "Mukhārvind"

The Jatipurā village (old Gopālpur), situated on the south-western border of the Govardhan hill, has largely been appropriated by the Vallabhite sectarians. The village itself contains three Vallabhite temples, known as *havelīs.*[10] But the pride of the village is the famous shrine known as "Girirāj kā Mukhārvind", lit. "the Lotus-Face (or "Sun-face") of Girirāj", or as "Bhog-śilā", lit. "the Food-Rock", i.e. "the Rock to be fed (by devotees)".

Concretely, the "Mukhārvind" refers to a crack in the rock at the bottom of the hill, beside the *parikrama* road. The object of worship is a large quadrangular slab of stone, forming, so to say, the "body" of the deity, on top of which a roundish rock has been cemented, so as to form the "head"—giving the strange assemblage a vaguely anthropomorphical appearance.[11] According to the Vallabhite tradition, the manifestation of the "Mukhārvind" of Śrī Nāthjī coincided with the arrival of the divine Master Vallabhācārya in Jatipurā.[12]

According to the custom prevailing in the Braj area, the rock deity is left bare for the morning *pūjā*, when devotees worship it with pots or buckets of milk thrown at the naked rock. The milk flows down through two cemented drains, in which it is eagerly lapped by dogs: the latter somehow seem to belong there and to have their proper place in the ritual.[13] In the evening, the icon is entirely covered with bright clothes, belonging to Kṛṣṇa-Gopāl's own attire. A raised limb, made of black stuffed cloth, is added to the deity's left side-recalling the *govardhana-dharaṇa* posture assumed by the hill deity when standing in the hill cave. Nowadays, the Jatipurā "Mukhārvind" is worshipped as a *svarūpa* icon of Lord Kṛṣṇa-Gopāl, Himself identified in Vallabhite belief with the Lord of the Govardhan Hill.

Now mainly a Vallabhite centre, Jatipurā is held as the most prestigious place for the celebration of the *Govardhanapūjā* or *Annakūṭ* festival in the Braj area. In Jatipurā, on that day, the Vallabhite *havelīs* are open to all Hindus without distinction of caste: all can watch the huge display of food, including *kaccā* food—normally protected from all impure looks—and the *prasād* food is distributed to all free of cost. On that day, even another *svarūpa* icon turns an onlooker: the Gokulnāthjī *svarūpa* icon, brought from Gokul for the occasion, is pompously led out of its nearby *havelī* and made to watch the ceremony from a raised platform especially built for the occasion.

The *Annakūṭ* celebration at Jatipurā appears as a kind of compromise between the archaic pattern of the festival, as celebrated by the pastoral population of Braj, and the Vallabhites' faith in their own *svarūpa* idols, the first and foremost of which is the famous "Śrī Nāthjī" icon, now housed in the Nāthdvāra temple in Mewar. Actually the Vallabhites, who worship their own *svarūpas* as well as their divinized "Mahārājas", could very well do without the Jatipurā Mukhārvind since, according to their belief, the Lord of the Hill, "Śrī Govardhannāthjī" *alias* "Śrī Nāthjī", emerged out of the hill long ago through the power of the Master Vallabhācārya, and was subsequently carried away to safety in Mewar. All the Vallabhite Mahārājas therefore celebrate the *Annakūṭ* festival in their own *havelīs* for the sake of their own adepts. The presence of three (secondary) *svarūpa* icons at the time of the *Annakūṭ* festival in Jatipur and the strange disguise of the old rock as an effigy of Kṛṣṇa-Gopāl Himself testify to the Vallabhites' lingering belief in the presence of an ancient deity within the sacred hill. The stuffed left arm is probably a late Vallabhite innovation meant to underline the identity of the Govardhan hill with Kṛṣṇa-Gopāl as *Govardhanadharī*, Himself identical with their own deity "Śrī Nāthjī".

2.4. The "Mukuṭ Mukhārvind" shrine in Govardhan town

The Mānasī Gaṅgā, a large pond within Govardhan town, is said to form the "mouth" of the Govardhan hill itself, more precisely of its southern half, in which the myth seems to be rooted.[14] The pond is situated in the middle of the rocky ridge, between its northern and its southern part (see map). The pond is called after the name of Manasā, a powerful snakegoddess, supposed to be the daughter of Śiva and the river-goddess Gaṅgā. Manasā Devī is said to be the greatest Devī of Braj (Mital 1966: 42) The Mānasī Gaṅgā is described as an "Ocean of Milk" as well as a magic pond: miraculous streams of milk are said to shoot from the pond now and then. The Manasā Devī temple is located on the south bank of the sacred pond, facing another important deity, Cakreśvar Mahādev, one of the four great "Mahādev" of Braj. This serpent goddess in her ocean of milk recalls the great Nāgas and Nāginīs of yore. She is also the tutelary deity of the local Pandas. The latter claim to be Vallabhites, though their way of worship owes much to the ancient traditions of pastoral Braj.

The Mukuṭ Mukhārvind temple is located right on the border of the Mānasī Gaṅgā. It is a rather small and unimpressive shrine, isolated from the town in the rainy season and early autumn, when the pilgrims have to wade through mud and knee-deep water to reach it. The shrine itself is the property of the Govardhan Pandas, who call themselves "Sāṇadhya Brahmans". They claim to be the oldest residents of the town and the descendants of the famous Saḍḍūpāṇḍe, who was responsible for the discovery of the sacred "Arm" of Śrī Nāthjī.[15]

The shrine, which is open to all and sundry, contains two Govardhan rocks emerging from the pond: (a) a low rock, showing a round depression in the middle and geomorphic cow-hoof imprint above it; (b) on the right side of the low rock, a high standing rock, showing on its smooth face a larger geomorphic impression evoking the elongated shape of a snake. The low rock is identified as the Mukhārvind", i.e. the "Sun-Mouth" or "Lotus-Mouth" of Lord Govardhan Himself, while the high-standing rock is said to be the *mukuṭ*, i.e. the "crown" or "canopy" of the Mukhārvind rock, though in fact interpretations differ.[16]

According to the prevailing pattern in the Braj area, in the morning the two rocks are left bare; in the evening, the lower rock is dressed up by the Pandas as befits Kṛṣṇa-Gopāl, in bright clothes complete with the flute placed across the round depression which is the Lord's "mouth". The upright stone is not dressed up, but is touched up with paint, so as to evoke the peacock feather (*mor*) which tops Kṛṣṇa-Gopāl's headgear. No artificial limb is attached, as it was the case in Jatipurā: the aniconic character of the double deity prevails. The lower rock is clearly identified with Kṛṣṇa-Gopāl by the local Pandas; the same Pandas deny that the high rock with the snake-like geomorphic imprint could be Baldev or Dāūjī, Kṛṣṇa's elder brother. Their Vallabhite conviction does not allow them to see anything in the high rock than an improbable "feather", which stands as the *mukuṭ,* i.e. the headgear of the double deity, now identified with Kṛṣṇa-Gopāl alone as the Lord of the Govardhan Hill.

At the "Mukuṭ Mukhārvind" great emphasis is placed on the divine mouth of the Lord: it is the very mouth which, in olden times, swallowed all the offerings of the Gopā tribe—the same tribal cowherd population which even now predominates in Goverdhan town around the Mānasī Gaṅgā. The Mānasī Gaṅgā itself is described as "an Ocean of Milk", milk being the favourite food of Kṛṣṇa-Gopal- and of all Nāga deities as well: it is the very essence of food. Every year in Kārttikka, pilgrims from all over Braj crowd at the Mānasī Gaṅgā and at "Mukuṭ Mukhārvind" to pour milk into the sacred "Mouth" before starting on the annual Braj *parikrama,* since that shrine stands as both the starting and the concluding point of the great autumnal pilgrimage.

In common Brajvāsī belief, Govardhan, the divine hill, stands at the centre of the holy Braj area and the two Govardhan stones in the "Mukuṭ Mukhārvind" stand at its epicentre. According to the belief prevailing in the area, the summit of the Govardhan hill is the highest point on earth, the original stones are its centre and the hole within the "Mukhārvind" lower stone is the "Navel", connecting the visible earth with the underworld (*pātāla*) which is the subterranean world of Nāgas (Cf. Toomey 1984, 62f.). In spite of the Vallabhite influence, the original myth which connected Govardhan, the anthill-shaped rock, with the subterranean ocean which is the realm of Nāgas, is not forgotten in Brajvāsī belief and practice.

In Braj language, the hole in the "Mukuṭ Mukhārvind" lower rock is referred to as *toṇḍ,* a word meaning both "navel" and "paunch". As we shall see,[17] this double meaning fits in well with the actual practice and ritual of the *Govardhanapūjā* or *Annakūṭ* as celebrated by the cowherd population in the area.

2.5. The Dān Ghaṭī Mukhārvind

Another less known "Mukhārvind" is signalled by Allan Entwistle (in his newly published work on Braj) at a place called "Dān Ghaṭī". Dān Ghaṭī is the name given to a stretch of the Mathura-Dig road (see map) that crosses over a break or low point of the Govardhan ridge. A disused and partly ruined temple, known as the original "Dānīrāy" temple, is found above Dān Ghaṭī. Entwistle remarks that the so-called "Mukhārvind" stone worshipped at Dān Ghaṭī "resembles a head surrounded by cobra hoods". According to the author's opinion, there may be no conclusive evidence that worship on the hill Govardhan was primarily a Nāga cult, yet "these associations indicate a degree of coalescence between the worship of Nāgas and the hill [...] Possibly the Nāga element had come to predominate in the period preceding the arrival of Mādhavendra Purī and Vallabha, under whose influence the worship of Govardhan became more closely linked with that of Krishna" (Entwistle 1987: paras. 7.4; 14.8; 14.9).

Our review of the oldest shrines on and around the hill, the two "Dāūjīs" and the three "Mukhārvinds", does support Entwistle's intuition.

3. The "Cowdung Govardhan"[18]

The *Annakūṭ* or *Govardhanapūjā* festival is celebrated in the Braj area on Kārttik śu. 1, i.e. on the day following *Dīvālī* (Aśvin Kṛṣṇa 15). In the whole area, *Annakūṭ* takes even more importance than *Dīvālī*. According to a local saying: "Girirāj is the bridegroom, *Dīvālī* is the bride" (Toomey 1984: 151). As noted by Toomey, "the festival is rooted in an ancient pre-krishnaite cattle-rite" (Toomey 1984: 148).

Annakūṭ, literally "*Mountain of Food*", primarily refers to the huge mound of rice placed in front of the Govardhan deity, behind which row after row of various foods, both *kaccā* and *pakkā* are displayed. In the *Annakūṭ* festival, Govardhan or "Girirāj" is simultaneously identified with the "mountain of food" and with the divine hill, as a source of wealth and sustenance.

The festival itself is diversely interpreted and celebrated by the Vallabhite and Gauḍīya Vaiṣṇavas on the one hand and by the Brajvāsī cowherd people on the other. The Vallabhite celebration is the richest and the most elaborate of all, followed by that of the Gauḍīyas. In both the sectarian traditions, the identity of Kṛṣṇa-Gopāl with the Lord of Hill is just taken for granted. In both, the celebration centres on the presentation of the food and their subsequent distribution as sanctified *prasād* to the participants. Though most local Brajvāsīs participate in those celebrations, especially at Jatipurā, they also flock to the "Mukuṭ Mukhārvind" shrine, described earlier, where the celebration is held with a simplified ritual. Most important of all, they celebrate their own *Govardhanapūjā* rites either in their village street or in the courtyard of their home, by moulding a "cowdung Govardhan". The rather shapeless effigy is made on the ground with cowdung paste. In the evening, the same "Govardhan" is ceremonially circumambulated by cowherds and cattle and then made to be trampled into the ground under the hooves of cattle. Songs in honour of "Girirāj" are part of the ceremony. No Brahman priest officiates (Vaudeville 1980: 2-4).

The cowdung Govardhan shows characteristic features: a large squarish "body" surmounted by a rounded head, features that recall the shape of the original Govardhan slab of stone worshipped at Jatipurā as "Mukhārvind". The Brajvāsīs' cowdung Govardhan adds two symmetrical "arms" raised at a straight angle from the "body" and two large feet below. Between the parallel feet hangs what looks like an oversize penis, the *lāṅgulā*, a word meaning both "penis" and "plough" [compare the pre-Śuṅga Nāga figure with an oversize penis, MM (Mathura museum), 17, 1303]. Just in the middle of the cowdung "body", a large round hole is made, referred to as *toṇḍ* and interpreted as the "Navel" or "Mouth" of the Govardhan deity. It is in the *toṇḍ* that milk is poured and that the other food offerings brought by the participants are piled up. All have direct access to the *toṇḍ*, just as all have access to the divine "Mouth" at the "Mukut Mukhārvind". The effigy is surrounded by an enclosure, also made of cowdung paste: within the enclosure, various ball-like cowdung objects are placed, apparently representing cowherds and cows as found in the ancient representation of the original Govardhan hill-cave. Interestingly, the cowdung fence around the effigy remains open just below the *lāṅgulā*, as if a secret passage existed linking the Govardhan cave itself to the lower world. On the "body" itself, high white sticks are planted bearing white tufts of cotton on top: the signification is not very clear, the most probable interpretation being the suggestion of fertile crops.

In India and elsewhere, *govar* (or *gobar*), i.e. cowdung, has been credited with magical fertility power. *Govar* appears as such in all the cattle festivals held in various parts of India, including some aboriginal festivals, with or without reference to Kṛṣṇa-Gopāl, though often the calendar dates of such festivals coincide with the Braj *Annakūṭ*: this is the case with the *Sohorai* festival held by aboriginals in Chota-Nagpur (Vaudeville 1980: 3). The pastoral cowdung rites clearly have an archaic, pre-Aryan character.

The presence of *two* symmetrical arms in the cowdung effigy of Govardhan in Braj does not reveal the deity identity: nowadays, Govardhan or "Girirāj" is identified with Kṛṣṇa-Gopāl, but it might just as well be identified with Baldev—or with both gods together. As we shall see, there are reasons to believe that the presence of Baldev is felt.

The songs sung by women during the ceremony are known as *hīro*, i.e. *abhīra* songs. According to S.K. Das, in Bihar and Bengal, the women sing obscene songs at the *Annakūṭ* festival, probably because the rite is a fertility rite (Vaudeville 1980: 3). This may also be the case in the Braj area and elsewhere. The aboriginal Cheros observe a similar festival in the bright half of the month of Śrāvan, i.e. on *Nāg-pañcamī* day, a day sacred all over India to snake-worship and held to be god Baldev's birthday (Vaudeville 1980: 3 and n. 28). Both cattle-worship and snake-worship are archaic fertility rites in which the women play a very significant part.

Songs of that type, known as "Lāṃguriyā" songs, sung during the Dussera festival at the Kailā Devī shrine in eastern Rajasthan, have been analysed and partly translated by Entwistle (1987: 85-101). In such songs, the Lāṃguriyā appears as a male attendant of the Devī, and an irregular sexual partnership, such as that of the *devar* and *bhābhī*, is often suggested. Some songs deal in sexually explicit terms with their relationship. As noted by the author, the *Lāṅguriyā* is the *lāṅgūlin*, literally "furnished with a plough", a word which occurs in the *Mahābhārata* and Purāṇas as an epithet of Balarāma. But *lāṅgūla*, "plough", also means "penis" and, most probably, the Lāṅguriyā in the songs means "the fellow with the [powerful] penis"—a nickname which fits god Baldev, as well as Bhairava, the Devī's attendant and lover.

The two symmetrical arms of cowdung are not present in all the cowdung effigies in Braj itself. A photograph taken by P. Toomey in a Braj lane shows male Brajvāsīs in the process of completing their cowdung Govardhan: only the *right* arm is raised, the left being turned down in the *abhaya* posture. The risen right arm can only belong to the Nāga god Baldev, since the posture is the same as that found in all Baldev icons all over the Braj area. The posture given to their cowdung deity by local Brajvāsīs, free from sectarian interference, re-inforces the hypothesis according to which the cowdung Govardhan effigy is originally based on the Baldev iconographical pattern rather than on the Śrī Nāthjī *govardhanadharī* pattern. As "Govardhanadharī", the Lord of the Hill reveals his presence and supreme power, whereas Baldev's lifted right arm expresses the benign protection He Himself extends to all Brajvāsī folk and cattle.

On the whole, the symbolism of the cowdung Govardhan is clear enough. The *toṇḍ* refers to Lord Govardhan's round and large "mouth", prominent in all the aniconic shrines already mentioned, where the divine mouth is called "Mukhārvind". As to prominent *lāṅgūla*, it must belong to god Baldev (Baladeva), also known as "Saṅkarṣaṇa", "the Drawer": Baldev is the Drawer of the subterranean waters, dwelling in the anthill cave. Through the Govardhan's "mouth" or "navel" milk flows down to feed the snakes in the underworld (*pātāla*) through the *lāṅgūla*, subterranean waters, relaying the rains, are drawn to fertilze the upper world during the dry season—a phenomenon symbolized by the well-known legend of god Balarāma alias Baldev dragging the Yamunā river with his "plough" to the centre of the Braj area.

The greatest feast in Braj after the *Annakūṭ* falls on Mārgaśīrṣa 15, i.e. on the Mārgaśīrṣa Pūrṇimā, which is god Baldev's main feast, corresponding to the beginning of the dry and cold season.[19] Enthusiastic crowds take the road to the Rīḍha village, in the south-eastern far corner of Braj, to pay their respects to god Baldev, since, in Braj parlance: "Braj is Baldev". The devotees are nearly all Brajvāsīs, mostly pastoral people. They are aware of Baldev's needs and tastes—especially of his taste for strong liquor—so they carry *madirā* for Baldev and also *gadalās*, a kind of stuffed cotton vest, to protect him from the incoming cold. The atmosphere is very gay and somewhat riotous, as the devotees consume the *prasād* of the *madirā* (i.e. *bhaṅg*) which they have offered to Baldev and his wife Revatī—both happily intoxicated. No pious Vaiṣṇavas are in sight. The attending *pūjārīs* at Baldev belong to an ancient tribe known as "Ahivāsis", who call themselves Brahmans and Snake-Worshippers. The impressive Baldev *mūrti* in the main temple is said to have been extracted from the near-by *kuṇḍ*. According to P. D. Mital, this icon "is probably the most ancient *mūrti* in the whole of Braj" (1966: 142). The well itself is known as Balabhadra *kuṇḍ*, Balabhadra being the ancient name of god Baldev (Vaudeville 1974: 102-3).

4. God Baldev, a Śaivite Deity

Nāga worship is very ancient in India and can be traced from the Indus Valley period. Both Buddhists and Jainas gave an important place to Nāgas and Mathura itself was an important centre of the Nāga cult. In the Braj area, anthropomorphic representations of Nāgas are found as early as the third century B.C. The importance of the Nāga cult in the area was confirmed by the excavations made at Sonkh by Härtel (1973).

Ancient symbolic representations of Baldev are found such as the Lion-Plough pillar capital (Kuṣāṇa period) and the Palm-Capital (Śuṅga period). Sculpturally, Baldev's icons go back to about the second century B.C. In the Kuṣāṇa period, his worship reaches its zenith. The Sangam literature of south India also refers to independent Balarāma temples, but, with the Gupta period, independent figures diminish in number. From the third-fourth century A.D., the Pañcarātras introduced the *caturvyūha* theory, in which the central figure is Vāsudeva-Kṛṣṇa: Baladeva-Saṅkarṣaṇa then is treated as a secondary form of Vāsudeva, from whom he is supposed to have sprung.

The rise of Vaiṣṇavism is closely linked to the Pañcarātra doctrine. But that doctrine, developed among Brahmanical circles, was bound to have but a limited impact on the tribal populations attached to their ancestral beliefs and the cult of their own Nāgas. In the Braj pastoral area, the old Nāga deity Baladeva or "Baldev" was never accounted as a *vyūha* or Vāsudeva-Kṛṣṇa: he kept his personality, though the ancient link between the twin deities Balarāma-Vāsudeva was never lost sight of. Though in the Kuṣāṇa period god Balarāma may have four arms, in popular iconography today Baldev is always two-handed, with his right arm stretched over the head, palm open, as in the very ancient Chargaon Nāga image.[20] Under the fond name of "Dāūjī", "the Elder Brother", Baldev remains immensely popular with the Brajvāsī pastoral population to this day.

Baladeva (Balarāma, Saṅkarṣaṇa) is usually interpreted as an agricultural god. According to N.P. Joshi, *Iconography of Balarāma* (Joshi 1979: 54-6), in spite of god Balarāma carrying the plough (*hala, lāṅgala*) and the pestle (*mūsala*) and having a very close relationship with earth and water, early works such as the *Arthaśāstra* and the *Harivaṃśa* do not associate him with agriculture, but rather with *madirā* (intoxicating drink) and with *sītā*, the furrow made by the plough according to the *Amarakośa* (Gupta period); another work, *Rājanirghaṇṭa*, tells us that *sītā* and *madirā* are synonymous. The standard image of god Baldev in the great "Baldev" temple, at Rīḍha and elsewhere all over Braj, always shows the god holding a flask of *madirā* in his left hand, while his right hand is being stretched over his head in front of his *nāga* canopy in the *abhayamūdra* gesture: *abhayamūdra* with the right hand and snake canopy are always present in the representation of god "Dāūjī".

The sectarian Vaiṣṇava—especially the Vallabhite—influence on the ancient Govardhan cult in modern times tends to relegate the cult of Baldev to a secondary place.

In the annual *Braj-yātra*, "Baldev" (a name which stands for the village as well as for the God) is included—yet sectarian maps of "Braj maṇḍal" often omit the Baldev temple.[21] In Braj today, god Baldev, though immensely popular with the local population, appears practically on his own.[22] The reason for this veiled ostracism is certainly linked with the god's ill reputation as wrestler and inveterate drunkard, addicted to liquor (*madirā*) and *bhaṅg* (cannabis), which makes him *persona non grata* with pious Vaiṣṇavas.

Baldev, as worshipped by common people in Braj, clearly belongs to the old Śaiva background. His relationship is with Rudra-Śiva as *Girīśa*, "Lord of the Hills", and with Mārtaṇḍa Bhairava, *alias* Mallāri, "the Enemy of [the mountain demon] Malla" (Sontheimer 1984: 155-70). Mallāri is a name of Kṛṣṇa-Gopāl, acquired in defeating the wrestlers Cāṇura and Muṣṭika, sent by Kaṃsa; it is also a name of the divinized Maharashtrian hero Khaṇḍobā. In the Krishnaite myth, both Kṛṣṇa and Baladeva are wrestlers,[23] and they have a connection with Bhairava. In the Maharashtrian calendar, Kārttikka *kṛṣṇa* 5 is dedicated to Kālabhairava and Mārgaśīrṣa *śukla* 1 to Mārtaṇḍa Bhairava, *alias* Mallāri. The fact that the latter coincides with the big feast celebrated in honour of god Baldev in the Braj area suggests an old link between Mallāri and Baldev.

Growse notes that the ancient site of Bhūteśvar, now about a mile from Mathura, preserves "what appears to be a relic of the ancient form of the Kṛṣṇa-Gopāl cult" (Growse 1974: 130-1). There a small temple is found, dedicated to Jagannāth, Baladeva and Subhadrā, while the principal temple is dedicated to "Bhūteśvar". At the side of the temple, a small shrine is dedicated to Baldev under the name of

"Dāūjī". The Bhūteśvar site preserves relics of an ancient cluster in which god Balabhadra *alias* Baladeva, is already integrated with Subhadrā and Jagannāth in what is known as the Jagannāth-Purī trio.

The integration of god Baladeva in the Bhāgavata synthesis is achieved by the mediation of the serpent deity Ananta, also a synonym of god Viṣṇu. The *Gītā* assimilates both theories when it tells us that Kṛṣṇa "is Ananta among the Nāgas". It appears that the superhuman act of Kṛṣṇa led to his association with Viṣṇu and similarly Baladeva came to be associated with Ananta. As we have seen, both brothers are initially Vrātyas, belonging to the ancient tribe of the Mallas, a guild of pugilists and wrestlers. In later times, however, Kṛṣṇa's tribal origins and his association with forests and mountains is blurred: he now is the darling child of Yaśodā and the Gopīs' lover. Yet his association with the Govardhan hill is not forgotten—so much that all pious Vaiṣṇavas maintain that He, Kṛṣṇa-Gopāl, is to be worshipped as Lord of the Hill.

Vaiṣṇava piety tends to eliminate Baldev. The old Nāga god, however, retains his popularity with the Braj natives, mostly pastoral people, who have made but superficial adjustments with upper caste sectarian Vaiṣṇavism: Hence the strange series of "Dāūjī" and "Mukhārvind" shrines found on the holy hill itself and all around in Braj.

5. The Śrī Nāthjī Icon: A Problem of Identity

5.1. The Manifestation of Śrī Nāthjī

The famous Śrī Nāthjī icon is a *pīṭhikā*, a low-relief quadrangular slab of stone of unknown origin, probably belonging to the Buddhist period. There are two main versions about its discovery: the Gauḍīya Vaiṣṇava and the Vallabhite versions.

According to the Gauḍiya tradition, the *pīṭhikā* was discovered by the Śaṅkarite ascetic Mādhavendra Purī (*c.* early sixteenth century A.D.) in a thicket in the vicinity of "Gopālpur" (now Jatipurā) village, following a revelation granted to Mādhavendra by "Śrī Kṛṣṇa" Himself about the place where the *pīṭhikā* was buried. It was Mādhavenda who first unearthed the icon, erected it on the Govardhan hill and started worshipping it as "Śrī Gopāl". Mādhavendra also undertook the *sevā* ("service") of the new deity and started cooking for it. According to the Vallabhite tradition, however, the deity itself objected to Mādhavendra's *sevā* and advised him to leave Braj. Meanwhile, He

("Śrī Gopāl" *alias* "Śrī Nāthjī") would feed solely on milk, waiting for the arrival of "Śrī Acāryajī", i.e. Vallabhācārya, an event which took place in 1549 V.S. (A.D. 1492). Mādhavendra was ordered by the deity to leave for a world tour—and he never came back.[24]

The Vallabhite version of the story is narrated at length in the *Śrī Nāthjī prakatya kī vārtā* written in Braj *bhāṣā* at the end of the seventeenth century (Vaudeville 1980: 19-23). According to the *vārtā*, the manifestation of the deity started in A.D. 1410 with the miraculous appearance of a bent "Arm" on top of the Govardhan hill on a *Nāg Panchamī* day. The wonder was discovered by a Brajvāsī cowherd, Saḍḍupāṇḍe, while looking for his stray cow: he found the cow spilling milk over a crack in the hill, out of which the divine "Arm" emerged. Henceforward the Brajvāsīs took to worshipping the Arm with oblations of milk, the hidden deity having let it known that the most sacred part of its body, its divine "Mouth", would only appear after the arrival in Braj of the divine Master, Vallabhācārya. According to the Vallabhite tradition, the manifestations of the "Mukhārvind", the "Sun-Mouth" of Śrī Kṛṣṇa, took place in A.D. 1479 on Vaiśākh *kṛṣṇa* 11—the very same day on which Vallabha Himself was born. In the *Puṣṭi-mārga-saṃpradāya* therefore, Vallabha is held as the *avatāra* of the divine Mouth *mukhāvatāra* of Bhagavān (Barz 1976: 22).

5.2. Characteristics of the Śrī Nāthjī icon

The representation of the Vallabhite Śrī Nāthjī includes three specific features: (a) the delineation of the moutain cave around the god's body; (b) the left hand of the deity raised above its head with the palm turned backward so that the five fingers pressed together are seen emerging from the cave; (c) a bunch of lotus stalks stuck in the god's right arm-pit, the hand resting on his waist.

Any number of chromos representing the famous deity are printed and sold in bazaars all over India. Some of these, especially common in Gujarat, represent the *pachīs darśan* of Śrī Nāthjī, i.e. the twenty-five different attires worn by the deity on twenty-five different feasts or occasions. We note that in twenty-three out of the twenty-five *darśans*, not only the Lord's body, but also the whole of the *pīṭhikā* are completely covered with clothes—only the nearly quadrangular black face of Śrī Nāthjī[25] (under a high turban and head-gear) and its feet emerge, besides the raised left hand. Two of those *darśans* however reveal a little more, since they are associated with Śrī

Nāthjī's ritual bathing, called *Snān yātra* and *Pañcāmṛta snān*: in both cases, the background cloth has been partially removed, uncovering the *pīṭhikā* and showing the rocky hill. The lotus stalks are missing. The deity wears a simple bathing *dhoti* and his hair is tied in cloth, out of which a strange kind of cap emerges carved in the stone itself.[26] Also carved in the stone is a kind of garland, which seems to emerge behind the covered legs, looking more like a rope or a snake, and passing over the lifted forearm.[27]

The Vallabhites are extremely secretive about their *svarūpa* icons and this is specially true of the famous Śrī Nāthjī which is the property of the "Mahārāja" of the first *gaḍḍī*, descendant of Viṭṭhalnāth's eldest son. Enclosed in its shrine at Nāthdvāra, Śrī Nāthjī can only be seen at appointed times, and normally only members of the sect can have the *darśan*. Particularities of the naked *pīṭhikā* therefore remain the secret of the Mahārāja and of the initiated priests attached to the Lord's service (Barz 1976: 20-5).

5.3. Śrī Nāthjī and Jagannāth

Śrī Nāthjī's extraordinary career cannot be understood unless we take into account the career of the self-divinized Master, Vallabhācārya, and the predominating influence of the ancient deity Jagannāth, "the Lord of the World", in eastern India, including Orissa and the Telugu area where Vallabha was born.

As Telugu Brahmans and devout Vaiṣṇavas, Vallabha's parents were devotees of Jagannāth. It is the course of a pilgrimage to Jagannāth, in A.D. 1479, that Vallabha makes his appearance in the world. According to the legend, the child was still-born—but he underwent a miraculous rebirth, which signalled his divine nature and announced more wonders: from this instant, Vallabha's biography is a succession of miracles.[28]

In A.D. 1489, Vallabha, ten years old, visits Jagannāth Purī, where he argues with the Māyāvādīs and defeats them all. He also manifests his nearness to Jagannāth -showing that he alone can read the Lord's mind. From A.D. 1493 to 1512, Vallabha undertakes three tours of India, arguing and preaching for *bhakti-mārga*. Traces of his holy presence are concretized by a number of *baiṭhaks*, lit. "seats"—not less than eighty-four in number—dedicated to him. In A.D. 1493, it is said that Śrī Kṛṣṇa Himself appears to Vallabha in dream and instructs him to go to Braj and to reveal the identity of the divine *svarūpa* that had appeared out of the top of the Govardhan hill, initially called "Devadaman". Vallabha informs the worshippers that the Devadaman icon is really a *svarūpa* of Śrī Kṛṣṇa in the act of holding up the mountain—therefore he should be called "Śrī Govardhananātha". The holy man looses no time in establishing the new religion, the *Puṣṭi-mārga-saṃpradāya,* imparting the *brahmasaṃbandha* initiation to his new disciples and receving the *svarūpa* around which the new *saṃpradāya* would revolve. In this way, Vallabha becomes the rightful owner of the divine *svarūpa* of Śrī Govardhannāthjī, with which he somehow indentifies himself. Nevertheless, Vallabha does not remain long in Braj. Between the years 1501-3, he reaches the holy city of Paṇḍharpūr in Maharashtra, whose presiding deity is Lord Viṭṭhalnāth or Viṭhobā, supposed to be identical with Śrī Kṛṣṇa.[29]

In Paṇḍharpūr, Vallabha allegedly asks Śrī Viṭṭhalnāthjī—a properly married god—about the opportunity of marrying, with a view to ensuring the promulgation of the *bhakti-mārga* after his own death. Implicit in this decision is Vallabha's desire to extend to his sons the supernatural status he had bestowed on Himself, necessary for administering the *brahmasaṃbandha* to his followers. But Vallabha goes further: he declares that "both the pride common to the state of *saṃnyāsa* and the duties of the state of *saṃnyāsa* are contrary to the *bhakti-mārga*"—an opinion unacceptable to all the other Vaiṣṇava bhakti sects (Eschmann, Kulke, Tripathi 1978: 106).

This last move and this new profession of faith mark the point of no return for Vallabhācārya, as far as the Hindu orthodox tradition is concerned. The *Puṣṭi-mārga-saṃpradāya* takes a new turn, away from traditional Vaiṣṇavism. "Śrī Nāthjī", the newcomer, joins forces with Jagannāth, the ageless tribal deity with a Tantric Śaiva background, dominant in Orissa and Andhra Pradesh. Behind Jagannāth is Narasiṃha, deity long identified with Śiva Himself in his Ekapāda Bhairava aspect, before he was incorporated into the Vaiṣṇava cult.

Narasiṃha, like Nāthjī is a mountain god: he is called *girija,* "Mountain-Born". Originally he is not thought to have been from the pillar but from a mountain cave, like Śrī Nāthjī Himself, and he is associated with Bhairava[30]. Another "hill deity" is Jagannāth Himself, earlier known as "the Lord of the Blue Mountain" (*nīlādrinātha*), referring to the hillock on which the Jagannāth temple at Puri now stands. Stietencron remarks that the word "Jagannāth", literally "Lord [or Protector] of the World", is unspecific. Other titles like *īśvara* or *parameśvara* were equally unspecific up to the post-Gupta period. In the beginning of the fourteenth century, the litle *īśvara* and its composite forms are used mainly for Śiva. After the decline of Buddhism in India, Śiva also acquires the monopoly on the title "Lokanātha", whereas "Jagannātha" becomes a term reserved for Viṣṇu alone. "It appears that the decisive factor in bringing about the correlation of Jagannāth with Viṣṇu was Śaktism". [31]

Unlike the *īśvara* title, the *nātha* title in Indian tradition has a Tantric flavour. It applies to the "nine Nāths", the most famous of whom is Gorakhnāth, themselves linked with the "eighty-four Siddhas", the old Tantric Masters inherited from the Buddhistic Tantric tradition. We find the number "eighty-four" much in honour in that tradition as well as in the *Puṣṭi-mārga-saṃpradāya* with Vallabhācārya's "eighty-four *baiṭhaks*" and "eighty-four [foremost] disciples".

5.4. The Blakaṭānanda "revelation"

Fortuitous circumstances and the help of an Indian friend in Vrindaban allowed the author to lay her hands on a rare and very badly printed book, which had been compiled by a former Administrative Manager of the Nāthdvāra Vallabhite *gaḍḍī*. In order to preserve his anonymity, the writer of the book had assumed the rather improbable name of "Blakaṭānanda". The book was printed by the Arya Bhushan Press in 1919 V.S. (A.D. 1862), with the promising title:

Vallabhakula chala kapaṭa darpana
athavā
Vallabhakula kā kacca ciṭṭhā

i.e. "The Mirror of the Lies and Treachery of the Vallabhites" or "The Detailed Account of the Deeds of the Vallabhites".

As a kind of preface, the author describes the former "Śrī Nāthjī" temple whose ruins are seen on the Govardhan hill at Anyor. According to him, the Anyor area was the principal place occupied by the Buddhists and the temple itself was built over an old Buddhist cave. In the first century B.C., Kanishka erected a *mūrti* of "Buddhadeva" on the spot. A number of Buddhist icons were found in the vicinity, "which somehow resemble Śrīnāthjī". Among the "Buddhist" icons, the author mentions Bhairava, Hanumān, some Yakṣas and a Yakṣinī Devī "to whom the Hindus gave other names".

According to the *Blakaṭānanda Purāṇa,* Mādhavendra Purī had discovered "a Bhairava *mūrti*" in a bush and had installed it in the former temple of "Budha Bhagavān". When Mādhavendra Purī left Braj, he entrusted the temple to some Bengali *pūjārīs,* whereas Vallabhācārya established himself at Aḍail. With a view to appropriate his father's riches, Vallabhācārya's second son, Gosain Viṭṭhalnāth, went to Girirāj where the Bengalis were worshipping "Bhairava Yakṣa" and "Kalyāṇī Yakṣinī Devī". They did not allow the Vallabhites to enter the temple. Then Viṭṭhalnāth recruited a crowd of "badmashes" to expel the Bengalis by force. Having succeeded in taking hold of the temple, Viṭṭhalnāth named the old Bhairvava *mūrti* "Devadaman", "because the latter had triumphed over Buddhadeva".

Viṭṭhalnāth then introduced changes: the red *tilak* (*sendur*) used by the Bengali priests was changed into *lāl rolī kā tilak*, another red *tilak* whose shape was *guptāṅk,* i.e. "cryptic". According to Blakaṭānanda, "up to these days the Vallabha *maṭh* is prevaded by strong *vāmamarga* (Tantric) flavour". A parallel is drawn by the same author with the Purī-Jagannāth temple: "As the Purī-Jagannāth temple is full of marks (*cinha*) of *Vāmamārga,* such is the case with the Nāthdvāra temple." Blakaṭānanda asserts that the *śikhara* on top of the Nāthdvāra temple is not [Vaiṣṇava] "Sudarśana" *śikhara,* but a "Bhairavī *cakra*".

After detailing the moral turpitudes of the *Vallabhakula* as he had seen them, our author sets about opening the reader's eyes on the "true" (*āsalī*) nature of Śrī Nāthjī, by giving a detailed description of the old *pīṭhikā.* This is done in a kind of sing-song.

> They call it Viṣṇu—but his marks are not of Viṣṇu, O Brother
> This is a mūrtī of Kālī Bhairava and his mother is Kālī!
> ...
> Viṣṇu wears no garland made of snakes, hanging from his neck—
> He wears a Kaustubha jewel of great brilliance.
> But this is a Bhairava *mūrti,* whose mother is Kālī!
> ...
> Who else is there, tell me on whose head a beautiful parrot stands?
> Why is his left hand risen?
> ...
> He has a dog near him, a serpent hanging from his neck:
> This is *mūrti* of Kāl Bhairava, whose mother is Kālī!

Blakaṭānanda, then, embarks on the comparison between Śrī Nāthjī and Śrī Dvārkānāthjī, the latter admittedly a truly Vaiṣṇava icon.

No one is obliged to take Blakaṭānanda at his word, especially as his narrative is rather confused and his knowledge about Buddhist icons and Buddhist names appears scanty. But we cannot doubt that he was in a position to observe the naked *pīṭhikā* at close quarters, and that he did his best about it. Unable to make a photograph of the naked *pīṭhikā,* he set about making a pen-sketch of it, which he incorporated in his book, side by side with a photograph copy of a Jaina "Baṭuk Bhairava" found in the Mathura Museum (D. 26). That Jaina Bhairava is a *śānta,* not an *ugra* icon, but the comparison between the Jaina Bhairava and the "Śrī Nāthjī" does show a general resemblance and the dog is present in both icons.

Studying the Blakaṭānanda pen-sketch of the Śrī Nāthjī *pīṭhikā,* we find, starting from below:

- lower left corner medallion: two cows
- lower right corner medallion: two birds (cranes or peacocks?)
- middle left medallion: a dog, with a snake head below
- middle right medallion: a dishevelled female face (Birakāl? with a snake head on top of the face.
- upper left medallion: a male sitting figure (a cowherd?)
- upper right medallion: two male sitting figures
- on top in the middle, above the god's head: a parrot.[32]

Under the Baṭuka Bhairava icon, the author writes (in Hindi):

> Readers! The two icons are alike. They seem to belong to Buddhist times. This one is Baṭuk Nāth, a Door-Keeper of the Jaina Tīrthaṅkaras, and admittedly the Buddhist icons are connected with the Jaina tradition—therefore the two icons can be traced to Buddhist times.

Under the right (Śrī Nāthjī) icon, he writes:

> Who will hear me? Whom shall I tell?
> One is deaf and the other is blind!
> Bhairon they call Viṣṇu—unable to reflect in their minds!

Blakaṭānanda then, who probably was a Gauḍīya Vaiṣṇava, comes back to the story of "Gosain Mādhavendra Purī", the Daśanāmī ascetic who was "the Guru of Caitanya Mahāprabhu". Then he once more expresses his indignation about the lies of the Vallabhites in these terms:

> Those [Vallabhite] gurus named the image according to their own mind: such people were forever changing the names, the places (*dhāma*), the images (*pratimā*), the castes (*jāti*), the stories (*bāt*), the fathers (*bāp*) and so on. How far shall I praise such "Ustāds"? But such is the fact. The above image [the pen-sketch] has been drawn according to the thorough investigation (testing) of the *Blakaṭānanda Purāṇa*.

Conclusion

Is the Blakaṭānanda "revelation" the last word on the problem of Śrī Nāthjī, the Lord of the Govardhan Hill? Is the mystery of his origins and acquaintances really solved? It is up to indologists to ponder the evidence I have collected and to try and elucidate the matter. As to myself, I am conscious that by attempting to draw evidence from a number of sources—including some unwritten ones—in order to elucidate the saga of the mysterious "Śrī Nāthjī", I have probably whipped up more problems about his identity than I have solved or tried to solve.

Yet, somehow, I am inclined to believe that such "unsolvable" problems may help us to keep awake as Indologists, since they force us to approach Hinduism on its own terms rather than on ours—without the support of a theoretical scheme. Hinduism, as we know, is not simply "a religion", not even a fascinating complex of religions "dont le centre est partout et la circonférence nulle part". Our Western minds somehow find it impossible to embrace it as a whole or even to give it consistency.

The case of the illustrious "Śrī Nāthjī" who once upon a time "emerged" from a crack in the rock of the Govardhan hill, was eventually carried away to Mewar in Rajasthan and made his residence at Nāthdvāra—yet remains to this day mysteriously present within the sacred hill with which he is identified—appears as a good example of the conflicting beliefs and the conflicting forces at work for many centuries within Hinduism as a whole.

NOTES

1. The word *govardhana* has been interpreted by Growse [1974 rpt of (1894): 5 and 169] as "a rearer of cattle" or "a nurse of cattle", an interpretation which suggests that the cows have not been just placed within the hill but that they actually "grow out of" the hill, which is endowed with the magical power of the

anthill as the seat of wealth; see Sontheimer, 1979: 2: "The origins of the god may also be found in the worship of the anthill...." Another interpretation of *govardhan*, as "wealth from cowdung", appears equally valid, in view of the importance which is attached to cowdung as a magical substance in the ancient pastoral tradition. Cf. *infra*, para. 3.

2. Cf. Coomaraswamy: *History of Indian and Indonesian Art*. 1927; Diskalar *et al.*, especially H. Goetz 1952: 51.
3. Mārtaṇḍa Bhairava, connected by tribals both with the hill and with the sun, Sūrya, was identified with Khaṇḍobā. Khaṇḍobā's association with the sun is supported by being worshipped on Sundays, like the Siddhanāth of Mhasvaḍ in Maharashtra, who is Kālabhairava. Sontheimer 1976: 27, 160.
4. In ancient iconography, only the hill-top is lifted, revealing the cave below. In more recent accounts and in modern iconography Kṛṣṇa-Gopāl uproots the whole hill, which he supports with a single finger.
5. At the earliest stage, Balarāma is not represented anthropomorphically, but in form of weapons, palm-capital and lion-plough; cf. N.P. Joshi 1979, 29-30.
6. "We are milkmen and we live in the forests and hills. Hills, forests and cattle, these are our supreme benefactors [...] from hills we derive the greatest of benefits. We should therefore start sacrifices in honour of the hills. Let cows and bulls decorated with autumnal flowers go round yonder hill", *HV* 59.
7. Apparently, in ancient times, it was primarily the southern part of the hill, from Govardhan town to Puñchri, which was held divine. It is also the area in which most Buddhist icons were found. The northern part of the hill was later colonized by the Gauḍīya Vaiṣṇavas, followers of Caitanya, who, to this day, worship the hill as divine and do not set foot on it (see map).
8. Cf. *infra*, para. 3.
9. Except on the *Annakūṭ* and *Makar Saṅkrānti* days, on which both *pakka* and *kacca* foods are offered to Baldev.
10. The icons are "Mathureśji", owned as a secondary *svarūpa* by the Tilkhayat of Nāthdvāra (first *gaḍḍī*); "Madanmohanji", owned by the Gosvāmī of the Ghanaśyām *gaḍḍī*, at Kāmban (Rāj) and "Gokulnāthjī", under the control of the Gokul Gosvāmī in Gokul (Braj). The first two icons remain in their respective temples, whereas Gokulnāthjī resides in Gokul: at the time of the *Annakūṭ* festival, Gokulnāthjī is brought from Gokul to Jatipurā in a procession and placed in his temple. The Gokulnāthjī icon is four-armed Viṣṇu-Kṛṣṇa, playing a flute.
11. This superposition is the common pattern prevailing all over the Braj area—though normally the roundish stone is just balanced on top of the quadrangular, higher one and is not cemented. Paul Toomey (1984: 167-9 and fn. 42) remarks that "unlike icons, Govardhan stones do not require formal consecration (*pratiṣṭhā*) when installed in a temple nor does their sanctity depend upon the continued ritual maintained by Brahman priest". Aniconic deities are not susceptible to caste pollution.
12. This event took place in A.D. 1492, according to *Śrī Nāthjī prākaṭya kī vārtā*, translated in Vaudeville 1980: 18-21.
13. On that particularity, cf. *infra*, para. 6, about the dog's presence on the famous *pīṭhikā* of Śrī Nāthjī.

14. Cf. *supra*, n.1.
15. About Saḍḍūpāṇḍe and his discovery, cf. Vaudeville 1980: 18-21.
16. The interpretations differ according to the Panda consulted. One of those told Toomey ([184 (MS), 61] that "the standing stone is Krishna and the lower stone is Govardhan" which does not make much sense. The "specialists" do not seem to know what to make of the higher stone. For the "vallabhized" Brajvāsī Pandas, both the stones ought to be one, since Govardhan and Kṛṣṇa-Gopāl are one.
17. Cf. *infra*, para. 3.
18. On the importance of cowdung as a fertiliser and the extraordinary virtues attributed to it in archaic societies all over the world, I have benefited from the penetrating study by René Gandillon (former Inspecteur général des Archives de France), published in 1978 in *Memoires de la Société d'Agriculture...* (Paris) and entitled: *La bouse de vache, Etude d' Ethnologie.*
19. Mārgaśīrṣa (or "Agahan") is said to be the best of the months in the *Gītā.* But all the twelve *pūrṇimās* of the Hindu year also belong to Baldev in Braj and many devotees visit the Baldev temple every month.
20. Belonging to the time of the Kuṣāna ruler Huviṣka; Cf. J.P. Vogel 1926: 42.
21. Typically, the name of the Baldev temple is omitted on the "Braj parikrama" map printed on the cover of P.D. Mital's book *Braj ke utsav, tyauhār aur mele* (1966), though in the book itself, the author notes the importance of the *melā* which takes place at "Baldev" on the god's feast day. But the offering of *bhaṅg* to Baldev, *horribile dictu,* is not mentioned.
22. A timid attempt at re-asserting the role of Baldev as protector of the infant Krishna is seen in a relatively modern shrine at Mahāban, in the Braj area.
23. Baldev seems to lead as a wrestler: according to the *Malla Purāṇa* (6.37-8, Sandesara, 1948) wrestlers should remember Balarāma and the serpent Vāsukī and put three knots on their crests (*śikhā*).
24. The story is told at length in *Caitanya-caritrāmṛta, Madhya-līlā,* 19-20.
25. The quadrangular black face of Śrī Nāthjī resembles the face of Jagannāth but for the head-dress and the shape of the eyes, which are not round but slanting.
26. In the Blakaṭānanda pen-sketch, the deity wears a curious type of cap or bonnet.
27. The author contacted a distinguished Vallabhite scholar who had seen the *pīṭhikā* naked. As the light was very poor, the gentleman could not distinguish clearly the motives carved around the *pīṭhikā.* All he could make out was a dog—which to him appeared rather puzzling.
28. This event occurs between A.D. 1501 and 1503, according to Barz (1976: 29).
29. Cf. Barz 1976: 33. Vallabha, a prolific writer, deals with the subject of pride and arrogance "that usually result from renunciation" in two of his works included in the *Ṣoḍoshagrantha* in the first of these, called *Bhaktivārdhinī*, Vallabha declares that living in solitude may be an obstacle to the practice of bhakti; the quotation above is found in the second book, the *Saṃnyāsanirṇayaḥ* (verse 13).
30. According to Eschmann/Kulke/Tripathi, (1978: 174), Narasiṃha can also be identified with Śiva in his aspect as Ekapāda Bhairava.
31. Stietencron (Eschmann *et al.*, 1978: 61-2) discussed the term *Jagannātha*, 'Lord of the world,' "applied to Buddha, to Śiva and Viṣṇu". The same author notes

that "the application of the term Jagannāth for Viṣṇu in Puri occurs for the first time in the early fourteenth century" and that "the correlation of Jagannātha with Viṣṇu was brought about by tantricism".

32. Blakaṭānanda does not comment on the strange half-conical cap or bonnet worn by Śrī Nāthjī.

REFERENCES

Barz, Richard 1976. *The Bhakti sect of Vallabhācārya.* Faridabad: Thomson Press.

Coomaraswamy, A.K. 1927. *History of Indian and Indonesian Art.* London.

Entwistle, A. 1987. *Braj, centre of Krishna pilgrimage.* Groningen: Egbert Forsten.

———. 1983. Kailā Devī and Lāṃguriyā. In *Indo-Iranian Journal,* 25, 85-101.

Eschmann, A., Kulke, H., Tripathi, G.C. (eds.) 1978. *The cult of Jagannath and the regional tradition of Orissa.* Delhi.

Goetz, H. 1952. The earliest interpretation of the myth of Kṛṣṇa-Govinda. In *Journal of the Oriental Institute* (Baroda), 1.

Growse, F.S. 1974. *Mathura: A District Memoir.* AES rpt, Asian Educational Services, Delhi 1974, (edn. of 1894 has been used).

Härtel, H. 1973. A Kuṣāṇa Nāga temple at Sonkh. *Mathura Centenary Number,* July-December.

Joshi, N.P. 1979. *Iconography of Balarāma.* New Delhi.

Leshnik, L.S. and Sontheimer, G.D. (eds.) 1974. *Pastoralists and Nomads in South Asia.* Heidelberg/Wiesbaden.

Mital, P.D. 1966. *Braj kā sāṃskṛtik itihās.* Mathura: Agravāl, Press.

———. 1966. *Braj ke utsav tyauhār aur mele.* Mathura: Sāhitya Saṃsthān.

Sandesara, Bh. (ed.) 1948. *Mallapurāṇa.* Ahmadabad.

Sontheimer, G.D. 1976. *Birobā, Mhaskobā und Khaṇḍobā,* Wiesbaden.

———. 1979. Some incidents in the history of god Khaṇḍobā. In *Asie du Sud. Traditions et changements* M. Gaborieau and A. Thorner (eds.), (VIth European Conference on Modern South Asian Studies 1978) Paris.

———. 1984. The Mallāri-Khaṇḍobā myth as reflected in folk art and ritual. In *Anthropos* 79, 155-70.

Toomey, Paul 1984. *Food from the mouth of Krishna* (MS).

Vaudeville, Ch. 1974. *The Cowherd-god in Ancient India.* In Leshnik and Sontheimer 1974: 102-3.

———. 1980. The Govardhan myth in northern India. In *Indo-Iranian Journal,* 22, 19-20.

Vogel, J.P. 1926. *Indian Serpent Lore.* London.

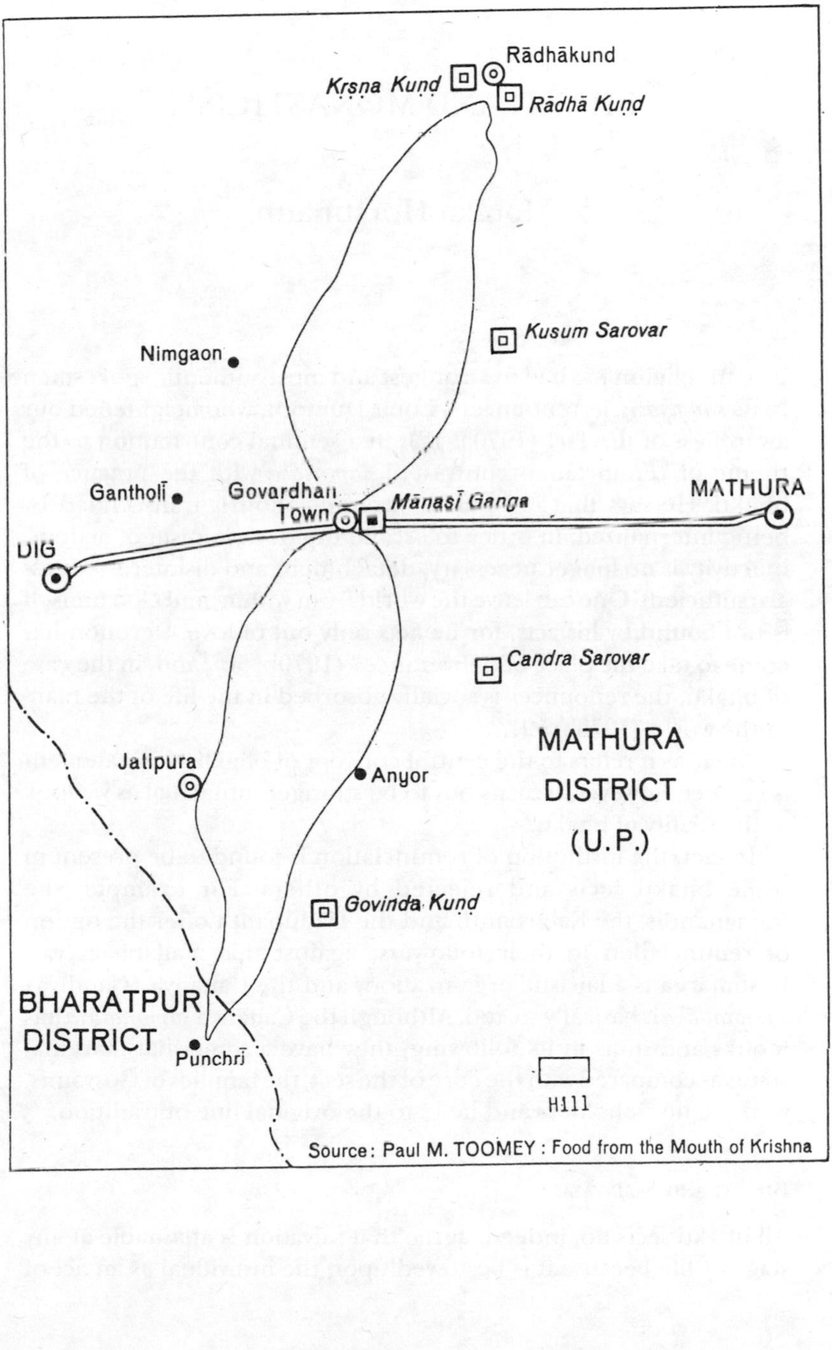

Source: Paul M. TOOMEY : Food from the Mouth of Krishna

BHAKTI AND MONASTICISM

Monika Horstmann

Indian religion has had its strongest and most authentic spokesmen in its *saṃnyāsīs*, its renouncers. Louis Dumont, who heightened our awareness of this fact (1970a: 12), in a seminal contribution to the theme of renunciation contrasted *saṃnyāsa* with the practice of bhakti. He says that in bhakti "...renunciation is transcended by being internalized; in order to escape the determinism of actions, inactivity is no longer necessary, detachment and disinterestedness are sufficient. One can leave the world from within, and God himself is not bound by his acts, for he acts only out of love. Devotion has come to take the place of deliverance" (1970b: 56), and, in the case of bhakti, the renouncer is socially absorbed in the life of the man-in-the-world (1970b: 59).

As far as it refers to the central concept of bhakti, this statement is correct; however, it turns out to be strangely unfactual as we look at the reality of bhakti.

In fact, the institution of renunciation is found to be present in some bhakti sects and rejected by others. For example, the Ramanandis, the Kabīrpanth and the Dādūpanth offer the option of renunciation to their followers; against this, Vallabhācārya's Puṣṭimārga is a laicistic organization, and the Caitanya (Gauḍīya) *sampradāya* is basically so, too. Although the Caitanya *saṃpradāya* has monks and nuns in its following, they have a somewhat marginal status as compared with the core of the sect, the families of Gosvāmīs, who are householders and heirs to the original line of tradition.

Bhakti and *Saṃnyāsa*

All bhakti sects do, indeed, agree that salvation is attainable at any stage of life because it is bestowed upon the individual as an act of divine grace. Nonetheless, all these sects arising in the middle ages were confronted with the institution of renunciation as it existed. As we shall see, it was not so much renunciation in itself that bhakti religion rejected but the soteriological and ontological concept on which *saṃnyāsa* relies. It was this concept that was found to be incompatible with bhakti.

Saṃnyāsa is based on the concept that liberation cannot be attained unless one gives up the life of a householder. The timeless, primordial status of being cannot, according to this concept, be attained with the caste-bound, ritual-bound relative status of a householder. A *saṃnyāsī* candidate has to die to the world during the various steps of his initiation into *saṃnyāsa.* However, his is not a negative status but at the same time a positive one since he ritually appropriates the world of the householder by interiorizing the householder's sacrificial fires, which constitute the central symbol of a householder's life. The *saṃnyāsī* becomes the repository of the whole world, here and beyond. He becomes the cosmic man himself. According to the early injunctions, if not necessarily in reality, he should roam about solitarily carrying the whole world with himself. *Saṃnyāsa* is to be an absolute state of freedom and perfect being. Against this, no bhakti follower can claim such a status, be he layman or monk. This would run counter to the principle of the Supreme Being's free grace which can be granted to anyone, householder and renouncer alike. Liberation granted in the process of bhakti cannot be confined to a ritual process. A bhakti devotee who is possessed by fervent devotion dies to the world too, but in so dying he cannot claim to possess an absolute status inaccessible to those who remain alive in the world.

The conceptually based adversity to *saṃnyāsa* of the orthodox type is expressed by its most shrewd critic Vallabhācārya, the founder of the Puṣṭimārga (1479-1531). Vallabha's position in this matter has been discussed earlier.[1] Here we may recall how he juxtaposes *saṃnyāsa* and bhakti in his treatise *Saṃnyāsanirṇaya:*

> It cannot be accepted that one should undergo *saṃnyāsa* in order to become accomplished in the nine-fold practice of bhakti, for the practice of the nine-fold bhakti must be observed in the company of helpful people and it must be observed continually. (3)

> Moreover, because there is pride inherent in *saṃnyāsa* and specific duties are imposed upon a *saṃnyāsī,* the two religious systems are incompatible. (4ab)[2]

Here Vallabha emphasizes two aspects of bhakti that are at variance with the principle of *saṃnyāsa.* (1) Bhakti is a type of religion wherein the devotee relies on the community of fellow-devotees who all work in common towards their spiritual betterment, whereas *saṃnyāsa* cannot be anything but a solitary affair. (2) *Saṃnyāsa,* Vallabha says, brings about conceit and a host of religious duties (such as the regimen of begging, roaming about, etc.), whereas bhakti means complete surrender to the Supreme Being and therefore rules out all other commitments.

The last-mentioned point Vallabha makes is directed against the practice of *saṃnyāsa* which produces conceit instead of non-attachment and an involvement in all sorts of religious duties in the name of liberation. More than one of the commentators on Vallabha's text have interpreted this point in a fundamentally conceptual way. In doing so, they once again underline the basic theological difference between *saṃnyāsa* and bhakti practice. One of them says:

> On embracing *saṃnyāsa* there arises conceit in oneself expressed in the idea 'This is I' brought about by the *mahāvākyas tat tvam asi* etc., whereas, on the path of bhakti and as soon as one has dedicated oneself totally to God, there arises a dependence of one's whole personality (*deha*), of one's life and senses on God, and therefore, due to one's subservience to God, there cannot be any conceit.[3]

A little further on, in the same context, he defines what it is that a devotee gives to God and contrasts it with *saṃnyāsa*: it is *parityāga,* giving oneself in an act of the total dedication (*sarvasamarpaṇarūpa*).[4] Finally, in the same paragraph he states that without the feeling of subservience to God, the devotee would be unable to perform the service of God which is rewarded by the devotee's being allowed to partake of the *ucchiṣṭas,* the remnants of the sacrificial matter enjoyed by God.

This criticism is directed against the very heart of the *saṃnyāsa* concept. The advaitic quotations mentioned are part of the central act of the *saṃnyāsa* ritual and are recited when the novice has deposited the sacrificial fires within himself and is on the point of undergoing ritual death in order to become a non-perishable being of a cosmic order, all this according to the treatises on *saṃnyāsa.*[5] That is to say, the theologians of the Puṣṭimārga do not denounce *saṃnyāsa* because of its insincere enactment but because they flatly deny that the concept of *saṃnyāsa* is valid. I think that it is not too sweeping a generalization to say that the bhakti approach to religion on the whole would be in agreement with the arguments of the Puṣṭimārgīya writers.

Bhakti and World-Renunciation

Yet, if we look closely enough at bhakti texts and at the lives of the paragons of bhakti, we cannot help admitting that bhakti cannot lead anywhere but to withdrawal from the world.

It is true that this tendency is counterpoised by the community aspects of bhakti practice, but ultimately, in its most radical form, seems to be incompatible with life in the world. Before proceeding to historical examples in evidence of this contention, let me just recall a passage from the *Bhāgavatapurāṇa* that forms a *locus classicus* for all treatises on the effects of bhakti. In this passage the nine items of bhakti practice are described and the effect of the bhakti practice on the devotee is described. In the last verse the ultimate state of bhakti is described as follows:

> Thinking of the lord they [i.e. the devotees] sometimes cry, sometimes they laugh, rejoice, talk—they are beyond the world (*alaukikāḥ*). They dance, they sing in praise of Him who was never born, they imitate Him, and they are struck dumb; having reached the Highest One they are at peace.[6]

No matter how much we may like to consider bhakti as a religion that can be practised by "leaving the world from within", as Dumont put it, we have to take passages such as these seriously because they prefigured the behaviour and conception of the historical *bhaktas* we are dealing with. The majority of these men and women whose charisma had its source in mystic experience had a tendency to break away from the world. It is obvious that this phenomenon lies at the core of all mystic experience. As universally testified to by the mystics themselves, the movements of mystical union are neither producible nor reproducible at will and are usually brief. This briefness and spontaneity are two of the genuinely religious traits they have that distinguish them from all other sensations metamorphorically related to them. This is why the mystic's career is set in the tension between the brief moments of mystic union and an ensuing incessant struggle for the renewal of the timeless state of union. This is what Indian literature describes as the dialectic between *sahaja* (mystic union) and *viraha* (separation). Even if the mystic slips out of the state of union and resumes his ordinary worldly life, he is unlikely to take a pre-mystic stance in approaching worldly matters.

For the time being, I will call the kind of withdrawal from the world that is caused by the mystical struggle "spontaneous individual renunciation" in order to distinguish it from organized forms of renunciation. This kind of renunciation is brought about by a feeling of loathing or detestation of the world (*ghṛṇā, nirveda*) or by a universal feeling of detachment (*vairāgya*). The term *vairāgya* is also used in *saṃnyāsa* texts where, too, it is called the prerequisite of renunciation. Besides this, *vairāgya* has also assumed the meaning of institutionalized renunciation, i.e. monasticism, and generally refers to Vaiṣṇava monasticism. To this we will turn presently. For the moment we will, however, briefly review a few historical cases of spontaneous renunciation.

One famous case is Caitanya (1486-1533), who under the influence of a *saṃnyāsī* called Mādhavendra Purī and expressing in a most radical way the bhakti propounded in the *Bhāgavatapurāṇa* passage quoted earlier, broke away from his life as a householder and became a renouncer.—Dādū (*c.* 1544-1604), a saint from north-west India, married and a father of four, likewise gave up his householder's status. He did not leave his family physically but transformed his family, along with the rest of his following, into a kind of spiritual family. A modern example would be Rāmakṛṣṇa who, though married, never consummated his marriage and established his wife as a sort of divine mother.

An especially interesting case of *vairāgya* depicted as the radical consequence of total bhakti is provided by a seemingly negative example, namely, once again, by Vallabhācārya. Neither was he himself a renunciate nor are the monks in his *sampradāya.* A very perceptive analysis, of which we will recall just the following, has been provided earlier (Barz 1976: 32-6). Unlike many other bhakti devotees, Vallabhācārya is not a *māyāvādin* who denounces the world as illusory. However, the whole world is thought to be in, and to rely on, God. Kṛṣṇa is the life of the world and therefore the giver of life. In consequence of this, the family as the worldly source of life is considered good. Moreover it provides the nucleus of the "company of the righteous", that is, the community of devotees. Lastly, only in the state of a householder can one fulfil the temple ritual and thus become fit to partake of the left-overs of the sacrificial matter (which is held to have already been enjoyed previously by God). On the other hand, Vallabha is also said to have originally had the intention of remaining unmarried in the interest of undivided devotion to Kṛṣṇa and, after having ultimately given in to a divine ordinance to marry, to have embraced *vairāgya* in the very final stage of his life. This is said to have happened in the manner he himself had considered to be the only condition providing for renunciation. Vallabha teaches that renunciation is only acceptable if a person is drawn away from life towards Kṛṣṇa by Kṛṣṇa himself and in a total act of *parityāga* (called *vyasana*, "obsession").[7]

However the cases of spontaneous renunciation may differ among themselves, they all share a common trait: in no case can a bhakti renouncer claim to have gained, out of his own accord, a superior state of existence. It is herein that we have to consider the essential difference between *saṃnyāsa* and the spontaneous type of individual *vairāgya*. In the *saṃnyāsa*-ritual the individual himself, or his guru on his behalf, bring about the candidate's ascent to the rank of a liberated being, while in bhakti only God's grace is thought to be able to bestow liberation. Liberation is not a ritual process but a lifelong struggle. Moreover, the reward of bhakti is bhakti itself, that is, the experience of the divine. Liberation is considered to be of secondary importance.

Bhakti and Institutionalized *Vairāgya*

The spontaneous *vairāgya* embraced by charismatic personalities like those mentioned tended to evoke like reactions on the part of their immediate following. A striking case is that of the six first-generation Gosvāmīs of Caitanya's sect who were the first propounders of Caitanya's doctrines. All of them were renouncers, while this was not the case in subsequent generations. In fact, Gosvāmīs of this sect are householders and the Caitanyite tradition is handed down within the various Gosvāmī families, who also provide the hereditary custodians of Caitanyite temples.

Other groups, however, in which the trend towards renunciation became institutionalized, developed regular orders of monks and nuns. The most common designation of these monks and nuns is *vairāgīs* and *vairāgiṇīs*, respectively.

As would be expected, the charismatic influence of an outstanding *bhakta* will rarely prevail much longer than the first generation of a newly emerging sect. It would further be expected that rules for the monastic life would evolve and also that there would be attempts to define the status of the renouncers as opposed to that of the laity. For, it would seem reasonable to ask, if both monk and layman have equal access to grace, what difference would there be between them other than a differing claim to intensity of devotion. It is hard to make out an essential soteriologically or ontologically founded difference between them.

The Dādūpanth: A Case Study

With this question in mind I looked at the Dādūpanth, a bhakti sect of western India with a following consisting of monks and laymen. On the basis of both sectarian writings (such as treaties on monastic life) and of actual observation I have attempted to study the problem as a double question: (1) What remains to be achieved by a layman, and (2) What is the relative position of householder and monk?

The sect was founded at the turn of the seventeenth century. Its founder, Dādū, died in 1604. The sect comprises *viraktas* (a variant of the term *vairāgī* and meaning a monk or a nun) who live in monasteries or convents; wandering ascetics who have their base in a monastery, but do not permanently live there; ash-smeared (*khākī*) *viraktas* who move about continually throughout the year, except during the ritually defined rainy season, and who have no permanent dwelling; *makānavāle viraktas,* monks who live in houses of their own and follow worldly occupations; and, finally, former warrior-ascetics, who may go on living in their monasteries, but nowadays mostly follow worldly occupations. The *makānavāle* monks and the former warrior-ascetics have no nuns in their following, while the others have, though not many. I concentrate here on the *viraktas* who live in monasteries and have no worldly occupations and are therefore the group most distinct from householders. Finally, I only rarely consider the ash-smeared ascetics who have not been made the object of any study so far and with whom I have had only superficial contact.

If a monk or a nun is asked what the characteristics of a perfect *virakta* are, he or she will reply (the replies hardly vary): (1) he finds the world detestable and shuns it because it is false and illusory; (2) he finds satisfaction in nothing but the Supreme Self; (3) he is pure (*śuddha*) and (4) he is peaceful (*śānta*). It was this often repeated minimal definition, which would hold good for any lay-

bhakta, too, which prompted me to investigate what the sectarian sources themselves have to say with respect to *vairāgya*.

The early sectarian sources illustrate very clearly how the monastic branch of the sect emerged. The first disciples were given an unelaborate *dīkṣā* during which Dādū put his hand on the novice's head.[8] There was no special monastic regimen, such as rules for conduct. All religious performance was meant to be interiorized[9] which is typical of the non-iconic bhakti Dādū adhered to. The only visible elements in religious practice would be listening to the bhajans and homilies in the *satsaṃga*, the community of the pious devotees. No matter how unelaborate the initiation into the monastic branch may have been, no matter how unstructured this branch itself may in the beginning have been, it is here that institutionalized renunciation starts.

Despite the charismatic atmosphere permeating the initial phase of this bhakti order, the main problem of such an organization existed from the very beginning. In many cases *vairāgya*, though it was claimed to have been embraced by individual choice and genuine desire, was in fact often adopted for semi-spiritual or even non-spiritual reasons. Hindu culture has always offered the option of institutional renunciation for the destitute and social drop-out. For this reason it was not all unusual that small children should become monks. They were made over to the order in fulfilment of vows, out of poverty, out of a pious inclination on the part of their guardians, and for many other reasons. Since in this sect nearly all male renouncers join during their childhood, it is obvious that there are more monks by habit than by genuine religious choice. The problematic practice of adopting novices at an age at which they are hardly able to understand what they are expected to become detached from, is reflected and somehow glorified in the many miracle stories relating to the precocious spiritual insight and scriptural knowledge which this or that saint attained during his childhood.

Householder versus *Virakta*: The Ideology of Their Ultimate Unity and Their Operational Duality

The problem of bhakti, then, is that the basic idea of the freely accorded grace of God in principle annihilates the mutual antagonism of householder versus renouncer. However, this is counteracted by the "radical" mystic *bhakta's* individual urge to renounce the world and the sometimes ensuing social momentum of an emerging body of fellow-renouncers. In consequence of this, we find in bhakti a conceptual egalitarian unity ("all men are dependent on God's grace") and a newly arising dual structure alike. There is a perpetual tension between a kind of *vairāgya* that allows for the fulfilment of the demands of the world and a radical type of *vairāgya*; this is evidenced very clearly in premodern and modern rules of conduct for *bhaktas*. Here I quote just one representative example from a non-sectarian source. There is a widely circulated Hindi catechism (issued by the famous Gītā Press) that says, under the heading of *Vairāgya*: "Wife and children who, from the point of view of an unenlightened person, seem enjoyable and happiness-granting, become detestable (*ghṛṇita*) and inflicting the cause of misery" as soon as one has *vairāgya*.[10] There is a footnote referring to this sentence: "From this nobody should draw the conclusion that one should detest wife and children in practice (*vyavahāra*). A pious householder should treat everyone as lovingly as he can but should remain detached [*vairāgya* is the word used in here] in his mind."[11]

So the difference between a householder and a renouncer is conceived of as an operational one (*vyāvahārika*). By the standard of unconditioned truth (*parama tattva*), as we would infer, they are identical; operationally they fall apart. A householder is a *virakta* in spirit, it is claimed; a monk is a *virakta* in spirit and flesh. In practice—that is, specifically in the way householders and monks interact—a clear-cut dual structure superimposed on the unifying principle is at work, as we shall now see.

Householder versus *Virakta*: Practice of a Dual Status

Initially, no much thought was given to a Dādūpanthī monk's status and rules. No rules different from those applying to a householder were enunciated. In other words, during Dādū's lifetime there did not yet exist specific monastic rules. The organization of the other was simply governed by the expressed rejection of sectarian emblems and by the injunctions that were in congruence with the popular religious literary genre of the rules of conduct for an "ideal Vaiṣṇava".[12] Rules enforcing celibacy or poverty were not even considered, for the charismatic influence of the founder was obviously so spiritually satisfying that straying from such basic injunctions was too insignificant to be worth recording. Since the last third of the seventeenth century, however, specific rules seem to have been in existence. Dādū also treats of them in his songs and in innumerable didactic verses. Here is a song of his which is illustrative of this genre:

REFRAIN

The chief ornament among saints is he who sings the excellencies of Govinda;

Who worships Rāma, forsakes worldly pleasures, and takes no thought of the self.

(1) He who speaks not idly with his mouth, and
slanders not another;
Who departs from evil and practices virtue,
whose heart is with Hari;

(2) He who bears enmity to none, esteeming other
spirits as his own;
Who, forgetful of self, seeks equally the good
of all;

(3) He, who beholding the divine presence in all,
makes no distinction between himself and others;
Who, sincere in his heart, speaks truth,
and devoutly meditates;

(4) He, who worshipping Him who is void of fear, is
himself set free and nowise entangled.
Says Dādū: In all the world perchance there is
such a one.[13]

Moreover, Dādū composed quite a few songs dealing with the above-mentioned rejection of all external Vaiṣṇava symbols. Texts like these, then, form the matrix of subsequent monastic rules, interspersed with more specific rules of conduct. I give here the schematic list of contents of one such manual, one Dāsa's *Grantha parakhyā*.[14] Even today it continues to be popular and has been reprinted in a monks' catechism circulated by one particular monastery.[15] In its stylistic make-up it is an exact replica of certain texts on the "ideal Vaiṣṇava", to the extent of having also their usual burden, namely "such a person is a Vaiṣṇava", albeit modified to run "such a person is a Dādūpanthī". Schematically arranged, the prescriptions refer to:

(1) the prime importance of belief in the *satguru* (the true guru who is identical with God) Dādū,
(2) the "ideal Vaiṣṇava" conduct, as already alluded earlier,
(3) single-minded concentration on Rāma, on the reiteration of his name and on sermons on him,
(4) abstaining from all *saguṇa* religious belief and practice (that is, from revering iconic representations of gods), from pilgrimages, from all Vedic formalism and from feeling subject to the social demands of the world (*loka vidhi*),
(5) improprieties such as singing love-songs and *saguṇa*-songs,
(6) discarding all external signs of renunciation,
(7) mendicancy: one should accept only as much as is necessary to satisfy one's hunger,
(8) the prohibition on the accumulation of wealth,
(9) chastity which, according to the author, forms the essential difference between the householder and monk; a householder has a single wife and considers all other women as either sisters or mothers, a monk has none.

Of the nine items I have listed only the last four refer to a monk while the rest apply to both laymen and monks. Among those referring exclusively to a monk, mendicancy linked with personal poverty and chastity figure prominently

Before I go on to evaluating this list, this is the proper place to refer to another treatise on the relationship between householder and *vairāgī*. It is by Sundaradāsa (*c*. 1596-1689), the most perceptive and academically best qualified Dādūpanthi author, who was an immediate disciple of Dādū. The text looks, at least at first glance, astonishingly simplistic. It is laid out as a dialogue between a householder, who praises the blessings of marriage in a rather homely way, and a monk, who tries, with modest success, to convince the stubborn householder that what he enjoys is just a disgusting lump of bones, flesh and foul fluids. The two positions in the dialogue with its stock motifs remain unreconciled until the *vairāgī* cuts the knot by making the following statement which marks the end of the text:

The householder says: "Great is the state of a householder; when
an ascetic comes to him [that is, to the householder],
He becomes satisfied since he obtains all alms". (17)

The *vairāgī* says: "This is just the way the body is made;
All five kinds of sins[16] vanish if an ascetic comes and obtains something". (18)

The way of life of a *virakta* is sustained by the householder and the *virakta* saves the householder.
As the forest protects the lion, so the lion protects the forest. (19)

The *virakta* is one who reveres only God; a householder serves the *virakta*;
The horse has two equal ears, and such is the difference between an ascetic and a charitable [householder]. (20)[17]

Taking into account also Sundaradāsa's statement, I will now resume the evaluation of the monastic rules.

Two rules emerge from the text that are fundamental; one is mendicancy plus personal poverty, the other is sexual abstinence. Other rules are of a more external nature. Also nowadays the commitments of a monk are specifically monastic only with regard to these two regulations. A monk's commitments today are

snāna, bathing
pāṭha, reading the scripture
ārāti, celebrating the (mostly communal) evening service
mendicancy
sexual abstinence
giving of *prasāda*, the "gift of grace".

A householder is bound to observe the first three prescriptions, too. In addition, like any other Vaiṣṇava householder, he should also observe sexual abstinence, unless he suspends it with the noble aim of creating offspring in mind. Finally, he too has to give what is called *bhemṭa*, "donation". So the difference between the state of a householder and that of a monk lies in

sexual activity versus abstinence (with an ideal shift toward abstinence on the part of the householder, too)
giving of *bhemṭa* versus giving of *prasāda*.

The double set of rules establishes a complementary relationship between householder and renouncer. It consists in the reciprocity of exchange. The householder provides material sustenance to the monk, and the monk is supposed to return spiritual benefit to him.

This exchange of material and spiritual (in fact, often also sanctified material) substance, respectively, is connected in an essential way with the complementarity of sexual activity and sexual abstinence. I have dwelt on this elsewhere (Thiel-Horstmann 1986: *passim*) and therefore can sum up briefly how the connection between sexuality and the exchange of substance is established. A householder can only give *bheṃṭa* because he possesses worldly goods that he gains on the basis of his being established in the world, that is, in a social and economic network. This network has no continuance unless he and his kin reproduce. His reproductivity and the obligations that ensue from it bind the householder to the world. Being bound to the world renders him "impure". The monk is "pure" because he is not enmeshed in worldly affairs. Sexual activity/abstinence have the symbolic function of grading a persons' purity. So the substance that enters the cycle of exchange on the part of the householder is given out of a state of relative impurity, the substance returned by the monk is given out of a state of purity.

Both rules are, therefore, not only complementary but also interconnected. They define the status of a *vairāgī* in relationship to the world but not in its own right. In connection with this, it is also easy to understand that the complementarity of material and spiritual exchange encourage the accumulation of wealth in monastic institutions, since wealth testifies to the generosity of the laity, and, therefore, implicitly to the spiritual benefit the laity receive in return. The interdependence resting on this double rule is prominent in the sedentary mode of life of many Dādūpanthī monks and nuns. They live in monasteries and convents, they practice mendicancy, they perform profitable religious duties within a certain geographical radius. So there exists a permanent localized pattern of regular exchange between groups who form each other's clientele.

Earlier I mentioned the ash-smeared ascetics who form a separate branch of the Dādūpanth. They enact *saṃnyāsa*- and *yoga*-ideals that have been fused with bhakti. They became incorporated into the sect in its formative phase, which was a period when the organizational and conceptual borders of the various religious bodies were still fluid. This is evidenced, for example, by juxtaposition of rulers for *saṃnyāsa* which employ Haṭhayoga Symbolism with a commentary in a Vaiṣṇava vein.[18] Thus there emerged sub-branches of renouncers who represent a stratum of different actual origin that has been incorporated into the bhakti sect in question as a somewhat marginal group. The ash-smeared ascetics also observe rules which are partly different from those of other Dādūpanthī *viraktas*. Unlike these, they apply ashes on their bodies and they maintain a fire. This is not done by *saṃnyāsīs*, who have internalized the fire and therefore never keep any fire, but by the Nāthyogīs, ascetics who practice Haṭhayoga.

In connection with the idea of ritual exchange that I have treated just now, it is revealing to observe how differently the ash-smeared ascetics and the *viraktas* of the sedentary type behave when they all gather together once a year at the headquarters of the Dādūpanth to celebrate the annual celebrations of their sect. The *khākī viraktas*, the ash-smeared ones, who move about throughout the year—except for the rainy season—hold themselves apart and aloof from the others.[19] They stay in an open space outside the temple called the *khākī cauk*, "the Square of Ash-Smeared Ones", which is their only permanent address. They never enter the precincts of the temple; they do not join the rituals there which are the most sanctified ones celebrated by the sect. They never join and never have joined in the *paṅkti*, a communal feast. The temple, on the occasion of the *melā* of the sect, houses thousands of laymen and renouncers other than the ash-smeared ascetics. Here is the place of material and ritual exchange where the laymen give their supposedly lavish donations and receive *prasāda* and spiritual gratification of various kinds. The highpoints of the display of wealth on the part of the householder are the *paṅktis* at which they feed hundreds of laymen and renouncers alike. This is considered a memorable meritorious act to which laymen and monks alike refer very often afterwards. "In this or that year so-and-so arranged a *paṅkṭi*. What a great *bhakta* he is!" The ash-smeared ascetics, however, cannot share in any such activities because the ritual exchange taking place within the temple is inconsistent with the concept of having died to the world and to all ritual performance.

In contrast to the absolute freedom demonstrated by the ash-smeared ascetics, the sedentary *viraktas* are not free. Along with their householder counterparts, they constitute a geographically defined network and must not risk the withdrawal of the laity's favour. The laity have, comparably, more freedom of choice. If they feel that the *viraktas* fail to fulfil their spiritual role properly and that they themselves can, in consequence of this, no longer be sure of receiving spiritual benefit in return for their material gifts, they can very well withdraw their gifts and make them over to other cults or groups. They may even choose to support ideologically more satisfying non-religious or semi-religious bodies that they consider better qualified to satisfy their needs. This is happening these days, to dramatic effect. Thus the *virakta* is as much bound to the world as the householder, albeit in a complementary way. The contrasting example of the ash-smeared renouncers shows the *virakta* to be, in fact, very much "alive" to the world as against those who conceive themselves as having died to it.

In the conceptual basis of bhakti also lies the solution to the bewildering fact that all measures directed against dissensions within the sect have failed.[20] Loyalties have always been bound to be divided because of worldly obligations, notwithstanding the fact that the *viraktas* constantly emphasize that they are totally detached. Within the concept of bhakti no conceptual re-orientation was at hand. The concept of God's free grace and its immediate accessibility was an impediment to according a monk an existentially real status of his own and restricted his role to that of a constituent in a dual structure. That is, it made his status a relative one (the hybrid ash-smeared ascetics of the sect are left out of consideration).

The dilemma of bhakti seems to be that, carried to its extreme consequence as we find it realized in the individual religious struggle of the mystics, it is compatible neither with communal life in the community of householders nor with that of a monastic order. It is only in ultimate withdrawal from the world that it can grant spiritual fulfilment.

It is probably due to this conceptual weakness inherent in bhakti that *vairāgya* looks so moribund. On the other hand, *saṃnyāsa*, despite the gross perversities in its spiritual aspirations which occur from time to time and the atrocities that have been committed in its name, has retained a remarkable vitality to this day.

NOTES

The author was enabled to do research on Dādūpanthī source material by a grant from the Deutsche Forschungsgemeinschaft for which she wishes to express her sincere thanks. An earlier draft of this paper was kindly read by R.K. Barz, Canberra, who provided valuable suggestions and also corrected the English of the manuscript. To him I likewise express my gratitude.

1. Cf. Barz 1976: 32-4.—More recently, James D. Redington in his unpublished paper "Vallabhācārya on how *Bhakti* matures and on *Saṃnyāsa*" (1984) has

analysed the theme of spiritual progress and renunciation as treated in Vallabha's *Bhaktivardhinī* and *Saṃnyāsanirṇaya*.

2. The text with eight commentaries was edited by M.T. Telivala and D.V. Sankalia in Bombay: Nirṇayasāgar Press, 1918. It was reprinted as part of volume 3 of Vallabhācārya, *Ṣoḍaśagranthāḥ*, ed. by Shyam M. Goswamy, 3 vols. Nāthdvārā: Motimahal 1980-1 (all texts published in this re-edition have retained their original separate paging). The Sanskrit text of the passage translated reads:

   śravaṇādiprasiddhyārthaṃ kartavyaś cet sa neṣyate,
   sahāyasaṅgasādhyatvāt sādhanānāṃ, ca rakṣaṇāt. (3)
   abhimānān niyogāc ca taddharmaiś ca virodhataḥ,...(4ab)

3. Op. cit., 31; the commentary on verse 4 is by Cācā Śrīgopeśa. The Sanskrit original reads:

   saṃnyāsagrahaṇānantaraṃ tattvamasyādivākyād ātmani soham ityabhimāno bhavati, bhaktimārge tu samarpaṇānantaraṃ dehaprāṇendriyādīnāṃ bhagavadadhīnatvaṃ bhavati, tadā dāsatvān na mametyabhimāna iti.

4. Cācā Śrīgopeśa, l.c. defines *partiyāga* as *sarvasamarpaṇarūpaḥ tyāgaḥ*.
   Apart from the conceptually based criticism of *saṃnyāsa*, Śrīgopeśa puts forth also moral criticism. He calls the renouncers *dharmadhvajins*, "those who display religion on their flags" (l.c.).

   In a very similar vein, also Śrīpuruṣottama denounces *saṃnyāsa* when commenting on the verse quoted in the text of this paper. Amongst other points he emphasizes, he places weight on the solitariness of *saṃnyāsa* as against the *satsaṃga*, "the company of the pious ones" a bhakta should resort to for his spiritual betterment.

5. Cf. for example *Paramahaṃsaparivrājaka-Upaniṣad*, para 3, [The *Saṃnyāsa Upanishads with the commentary of Śrī Upanishad-Brahma-Yogin*, ed. by T.R. Chintamani Dikshit, Madras: The Adyar Library (Theosopical Society), 1929, 164].

6. XI, 3, 32; the Sanskrit text says:

   kvacid rudantyacyutacintayā kvacid dhasanti nandanti vadantyalaukikāḥ,
   nṛtyanti gāyanty anuśīlayantyajaṃ bhavanti tūṣṇīṃ param etya nirvṛttāḥ.

7. Vallabha, *Bhaktivardhinī*, verse 5, op. cit. (cf. note 4). "Obsession" is the stage at which one cannot exist any more without Hari.

8. The earliest hagiography of Dādū is by Janagopāla and is entitled *Dādūjanmalīlā*. A critical edition by W.M. Callewaert is forthcoming. The text was probably written shortly after Dādū's death. Cf. 4,6,6 (an interpolated passage). Cf. also ms L 113 of the Dādū Mahāvidyālaya Collection, Jaipur, scribed in 1827 V.S. (*c.* A.D. 1770).

9. This is emphasized in the text *Dou bacan*, for which cp. Thiel-Horstmann 1991, pp. 108-10. Thus the guru should take the place of the sectarian mark (*tilaka*); the *mana*, the purified mind, that of the rosary (*mālā*); the remembrance of the name of God that of vows (*vrata*); and the company of the pious (*satsaṃga*) should take the place of the pilgrimage [*tīrtha* (*yātrā*)]. Thus these bhaktas set themselves apart from iconic forms of worship as practiced by the *saguṇa* Vaiṣṇavism.

10. Jayadayāla Goyandakā (ed.), *Tattva-cintāmaṇi*, vol. 1. Goṛakhapura: Gītā Press, 18th ed, *c.* 1983, 224.
11. L.c.
12. F. Mallison (1985) gives an excellent survey of such texts and research done on them so far, along with an evaluation of their subject matter.
13. Dādū, *pada* 20, 15 (ed. P.R. Caturvedī; Dādūdayāla, *Granthāvalī*, Vārāṇasī: Nāgarī Pracāriṇī Sabhā, 2023 V.S.). The English translation is that given by W.G. Orr 1947: 122-3.
14. The author of the treatise, Dāsa, wrote probably between 1720-30 V.S. (c. A.D. 1663-73); cf. Surajanadāsa Svāmī (with collaboration of Keśavadāsa Svāmī) (ed.), *Śrī Dādū Mahāvidyālaya rajata-jayantī grantha*. Jaipur: Śrī Dādū Mahāvidyālaya Rajata-Jayantī Mahotsava Samiti, 2009 V.S., 80 (no. 34). The text has been edited, translated, and discussed by Thiel-Horstmann (1991).
15. Haridasa (ed.), *Mahāmahima Śrī Sukharāmajī Mahārāja kā jīvana-caritra*. Kācarodā (Phulerā): Bābā Thaṇḍīrāmajī kā akhāṛā, 2021 V.S., 82-93.
16. These sins are: maintaining a kitchen fire, grinding of food-grain (between the millstones), using a broom, pounding grain, etc., in a mortar, and keeping pots filled with water. In all these cases a househoder incurs the risk of killing insects.
17. "Gṛhavairāgabodha", *Sundara-granthāvalī*, vol. 1. ed. by H.N. Śarmā, Kalkattā: Rajasthan Research Society, 1993 V.S., 309-12; the passage quoted is to be found on pp. 311-12.
18. "Nirvāṇopaniṣat". The *Saṃnyāsa Upanishads* with the commentary of Śrī Upanishad-Brahma-Yogin. Ed. by T.R. Chintamani Diksit. Madras: Adyar Library (Theosophical Society), 1929, 134-48. The Dādūpanth is influenced in many ways by the Haṭhayoga, and its rules, as contained in the manual as mentioned before, seem to be mostly adaptions from rules for *Saṃnyāsīs*, unless they belong to the nucleus of the genre of the "ideal Vaiṣṇava" precepts.
19. The ash-smeared ascetics have similarity with the Ramanandi renouncers, for whom cf. Burghart 1983: 361-80; especially 362-7 for the external aspects of their mode of life. The extent of this similarity is unknown for there exist no studies of these ascetics.
20. According to sectarian sources, the sect nearly broke up in 1750 V.S. under the newly elected abbot-in-chief Jaitarāma who had tried to remedy schismatic symptoms by issuing rules regulating the external marks of a monk, the appropriate procedures for the investiture of abbots, hierarchical rules for holding *paṅktis* a.s.o. This semi-schism seems to have been superficially plastered over five years afterwards (1755 V.S.). In 1789 V.S., however, another case of dissent entailed a split-up of the community residing in the headquarters of the sect. Finally, after 1810 V.S. a third fight among factions occurred when a new abbot-in-chief was to be elected. For details cf. Orr 1947: ch. 10, 191ff.; Thiel-Horstmann (1985); Sv. Kanirāma Dādūpanthi, *Śrī Jayata prakāśa*, Bhivāṇī (Hariyāṇā): Śrīcanda Goyala, 1986, in which the author also publishes portions of Jñānadāsa's records of the reforms introduced by the abbot-in-chief Jaitarāma (abbotship: A.D. 1693-1732).

REFERENCES

For references to text editions see notes.

Barz, R. 1976. *The Bhakti sect of Vallabhācārya*. Faridabad, 1976.

Burghart, R. 1983. Wandering ascetics of the Ramanandis. In *History of Religions* 22/4 (May).

Dumont, L. 1970a. For a sociology of India. In *Religion, politics and history in India: Collected papers in Indian sociology*. Paris/The Hague: Mouton.

———. 1970b. World renunciaton in Indian religion. In *Religion, politics and history in India: Collected papers in Indian sociology*. Paris/The Hague: Mouton.

Mallison, F. 1985. The definition of Vaiṣṇava according to medieval Gujarātī devotional literature. In *Proceedings of the third international bhakti conference*, December 1985 (unpublished ms.).

Orr, W.G. 1947. *A sixteenth-century mystic*. London/Redhill: Lutterworth Press.

Redington, James D. 1984. Vallabhācārya on how *bhakti* matures and on *saṃnyāsa* (unpublished ms.).

Thiel-Horstmann, M. 1985. Warrior ascetics in 18th century Rajasthan and the religious policy of Jai Singh II. In *Proceedings of the third international bhakti conference*, December 1985 (unpublished ms.).

———. 1986. *Symbiotic antinomy: The social organisation of a North Indian sect*. Canberra: Faculty of Asian Studies.

———. 1991. Treatises on Dadupanthi monastic discipline. In *Pathways to literature, art, and archaeology: Pt. Gopal Narayan Bahura felicitation volume*, vol. I, Jaipur 1991, pp. 95-113.

STAYING ON THE GODDESS'S EYELID: DEVOTION AND REVERSAL OF VALUES IN HINDU BENGAL

Serge Bouez

The theoretical approaches to the problem of the Hindu goddess can be roughly divided into three main streams. The oldest, with which we shall be little concerned here, may be conveniently labelled the mother-goddess theory;[1] this point of view has been reshaped, in the projective hypothesis of G. Obeyesekere (1983). This is clearly a second approach in its own right, since this author has produced new tools and new terms for his analysis. The third hypothesis, which directly contradicts the first two, has been systematized by M. Biardeau. Being conversant with Hindu classical mythology, she puts forth the idea of a unique and mediating Goddess: in the same way as bhakti mediated between the transcendent aspirations of high caste Hinduism and popular religion, the goddess mediates between the earthly desires she can fulfil and the ideal of salvation.[2]

Despite the elegance of this encompassing scheme and its philosophical congruency, it fails to be adequate at the popular level because the author presupposes a general homology between pantheon and society, so that the demons would be the gods of the Untouchables (Biardeau 1981: 16), the high gods being conversely the deities of high caste people. The principle of this homology runs directly along the line of the pure/impure distinction, low gods being ascribed to those who perform impure functions, high ones to those who perform pure functions, especially the brahmins. However, recent studies have given strong evidences of an underlying equivalence between the extremely high and the extremely low in the Hindu hierarchy, because both categories of people have mediating functions that limit their access to the transcendant plane.[3] This logical argument is enough to cast a doubt on the encompassing capacity of the pure/impure dichotomy, a capacity that is even more undermined by some recent studies showing how this opposition is cut across by the dimension of auspiciousness.[4] We can also find, especially in the historical field, a good deal of factual evidence showing its limitations. Historical studies, when conducted with special attention to the problems of the political legitimation have shown the importance of locality in the shaping of goddess' identity, an hypothesis which, in turn, has shed some light on regional specificities in Hinduism.[5] If we are to take into account the historical dimension in the development of the mythology of the goddesses in Bengal, we should certainly distinguish between the local, folk level, and the sanskritized layer which has remodelled the former according to standard pan-Indian pauranic ideas.[6]

Such kinds of narratives, amongst which the most famous are the *Maṅgulkāvyas* (epic poems) on deities like Dharma, etc., display some kind of separateness between their popular core and their brahmanic overlay. Such is not the case in devotional literature for the latter closely intertwines both levels: brahmanic concepts are integrated in popular devotion but, as we shall see here, they are, more often than not, twisted off to the extent of going beyond the frontiers of orthodoxy.[7] How can this distortion take place and give to popular devotion a kind of universal character difficult to achieve in the Hindu hierarchized context? First of all, through the ambiguity of the Goddess's identity as a mother.

1. Mother as Goddess, but which Mother?

We can observe in the religious literature, even in very classical texts, a certain maliciousness in making the identity of the mother rather uncertain: "The husband enters as an embryo in his wife, who becomes his mother." The well-known commentary of this verse being that the husband is equated with the seed he gives to his wife, the latter's womb becoming in this way like the sacrifice out of which the sacrificer is reborn (O'Flaherty 1981:21).

No doubt, the address term *mā* borrowed from the vocabulary of kinship has too wide-ranging connotations to be used as a proper guide here: besides the mother's younger sisters who are called *mā*, can be the daughters-in-law,[8] and also a guru's wife.

As we shall try to demonstrate in this paper, the mother-infant relation is partly used as a manifest symbol for imaginary transgressive relations; it would be limited to perceive the symbolic bond between the devotee and his goddess as a mere reflection of genuine reciprocal affection between mother and son. As we know, this is the basic postulate of the projected hypothesis the general frame of which we shall, however, keep since it has proven a maximal validity as a comparative tool for analyzing the religions of South Asia, especially in the beautiful way it has been systematised by G. Obeyesekere (1983). Let us briefly summarize his main argument: in north India, the daughter has to leave her parent's home and go to a stranger's place at the time of her marriage, in this patrivirilocal context this place is her husband's father's, where she will have to stand the pressures of a hostile kinship group; therefore, the only recipient to channelize her frustrated affective needs are her children, especially her son.

There is much truth in this statement, since we can roughly observe a greater preeminence of the goddess when the father/son relation is socially strained, which is particularly the case in Bengal where the particularity of the inheritance system[9] prevents sons from sharing paternal property before the death of their father.

The restriction we can propose to this socio-psychological explanation is that the reverse situation fails to obtain: a matri-uxorilocal residence does not generate so systematically a masculine oriented pantheon. This is due to an impossibility of reducing the devotional content of the goddess/devotee relation to a mother/child relation. The erotic and aggressive overtones of the former bond, make the projective hypothesis all the less sufficient, since the goddess is often, especially in tantric fashion, a child-eater, wandering about, dishevelled and uncontrolled.[10]

These "bad" attributes naturally put the goddess on the tantric track, where she may achieve over the gods in the *śakta* tradition (a point we shall discuss in more detail in section 3), here we can just observe that the tantric atmosphere is well fit to allow for an expression of devotion in terms of madness (*mādana*). We will subscribe to L. Dumont's view (1966: 343) on tantrism according to which this system conveys a reversal of the values of purity. This reversal takes a systematic and elaborated turn in the sectarian *śakta* tradition, but can also be more directly expressed in transgressive attitudes some of which we shall discuss here.

In fact, *tantrik* is most often a term of abuse, especially when used by Vaiṣṇavas against their *śakta* opponents or the performers of blood sacrifices irrespective of their caste-origin. Orthodox Brahmins may use the word to charge, for instance, a distant member of their own family line (*kula*) they are trying to separate with in order to achieve a better status. The main point to be emphasized here is a double and seemingly contradictory process of maximal segmentation and maximal integration. Left unruled by a king of their own due to Muslim domination from the early twelfth century, Hindu Bengalis have seen their society split off to the last due to the tremendous fissiparity of social groupings; on the other hand from the fifteenth century onwards a Bengali identity has developed strongly channelized by the Gauḍiya Vaiṣṇava movement. Thanks to recorded devotion poetry dedicated to the Goddess, this move has been partly taken over by a cult to the Goddess which is known today as the hallmark of Bengali religion (everyone in India knows that Durgā *pūjā* is the *pūjā* of the Bengali).

Whether exacerbated or alleviated, hierarchy has failed to provide a totally encompassing grid for structuring the whole of the society,[11] the result being a discrepancy between labels and things, which explains the homology between religion and society does not so directly obtain as in the rest of India. This blurring situation gives to the term devotion its particular meaning here, resting at the junction between formal observance of social rules and deliberate transgression.

2. Devotion and Transgression of Social Rules

As we have just observed, the label *tantrik* is primarily a term of abuse, but the observation of actual behaviour shows a good deal of inconsistency, for instance a brahmin, vegetarian at home and expressing outer disapproval for blood sacrifice would act as a *jajman* of this type of rite at a place where he is unknown. He acts in this way for the practical results to be obtained out of the sacrifice: healing a parent, solving a money problem, the most frequent rationalization for this kind of behaviour being that the goddess (most of the time Kāli, but not always) can be called for only in such a fashion.

By having blood sacrifice performed far from his home, a Bengali brahmin can thus save his purity and look for some kind of auspiciousness (*śubha*), but it is significant that the latter can be achieved only through a prohibited practice (animal sacrifice). This also means that the outer display of shastric orthodoxy only concerns the social side of things, the religious dimension being encapsulated in what the social code disapproves of. In Bengal, sectarian tantrism allows for a transgression of social rules insofar as it is more a symbol of prohibited behaviour than an actually prohibited practice, and thus it indicates that such a practice can take place: you frequently hear this kind of statement "His behaviour is like a *tantrik's.*"

A very orthodox (*kulin*) family having a well known *śakta* (indulging in healing rituals) member will manage to save its reputation by saying "this *śakta* is also *saṃnyāsī,* so it is all right, had he been just a *tantrik,* it would not have been all right".

In fact, what orthodox people (or those taking orthodoxy at its face-value) deny in the *tantrik* is exactly what is necessary for devotion to be efficient: a minimal degree of transgression of normal social rules. From this point of view, it is significant that the most popular poets in Bengal owed their fame to a deliberately transgressive behaviour, a famous example is provided by *Candidās,* a Kṛṣṇa devotee who took as his second wife a beautiful woman of the *ḍom* caste whom he used to worship as a goddess.

Transgression of endogamy rules related to caste hierarchy finds an echo in the infringement of kinship rules, which we can illustrate by taking a famous literary example, the novel *Devi* by Rabindranath Tagore. Here we are told how a rich zamindar feels some attraction for his daughter-in-law and how he is unable to express this in an erotic idiom (since he is supposed to act towards her in accordance with an avoidance behaviour). To obviate such a difficulty, he turns his daughter-in-law into a goddess (*devī*). To achieve his purpose, his first care is to cut her off from any relations with her husband, namely his own son. Soon the young incarnate goddess is believed to possess some miraculous powers and crowds of pilgrims flock to her shrine. Unfortunately, she fails to heal the baby of her sister-in-law (therefore a grandson to her father-in-law-cum-devotee). The baby dies and her father-in-law throws her out of the house calling her a witch (*rākṣasī*).

In this example, too briefly summarized here, we can see that the sacredness of the young bride (it is noticeable that she has not had a child yet) is the produce of an extreme situation of transgression of the prescribed relation between affines. I would argue that such a transgression is structurally equivalent with the liminal situation characteristic of blood sacrifice and tantric practices in general. All of them have to be very carefully handled, otherwise, the expected auspicious result may turn into its contrary. In our last example, Devi failed because she was doomed to fail: by excluding his daughter-in-law from the field of normal social relations, her perverse devotee has sealed her destiny: she obtained nothing, but the extremes, starting as a Devi, she ends up as a Rākṣasī.

During my last fieldwork.[12] I came across an equivalent case, although less beautifully structured than Tagore's novel. There was a man of the *tili* caste named Shonkor who was very fond of his younger brother's wife, Lalati. As we know, Hindu custom proscribes any relation between people related in such a way. Ideally, they should not even talk to each other, so that if they want to communicate, they need to seek the assistance of a go-between. This was extremely difficult in our case, since the trio was living in a very small house a little apart from the village. Shonkor's feelings towards Lalati were reciprocal, a fact easily understandable when we know that the younger brother (Lalati's husband) was a rather unrefined youth who often used to leave his wife alone, to go around with friend, whereas Shonkor was a still a good-looking widower. Moreover he was much more responsible than his sibling, and had a fixed job as a Railway employee at Bolpur station.

The only way available for the expression of this reciprocal attraction was the religious medium: Shonkor acted as the devotee of his younger brother's wife. He especially used to bring her good fruit (such as mangoes, costly for his means), but as he was forbidden to give them directly to her, he used to put them on the threshold of the house saying in a rather neutral voice: "there are fruits for the *pūjā* to *mā*". But who was *mā* in this case? In fact for Shonkor this word had two meanings. *Mā* was, on the first, explicit level, the goddess *Aparājitā* represented on a cheap calendar hanging in the small inner-room of Lalati. The typical way the *pūjā* was enacted seems to militate in favour of this argument. After cutting the fruits on a leaf-plate, Lalati used to put them in front of the image of the Goddess whom she honoured by making *ārati* with incense sticks. Some bits of food being left in the plate, she would take the rest in her right hand. Meanwhile Shonkor kneeling down and touching Lalati's *sari* with his forehead, would mutter: "O *mā, prasad dao, prasad dao*" (*O mother give the prasād*), then very unexpectedly as he raised up his head and body, Latati put some bits of food directly into his mouth saying "*prasad khao, betā*" (Son, eat the *prasad*). Once Shonkor objected "*mā, khete parbo no, apni khan.*" (Mother I cannot eat it, you eat it). On this occasion he used the respectful form to address Lalati, clearing away any doubts about the goddess identity he was attributing to her at that time.

The pair avoided Lalati's husband being present at their ritual sessions; if he happened to be there, there was either no *pūjā* at all, or Lalati performed it in a very different style; she was mechanical, showed less devotion, and last but not the least, neither her husband nor his brother showed off towards her as a *mā's* devotee on such occasions.

Therefore, it is very plausible to draw an equivalence between *intense* devotion to *mā* and the ritualized transgression of kinship prohibitions. This is only possible because of the wide range of connotations of the word *mā*, such wideness, allowed for ambiguity to be expressed each time the word was used to channelize, in religious language, feelings that Shonkor and his younger brother's wife could not express directly.

So far we have come across cases of transgression of kinship rules through a religious idiom, namely the devotion to *mā*. But this devotion can also take the lawful path of the relation to *guru mā*, the guru's wife who is also addressed as *mā*. As a guru is like a god to his disciple so his wife is like a goddess. Theoretically there should be between guru's wife and the former's disciple an avoidance relation. A sexual affair between the two is counted among the five great sins (*mahāpātaka*) according to the old Hindu law code (*dharmaśāstra*), remarkably enough if this happens with a true mother it is not considered so grave.[13]

Day-to-day behaviour between the guru's wife and guru's *siṣya* (pronounce *siṣ:o*) shows a pattern rather different from the prescribed behaviour; no doubt the disciple shows to his master's wife a devotion of an almost religious nature, but this devotion is not enacted at all according to an avoidance pattern. On the contrary, observation reveals a good deal of familiarity, not to say intimacy, between the two: here it should be remembered that the disciple stays in his guru's house, which gives him all opportunities to show his eagerness to serve his *guru-mā*. In return the latter is very often kind with him, avoids using harsh words when she orders him. Moreover, the guru's wife is often quite younger than her real or spiritual husband, which counts also in the mutual attraction she may feel for her husband's *siṣya*. I would suggest here that, far from impeding the development of a religious sentiment between them, it can be the very root of it.

Here the Vaiṣṇavites seemed to be more at ease to express this fact, as a certain Robi Das from Jayadeva explained to me: "My mother (*nijer mā*) has thrown me into *saṃsāra*—when she gave birth to me—, my *guru-mā* will liberate me from *saṃsāra,* she will be my true (*sat*) life-giver (*jononi*)." He further explained that she would give him a new life (*nuton jibon*). These qualifications are enough to give the *guru-mā* the status of a goddess. However, I never met with any direct statement about it, whereas the expression *guru deber moto* (guru is like god) can be heard sometimes. After all this is not so surprising, as too direct an expression of the godly nature of the *guru-mā* could be but suspect. I would even argue that the transgression of social rules inherent in the relation to the *guru-mā* can be kept up only if the devotion towards her does not take on too overt a sentiment, otherwise what occurred in the novel to Devi would probably happen. To understand such facts, we have to keep in mind the extreme plasticity of the Hindu mind, fond of paradoxes: the eroticism inherent in the three situations we have just described is not purely a sublimation of cruder feelings, nor are these really erotic feelings a heretical deviation of the religious sentiment they convey.

The explanation for such paradox lies in the liminality pattern the three cases present. The partners to the prohibited relations are always on a threshold; they theatralise the prohibition which their actual behaviour already transgresses, and it is because this failure is always possible, that we find a sublimation of human attraction into religious feelings. The ambivalence of "religious love" is exactly the same as that imbedded in power and sacrifice: impurity is attached to these two, but life and regeneration are only possible through them. As for sacrifice, the difficulty is most of the time solved by the mythic and ritual treatment of impurity; in the case of the religious expression of unlawful sentiments, the matter is more tricky, especially in our material because it is one and the same person who bears the qualification of a goddess. This is also why she, like the goddess she represents, is made up of contradictory qualities: she is at the same time a *devī* and *rākṣasī,* a divine mother and a whore (most of the time the female-companion of a renouncer is suspected of prostitution). All these contradictory and extreme qualities contributed to make the devotion greater, exactly in the same way as blood sacrifice is very efficient and very impure.

If the transgression between disciple and guru's wife becomes real, the penance to be endured is one of the most degrading "the disciple will have the mark of a female organ impressed on the forehead with a hot iron" (Manu IX.237). Here, I would argue that in its crudeness, the punishment has something to do with the fault which it is supposed to chastise.

3. God and Goddess: The Fight for Supremacy

From the standpoint of hierarchy, the three case studies I have too briefly reported here show a very strong ambiguity concerning feminine identity in Bengal. When taken as religious objects, women are either over- or underestimated according to the standard value they represent in the social system. Truly this standard value is a low one, lower than the female lot in south India, for instance. The main reason for the low secular status of women in Bengal is to be sought in the strong remodelling of Hindu orthodoxy by the Sena kings in the twelfth century. Inferior status in society, superior rank among divine people, and one unlasting move from one position to the other which accounts for the fact that the Bengali goddess is *at the same time* terrific, cannibalous, and benign and even salvation-giving.

Tamil Hinduism has coped with this ambivalence in more clear-cut fashion, a process which has been beautifully described by D. Shulman (1980). In the first stage, there was a local virgin goddess whom the gods coming from the north tried to seduce in order to make her loose her power which was directly linked to her chastity. Such endeavours generally ended up with the death or castration of the god(s). At a second, more Sanskritized stage, the goddess is inferior to the god, because the latter has tamed her, through a dance-contest for instance. At this crucial moment, when she achieves a respectable sanskritic identity, the goddess leaves her former, local and impure characteristics to the god's second wife who bears a pure Tamil name (for instance Vaḷḷi). At the same time, the theme of the castration of the god undergoes significant changes. It is no more a great god coming from the north who is castrated, but a local demon who is inferiorized in this way (Shulman 1980: 317-19).

This recurrent pattern is understandably a very useful device for avoiding paradoxical beliefs about one and the same goddess, which occur so drastically and beautifully in Bengal. Here I do not subscribe to Fr. Bhattacharya's hypothesis according to which the terrific aspect of the goddess is only subservient to her benign, salvific characteristics (1981: 17-54). This argument has been nurtured by the too-clearly neo-vedantic orientation of Professor Biardeau, since it reminds us too much of the idea of the so-called true nature of the god hidden by the veil of *māyā*.

For the ordinary devotee of Kālī, this intensity of his devotion is conveyed directly through the terrific and erotic appearance of the goddess "O mother, please, put some clothes on—since you are naked—" or "mother, you are a fake-mother, you left your children to go to your lover." Bengali devotional songs are full of abuse and expressions of surrender, and this double tone reminds us very much of the two mothers of M. Klein. Insofar as the Bengalis are coping with a universal problem in the devotion to their goddess(es) I would argue that these two mothers are no mothers at all—as the Bengalis perfectly know. The biological mother fades away when imaginary structures take over what is supposed to be her very name, *mā*.

There is an additional problem: in the neo-classical literature of the pauranic type, the goddess is not every often called *mā*, which does not, however, prevent brahmins of the most orthodox obedience from calling her *mā* on non-ritually codified occasion. Then we must try to be a little more precise about what we mean by popular devotion in Bengal. This devotion does not seem to be very much opposed to a sanskritic type of culture. The contrast lies somewhere else: between general (cutting across caste-lines) devotion and an esoteric knowledge, even though the two may have the same object, namely the goddess. As we have tried to show in this paper, popular (read "general") devotion achieved its symbolic efficiency through a pattern of transgression of normal social rules. At the esoteric level, we find an analogous type of reversal of values. One of the most typical is given in the theme of the demon-devotee (section 62 of *Kalikā Purāṇa*).[14]

Here we are told how the demon *Mahiṣa* is killed twice by the goddess. This re-killing seems to puzzle Sagara (62/ 81-3). In fact, after being killed once (62: 60-1), *Mahiṣa* is reborn as the son of *Raṃbha* (a devotee of Śiva) and of a buffalo-cow, a part of which was Śiva himself (62: 146-7). Then this *Mahiṣa* is killed by the goddess who appeared to him in the double form of the terrible *Ugracaṇḍā* and the benign *Bhadrakālī*. Through this killing, the goddess gives him release (62: 133), and also (156-60), we are told that "The demon now remains under the soles of the goddess. There is no birth for him anymore." But in 161 we are told that Śiva himself has been killed by the goddess for the sake of his own release. We know also from popular comment that this position of the god is also a metaphor for the *viparītām* form of love-making. I would suggest that these two views of the under-position of the god are not so foreign to each other. Whether Śiva be the demon-devotee achieving *mukti* through his being killed by the goddess (his own wife after all) or the masochist lover being under the woman, we are always faced to an equivalence of man being subservient to the woman. In structural terms the complementary (and seemingly contradictory) qualities of Śiva as the foremost yogī (able to give release to his devotees) and foremost lover[15] are transferred on the feminine figure of the goddess.

However, this translation is not easy to work out. For Śiva the model is rather simple: keeping back his seed through *tapas* enables him to become a foremost lover (*tapas* and love-making being sometimes distributed in an exact balance of time). Hinduism does not apply such a bold model to female divine identity; the latter is split into several symbols which are far from being so complementary as in the case of the male *sannyāsi*-lover. The main symbols are the faithful wife (*sati*), the erotic lover (*ramaṇi*), the nurturing mother (*mā*), the forbidden mother (*bau mā*), and of course the most ambiguous figure of the *guru mā* (the guru's wife).

In other words, not being able to achieve a complete renouncer identity which could be used as a non-equivocal symbol for liberation, the goddess cannot totally give up her role as wife and mother. As we suggested in this paper she has to be a mother making her son-devotee escape rebirth, which Ramprasad Sen very aptly expressed in this short expression qualifying the goddess: *janmaharā jananī* (lit. "a birth-giver taking away birth"). Even, though the ways to express her affiliation to the values of renunciation are ambiguous when compared to her masculine counterpart (Śiva is the "King of the yogīs," a very simple and not too equivocal statement), they are inescapable. Moreover, in Bengal they give a very radical turn to renouncement when compared to the rest of India: the meaning of a reversal of the values of the caste-system. If his devotion to the goddess truly overwhelms him, the brahmin devotee is driven away from his caste-origin, "I was a household master, but the 'great-she-Destroyer' turned me into a *sannyāsi*."[16]

4. The Snake-goddess Manasā: A Scape-goat for the Bad Divine

With all her negative attributes (putting her close to blood-eating goddesses and heretic renouncers) likely to be turned into good qualities as they emphasize the relativity of this manifested world, *mā* the goddess is good in the end. But insofar as we assume a certain logic in the Bengali views about goddesses, we have to explain where her residual bad attributes are located. To put it in cruder terms, we have to look for a negative form which can function as the scapegoat embodying most bad qualities and allowing for all other forms to appear as manifestations of this good and great goddess of sanskritic extraction.

From all expectations, this "bad", scapegoat goddess is likely to be of local and low origin, and that is what she is: the goddess of snakes, Manasā. The narrative of the goddess Manasā is one of the most popular pieces of medieval literature in Bengal. The following is a brief summary of the main core of the story which I have studied in more detail elsewhere.

Śiva left his wife Durgā to go to the lake of Kalidaha for the sake of meditation. She came there to meet him disguised as a she-dancer. Overcome with desire, Śiva emitted his seed which fell down on a lotus, and soon after it went down to the infernal world (*pātāla*) along the stalk of the flower. There the King Vasuki turned the seed into a beautiful Goddess, Manasā, to whom he gave command over all the snakes in the world.

After some unsuccessful attempts to live with her father and step-mother, Manasā wanders about in the world eager to be worshipped by mankind. Her first devotees are significantly low caste women and some Muslims. But Manasā has higher ambitions, she particularly wants to receive a cult from Chando, rich merchant who is an exclusive devotee of Śiva, her own father.

Chando resists her with obstinacy for a long time, standing valiantly up to all the miseries she causes to him: she destroys all his riches, has his seven sons killed, the seventh in a very particular way which deserves to be mentioned here.

This son, named Lakhindar, is killed on his wedding night by a small snake dispatched by Manasā which enters the iron room where the new couple has been put to escape precisely such a danger.

The strong-hearted bride, Behulā, insists upon accompanying her dead husband's body, floating down on a raft, to the city of the Gods, where she will try to make Lakhindar live again.

After this positive result has been obtained (in fact it is Manasā herself who is compelled by Indira to revive Lakhindar), the couple goes back to the boy's house in the disguise of a *yogī* and a *yoginī*. There Behulā convinces her father-in-law, Chando, to give a regular cult to the goddess Manasā. In the end, the merchant reluctantly surrenders, since he accepts to present offerings to the goddess only with his left hand (the impure hand in Hinduism).

In a tentative analysis made of this narrative I suggested that Manasā is the negative feminine counterpart of Śiva. Whereas the latter is unable to keep back his seed in his body as his qualification as a yogin would require him to do, Manasā, born from this very mistake, has an absolute control over venom, the latter substance being the structural reversal of seed. It is a substance she is able to keep back successfully in her body (as *viṣadhari*, one of her names, strongly suggests). She stores this venom in her left eye, a kind of counterpart of Siva's third eye, since a single glance of it is supposed to bring death.

Therefore, Manasā has control over the venom, a destructive substance in the very same way her father should have had control over the seed, a creative substance. It is through this inversion that Manasā, from the very beginning of the story, takes over the yogic power of Śiva, which explains why she is able to take away from him his best devotee.

Another significant dimension of this myth is the splitting of the feminine identity into the negative figure of Manasā on the one hand, and the positive symbol of Behulā on the other. The latter is the courageous daughter-in-law of the merchant Chando and she is also endowed with definite yogic qualities: she is able to stay for six months on the raft carrying her husband's dead body (a strong reminder of cremation grounds). She is even said to be a *siddha yoginī*. But all that Behulā does (not to speak of more deviant behaviour) she just does it for the sake of *dharma*, whereas Manasā is just acting on her own behalf, to get devotees for herself.

However, the narrative concludes with a woman (Behulā) giving her father-in-law as a devotee to the Goddess Manasā, whereas the latter gives back her husband Behulā. Here men are objects of exchange, and women the actors of the transaction, a rather unexpected pattern according to the standards of Hindu orthodoxy. In terms of the power of women, Behulā and Manasā are almost identical, only they seem to be distinguished for the sake of making *dharma* and *adharma* different. After all, the story insists upon the fact that Manasā curbs herself only in front of another woman Behulā, so similar to her that she seems to be her mirror-image.

More generally, the myths of Manasā seems to aim at making *yoga* subservient to *dharma* by presenting the first one in its most negative character (Śiva as a bad and lustful *yogī* and Manasā as a strong kind of *yoginī*, but a very ill-hearted one), and only allowing *yoga* to appear when it has *dharma* as its goal as the character of Behulā exemplifies.

So at the end, *dharma* wins, but it has to give up a part of its kingdom to *yoga*, and a *yoga* which from all appearances is not of a very respectable Hindu standard. This sharing of opposite values releases the tension and winds up the narrative, but does not totally suppress it, as is shown by the fact, that Chando only accepts to give offerings with his left hand.

Manasā is not only the scapegoat of the bad side of the Bengali goddess-mythology, the very type of devotion she receives has also very strong negative overtones, it is *bhor* (possession) most of time enacted by low-caste-women. In the case of Manasā, there is no need for devotion to be used as a clothing for the expression of negative or prohibited feelings, because she is already on the bad, impure, side of Hinduism. With her, no question of mystic surrender, what we get are just exchanges taken at their face-value (protection against offerings) or mad possession to fill up the distance between man and the divine.

5. Unorthodoxy and Reversal of Values

In this paper, I have concentrated on personal devotion, willingly leaving aside temple rituals such as the performance of the Durgā *pūjā*. This would constitute another work in its own right and would lead us to re-examine the lengthy process of re-orthodoxization of left-hand tantricism. We want now to concentrate on the first stage of the process in trying to show how the rejection of some Hindus from the pale of orthodox Hinduism leads them to a radicalization of their tantric-like behaviour.

For Vaiṣṇava devotees in general, devotion always encompasses renunciation in terms of a total amorous surrender to Kṛṣṇa, which should be done regardless of any prospect of personal release (from *saṃsaric* bonds). In the Gauḍīya Vaiṣṇava movement, the renouncer's path was slightly undervalued when compared to the status of the householder devotee, especially when the latter was a brahmin, popular Caitanya biographies often equate *vairāgi's* styles with *aul's* fashion, a clearly derogatory comparison.[17] The evolution of the sect shows that this devaluation has not so much theological foundation as the main concerns of the high caste members of the sect were chiefly to merge sectarian rules with brahmanic orthodoxy.[18] Quickly Caitanya's followers did better than ordinary brahmins, whom they overcome in their care for purity and non-violence. This orthodox move was orchestrated by Caitanya's most conservative disciple Advaita (a converted *sannyāsin* as his name indicates).

The result of such a merging (of sectarian and brahmanic orthodoxies) was a double rejection. One was internal to the sect: Advaita's followers, most of them being brahmins, discarded the most popular branch of the sect, conducted by Nityānanda. The second exclusion runs along the lines of sectarian antagonism: Gauḍīya Vaiṣṇavas reject renunciation and also tantricism, since they consider both of them grounded on a selfish quest, whereas they, Vaiṣṇavas, are simply looking for total refuge (*śaraṇa*) in God's compassion (*karuṇā*), they just want to be lifted up (*uddhāra*) from their wretched condition of being sinners.[19]

Truly, both *saṃnyāsī* and tantric *yogi* do not have devotion as their primary goal, their bhakti is most of the time subservient either to a quest for salvation or to some practical end. Moreover both of them share a common disdain for this world of illusion (*māyā*), an attitude that produces low concerns with purity. It is at this very point that popular devotion merges with the ideal of renunciation and tantricism, since the low are natural transgressors (of brahmanic orthodoxy) and the *saṃnyāsi-yogīs* cultural transgressors. The low castes transgress according to Hindu standards because their deviant behaviour is encoded in their *svadharma*, but the *śaktas* transgress willingly rules of brahmanic purity. The main point to be stressed here is that both categories are merged because of the common rejection they had to stand from the Vaiṣṇavas.

Truly an advocate of the holistic theory will object that we are not facing cases of exclusion, that all practices are integrated and hierarchized in the pale of Hinduism. This point of view is not relevant in our case which reveals a real infringement of a universal law, the *sanātana dharma*. Vaiṣṇavas and tantrik *yogīs* think that *sanātana dharma* is theirs but in very different ways: for a Vaiṣṇava this *dharma* is all embedded in his devotion to Kṛṣṇa, for a *tantrik*, it is contained in the reversal of values he achieves in his practice and meditation. What is interesting here is that we find "universal Law" either at the apex of orthodoxy or in its contrary.

If this observation is accepted, it means that orthodoxy and unorthodoxy, lawfulness and transgression are related to each other in terms of semantic complementarity, which at the same time allows for positioning that transgression behaviour as an incentive to authorized devotional feelings. In fact, lawful devotion seems to be related to unconscious transgression almost in the same way as is right-hand tantricism to its left-side counterpart: the former finds in the latter a symbolic efficiency which was to be kept secret, unavowed.

Significantly, the cases we have briefly evoked in this paper, whether drawn from field observations or form literary example, display this kind of logic, as we can see in the set of contrasted items listed below:

pure	impure
goddess	god
female	male
renouncer	householder
venom	seed
low caste	high caste
left hand	right hand
daughter-in-law	father-in-law
tantric yoga	*dharma*

Among the above items, all those of the "left" column display more power than their right column counterparts.

The goddess, despite belonging preferentially to the left side also mediates between both, and through this mediation she provides an outlet for the release of the tensions produced by hierarchy. Since she endows the encompassing form of the manifested world (*saṃsāra*), she has command over it (she is often termed *saṃsāra thākurani*), which accounts for her ability to turn bad into good on behalf of her devotee.

Since the goddess's body is the world, truly a world of illusion, there are two ways of escaping it, renunciation and devotion, but as we have seen here the latter is grounded on transgressive behaviour, which makes the devotion path the exact contrary of renunciation: to escape *māyā*, the devotee deepens into it, craves for the goddess's body. The latter is often incarnated in some prohibited beautiful female-in-law, a desire so unlawful that it has to be clothed in the benign metaphor of affection towards one's mother. What relates these women together is that they always belong to another man, whether father, son or younger brother. Conversely, we never came across a case of a sister or wife being turned into a goddess, which is understandable: a male Ego is already one with the former and the latter is one's own by marriage with a consanguinal relative.[20] In the same way his elder brother's wife, who potentially belongs to him never acquires a godly status.[21]

By giving hints of the transgressive nature of the devotion to the goddess, we arrived at this surprising evidence: the goddess's divine body, all shaped through illegitimate desires has little to do with a maternal body which appears as but a decent metaphor for an inaccessible reality.

The hyper-realistic way goddesses are represented in Bengal is but a consequence of this ambivalent identity of the feminine divine. The *mūrti,* the *pratimā,* stands for something else, an entity which is beyond reach both in metaphysical terms and in the language of desire. This is the point of view of sophisticated devotees, *saṃnyāsīs* and tantric *yogīs.* For the common folk, the *mūrti* is a house the goddess will occupy for the time of a festival. We would have probably been at loss concluding this paper in terms of a radical heterogeneity between folk and Sanskritized levels, had we not been rescued by the goddess's eyes. These eyes are an area of rich symbolism uniting both the folk and sophisticated levels in graduated images. The former is most present in the rite of *jāgāraṇ,* when the status of the deity is "awakened" by having the last touch of paint put on its eyes. Again in this benign symbolism, we find the metaphor of eyes being a "house of affection" (*sneha ghar*) for the devotee.

At the other end of this eye symbolism continuum, where the ferocious attributes of the goddess unite with her liberation-giving qualities, we shall find that a single glance of hers can burn the whole world in a conflagration *pralaya*[22] or enflame the devotee with *kāma* (desire).

So the glance of the goddess is eagerly looked for and at the same time inspires awe, from whence the quality of the eyelid is a strategic shelter. From her eyelid, the goddess lets her cooling tears run down, thus pacifying her burning devotee. This part of her face is also the spot from where the river of liberation[23] springs forth.

NOTES

1. This approach is moulded in a more or less explicit naturalism insofar as it tries to derive the identity of divine beings from natural entities such as sun, mountains, rivers, etc. Typical of this kind of endeavour for Bengal materials is A. Bhattacharya 1977.
2. "The complementarity of the great gods and the goddess then takes on another meaning: the latter is an indispensable mediator between what is extremely pure and what is extremely impure, between man's ultimate goals (amongst which rank the gods) and the more immediate necessities of life", M. Biardeau 1981: 16.
3. An idea well argumented by D. Shulman 1984: 17-18.
4. A recent collection of essays shed a new light on this subject, see J. Carmen and F. Marglin (eds.) 1983.
5. For a striking example, see H. Kulke 1978: 29-38.
6. Many evidences of this process are provided by W. Smith, *The one-eyed goddess: a study of the Manasa Mangal.* Stockholm: Stockholm Oriental Series, 1980.
7. The notion of orthodoxy in Hinduism is so different from its Western counterpart that it has been for long denied any heuristic value. For new approaches on this notion in India, see Eisenstadt *et al.* (op. cit., see note 3) and also S. Bouez (ed.), *La solitude bien ordonnée: ascèse et renoncement en Inde.* Nanterre: Société d'ethnologie.
8. In reference, they are termed *bau-mā.*
9. In India, the Bengali Hindus are the only ones to follow the *Dāyabhāga* school of inheritance according to which a man gets full control over his property till his death, other Hindus follow to *Mitākṣara* rule which gives a son the opportunity to demand his share of the paternal estate as soon as he is married.
10. *elokeśi* (dishevelled) is one of the most frequent epithets of Kali.
11. For some detalis on this problem, see S. Bouez, 1985: 23-48.
12. In West Bengal (April-May 1985).
13. For the sin of having an affair with the guru's wife, see Manu (XI. 104-7).
14. References to the Kālikāpurāṇa will be here made through K. Van Kooij, (Leiden 1972).
15. This is probably the central argument of W. O'Flaherty in her *Asceticism and eroticism in the mythology of Śiva.* London: Oxford University Press, 1973.
16. Ramprasad Sen, song 90 of the collection translated from Bengali into French by M. Lupsa, *Chants à Kali de Ramprasad.* Pondichéry: Institute Français d' Indologie, 1967.
17. *aul* is derived from the Arabic *aulia,* itself the plural of *wali* (a saint), without being clearly aware of this foreign origin, orthodox Vaiṣṇavas apply the term to popular Vaiṣṇavite mendicants.
18. Brahmanic orthodoxy is focused on the respect of the principle of caste (*varṇāśrama dharma*) and rules of purity.
19. This notion of "elevation" as an essential concept in Gauḍīya Vaiṣṇava theosophy has been put forward by J. O'Connell (1980: 124-35).
20. As a consanguinal relative, a sister is *ātmiya-svajan* (lit. "an own and one's person").
21. A joking relation prevails between a man and his elder brother's wife.

22. *pralaya* is the destruction of the universe (mainly achieved through an all-consuming fire at the end of a cosmic era (*kalpa*).
23. *nayaner mud theke mukti nadi cole jabe* (personal recording to devotional songs, Birbhum, 1985).

REFERENCES

Bhattacharya, A. 1977. *The sun and the serpent lore.* Calcutta: Firma K.L. Mukhopadhyaya.

Bhattacharya, Fr. 1981. 'La déesse et le royaume selon le Kalaketu Upakhyana du Candi Mangala. In *Puruṣārtha* 5, pp. 17-54 (Autour de la déesse hindoue).

Biardeau, M. 1981. "Introduction." In *Puruṣārtha* 5, pp. 9-16 (Autour de la déesse hindoue).

Bouez, S. (ed.) 1985. Le prix de la pureté: isogamie et hypergamie chez les brahmanes rarhi du Bengale. In *L'Homme,* 25, 4, pp. 23-48.

———. 1986. Le sperme et le venin: sur la nature ambigu' de le déesse bengalie Manasā. *Puruṣārtha* 18.

———. (ed.) *La solitude bien ordonneé: ascése et renoncement en Inde.* Nanterre: Société d' ethnolgie.

Carmen, J. and F. Marglin (eds.) 1983. *Purity and auspiciousness in Indian society.* Leiden: E.J. Brill.

Dumont, L. 1966. *Homo Hierarchicus.* Paris: Gallimard.

Kooij, K. van 1981. *Worship of the goddess according to the Kalikapurana.* Leiden: E.J. Brill.

Kulke, H. 1978. Early state formation and royal legitimation in tribal areas of eastern India. In *Aspects of tribal life in South Asia I: Strategy and survival* (eds.) R. Moser and M.K. Gautam (Studia Ethnologica Bernesia, I) Bern 1978, 29-37.

Obeyesekere, G. 1983. *The cult of the goddess Pattini.* Berkeley: Berkeley University Press.

O'Connell, J. 1980. Gauḍīya Vaiṣṇava symbolism of deliverance from evil. In *Journal of Asian and African Studies.*

O'Flaherty, W.D. 1973. *Asceticism and eroticism in the mythology of Śiva.* London: Oxford University Press.

Id. 1981. *Women, androgynes and other mythical beasts.* Chicago: Chicago University Press.

Sen, Ramprasad 1967. *Chants à Kali de Ramprasad.* Transl. M. Lupsa, Pondichery: Institute Français d'Indologie.

Shulman, D.D. 1980. *Tamil temple myths.* Princeton: Princeton University Press.

———. 1984. The enemy within: Idealism and dissent in South Indian Hinduism. In *Orthodoxy, heterodoxy and dissent in India* (eds.) S. Eisenstadt, R. Kahane and D. Shulman. Berlin: Mouton.

Smith, W. 1980. *The one-eyed goddess: A study of the Manasa Mangal.* Stockholm: Stockholm Oriental Series.

HINDUISM IN DIASPORA: THE TRANSFORMATION OF TRADITION IN TRINIDAD

Steven Vertovec

A central theme in "reconsidering Hinduism" is the attempt to come to terms with the tremendous variety of practices and beliefs subsumed as "Hindu". Considerable debate has waged through the years over whether or to what degree highly localized religious phenomena are integrated into philosophically broader or socio-cultural far-ranging institutions. Most often the issue has been set in the framework of the Hindu "Great Tradition" versus the "Little Tradition". The Great Tradition of Sanskritic literature and deities, Brahmanic rites, national pilgrimage sites and widely recognized religious calendar is, in this approach, set out as characteristically distinguishable from the Little Tradition of tutelary deities and a host of supernatural beings, folklore charismatic or shamanic practices, local sacred sites and a calendar with these village-level idionsyncracies. Most scholars assure us that both traditions are in symbiotic relationship: that they are "mutually necessary conditions of each others' existence" (Marriott 1955: 191), complexes which are "complementary, each serving important but differing religious purposes" (Mandelbaum 1964: 11), and "two currents of thought and action, distinguishable, yet ever flowing into and out of each other" (Redfield 1956: 42-3). Such an approach is found outside of Indian studies in cross-cultural discussions about official versus popular religion or textual versus contextual religious culture. Yet some students of Hinduism see the local or "ground-level" phenomena as so diverse and divorced from Sanskritic or Brahmanic tradition as to claim they are wholly distinct (e.g. Miller 1966). By the same token, then, some suggest that a single rubric "Hinduism" is consequently a misnomer (see von Stietencron or Frykenberg, elsewhere in this volume).

Perhaps the most prominently differentiating feature is the so-called Little or local tradition's pragmatically focused attention to a huge variety of minor deities, demons, spooks, saints, ancestors and miscellaneous spirits. Such beings may be blood-demanding, meat-eating, or vegetarian; they may interact with persons of specific lineage or place, or with whoever happens-by. They may be propitiated personally (*iṣṭadevatā*), by families or clans (*kuladevatā*), or by the entire village (*grāmadevatā*). A range of mother goddesses, who may or may not be conceived of as manifestations of the Divine Mother, Durga, Kali, or cosmic energy (*śaktī*), are also recipients of many prayer offerings. Scores of supernaturals are also significantly regarded from day to day, from ferocious godlings to beatified historical figures of the neighbourhood to ghosts of the recently deceased. All of these beings may be associated with particular places in a village or vicinity, in a temple, shrine, mound, tree, or river. Religious practitioners, both brahman and low caste, conduct specified rites to worship or drive-away one supernatural or another. Yet numerous other acts and sentiments towards area-specific supernatural and divinities preoccupy the daily lives of Hindu villagers: "Although they are not ceremonies in any strict sense, there are a number of kinds of religious behaviour which feed the stream of religious consciousness" (Opler 1959: 225). The heterogeneity of religious customs and duties are made even more complex by variations according to caste.

Srinivas (1952: 214f) suggested that patterns of Hindu religious belief and practice can be grouped in a social geographic manner: "local Hinduism" consists of parochially idiosyncratic phenomena, "regional Hinduism" denotes institutions found through a cultural linguistic area, "peninsular Hinduism' points to major differences in religious style throughout south India as opposed to the north, while "All-India Hinduism" generally refers to the fundamental (usually described as Sanskritic) pantheon and corpus of literature and rites. "In a very broad sense," Singer writers (1971: 44), "Srinivas believes that, as the area of spread decreases, the number of ritual and cultural forms shared increases; as the area increases, the common forms decrease." Considerable debate has subsequently followed, as anthropologists, historians and others have argued whether or not various Hindu features are found within certain castes, locales, lore, or literature.

On occasion, anthropologists have described processes whereby change has occurred in the direction of Great or Little Tradition or vice-versa. That is, the socio-religious phenomena found throughout India in philosophical literature and culture-wide institutions have been seen to become particularized in unique village-level forms, while conversely, attributes of an area-specific religious complex have been broadly adopted by Hindus far afield (cf. Srinivas 1952, Marriott 1955). Another, perhaps more contemporary trend seems to evidence the gradual disregard of many magico-religious practices and beliefs in favour of ones more widely acceptable or respected. Often described as "Sanskritization", this trend, through which low status individuals gain prestige by acquiring high status doctrines and practices, may be slowly changing the face of Hinduism in India.

> The spread of Sanskritization and Westernization across the country and to different structural levels is beginning to produce nationwide uniformities in religion and culture. Everywhere village deities traditionally associated with epidemics of diseases such as plague, smallpox and cholera seem to be losing ground, while the prestigious Sanskritic deities are becoming more popular. Blood sacrifices and offerings of liquor are also becoming less popular. The horizon of the peasant is widening, and the richer peasants now visit pilgrimage centres several hundred miles away from their villages. Films, radio, textbooks, newspapers, journals, and paperback books are strengthening "regional" and "All-India" Hinduism, at the expense of the strictly local forms. (Srinivas/Shah 1968: 365)

The motivation to adopt generalized Sanskritic traits and to forego particularized village ones is catalyst to an interesting type of religious or cultural blending. Such blending within Hinduism is different from instances of syncretism with non-Hindu phenomena, a capacity for which the religion has become notorious. Instead, this form of change sees Hindus rallying around mutually accepted or commonly venerated religious and cultural institutions and tenets. "It has canalized the change in such a way that all-Indian values are asserted and the homogeneity of entire Hindu society increases" (Srinivas 1956: 493). Originally, as Srinivas and others have proposed, its process must have been set in course for the purpose of advancing individual or caste group prestige. Now, heightened, senses of communalism and radical Hindu fundamentalism are affecting similar results in India.

Yet among the considerable overseas Hindu population, parallel processes of Sanskritization and homogenization have occurred for altogether different reasons. Hindus in numerous places outside

India have been subject to changes which have "led from village and caste beliefs and practices to wider, more universalistic definitions of Hinduism that cut across local and caste differences" (Jaywardena 1968: 444). In South Africa, for instance, Kuper (1957: 229) portrays the emergent form of religion among Indians as a new variety of "regional Hinduism" similar to the shared patterns of wide areas in India. Bharati (1970: 28-9, 38-40) describes a "complete fusion of 'big' and 'little' tradition elements" among Hindus in East Africa. In virtually every case, Hinduism in Diaspora has developed substantial modifications from the traditions originally carried abroad.

In Trinidad, a Caribbean island of 1,864 square miles off the coast of Venezuela, like transformation of Hindu tradition have taken place. In today's Trinidadian population of over 1.25 million, 40.7 per cent are descendants of Indian immigrants (a further 40.8 per cent are of African origin, 16.3 per cent of various mixed descent, 0.9 per cent whites, 0.5 per cent Chinese, and 0.8 per cent other; the island of Tobago, almost wholly African in population, is also part of the Republic). Hindus comprise 25 per cent of the total religious makeup of the island (with Catholics 33.6 per cent, Anglicans 15 per cent, Muslims 5.9 per cent, Presbyterians 3.9 per cent, and other Christian denominations 16.6 per cent). Currently, a kind of "Hindu renaissance" or self-proclaimed "revival" is underway among Trinidad Hindus. *Bhajan* groups, summer Hindu youth camps, weeklong *yagnās* or *Rām Līlās*, family *pūjās* of newfound variety, *Rāmāyaṇa satsangs*, fund-raising *Melās*, personal Mandirs—all these and more features of Hindu social and cultural activity now proliferate under the banner of *Sanathan Dharma* throughout this small island. Yet those Hindu forms which exist in Trinidad today have been culturally siphoned through specific historical conditions and elaborated in response to circumstances of social pluralism. It is Hinduism unlike that found in any particular part of India, but it is fundamentally Hindu. Like other aspects of culture among Indians abroad, it has been forced to evolve " a style which was certainly 'creolized' but which was still uniquely Indian" (Tinker 1974: 210).

Indian Migration to Trinidad

After the abolition of slavery in British colonies (1834-8), acute labour shortages occurred on sugar plantations around the world. Numerous schemes for gaining local free migrant labour were unsuccessfully attempted in the various colonies affected. Though necessitating considerable investment by planters and colonial administrators, the migration of people from the subcontinent of India proved to be the salvation of the British sugar industry. The migrants accepted contracts whereby they would be shipped to sugar colonies to labour usually for a period of five years, guaranteed pay, housing, and medical services, and provided a return passage to India following the expiration of indenture (yet often with the stipulation of an additional five years free labour in the colony). Though many regulations and interviews in the ports of embarkation, Madras and Calcutta, sought to ensure complete willingness and understanding of the contracts on the part of the migrants, only few realized all implications of their moves to such distant lands.

Mauritius received the first indentured Indians for plantation work in 1834. Indentured migration to British Guiana (now Guyana) began in 1838, then to Trinidad in 1845, to South Africa in 1860, to Dutch Guiana (now Surinam) in 1873, to Fiji in 1879, and to East Africa in 1896. All indentured migration from India ceased in 1917, due primarily to pressures from leaders in India to put a halt to what they saw as a degrading institution (especially given the situation in South Africa around that time).

TABLE 1: INDIANS IMMIGRATED INTO TRINIDAD, 1845-1917

Years	*Numbers*	*Years*	*Numbers*
1845-50	5,568	1886-90	13,988
1851-5	5,054	1891-5	13,565
1856-60	11,208	1896-1900	7,414
1861-5	7,474	1901-5	12,433
1866-70	11,836	1906-10	12,547
1871-5	11,868	1911-15	4,051
1876-80	12,763	1916-17	2,619
1881-5	11,551		
Total			143,939

(Source: Roberts/Byrne 1966: 129)

TABLE 2: INDIANS RETURNED FROM TRINIDAD TO INDIA

Years	*Numbers*	*Years*	*Numbers*
1845-50	—	1881-5	2,265
1851-5	1,395	1886-90	2,924
1856-60	982	1891-5	3,775
1861-5	817	1896-1900	3,638
1866-70	722	1901-5	3,838
1871-5	970	1906-10	3,471
1876-80	1,875		
Total			26,672 (20% of 143,939)

(Source: Roberts/Byrne 1966: 133)

Between 1845-1917 over 140,000 Indians came to Trinidad as indentured labourers (see Table 1). The immigrants were housed on estates in rows of wooden barracks, labouring amidst conditions of great poverty, poor sanitation, vitamin deficiency and disease. After their period of indentureship, however, only about one in five chose to return to India (Table 2). The vast majority remained working on plantations as wage labourers, cultivating their own gardens while continuing to live in the barracks. Towards the end of the nineteenth century, however, Crown lands were made available for lease or sale, and many Indians took advantage of the situations by gaining their own property in areas adjacent to estates. Subsequently, they formed their own homogenous village settlements while continuing to work part-time on plantations. Eventually, through their successful shift into independent cane farming, the Indians in Trinidad became a key component of the island's economic structure before the turn of the century.

Many social historians have naively asserted that once the immigrant Indians left the estates and established their own village, they were readily able to reintroduce traditional patterns of Indian society and culture. Later, some anthropologists would point to aspects of Trinidad Indian values and behaviour as prime examples of cultural persistence. This led to academic debates over the nature of the culture change, retention, and creolization. Most writers on the subject have simply assumed that Indians in Trinidad picked up where they left off in India, reinstating familiar cultural institutions, such as religion, as best they could given the structure of the colonial society. Subsequent change under this view then, has been seen to result from this transplanted "traditional" culture being passively "acted upon by forces" of acculturation and assimilation. Yet the Indian culture practiced by the early migrants and their descendants must have actually been an amalgamation or homogenized set of institutions necessitated by the casting together of a diverse range of Indian peoples. Change since the immediate post-indenture period has been actively conducted by Indians as they became increasingly well organized and conscious of their identity within the multicultural island setting.

Perhaps the foremost social problem the Indian immigrants had to overcome during their settlement period in Trinidad was their sheer diversity. In India, local recruiters were hired to contract labourers and deliver them to a depot at the port of embarkation. The recruiters travelled far and wide in their task: the result was a tremendously heterogeneous assembly of migrants. In the initial years of indentured immigration to Trinidad, Indians embarked from two different ports, Calcutta and Madras. Far more came through Calcutta, from the vast Gangetic plain of north India, than from the coastal and urban areas of south India near Madras (Table 3). Fundamental socio-cultural differences existed between the Indians from the north and south, as there remain today. These include dissimilarities in economic exchange and agricultural bases, *varṇa* structure, basic religious orientations, religious structure and religious activity, degree of Brahmanization, the nature of kingship, architecture, degree of influence by Islamic culture, and fundamental linguistic differences (Indic/Hindi versus Dravidian language families). Moreover, the north Indian migrants were primarily rural villagers, while those from the south, it is believed, tended far more often to be urban dwellers from the immediate vicinity of Madras itself (Gamble 1866: 33-4; Wood 1968: 139-40). The cultural gulf between immigrants from these two areas must have been exceedingly difficult to overcome in the rigid and repressive conditions of the sugar estates. Estate owners regarded south Indians as having particularly filthy habits, as troublesome, and as labourers more likely to run off and break their indenture contracts. So great were the complaints against "Madrassis' that migration from Madras to Trinidad was terminated after 1870 (cf. Brereton 1981: 103).

TABLE 3: EMIGRANTS FROM INDIA TO TRINIDAD
BY PORT OF EMBARKATION, 1845-70

Port	*Men*	*Women*	*Children*	*Total*
Calcutta	25,059	8,023	4,445	37,527 (88.2%)
Madras	2,971	1,257	764	4,992 (11.7%)
Total	28,030	9,280	5,209	42,519 (99.9%)

(Source: B.P.P. 1874: 496)

The fact of common port of embarkation, Calcutta, by no means meant that the vast majority of Indian migrants shared a common culture. On the broadest level, the variety of regions and provinces from which they came saw to considerable cultural differentiation. Table 4 gives migrants' regions of origin between 1845 and 1871, while Table 5 shows their home provinces from 1875 to 1917.[1] Indians emigrating from so many different areas would be used to considerably different political structures and styles of colonial administration, agricultural activities and modes of distributions, land tenure systems, village structure and house types, diets, religious sects and pilgrimage sites, languages and dialects. In the last decades of indentured migration, a number of tribals (called *jangli* to this day

TABLE 4: EMIGRANTS FROM INDIA TO TRINIDAD FROM PORT OF
CALCUTTA BY REGION OF ORIGIN, 1845-71

North-West Provinces[1]		
Oudh, Central India	16,027	(41.7%)
Beha	11,278	(29.3%)
West Bengal	8,396	(21.8%)
Central Bengal	1,305	(3.3%)
East Bengal	176	(0.4%)
Orissa	378	(0.9%)
Elsewhere	853	(2.2%)
Total	38,413	(99.6%)

(Source: B.P.P. 1874: 497)

[1]Known as "United Provinces of Agra and Oudh" after 1902 (today's Uttar Pradesh).

in Trinidad) came to the island; their linguistic, behavioural, and religious differentiation from the rest of Indian society is well noted. The varying ratio of emigrants' home regions over the years (a variation due to changes in recruitment strategies, shifts in migration caused by local famines and economic depressions, etc.) meant that Indians already in Trinidad continuously met a constant stream of newcomers from unknown places and subcultures.

Furthermore, a shared province of origin did not guarantee complete cultural familiarity either. The greatest proportion of

TABLE 5: EMIGRANTS FROM INDIA TO TRINIDAD BY PROVINCE OF ORIGIN, 1875-1917

Province	*1875-85*	*1886-95*	*1896-1906*	*1907-17*	*Total*
North-West	12,613	15,395	9,865	9,9117[1]	47,590
Provinces[1]	(48%)	(59%)	(46%)	(52%)	(52%)
Oudh	5,579	1746	5,217	5,26[1]	20,803
	(21%)	(18%)	(25%)	(28%)	(23%)
Behar	5,482	5,035	1,145	1,722[2]	13,384
	(21%)	(19%)	(5%)	(9%)	(13%)
Central India	394	107	2,790	440	3,731
	(2%)	—	(13%)	(2%)	(4%)
Nepal & Native	87	231	1,320	1,014	2,652
States[3]	—	(1%)	(6%)	(5%)	(3%)
Punjab	697	111	766	265	1,839
	(3%)	—	(4%)	(1%)	(2%)
Bengal	850	333	46	76	1,305
	(3%)	(1%)	—	—	(1%)
Miscellaneous	472	111	56	64	703
incl. Bombay	2%	—	—	—	(1%)
Orissa	54	38	47	52	144
Ajmere	—	—	33	59	92
Total	26,228	26,107	21,285	18,623	92,243

(Source: Protector of Emigrants, 1876-1918)

[1]Known as "United Provinces of Agra and Oudh" after 1902. Tabulated with Oudh in 1910 and 1911.

[2]Tabulated as "Bihar & Orissa" between 1912 and 1917.

[3]Recruitment of Nepalese was prohibited after 1895.

TABLE 6: SAMPLE OF EMIGRANTS FROM INDIA TO TRINIDAD BY DISTRICT OF REGISTRATION, 1881-91[1]

NORTH-WEST PROVINCES

District	*1881*	*1882*	*1883*	*1884*	*1885*	*1886*	*1887*	*1888*	*1889*	*1890*	*1891*	*Total*
Agra	104	65	4	85	32	176	234	265	79	34	88	1166
Allahabad	150	122	146	76	17	9	40	84	33	64	75	766
Aligarh	203	75	39	...	...	...	28	21	...	...	24	390
Azimgurh	30	44	50	36	12	...	212	33	114	238	515	1284
Badaon	...	13	...	...	...	...	...	...	...	...	...	13
Banda	...	5	1	...	...	...	...	...	...	...	...	6
Barielly	80	128	107	11	...	...	10	60	...	129	90	615
Basti	5	...	55	56	56	108	67	12	127	346	818	1650
Benares	30	...	392	161	174	332	240	534	539	848	665	3921
Bulundshahar	43	...	...	...	...	...	...	...	...	...	...	43
Cawnpore	240	241	159	83	201	126	166	235	277	239	161	2128
Etawah	210	114	134	13	21	...	39	34	...	...	...	565
Fattehpore	55	2	3	...	...	...	...	...	...	...	...	60
Farrackabad	147	91	...	...	4	...	...	...	...	...	...	242
Goruckpore	35	...	...	22	18	12	46	...	57	104	...	294
Gazeepore	28	82	...	48	...	46	129	223	376	555	749	2236
Itah	...	...	14	...	...	...	...	...	...	...	...	14
Jaunpore	...	...	45	59	40	65	79	170	241	340	694	1733
Mainpuri	...	28	...	...	...	...	...	...	...	...	...	28
Munipore	71	...	...	...	...	...	...	...	...	...	...	71
Mirzapore	...	...	3	...	...	...	...	...	...	...	...	3
Mooradabad	48	37	20	...	...	...	...	...	...	...	...	105

TABLE 6 (CONTD)

District	*1881*	*1882*	*1883*	*1884*	*1885*	*1886*	*1887*	*1888*	*1889*	*1890*	*1891*	*Total*
Muttra	172	128	276	17	...	75	114	46	...	...	...	828
Shajihampore	27	60	15	8	...	4	...	...	...	...	...	114

It should be noted that the District of Registration is not necessarily the same as the district of origin. That is, many migrants were recruited and registered for emigration in places which were not their home districts. This refers especially to the larger towns and cities, such as Benares, Patna, and particularly the 24 Pergunnahs surrounding Calcutta: individuals would have travelled from their rural home to these places in search of employment and opportunities, eventually to be recruited and registered for emigration there.

BENGAL & BIHAR

District	*1881*	*1882*	*1883*	*1884*	*1885*	*1886*	*1887*	*1888*	*1889*	*1890*	*1891*	*Total*
Bettiah	1	...	...	...	...	...	...	...	...	...	...	1
Bhagulpore	...	...	58	172	113	33	25	...	...	...	...	401
Burdwan	...	...	...	...	151	...	...	...	...	...	...	151
Buxar	...	6	...	...	...	...	...	...	...	...	...	6
Chumparun	5	...	...	9	...	...	...	...	...	...	...	14
Dinapore	...	64	...	...	...	...	...	...	...	...	...	64
Durbhunga	...	...	121	219	195	145	42	47	48	20	32	869
Gaya	...	...	...	585	235	15	...	44	13	60	...	952
Hazarbagh	...	...	...	131	19	11	...	...	...	...	...	161
Monghyr	...	...	...	15	88	17	...	4	97	38	17	276
Patna	...	...	282	255	245	234	267	277	324	481	172	2537
Sarun	30	2	...	12	...	44	1	7	...	...	...	96
Shahabad	20	...	...	69	245	279	245	496	970	478	462	3264
24 Pergunnahs	106	147	264	716	424	629	447	496	789	347	311	4676

TABLE 6 (CONTD)

District	*1881*	*1882*	*1883*	*1884*	*1885*	*1886*	*1887*	*1888*	*1889*	*1890*	*1891*	*Total*
OUDH												
Bahraich	80	11	...	...	...	...	...	...	...	...	...	91
Barabanki	40	8	10	...	...	...	...	...	...	...	...	58
Fyzabad	300	272	244	154	123	132	188	118	159	421	736	2847
Gonda	18	77	57	55	16	28	25	60	103	128	157	724
Hardui	11	16	...	...	...	...	...	...	...	...	...	27
Lucknow	315	505	262	148	22	243	199	55	73	128	357	2347
Sultanpore	79	43	32	9	19	...	5	...	...	...	...	187
Unao	7	...	...	7	...	...	...	1	...	...	...	15
Raibaraili	...	3	...	...	...	...	...	...	...	...	...	3
Sitapore	...	...	...	...	...	8	...	...	...	...	...	8

PUNJAB

District	*1881*	*1882*	*1883*	*1884*	*1885*	*1886*	*1887*	*1888*	*1889*	*1890*	*1891*	*Total*
Delhi	440	184	121	36	...	...	...	...	...	...	...	781
Umballa	105	...	...	...	...	...	...	...	...	...	...	105
Gargaon	...	...	...	38	...	...	...	...	...	...	...	38

GENERAL INDIA

District	*1881*	*1882*	*1883*	*1884*	*1885*	*1886*	*1887*	*1888*	*1889*	*1890*	*1891*	*Total*
Jubbulpore	...	...	14	...	...	...	...	...	...	...	...	14

TABLE 6 (CONTD)

BOMBAY

District	*1881*	*1882*	*1883*	*1884*	*1885*	*1886*	*1887*	*1888*	*1889*	*1890*	*1891*	*Total*
Ahmedabad	...	...	140	...	...	...	...	....	...	...	...	140

RAJPUTANA

District	*1881*	*1882*	*1883*	*1884*	*1885*	*1886*	*1887*	*1888*	*1889*	*1890*	*1891*	*Total*
Nemuch	...	...	36	...	...	...	...	...	...	...	...	36

GANJAM

District	*1881*	*1882*	*1883*	*1884*	*1885*	*1886*	*1887*	*1888*	*1889*	*1890*	*1891*	*Total*
Ganjam	...	...	89	...	...	...	...	...	...	...	...	89

(Source: Protector of Emigrants 1882-92)

immigrants to Trinidad came from what was then called the "Northwest Provinces" (today known as Uttar Pradesh). But within even such a single state, the emigrants belonged to a multiplicity of distinct towns, districts, and local areas (*tālukā*).

Table 6 provides a sample of the distribution of emigrants' home districts over a ten-year period. District by district, the Indians coming to Trinidad would have known different caste and sub-caste compositions, caste and local dialects, caste hierarchies, population densities, lineages and clans, inter-village networks for economic exchange, exogamous unions, and religious festivals, feuding relationship within and between village groups, and complexes relating to folklore, sacred sites, supernatural beings and protective godlings particular to each village and vicinity. Thus the immigrants to Trinidad, thrust together on plantation estates halfway around the world, were faced with overwhelming complexities for establishing a shared social and cultural system.

Aspects of Cultural Blending among Trinidad Indians[2]

Even before leaving India, the migrants had to begin modifying their traditional ways. Recruiters would bring individuals from their home areas to a depot at the port, where they would be housed together with people from other regions who had also contracted themselves as indentured labourers or "coolies".

> While under the control of the recruiter, the coolie was at least in the company of people who were of his *janambhūmi*, his own country, and who spoke his own dialect, though they were strangers of different castes. But now he was surrounded by folk whose speech was unintelligible, and whose physical characteristics appeared foreign, while their ways of eating and other habits would seem all wrong. However, he would have to conform to these strange ways.... (Tinker 1974: 140-1)

Confusion and anxiety were doubtlessly widespread among the contracted Indians in the depots. The situation would grow worse for the unaccustomed villagers on the one-hundred-day voyage around the treacherous Cape of Good Hope; not only was the passage long, dangerous, and often disease-ridden, but the act of crossing the sea, the *kālī pānī* ("black waters"), was considered an utmost act of ritual defilement. Yet the harrowing experience did serve to instill comradery among the heterogeneous set of Indians.

A feeling of solidarity did arise in the group emigrants. They were all in the same boat, not only in the literal sense, but also in being victims of their own impulse. The long voyage, and uncertainty about the future strengthened cohesion between them. (Speckmann 1965: 25)

The deep friendships forged between diverse individuals (even Hindu-Muslim) on the voyage abroad became known as *jahāzī bhāī* or "ship brothers"; after the period of indentureship they would often settle near each other, and their subsequent progeny would continue to treat each other's families as *nata* or fictive kin (cf. Jayawardena 1968: 435f.; Mayer 1961: 6). These strong emotional bonds were an important foundation for later moves by the Indians to arrive at common social and cultural institutions.

One of the primary and most formidable hurdles to overcome was the linguistic differentiation found among such a wide spectrum of Indian peoples. The tongues spoken by migrants of Trinidad included the individual languages of Bengali, Punjabi, Hindi, Bihari, Oriya, Gujerati, Telugu, Tamil, and the tribal languages of the Oraons, Santals, and Mundas. This tremendous range of spoken languages was multiplied by the distinct dialects of Vanga, Radha, Varendra, Rajbanghsi, Magahi, Shadri, Bhojpuri, Eastern and Western Hindi, Bangaru, Ajmeri, and Tondai Nadu (cf. Schwartzberg 1978: 100). Further, each of these would be internally diversified by local and caste dialects.

In Trinidad, as in most sugar colonies with indentured Indian labourers, there was a great need among these immigrants to create a common speech, often referred to as "plantation Hindustani" (see Tinker 1974: 208, 211). A pidgin English sufficed for important economic transactions and other relationship with plantation staff, yet the Indians gradually developed a shared language amongst themselves which facilitated communication irrespective of caste or regional origins. Bhojpuri, the dialect of eastern Bihar, became the basis for this India *lingua franca* in Trinidad. Bhojpuri shares certain characteristic features with both Bengali and Hindi, and thus naturally became a kind of linguistic middle ground: it was sifted and refined by reducing the number of non-semantic utterances (articles, prepositions, inflections) to promote accessibility to non-Bhojpuri speakers (Durbin 1973). Today's "Trinidad Hindi" which survives essentially only among the over-40 year old generation, is the resultant, creolized Bhojpuri (see Mohan 1978).

Another important aspect of language change and cultural blending among immigrant Indians, which Durbin (1973) points out, concerns the disintegration of the caste system. As part of the trend towards common linguistic forms, caste dialects were dropped. Further, the speech indicator conveying higher-lower caste status were eliminated in favour of inter-caste forms. This may have provided social modifications functioning to allow greater attitudes of commonality and equality. Of course, such a shift was not causal in the breakdown of caste overseas, but certainly it may be seen as augmentative.

The dissolution of the caste system among overseas Indians represents an important subject unfortunately too broad and complex to treat in the present article (see especially Pocock 1957b, Schwartz 1967a, Jayawardena 1979). A brief summary of the causes of its collapse is, however, warranted. In most overseas contexts where indentured migration and plantation labour obtained, the processes affected traditional Indian social structures were very similarly.[3]

The alien conditions produced by indentured migration and estate life militated against practically all the most characteristic features of the caste system. Fundamental standards involving purity, pollution and ritual status could not be maintained among indentured migrants; in the depots, on the ships, at the estates, and within the barracks, Indians of all castes and statuses were haphazardly assembled to eat and sleep together, necessarily causing mutual defilement. The lack of proper sanitary provisions meant considerable bodily pollution in terms of traditional practice. The age-old occupational specialization and exchange of service (*jājmānī*) could not function either, due to generalization of tasks on sugar plantations; the few specialized or high status jobs appointed by white supervisors were certainly not done so with reference to high caste. Even after the indenture period, when Indians established their own communities, the majority of individuals continued to remain agricultural labourers instead of resuming their pre-migration occupations.

Perhaps even more important than the constraints of the new environment, the tremendous pre-migration regional diversity, presented a situation whereby caste as witnessed in India simply could not persist. From throughout north India between 1875-1917, the castes brought to Trinidad can be categorized as 14 per cent Brahman, 30 per cent "agricultural castes", 7 per cent artisans, and 35 per cent "low castes" (with an additional 14 per cent Muslims;

Protector of Emigrants 1876-1918). But the caste hierarchies are essentially local phenomena: standards of behaviour, interactions, avoidance, inclusion and exclusion, prestige and position are claimed and contested wholly within the village and regional locality (Pocock 1957a, b; Dumont 1970: 79-91). "It follows", Dotson (1968: 144) writes, "that claims validated in one region are not necessarily negotiable in another and that in the last analysis no university agreed-upon hierarchy or rank order for various groups really exists." Once randomly mixed together on Trinidad sugar estates, Indians were unable to create a mutually recognized caste structure given so many diverse castes and sub-castes, many of which were never even heard from one area in India to another.

However, an "All-India" or Great Tradition form of hierarchy did exist whereby caste groups could be readily ranked. This was the fourfold *varṇa* system of Brahman, Kshatriya, Vaishya, and Shudra. In the subcontinent,

> the importance of the *varṇa*-system consists in that it furnishes an All-India frame into which the myriad *jātis* in any single linguistic area can be fitted. It systematizes the chaos of *jātis* and enables sub-castes of one region to be comprehended by people in another area by reference to a common scale. (...) This has helped the spread of a uniform culture throughout Hindu society. (Srinivas 1952: 24-5)

In overseas contexts, the ideological framework of *varṇa* is actualized in social practice: *varṇa* comes to "replace" caste as the endogamous unit and status referent (see Mayer 1967; Clarke 1967; Dotson 1968). However, in Trinidad today, little remains of caste or *varṇa* as significant behaviour or social relation-modifying structures. Ritual status became an individual matter based around abstention; social and occupational status became a matter of individual achievement; internal differentiation within the community became dysfunctional when they faced a situation of common discrimination by the rest of the society. Only the extreme ends of the caste continuum (Brahman-Chamar) are now sometimes taken into account in allocating social status. Traditionally-minded parents sometimes, too, insist on *varṇa*-endogamous marriage among their children. And considerable debate still occurs over the question of non-Brahman pundits. But in terms of occupational ascription, inter-personal relationships and avoidance, ritual purity and pollution, generally no account is taken of individuals' caste descent.

Just as the over-arching categories of *varṇa* once provided a means of mutually organizing the amalgam of castes among migrants to Trinidad, the central features of the so-called Hindu Great Tradition allowed people from an unknown number of Little Traditions to reach some consensus on methods and focuses of worship. On the sugar estates so far from the villages of their birth, Hindus in Trinidad needed some continuity in religious expression; yet gone were their familiar local shrines and sacred sites, tutelary deities, and parochial supernaturals. Few could recognize each other's family and village deities. Yet virtually all would know of Ram, Krishna Durga, and Kali, and all would have heard the *Rāmāyaṇa*, the *Bhāgavad Gītā* and one or more of the *Purāṇas*. All would have celebrated in some fashion the holy days of Diwali, Holi, Shivratri, Ramnavami, and others. And all would revere the Brahmanic rites involving *havan* and Sanskritic *mantrās*.

However, reaching a consensus religion doubtlessly proved no easy task. In addition to the linguistic divisions, ritual specialists from various places would vary in their methods of ritual and discourse. Prominent sects also came to Trinidad, including the Ramanandi, Kabir, Swami Narayan, and Aghor *panths*. On even broader levels, Vaishnavism, Shaivism, and Shaktism were all represented as well. An early Christian missionary to British Guinea described the confusion among Indians there, as in Trinidad, noting how followers of various sects and cults vied with one another, "each strenuously contending for the supremacy of the chief object of their worship, and the consequent inferiority of the other" (Bronkhurst 1888: 17).

In the early years of Indian presence in Trinidad, the bulk of Hindu religious activity probably revolved around individual pundits and their clients from the same general regions of origin. As linguistic and cultural homogeneity gradually increased, these pundits could "cast wider nets", as it were, gaining clients from other parts and traditions of India. Pundits cabable of broader appeal were more successful, for a new market-type situation existed among individuals separated from their original *guru-chelā* relationships in India. Further, those pundits who could promulgate "higher class" religious teachings and rites to the bulk of appreciative low caste migrants would gain better following (cf. Jayawardena 1966: 227-8). Throughout the north of India from whence most migrants came, a well respected Vaishnavite bhakti orientation was prominent. This tradition provided the core of Trinidad Hinduism. Loving devotion to the *avatār Rām*, as preached especially by the Ramanandi *panth*, eventually had the most popular, cross-caste and interregional appeal. Tulsidas' *Rāmāyaṇa* became the cornerstone of Trinidad Hinduism. The Ramanandis' characteristic greeting "Rām-Rām" or "Sītā-Rām" is still said by practically every Hindu on the island today (with the exception of the few remaining Kabir *panthīs* and Ārya Samājis). The blood sacrifices and ritual devotion to lesser deities increasingly became looked down upon as low religion, while unitary devotion to God as Viṣṇu was adopted as the ideal religious path.

We know that plantation owners did little to stifle religious activities among their Indian workforce, unless the activities interfered with labour requirements. Celebrations and rites for major religious days occurred on the estates and in the nascent villages. Soon after settling in their own communities, Indians built *kūtīs* or small temples which also function as meeting places and shelters for wandering *sādhūs* (ascetics); these had been important features of villages in Bihar and elsewhere (Grierson 1885). The *kūtīs* and calendrical rites acted to religiously communalized Indian migrants in the years following indentureship, as did the revitalized institutions of *pancāyat* (village councils) and *aguās* (matchmakers).

The subsequent history of Indians in Trinidad tells of growing solidarity and organization. Around the turn of the century, national Indian associations were formed to lobby on behalf of immigrants' rights. Massive strikes by Indian workers came to plague the plantocracy. Indians gained representation on the colony's Legislative Council, and Indian newspapers were founded by the 1920s. Hindu missionaries visited the island periodically and, inspired by their lectures, Trinidad Hindus organized national religious bodies in the early 1930s. The 1930s, however, proved to be both organizationally ground-breaking and communally divisive.

In 1932, two rival Hindu organizations were established (the Sanathan Dharma Association and the Sanathan Dharma Board of Control), each claiming to represent orthodox Hindus. (It is evident that by that time, Hinduism in Trinidad had been fully consolidated into a single tradition, demanding equal standing to the island's other major religions, Catholicism and Anglicanism.) Divided more by personalities than by ideological prediction, these bodies shared a common antagonist, the reformist Ārya Samāj.[4] Although the Hindu community became divided between these three associations, their confrontations and debates "spearheaded a Hindu renaissance and socio-religious reforms while also providing an orthodox counter-reformation" (Forbes 1984: i). The Ārya Samāj harkened the high civilisation of India's past, inspiring the Trinidad Indians and introducing previously unfamiliar philosophical concepts and Vedic teachings to the rural migrants and their children. The Sanathan Dharma organizations, in turn, were forced to defend their blend of Great Tradition tenets and to bolster their *pūjā*-centred orthopraxy. A growing sense of identity and pride within the Hindu populace was one positive consequence of the competition between these bodies.

Indian consciousness grew considerably in the 1940s with the legal recognition of Hindu marriages in 1945 (Muslim marriages had been recognized in 1936), with a successful battle for the removal of language test in the first federal elections with universal suffrage (in which the Indian candidates fared well), and with the communal excitement brought about by the independence of India in 1947. Yet it was in the 1950s that a burgeoning ethnic identity took full organizational and political manifestation.

In 1952 the two orthodox Hindu organizations were united as the Sanatan Dharma Mahā Sabhā under the strong arm of Bhadase Sagan Maraj. Maraj was a self-made millionaire and head of the Indian-dominated All-Trinidad Sugar Estates and Factory Workers Union. Under his leadership, the Mahā Sabhā quickly built 31 Hindu schools between 1952-6. A number of temples were also built, and most of those already existing became affiliated to the national body. A single pundit's *pariṣad* or council was also formed to coordinate activities and standardize practices. The effect was a Christian like congregationalizing of Hinduism: temples were constructed in the pattern of Christian churches, Sunday schools became the norm, and pundits often functioned like parish priests. Further, a single creed was promulgated and published in the Mahā Sabhā's Prayer Book of Sanskrit *mantrās* (with English translations). The creed, still learned in Hindu schools throughout Trinidad, provides a seven-point declaration of faith in:

(1) God as an immanent and pervasive Divine Essence
(2) manifestations of God as creating, preserving and dissolving powers of the universe
(3) *avatār* (incarnations of God from time to time)
(4) *ātma* (individual soul)
(5) that *ātma* is a part of the Divine Essence
(6) the law of *karma*

(7) the belief "that the Vedas, Upanishads, the Shāstras, the *Mahābhārat*, the *Rāmāyaṇa*, and the *Bhāgavad Gītā* contain all the eternal truths of religion".

It is clear that Hinduism in Trinidad, as evidenced by the working of the Mahā Sabhā, had become a condensed and coherent religious tradition which united the second and third generations of Indians following the initial generation of heterogeneous migrants.

Indian identity, carrying with it important ramifications for the perpetuation of Hinduism, continued to consolidate through the 1950s. In 1953, Maraj launched the People's Democratic Party (PDP), an Indian-based political body structured around the Hindu elite. As it happened, the PDP and the Mahā Sabhā were inextricable social entities, serving to politicize Trinidad Hinduism.

> The PDP in fact had never really functioned as an autonomous political party with a constitution and a grassroots organization. It felt no real need to organize since the branches of the Mahā Sabhā and the priesthood were easily convertible into political instrumentalities. Apart from the role which the Hindu priesthood played in keeping the flock together, it has always been the source to which politicians turned for help in their political careers. Pundits were among the principal opinion leaders within the Hindu community, and a few of them used this advantage to seek political office.
>
> There is considerable evidence to support the charge that many religious meetings in temple and in homes became political meetings, and that Hindus were enjoined to support their religion by ensuring that Hindus were elected to public bodies. Pundits were known to make individuals swear on the *loṭāh* (a holy Hindu vessel) to support candidates, and would threaten religious sanctions for broken pledges. (Singh 1985: 54)

Beginning with the 1956 elections, when the PDP challenged the African community-based People's National Movement (PNM), a renowned condition of racially-polarized politics has existed in Trinidad until recent times (see Bahadoorsingh 1968, Ryan 1972).

The 1960s and early 1970s witnessed a decline in Hindu communal spirit. The PNM led the country to independence in 1962, and continued to strengthen its grip on local and national politics. The island's economy was in decline, particularly the sugar industry which provided employment for the bulk of rural Indians; racial discrimination and other employment inequalities kept the Indian minority on the bottom of the country's socio-economic structure (cf. Harewood 1971; Malik 1971). Fundamentalist Christian missions from the United States made considerable inroads into the staid Indian community, converting a conspicuous number of Hindus. The Mahā Sabhā fell claim to allegations of corruption and mismanagement, while the Democratic Labour Party (DLP), heir to the PDP, ceased to be an effective opposition party by the late 1960s. In 1970, the radical Black Power movement rocked Trinidad, frightening and alienating much of the Indian population. Finally, the 1971 elections, boycotted by opposition parties and consequently granting sweeping powers to the PNM, "virtually finished off the East Indians as a political factor in Trinidad" (Tinker 1977: 82; cf. Ryan 1972: 462-89).

With the weakening of the Indian community many observers thought Hinduism in Trinidad was on its last legs. Schwartz, an anthropologist, identified "infrequent and selective commitment to Sanatanist beliefs and practices" among Hindu priests and laity alike (1967d: 245), as well as an overall decline in Hindu religious motivation in response to a greater move "in the direction of increased economic and political opportunities" (1964b: 13). Growing dissatisfaction with the Mahā Sabhā and its "Brahmanization" of Hinduism (insisting on the high status and ritual monopoly of Brahmans; cf. van der Burg/van der Veer 1986) further perpetuated a sense of malaise among average village Hindus. Indians began the 1970s in this down-trodden mood, but their condition would soon change rapidly.

Contemporary Trends in Trinidad Hinduism

In the mid- to late 1970s, the small republic of Trinidad and Tobago was the recipient of an unparalleled economic boom. It had been an oil producer since the turn of the century at least; yet following the OPEC price hikes and the world oil crisis beginning about 1972, the value of the country's oil exports skyrocketed. In 1970, Trinidad and Tobago earned 29.6 million from oil production and refining. By 1979, the income topped 920.8 million (Taylor 1980: 13). The massive economic injection provided for largescale public work schemes and rapid expansion in construction, transportation, retailing, and other sectors. By the late 1970s, the "petrodollars" had "soaked through the economy, raising the standard of living even at the bottom" (ibid., 14).

Simultaneously, an international rise in sugar price brought widespread benefits to Indian-dominated sugarcane areas. In 1974 alone, the price paid to cane farmer more than doubled (from 18.25/ton to 40.78/ton). The price further rose to over 100/ton by 1982 (Caroni Ltd. 1979, 1984). By one way or another, even the poorest villagers gained substantially through the course of the decade. Electricity, refrigerators, TVs, and cars, became village norms by the early 1980s.

Yet rather than acting to dissolve Hinduism through rapid Westernization, as some had predicted, the economic boom in Trinidad actually served to restore the Hindus' spirit and organizational strength. During ethnographic fieldwork carried out in 1973, Nevadomsky (1983: 77) noted some reluctance on the Hindus to spend money on religious ceremonies. That situation was completely reversed by the end of the decade, when individuals were spending thousands of dollars on lavish Hindu rites and celebrations.

Initially in the mid-70s, the *nouveau riche* of local communities would sponsor large *pūjās* or week-long *yāgnās* for the benefit of all; the sponsor would conceivably gain spiritual merit, but the achievement of conspicuous status was a motivating force as well. Since the earliest days of post-indenture settlement, *pūjā* had been refined to a basic ritual complex: the sixteen offerings (water, cotton, flowers, etc.) with accompanying *mantrās* were directed to Hanuman on Fridays, Satnarayan on Saturdays, and Suruj Narayan on Sundays; coloured *jhandī* or flags (red, white, and yellow respectively) were raised for each deity outside of the sponsor's home. *Yāgnās* (named after but not really resembling Vedic sacrifice) were rare, seven or fourteen-day occasions during which *pūjā* was performed and a sacred text, usually the *Bhāgavad Purāṇa* was read and interpreted daily by a pundit. With the newfound wealth of the 70s, these rites gained in frequency, decoration, scale of attendance (with *praśād* and qunatities of food for up to 1000 people), and diversity. *Pūjās* were soon held for Lakshmi, Saraswati, Ganesh, and others (represented by a virtual rainbow of *jhandīs*), and *yāgnās* are now held for the reading and interpretation of the *Rāmāyaṇa, Śiva Purāṇa, Mahābhārata, Bhāgavad Gītā, Vedās,* and other Sanskritic texts. So popular were the newly elaborated events that they quickly became institutionalized as the foundations of a religious revival.

This accelerated evolution of Hindu activities in Trinidad

developed a unitary, Great Tradition-style of orientation to an even greater degree. The remaining minor Hindu sects in Trinidad—the Ārya Samāja, Kabir *panth*, and Swami Narayanis (the Aghor *panth* has faded into obscurity)—have been peripheralized completely; moreover, their members take part in almost all Sanatanist activities. Even the recent Satya Sai Baba movement has failed to breach the stronghold of orthodox Trinidad Hinduism in any significant way. Vestiges of the so-called Little Tradition, interestingly, have remained in some isolated pockets; but these are viewed by the majority as low or impure. Such religious remnants included annual sacrifices to "Dih Baba" (a *grāmdevatā* found in Bihar, see Crooke 1896: 95), sacrifice of a hog to Parmeshwari by Chamars (exactly as conducted in parts of Uttar Pradesh; see Planalp 1956: 1668), south Indian-style cults involving possession by Badra Kali, preventative magic (*ṭoṭkā*) and healing by *mantrās*, use of black magic by specialized practitioners (*ojhā*), and pilgrimage to a Catholic shrine for a child's first haircutting *saṃskārā* in front of a miraculous statue, deemed *Sipari Mai.* Practically all of these isolated religious phenomena, however, are neglected by the younger, well-educated Hindus whose interests take them more in the direction of philosophy than of pragmatic ritual.

Since around 1982, the oil and sugar industries have fallen into steep decline, and a long and bitter economic recession has overwhelmed Trinidad and Tobago. Yet unemployment and a reduced cash flow have not stifled Hindu vivacity. A kind of momentum prevails. Though individuals are now less able to sponsor religious events, numerous local groups have been founded to raise funds and sponsor *yāgnās, melās* (festivals), song contests, plays, *bhajan* (hymn) and *satsang* (religious reading) groups. Hindu youth associations and national Hindu bodies alternative to the Mahā Sabhā currently organize a number of religious, educational, and cultural activities. Indian newspapers and other publications have also been founded of late. All of the institutions collectively represent and propagate a single social and cultural system, Trinidad Hinduism.

Conclusion

The phenomenon of Hinduism in diaspora presents students of Indian culture and society with unique, almost laboratory-like situations for analysing the impact of varying conditions on processes of retention and change. Processes such as the homogenization of

Indian culture towards "All-India" forms are presently underway in India, and observations of similar trends as they have occurred within overseas Indian communities may provide glimpses of future patterns on the subcontinent. Yet Indians overseas, faced with a contraposition to other religious traditions and most often relegated a minority ethnic status, have developed Hinduism into an "ethnic religion" (cf. Burghart 1987). That is, adherence to Hindu religious beliefs and practices (however refined, blended, or syncretized) becomes a fundamental criterion of affiliation to a specific ethnic group. This has been the case in Trinidad, where was an initial generalization of religion and culture around north Indian Great Tradition forms. Subsequently, institutionalization and psychological strengthening of Hindu identity have ebbed and flowered with the political and structural condition of Indians within this multi-ethnic society. Likewise in each overseas Indian community, specific historical conditions and the changing status of Indians vis-a-vis other segments of the host society combine to produce different manifestations of Hinduism and Hindu identity.[5]

The study of social and cultural transformation within Hindu populations, at home or abroad, should take precedence over the endless task of categorizing religious phenomena into schemes such as Great vs. Little, priestly vs. folk, literate vs. customary. Outside India, changes in Hinduism may actually produce a more "heightened sense of religiosity than among similar social strata in India" (Bhardwaj/Rao 1983: 2) In India itself, changes such as the spread of philosophical ideals among low castes or the growing militancy of certain Hindu organizations may be fundamentally altering the structure of Indian society. It is equally the nature of our social scientific attention, as much as the nature of the Hindu tradition, which must be reconsidered.

NOTES

The author conducted ethnographic fieldwork in Trinidad between October 1984–December 1985 under grants from the following bodies, to whom he is grateful: Philip Bagby Bequest, Nuffield College, Oxford, Sigma Xi Society, Oxford University Graduate Studies Committee, and the Spalding Trust. He also thanks Nick Allen, David Mosse, and Helen Lambert for their helpful information and advice concerning this article.

1. There are no available records between 1871-5. The colonial sources from which this data is derived, it should be noted, are not precisely reliable, but serve to provide significant proportional indicators.
2. Speckmann (1965: 37) lists a number of conditions which retarded or accelerated acculturation among overseas Indians. His list includes: absence of normal family relations due to unequal sex ratios (usually at least two or three males per female), rigid organizational structure of plantations, and geographic isolation from the rest of the colony. Similarly, Jayawardena (1986) discusses four variables affecting the kind of socio-cultural change among Indian migrants: (a) type of migration, (b) extent of remaining ties with India, (c) type of enterprise engaged in overseas, and (d) structure and polity of host society. Neither of these authors describes the amalgamation of Indian subcultures, however.
3. The caste system can and does survive within some overseas contexts primarily among business classes and in some western countries. Kuper (1960: 31) suggests that caste survives outside India if Indians "(1) can maintain a ritual exclusiveness from the time they leave India, (2) hold a privileged position in the economic organization and avoid proletarianisation, (3) retain ties with a protected caste nucleus in India, and (4) isolate their women from intimate cross-caste contact". Regarding the retained functions of caste among Indians in Uganda, Morris (1967: 275-7 and 1968: 27-8) points out that the system remained almost intact by virtue of the proximity to India for frequent visits, cordial race relations in the early years of migration (which then allowed for internal diversity within the Indian population), and caste representations large enough to remain distinct communities. None of these factors obtain for sugar colonies like Trinidad.
4. A sect founded in India in 1876 by Swami Dayanand Saraswati, the Ārya Samāj advocates a return to the basic tenets of the Vedas and, among other things, criticizes the worship of idols.
5. This is the central argument made by Jayawardena (1980) in contrasting Indian ethnicity in Fiji and Guyana. Drummond (1981) criticizes Jayawardena's methodology, adding that it is not only historical conditioning but continued representation of Indianess vs. Africanness which underscores ethnicity in Guyana (cf. Drummond 1980). Norton (1983: 191) reasserts Jayawardena's earlier thesis about places like Guyana (and Trinidad), writing that Indians, "having experienced an early erosion of much of their traditional social life, recreated an identity that has mythic qualities, and asserted this to establish a sense of their worth and strength in the wider society". Hinduism functions in a similar manner in South Africa, according to Kuper (1960: 215-16). Tinker (1977: 13) also points to religion as providing "the most important source of identification for the more tradition-minded among Indians overseas".

REFERENCES

Bahadoorsingh, Krishna 1968. *Trinidad electoral politics: The persistence of the race factor.* London: Inst. of the Race Relations.

Bharati, Agehananda 1970. "A social survey". In *Portrati of a minority: Indians in East Africa.* Ed. by Dharam P. Ghai and Yash P. Ghai, Nairobi: Oxford University Press, pp. 15-67.

Bhardwaj, Surinder M./Madhusudhana Rao 1983. "Religious rekniting of ethnic Hindus in the 'New World'". Paper presented at the annual meeting of the Association of American Geographers, Denver, April 1983.

Brereton, Bridget 1981. *A history of modern Trinidad 1783-1962.* London: Heinemann.

British Parlimentary Papers 1910. Report of the committee on emigration from India to the crown colonies and protectorates. XXVI (*c.* 5194).

Bronkhurst, H.V.P. 1888. *Among the Hindus and Creoles of British Guiana.* London: T. Woolmer.

Burg, Corstian van der/ Peter van der Veer 1986. "Pandits, power and profit: Religious organization and the construction of identity among the Surinamese Hindus". In *Ethnic and Racial Studies* 9: 514-29.

Burghart, Richard (ed.) 1987. *Hinduism in Britain.* London: Tavistock.

Caroni (1975) Ltd. 1979. *Annual report.* Brechin Castle, Trinidad.

———. 1984. *Annual report.* Brechin Castle, Trinidad.

Clarke, Colin 1967. "Caste among Hindus in a town in Trinidad". In *Caste in overseas communities.* Ed. by Bartom M. Schwartz. San Francisco: Chandler, pp. 165-99.

Dotson, Floyd/Lillion O. Floyd 1968. *The Indian minority of Zambia, Rhodesia, and Malawi.* New Haven: Yale Univ. Press.

Drummond, Lee 1980. "The cultural continuum: A theory of intersystems". In *Man* (N.S.) 15: 352-74.

———. 1981. "Ethnicity, 'ethnicity' and culture theory". In *Man* (N.S.) 16: 969-72.

Dumont, Louis 1970. *Homo Hierarchicus.* London: Weidenfeld & Nicholson.

Durbin, Mridula Adenwala 1973. "Formal changes in Trinidad Hindi as a result of Language adaption". In *American Anthroplogist* 75: 1290-1304.

Forbes, Richard 1984. *Arya Samaj in Trinidad: An historical study of Hindu orgnizational process in acculturative conditions.* Unpublished Ph.D. thesis, Univ. of Miami.

Gamble, W.H. 1866. *Trinidad: Historical and descriptive.* London: Yates & Alexander.

Grierson, George A. 1885. *Bihar peasant life.* London: Truebner.

Harewood, Jack 1971. "Racial discrimination in employment in Trinidad and Tobago". In *Social and Economic Studies* 20: 267-93.

Jayawardena, Chandra 1966. "Religious belief and social change: aspects of the development of Hinduism in British Guiana". In *Comparative Studies in Society and History* 8: 211-40.

———. 1968. "Migration and social change: a survey of Indian communities overseas". In *Geographical Review* 58: 426-49.

———. 1979. "Social contours of an Indian labour force during the indenture period". In *Rama's banishment*. Ed. by Vijay Mishra. Auckland: Heinemann, pp. 40-65.

———. 1980. "Culture and ethnicity in Guyana and Fiji". In *Man* (N.S.) 15: 430-50.

Kuper, Hilda 1957. "An interpretation of Hindu marriage in Durban". In *Afrian Studies* 16: 221-35.

———. 1960. *Indian people in Natal.* Durbar: Natal University Press.

Malik, Yogendra 1971. *East Indians in Trinidad.* London: Oxford University Press.

Mandelbaum, David G. 1964. "Introduction: Process and structure in South Asian religion". In *Religion in South Asia.* Ed. by Edward B. Harper. Seattle: University of Washington Press, pp. 5-20.

Marriott, McKim 1955. Little communities in an indigenous civilization. In *Village India.* Ed. by McKim Marriott. Chicago: University of Chicago Press. pp. 171-223.

Mayer, Adrian 1961. *Peasants in the Pacific.* London: Routledge & Kegan Paul.

———. 1967. Introduction. In *Caste in overseas Indian communities.* Ed. by Barton M. Schwartz. San Francisco: Chandler, pp. 1-19.

Miller, Robert J. 1966. "Button button...great tradition, little tradition, whose tradition?" In *Anthropological Quarterly* 39: 26-42.

Mohan, Peggy Ramesh 1978. *Trinidad Bhojpuri: A morphological study.* Unpublished Ph.D. Thesis, University of Michigan.

Morris, H.S. 1967. "Caste among the Indians of Uganda". In *Caste in overseas Indian communities.* ed. by Barton M. Schwartz. San Francisco: Chandler, pp. 267-82.

———. 1968. *The Indians of Uganda.* London: Weidenfeld & Niccolson.

Naidoo, N.B. 1959. "The survival of Hindu institutions in an alien environment". In *Eastern Anthropologist* 12: 171-87.

Nevadomsky Joseph 1983. "Economic organization, soical mobility, and chaning social status among East Indians in rural Trinidad". In *Ethnology* 22: 63-79.

Norton, R. 1983. "Ethnicity, 'ethnicity' and culture theory". In *Man* (N.S.) 18: 190-1.

Opler, Morris. 1959. "The place of religion in a north Indian village". In *South-western Journal of Anthropology* 15: 219-26.

Pocock, David F. 1957a. "Inclusion and exclusion: A process in the caste system of Gujerat". In *Southwestern Journal of Anthropology* 13: 285-300.

———. 1957b. "'Difference' in East Afirca: A Study of case and religion in modern Indian society". In *Southwestern Journal of Anthropology* 13: 285-300.

Protector of Emigrants, Government of Bengal (1875 to 1918). *Annual Report(s) on emigration to British and foreign colonies from the port of Calcutta.* Calcutta: Bengal Secretariat.

Redfield, Robert 1956. *Peasant society and culture.* Chicago: University of Chicago Press.

Roberts, G.W./J. Byrne 1966. "Summary statistics on indenture and associated migration affecting the west Indies". In *Population Studies* 20: 125-34.

Ryan, Selwny 1972. *Race and nationalism in Trinidad and Tobago.* University of the West Indies: Inst. of Social and Economic Studies.

Schwartz, Barton M. 1964. "Ritual aspects of caste in Trinidad". In *Anthropological Quarterly* 37: 1-15.

———. 1967a (Ed.). *Caste in overseas Indian communities.* San Francisco: Chandler.

———. 1967b. "Differential socio-religious adaption". In *Social and Economic Studies* 16: 237-48.

Schwartzberg, Joseph E. (Ed.). 1978. *A historical atlas of South Asia.* Chicago: University of Chicago Press.

Singer, Milton 1971. *When a Great Tradition modernizes.* New York: Yeager.

Singh, Kelvin. 1985. "Indians and the larger society". In *Calcutta to Caroni,* Ed. by John LaGuerre, St. Augustine: Extra-Mutual Studies Unit, University of the West Indies, pp. 33-60.

Speckmann, Johann D. 1965. *Marriage and kinship among Indians in Surinam.* Assen: van Gorcum.

Srinivas, M.N. 1952. *Religion and society among the Coorgs of South India.* London: Oxford University Press.

———. 1956. "A note on Sanskritization and Westernization". In *Far Eastern Quarterly* 15: 481-96.

Srinivas, M.N./A.M. Shah. 1968. "Hinduism". In *International Encyclopedia of the Social Sciences,* Vol. 6. pp. 358-66.

Taylor, Jeremy. 1980. "Drowning in Petrodollars". In *New Internationalist* 94: 13-14.

Tinker, Hugh. 1974. *A new system of slavery.* London: Oxford University Press.

———. 1977. *The Banyan tree.* Oxford: Oxford University Press.

Wood, Donald. 1968. *Trinidad in transition.* London: Oxford University Press.

THE POLYTHETIC-PROTOTYPE APPROACH TO HINDUISM

Gabriella Eichinger Ferro-Luzzi

Introduction

The clear definition of one's subject matter has long been thought to be an indispensable condition of any scientific investigation. Students of Hinduism with its bewildering variety have found this requirement problematic. Undeterred, some have nevertheless attempted definitions, others have preferred to speak of Hindu way of life rather than the Hindu religion or to define Hinduism by reference to history and geography leaving aside content (Basham, quoted after Sharpe 1970: 6). Blame for the difficulty to define the religion has even been put on the term "Hinduism" said to be "a false conceptualization incompatible with any adequate understanding of the religious outlook of the Hindus" (Smith, quoted after Sharpe 1970: 1-2).

In the following, I wish to show that it is not necessary to abandon the term Hinduism or deny it the status of a religion. What should be abandoned instead is the conviction that all concepts can be defined because they must possess common attributes and clear-cut boundaries. In the West this conviction has been attested from the times of ancient Greek philosophy. It goes to the credit of the medieval Indian philosopher Śrī Harṣa that he noticed an overlap between certain concepts, but he put this observation into the service of his *advaita* view that the world is an illusion and "the existence of the objects of our world is not defensible" (Granoff 1978: 11-13). It is as if he had argued that the existence of colours in the rainbow is not defensible because the colours of the rainbow flow into one another. The rectification of our thinking about concepts had to await Wittgenstein's discovery that concepts need not have common attributes and clear-cut boundaries but may be held together by "a complicated network of similarities overlapping and criss-crossing" (Wittgenstein 1976: para 66), in other words that a "family resemblance" may exist among their members. Concepts formed in such a way now called polythetic (Needham 1975: 349-69) cannot be defined but only exemplified.

This fact has been intuitively understood by Srinivas when he wrote: "It is impossible to define Hinduism because there are no beliefs or institutions which are common to all Hindus, and which mark them off from others" (Srinivas 1960: 574). The Indian scholar stopped short of explaining how such a vague concept can be understood, but otherwise his words correspond exactly to Wittgenstein's notion of "family resemblance" (idem, 1967). Srinivas further stated: "While it is not possible to define a Hindu, it is not very difficult to identify a person as a Hindu" (1960: 575). This again corresponds to the notion of "family resemblance". While a "family resemblance" cannot be defined by any constant attribute, it is often possible to identify a person as belonging to a certain family.

Traditional Approaches to the Understanding of the Concept of Hinduism

Before presenting my polythetic-prototype view of Hinduism, I want to point out the inadequacy of traditional approaches to it. Confronted with the kaleidoscopic variety of things a traditional non-Wittgensteinian stratagem has been to postulate two levels of understanding. Confusion is said to lie only at the surface, while at a deeper level there is unity and order. Whoever had made this claim has usually been praised for profound wisdom. Several scholars like Max Weber, S. Radhakrishnan, Tucci, Zaehner, to mention but a few, have tried to arrive at an understanding of Hinduism in this way. Their writings are studded with expression like "seeming diversity" "apparent incoherence", "hidden unity", "hard core" and so forth. Unfortunately for the credibility of their solutions to the problem of Hinduism the unity or hard core proposed has varied from scholar to scholar. For Max Weber, for instance, the structural core of Hinduism was "the transmigration of souls and the derived karma-doctrine" (1958: 28). Radhakrishnan found the "unity of spirit binding its different expressions ... into one organic whole" in Śaṅkara's monism according to which the world is an illusion (1931:

12, 22, 25-7). This doctrine was also singled out by Tucci; but he also claimed that if he had to express the essence of Hinduism in one word, he would choose the word *yoga* (1940: 50-1). Zaehner noticed correctly that "pantheistic monism is only one strand among many that go to make up the rich tapestry that is Hinduism" (1966: 3, 10, 187-9). Nevertheless he did not give up the conviction that Hinduism possesses an eternal and unchanging essence and found it in the fusion of theism, bhakti, and *advaita* philosophy in the manner of Ramanujan's qualified monism (*viśiṣṭa advaita*).

Zaehner's view lends itself to counter a possible objection that might be raised against my polythetic-prototype approach. Since the scholars mentioned have mostly declared the feature of Hinduism they personally favoured to be its core, it might be assumed that I am doing the same. However, if I had to choose among *advaita, dvaita* and *viśiṣṭa advaita* worldviews, like Zaehner I would choose the latter but for very different reasons. Contrary to him I hold qualified monism to be far from essential to Hinduism, since it seems to have even fewer adherents than monism and dualism. My reason for preferring a worldview which conceives of things as simultaneously similar and different is that it can be rationally defended and empirically demonstrated. All living beings consist of the same amino-acids and the whole universe is made up of the same elements and atoms. In this sense, therefore, everything is the same; but nothing authorizes us to disregard the different proportions and spatial arrangements of these common features. By taking them into account everything is different. I do not claim, of course, that this interpretation of qualified monism corresponds to the Hindu one, which is mystical, "a secret only sages can comprehend" (Zaehner 1966: 89).

The defining attributes of Hinduism proposed by the various scholars such as *karma* and rebirth, *yoga, advaita* and *viśiṣṭa advaita* views are all inadequate for the same reason: they do not apply to all Hindus and partly extend beyond to the followers of Buddhism and Jainism. Common denominators have been proposed not only for Hinduism as a whole but also for parts of it with the same lack of empirical support. For Max Weber, for intstance, "the core substance of [Hindu] mass religiosity is the the magical spell" (1958: 335), i.e. the *mantra* while Wadley says that "the notion of power is the defining characteristic of Hindu deities" (1975: 54). *Mantras*, however, are also muttered by the Hindu spiritual *élite*, whereas not all illiterate villagers are familiar with them. Although power characterizes all Hindu deities, it cannot strictly speaking define them for two reasons: firstly, power is vested also in many things other than deities; secondly, belief in the willingness of the gods to help seems to be more crucial for the relationship of the Hindu to his gods than their power. If the pragmatic Hindu villager—the one with whom Wadley is mostly dealing—conceived of the gods as powerful but otiose, he would not see any reason to worship them.

There is a second way of postulating unity in face of diversity. It consists in climbing to a higher taxonomic level or in fusing differences into a synthesis. While propounders of underlying unity generally stick to the numbers one or two (the one essence or the binary structure), propounders of synthesis favour the number three in the triad: thesis, antithesis and synthesis. Gonda chooses this second way to arrive at the unity of Hinduism. He is aware that "nearly all general statements about it have only relative validity" (1960: 347). Nevertheless, he remains convinced that Hinduism "only *seems* [emphasis added] to be a cultural mosaic of ill-fitting parts, but by nature it is unity.... This unity, however, is not uniformity but ... a synthesis" (1960: 355). Undoubtedly, there have been some attempts at synthesis in Hinduism, for instance the figure of the *trimūrti* also mentioned by Gonda. But the *trimūrti* is a rather artificial synthesis putting at the same level Brahmā, who has only two temples in the whole of India, Śiva and Viṣṇu, who can boast of thousands of temples.

To my mind, one of the characteristics of Hindu thought is precisely that it does not normally aim at a synthesis. Despite the glaring contradiction between belief in *karma* (the rigid autodetermination of one's fate) and *līlā* (the indetermination of one's fate because it is subject to the whims of a playful god) the Hindus may accept them both (Eichinger Ferro-Luzzi 1983: 289). Of course, the simultaneous espousal of contradictory beliefs is not limited to the Hindus, a finding which has greatly intrigued anthropologists. Perhaps the most sophisticated attempt at solving the problem has been to attribute to people holding such beliefs a non-standard logic that employs the third truth-value "indeterminate" in addition to true and false (Cooper 1975: 238-56). For my part, I cannot see any evidence that ordinary Hindus use this third truth-value which is just another type of synthesis. It rather seems that they manage to hold contradictory beliefs because they keep them separate. This claim might sound more persuasive if we remember that multilingual speakers effortlessly accomplish the same thing. They have no difficulty to consider a double negation an affirmation in one language and a negation in another or to conceive death, the sun or the moon as male in one language and as female in another. Just as multilingual speakers do not fuse different languages into a synthesis (even though some interferences may occur) so the Hindus need not aim at a synthesis of their various beliefs in a coherent religious whole.

The clinging of so many authoritative students of Hinduism to the idea of its unity obviously does not depend on their inadequate scholarship. They probably have been led to this position by their uneasiness when confronted by disorder and their preference for reductionism. Without the help of Wittgenstein's insight they also could not imagine in what other way Hinduism might be understood.

The Polythetic Approach to Hinduism

In the following, I shall give a few examples showing how disparate aspects of Hinduism can be thought to be held together by sporadic overlapping similarities rather than a common denominator at a deeper or higher level of analysis.

Village Hinduism with its worship of mostly bloodthirsty goddesses who have to be placated and Sanskritic rites addressed to gentle gods like Kṛṣṇa have nothing in common as long as we remain on this general level of description. Every form of Hinduism (as well as other religions), however, for heuristic purposes can be broken down into smaller constituent units and by doing so multiple overlapping strands become apparent. The fact that one deity is female and the other male creates no problem because a village goddess often has male servants who participate in her offerings and Kṛṣṇa may be worshipped together with Rukminī or Rādhā. Another overlapping similarity consists in the fact that non-Brahman *pūjāris* just like Brahman temple priests approach their respective deities in a state of ritual purity, though the purificatory rites of the latter are more elaborate. Furthermore, the blood demanded by the goddess and the milk pudding relished by Kṛṣṇa (Eichinger Ferro-Luzzi 1977: 544) may either be subsumed under the heading of food or it may be pointed out that, while Kṛṣṇa never accepts any bloody offering, village goddesses enjoy both blood and sweet dishes.

Many Hindus who believe in the cycle of rebirths (*saṃsāra*) strikingly agree on the negative evaluation of it and on desire for immediate liberation (*mokṣa*). Tukārām, the seventeenth century Maratha saint poet, however, *wanted* to be reborn in order to go on singing the praise of god (Zaehner 1986: 142) and his contemporary, the Tamil saint poet and *yogin* Tāyumāṉavar "prayed for further births to serve the suffering humanity" (Meenakshisundaran 1976: 50). Desire for rebirth and no desire for rebirth as opposites in the positive-privative form cannot have any common denominator; there also is no need for one. Despite their aberrant beliefs (from an Indian point of view) Tukārām and Tāyumāṉavar remained within the fold of Hinduism because they did not deny all its aspects simultaneously. They rather preserved ties with other less aberrant Hindus or Hindus aberrant in other respects: Tukārām, for instance, through his worship of Viṭhoba as Viṣṇu or Rāma and his *bhakti* spirit; Tāyumāṉavar, for instance, because he was a devotee of Śiva and a *yogin*.

Rebirth has not only been idiosyncratically evaluated by some Hindus, but belief in it has also been repeatedly rejected, for instance, by Rammohun Roy, the nineteenth century founder of Brahmo Samāj. Since Roy based his teachings on the Vedas he indisputably was a Hindu and even thought himself as an authentic one. Doctrines of both *karma* and *saṃsāra* were negated, for instance, by the north Indian mediaeval Kāpālikas. Despite these and other revolutionary ideas, however, they squarely remained within the Hindu fold as Śaivites and *yogīs*.

Nobody will deny the importance of purity and pollution in Hinduism, but there are Hindu rites which do not require purity like the Tamil worship of crows as the representatives of the ancestors. Preoccupation with pollution has also been repeatedly denied by devout Hindus. The Liṅgāyats, for instance, do not feel polluted by death. Liṅgāyat priests officiating at Śrīsailam, Andhra Pradesh, have no objection if worshippers touch the liṅgam in the temple, which would elsewhere be held to pollute the idol. Some mediaeval south Indian *siddhas* (saint poets and *yogic* physicians) made fun of the Hindu horror of saliva and caste pollution (Zvelebil 1973: 229: 31). Their poems, however, are popular to this day as a perfect expression of Śaiva *bhakti*. Also Gandhi, who in the eyes of many Indians and Westerners is a typical Hindu, did his best to abolish caste pollution.

One of Gandhi's traits which made him a typical Hindu was his ascetic bent. Asceticism, however, is rejected, for instance, by the Tantrics who otherwise preserve many features of traditional Hinduism like *yoga* and the worship of the godhead in female form, which also characterizes village Hinduism.

It might be objected that by dissecting Hinduism into minute fibres, some of which break off at a certain point while others continue, it will no longer be possible to draw a line between Hinduism, Jainism, Buddhism and other religions. But it has precisely been my purpose to demonstrate that all boundaries of polythetic concepts are fuzzy. Buddhism and Jainism are separate religions because of their members' wish to be separate and not because of any intrinsic criteria justifying their separate status. For instance, the rejection of the authority of the Vedas and of Brahman priesthood, the major ground on which Buddhists and Jains base their separateness, also characterize certain sections of Hinduism. This is not to say, of course, that Buddhism and Jainism have no features distinguishing them from Hinduism. The Buddhist denial of the existence of an eternal soul and the Jain extension of *ahiṃsa* (non-violence) to the vegetal and mineral world are cases in point. But a community's possession of such distinctive features is no sufficient criterion for being classified as a separate religion. Also Hindu communities have distinctive characteristics, as we have seen, and yet they do not leave the Hindu fold. The decision to call a religious community a sect or a separate religion is similar to the decision to call a linguistic community a dialect or a separate language. Low German, for instance, has phonological features distinguishing it from High German and linking it to Dutch, but Low German counts as a German dialect while Dutch counts as a separate language. Also in this case there is no intrinsic criterion in the speech forms that decides classification but the people's wish to be separate or not. When similarities are few as between Hinduism and Christianity, it is, of course, reasonable to speak of different religions, but the decision where to draw the line is always subjective and hence more or less arbitrary.

Prototypical Features of Hinduism

So far I have been concerned with illustrating why Hinduism should be considered a polythetic concept made up of a criss-cross of overlapping strands rather than a bounded unit possessing essential features. But I have called Hinduism a polythetic-prototype concept.

Most polythetic concepts, in fact, are not uniformly vague throughout their extension. Prototype, in the binominal polythetic-prototype, refers to a collection of the most frequent features reducing the vagueness of the polythetic notion. I am aware that the term 'prototype' might cause confusion and erroneously suggest the original model. It cannot easily be changed, however, because it has been used in this new sense for about ten years by American psychologist (Rosch *et al.* 1976, Osherson and Smith 1981: 35-58) and I have also done so several times.

As long as any claim to essentiality is abandoned all criteria that have been pointed out by various scholars as characteristic of Hinduism and useful to identify a Hindu remain valid as prototypical features. In language the term most frequently used for a domain tends to coincide with its most characteristic and prestigious features. For instance, in the West the rose is the prototype of a flower. Even though there are more daisies than roses, in our minds the rose stands foremost. We speak more often about roses than daisies and are likely to start with the rose when asked to list flowers. The case of Hinduism obliges me to qualify this seemingly indissoluble link between prototype, prestige and frequency of use. Some characteristic features of Hinduism are prototypical in the sense of combining high frequency of occurrence and prestige, others are not. For instance, Siva, Kṛṣṇa and Gaṇeśa as high gods venerated by a majority of Hindus, temple worship and the practice of pilgrimage belong to the former category. The concepts *dharma, karma, saṃsāra, mokṣa, brahman* as well as *advaita, viśiṣṭa advaita* worldviews, etc. I would include in the second category. Even though only a minority of Hindus believes in them or even knows them, they enjoy the greatest prestige both among educated Hindus and Westerners. Besides, their influence on the Hindus tends to increase now with the spread of education. The prototype of a Hindu might be a person who worships the above deities, visits temples, goes on pilgrimage and believes in the above concepts. Undoubtedly, such persons exist but they are only a minority among Hindus.

There is a second group of prototypical elements of Hinduism that enjoys great prestige though it does not apply to the majority of Hindus. I am referring to asceticism and vegetarianism. In their case, however, the relatively small number of followers does not owe to lack of knowledge but to lack of rigour. On a national average not more than about 30 per cent of Hindus are vegetarians by religious conviction (Gopalan *et al.* 1969:L 45) and strict ascetics are certainly much fewer still. Contrary to Western meat-eaters, however, non-vegetarian Hindus normally agree with their vegetarian correligionaries that abstaining from meat, fish and eggs is better than eating them and during most religious festivals they temporarily adopt a purely vegetarian diet. Similarly, the normally non-ascetic Hindu householder admires the ascetic world-renouncer and may occasionally submit himself to limited forms of *tapas* (austerity).

Final Remarks

In stressing that Hinduism should be understood as a vague polythetic-prototype concept, I might have given the impression that I hold all concepts to be such. But this is not so: a distinctive feature of a polythetic approach is precisely that it avoids absolute statements. Christianity and Islam, for instance, are clearly not polythetic. Even though they possess numerous elements overlapping with other religions, they also have essential ones that permit the minimal definition. Amongst other things, a Christian is a person who believes in God, Christ and the New Testament, and a Muslim is a person who believes in Allah, his prophet, and the Koran.

Since several scholars have doubted that Hinduism can be defined, and Srinivas has explicitly said so, my anti-essentialist view of it might not meet with too strong a resistance. Once it has been recognized that an undefinable concept exists, it should stand to reason that Hinduism is not the only one. Whenever definitions have varied from scholar to scholar it seems likely that we are dealing with an undefinable polythetic or polythetic-prototype concept. It should be clear, for instance, that Humphrey's attempts at defining beauty (1983: 121-37, cf. also Eichinger Ferro-Luzzi 1984: 639-94) are doomed to failure because without reference to a specific cultural context, beauty is a fully polythetic concept devoid of any privileged criterion of identification. It should be equally clear that evil eye beliefs and practices (Maloney 1976: viii) have no core and essential meaning (apart from referring to the eye) but only prototypical attributes. Hopefully, the example of Hinduism will facilitate the acceptance of my earlier proposals to consider also caste (Eichinger Ferrro-Luzzi 1983a: 129-59, 1986) as well as myth and other types of folk narrative (Eichinger Ferro-Luzzi 1983b: 437-58) as undefinable polythetic-prototype concepts.

To abandon the idea that patently different things called by the same name must have some kind of unity and to accept vagueness and disorder for what they are is not the end of the scientific endeavour but a new start. Freed from the old errors we can now study degrees of disorder and try to discover at what points and in which fields tolerance for imprecision tends to decrease.

NOTE

I should like to thank all participants in the discussion following the presentation of this paper and in particular Monika Thiel-Horstmann for her helpful comments.

REFERENCES

Cooper, David E. 1975. "Alternative logic in 'primitive thought'". *Man* (N.S.) 10, 238-56.

Eichinger Ferro-Luzzi, G. 1977. "The logic of South Indian food offerings". IN *Anthropos* 72, 529-56.

———. 1983a. *Cool fire: Culture-specific themes in Tamil short stories.* Aachen: Rader Verlag.

———. 1983b. "Strands versus structure in the theory of myth". In *Anthropos* 78, 437-58.

———. 1984. "Review of Humphrey, N., Consciousness regained". In *Anthropos* 79, 639-94.

———. 1986. "The polythetic prototype concept of caste". In *Anthropos* 81, 637-42.

———. 1987. *The self-milking cow and the bleeding Liṅgam: criss-cross of motifs in India temple legends.* Wiesbaden: Harrassowitz.

Gonda, Jan 1960. *Die Religionen Indiens.* Bd. I *Veda und älterer Hinduismus.* Stuttgart: Kohlhammer.

Gopalan, C./Balasubramanian, S.C./Ramasastri, B.V./K. Visweswara Rao 1969. *Diet atlas of India.* Hyderabad: National Institute of Nutrition.

Granoff, Phyllis 1978. *Philosophy and argument in late Vedānta: Śrī Harṣa's Khaṇḍanakhaṇḍakhādya.* Dortrecht: D. Reidel.

Humphrey, Nicholas 1983. *Consciousness regained: Chapters in the development of mind.* Oxford: Oxford University Press.

Maloney, Clarene 1976. "Introduction". In *The evil eye* (ed.) C. Maloney, pp. iii-xvi. New York: Columbia University Press.

Meenakshisundaran, T.P. 1976. *Tamil: A bird's eyeview.* Madurai: Makkal Nalvaalvu Manram.

Needham, Rodney 1975. "Polythetic classification: convergence and consequences". In *Man* (N.S.) 10, 349-69.

Osherson, Daniel N./Smith, Edward E. 1981. "On the adequacy of prototype as a theory of concepts". In *Cognition* 9, 35-58.

Radhakrishnan, S. 1931. *The Hindu view of life.* London: Allen and Unwin.

Rosch, E./Mervis, C.G./Gray, W.D./Johnson, D.M./Boyes-Braem, P. 1976. "Basic objects in natural categories'. In *Cognitive Psychology* 8, 382-439.

Sharpe, Eric J. 1973. "Introduction to Hinduism". In *Hinduism* (eds.) J.R. Hinnells and E.J. Sharpe, pp. 1-7. Newcastle upon Tyne: Oriel Press.

Srinivas, M. N. 1960. "Hinduism". In *Encyclopaedia Britannica.* Vol. 11, pp. 574-7.

Tucci, Guiseppe 1940. *Forme dello spirito asiatico.* Milan: Casa editrice G. Principato.

Wadley, Susan Snow 1975. *Shakti: Power in the conceptual structure of Karimpur religion.* Chicago: Department of Anthropology.

Weber, Max 1958. *The religion of India. The sociology of Hinduism and Buddhism.* (trans. and ed.) H.H. Gerth and Don Martindale. New York: Free Press.

Wittgenstein, Ludwig 1976. *Philosophical investigations,* (trans.) G.E.M. Anscombe. Oxford: Basil Blackwell.

Zaehner, R.C. 1966. *Hinduism.* London: Oxford University Press.

Zvelebil, Kamil 1973. *The smile of Murugan: On Tamil literature of South India.* Leiden: E.J. Brill.

HINDUISM: THE FIVE COMPONENTS AND THEIR INTERACTION

Günther-Dietz Sontheimer

1. Hinduism and the Study of Hinduism

The approach to Hinduism here is not to work out another monolithic conceptualization, but first to distinguish the different layers, levels, strands, currents, or, as I shall call them, *components*, and to treat each of them in its own right. They will then, however, not be viewed as watertight compartments, but rather as presenting a continuum and as interacting among themselves in a fluctuating process over thousands of years.

There is no comparable theology or religious conceptual framework or even terminology in Western religions which completely fits what we call "Hinduism", this has made comparative religion hazardous. There may be an underlying unity of Hinduism, expressing itself in a statement such as "India is one". But this unity is often postulated more or less on the basis of partial and selective evidence. Modern scholars have made many important and stimulating contributions towards understanding Hinduism, but their methodological approaches and key concepts are open to criticism and rarely stand the test of time. The study and understanding of Hinduism are handicapped not only by the vastness of divergent material and sources, but also by the compartmentalization of academic specialization such as philology, anthropology, sociology, religion, philosophy, psychology and so on. But Hinduism necessarily partakes of all these fields. In the past Hinduism was comprehended by the term *dharma*, but *dharma* did not mean the same thing at all times in all contexts for all people. It had to be defined again and again, not only from case to case, but also at several levels. It has been suggested that Hinduism is *sanātana dharma*: this may mean the conformity to old customs and the preservation of the solidarity of society not only at any given time, but also through time. The stress was on maintaining eternal *dharma*, deviation from which spelled personal and social ruin (Creel 1977: 20f). Nowadays it is stressed that it is ultimate reality which is eternal changeless, but that there is no ultimatacy about socio-religious institutions and customs (Creel 1977: 46 citing T.M.P. Mahadevan).

Ultimately the nature of Hinduism as a comprehensive religion is characterized by features which would make some say it is no religion (in the Western sense), namely the absence of dogmatic tenets or an overarching authority, however influential a particular belief may be, e.g. the belief in the authority of the Veda. But, as has been pointed out, one can be a good Hindu without believing in the Veda. Marglin formulates this aptly: "... to conceptualize the Hindu life-world from a single consistent point of view is to ignore the fact there is not one privileged point of view from which to look at things. The 'objective' non-situated viewpoint is a myth dear to the Western scientific life-world but I would suggest not to the Hindu life-world" (Marglin 1985: 289).

We have tried to distinguish five components which appear whenever one investigates Indian religious phenomena (cp. Kelkar 1977: 23f, who speaks of three elements). Our approach is motivated by a desire to teach Hinduism systematically to students and by uneasiness which comes from seeing that some components are often ignored or misunderstood for various reasons. Such "endocentric" perceptions of the multiple elements or strata of Hinduism as *mārga* ("classical") and *deśi* ("folk"), *dharma* and *deśadharma* (cp. Wezler 1985: 1ff), Sanskrit and Prakrit, *saumya* = "peaceful", "auspicious", etc., and *ugra* are extremely useful and have hardly been systematically explored, but we have to be cautious whose "endocentric" view we take. Thus, for example, a "lower" deity would be called by some *ugra* = "fierce", "ferocious", "ogre-like", "appalling", "shocking", etc. (Molesworth 1857: 86). But this might not be acceptable to the actual adherent of such a deity, for whom *ugra* (if he knows the term) would imply "powerful", "mighty", "strong", "high", "noble" (cp. Monier Williams 1956: 172). And we may take a contextual view, as did, e.g. the Maharashtrian saint Rāmdās (1608-81): in one place he lists the famous folk deity Khaṇḍobā amongst the ghosts (*Dāsbodh* 3.2.29), but nevertheless sees him elsewhere as powerful enough to grant children (ibid.,

3.3.47), and in yet another context even identifies him with Rāma (Sontheimer 1986a: 19). Khaṇḍobā, God as king, and Rāma, the ideal king, thus share an essential element of successful kingship, i.e. both are *ugra.*

Indian religious phenomena may partake of some or all of these components, but the important point is *which component is emphasized and which may be just secondary, subordinated, peripheral, or amounting to lip service in a particular case or at a particular time.* Once the components are distinguished we can use "endocentric" perceptions and also test and apply the theories developed by modern scholars as far as they are relevant to the interaction of the different components. I shall list some of the most important theories later. I shall not try to be exhaustive, because this is not the main concern of this paper. It may seem superfluous to summarize the contents of some well-known theories, but that has to be, because they may not be so well-known to followers of other disciplines. It may also be unnecessary to reiterate that theories are often based on the approach and object of *one* discipline and cannot explain the *whole* phenomenon of Hinduism. In this context it is tempting, though admittedly arrogant in view of the path-breaking but restricted contributions which scholars in various disciplines have made, to recall the famous parable of the "Elephant and the Blind Men" (*Udāna* 6, 4 and elsewhere).

We may start with the well-known concept of *Sanskritization* developed by M.N. Srinivas (1952; Staal 1963: 261ff). According to him Sanskritization is a process by which a lower caste tries to raise its status and to achieve a higher position in the caste hierarchy. Sanskritization can happen by adoption of vegetarianism, teetotalism, worship of Sanskritic deities, or employment of Brahmins for ritual purposes. It can refer to ritual and custom, ideas and beliefs, as well as to the pantheon. The material to which Sanskritization applies consists of non-Sanskritic gods, beliefs, and rituals, e.g. the worship of village deities, ancestors, trees, rivers, mountains, and generally local cults. Sanskritization happens *at the expense of* non-Sanskritic elements.

Following Robert Redfield and Srinivas, Milton Singer introduced the distinction between "Little Tradition" and "Great Tradition". The "Great Tradition" was identified with Srinivas' Sanskritic Hinduism, i.e. the generalized practice and beliefs which have an All-India spread. The local forms of Hinduism can be seen as the "Little

Tradition", and Sanskritization becomes the process by which the "Great Tradition" spreads to the "Little Tradition" and absorbs it (see summary in Staal 1963: 263f.).

McKim Marriott (1965: 171-222) pointed out that Sanskritization does not necessarily take place *at the expense of* the little tradition, and that the identification of a local deity with a universal deity is one of the main techniques of Sanskritization. He introduced instead the concepts of universalization and parochialization. One finds in an Indian village a transmutation and transformation of great and little traditions resulting from upward universalization (the carrying forward of religious contents which are already present in the little traditions to the levels of the literate Sanskritic great traditions of Hinduism under the influence of the latter) and parochialization (downward evolution of great traditional elements and their integration with the little traditional elements). But it is difficult to know whether the present religious tradition of a community is the result of one, and not also the result of the other, of these two processes. After all, as Staal reminded us (1963: 269), Sanskrit culture itself originated from the little tradition and these origins are generally visible in a later stage.

Another concept relevant in our context is "Inklusivismus". This is a term which Paul Hacker uses to describe data

> aus demjenigen Bereich, den wir indische Religionen und speziell indische Religionsphilosophie nennen. Inklusivismus bedeutet, dass man erklärt, eine zentrale Vorstellung einer fremden religiösen oder weltanschaulichen Gruppe sei identisch mit dieser oder jener zentralen Vorstellung einer Gruppe, zu der man selber gehört. Meistens gehört zum Inklusivismus ausgesprochen oder unausgesprochen die Behauptung, dass das Fremde, das mit dem Eigenen als identisch erklärt wird, in irgendeiner Weise ihm untergeordet oder unterlegen sei. Ferner wird ein Beweis dafür, dass das Fremde mit dem Eigenen identisch sei, meist nicht unternommen. (Hacker 1983: 12)

Hacker uses the term "Inclusivismus" mainly in textual criticism of Sanskrit literature and in the field of theology and philosophical ideas expressed in texts. Hacker's views have been reviewed by Halbfass, Oberhammer and Wezler (Oberhammer: 1983). According to Wezler, *inclusivism* mainly implies a relationship of tension between the *old* and the *new, tradition* and *change*. He extends the theory to psychological, social and similar conditions which he considers responsible for the *practice* of inclusivism. For example, the strict tradition of family values handed down in the joint family might psychologically generate the attitude of inclusivism which leads to taking over the new without radically abandoning the old. We are reminded here of the suggestion of McKim Marriott, who proposes the term "dividuality" of the person "in the flow of social relationship" (1976: 196)—for example, a member of a joint family may belong at the same time to a sect which may transcend family, caste and religion (cf. Derrett 1976: 60f.).

Modifying Dumont's theory of the dichotomy of pure and impure based on one model of hierarchical Hindu society, i.e. the *varṇa* model (Dumont 1966), Burghart (Burghart 1978) has suggested that there are three hierarchical models, which are incongruent: (a) the Brahmanical organic model of the sacrificial body of Brahmā as the cosmic-based social organism composed of four *varṇas*; (b) the continuum of the incorporated *jīvas* which are separate from the ascetic, who ranks highest in this hierarchy; and (c) the king who rules over the earth (*bhūpati*) and men irrespective of caste, tribe or sect, differentiated by their respective rights and duties towards him.

Brahman, ascetic and king each claim their highest rank and godhood within the respective hierarchies. But the hierarchies do not face each other as rigid structures, but rather interact (in a typically Indian way?). Elements of the codices of another hierarchy were incorporated into each one's own hierarchical model, and the highest ranking person of the other hierarchy was assigned an honourable but subordinate rank within the enlarged model (Burghart 1978).

Recently A.K. Ramanujan has presented the important theory of "reflexivity" for the interactions between different Indian literatures, oral and written. Unfortunately the paper is as yet unpublished (Ramanujan 1985a). Ramanujan says that similar observations can be made about other aspects of the culture, such as ritual, philosophy, eating, or socio-linguistic patterns. He states: "Reflexive elements may occur in various sizes: one part of a text may reflect on another part; a whole tradition may invert, negate, rework and revalue another. Where cultures (like the 'Indian') are stratified yet inter-connected, where different communities communicate but do not commune, the texts of one strata tend to reflect on those of another: encompassment, mimicry, criticism and conflict, and other power relations are expressed by such reflexivities. Self-conscious contrasts and reversals also mark off and individuate the groups.... Stereotypes, foreign views, and native self-images on the part of some groups, all tend to think of one part (say, the Brahmanical) as original and the rest as variations, aberrations: so we tend to get monolithic conceptions. But the civilization, if it can be described at all, has to be described in terms of all these dynamic interrelations...." It follows that a view of what Hinduism is cannot be exclusively derived from the attitudes, written and/or oral texts, or statements or members of one group, however articulate they may be. Admittedly, modern middle class notions favour certain aspects of Hinduism; these may be summarily circumscribed by the preference for "Rāmrājya", Kṛṣṇa, the *Bhagavadgītā* (now nearly a "scripture" like the Bible), bhakti, sectarian guru worship, and emphasis on the spiritual and philosophical contents of Hinduism, especially the Vedānta of "Neohinduism" (cf. Derrett 1968: 560). In this process, much of the ritual world (the *karmakāṇḍa*) of the Smṛtis or the culture of the "Little Traditions", for example, get out of focus or even disappears, along with its enormous oral literature, whereas middle class notions become more and more assertive and dominant, if not monolithic. All the more does the past of Hinduism have to be studied and recorded taking *all* components and their interaction into account, so that we can isolate modern trends towards reductionism, and detect change or persistence.

These theories and concepts, as well as the five components which I shall outline below—must also be reviewed in the context of time and space. Mythological, astrological, sacred and historical/secular time have to be taken into account. The element of time plays a role, e.g. in the fixing of festivals: for example tribal festivals especially are seasonal, and every year the exact dates for the *madhais* in Bastar in the month of Māgh are fixed *ad hoc* by a secular body at the end of the harvest season. All-India festivals are determined by astrological considerations. Equally important is the dimension of space. The old Tamil theory of the landscapes (*tiṇai*) may be referred to here. The *tiṇai* theory may have become just a literary convention, but I would still maintain that it was based originally on direct observations of facts which persisted in later times. Each of the five landscapes (*kuṟiñci* = the densely forested, hill region, *mullai* = the pastoral region, *marutam* = the riverine agricultural region, and *pālai* = the "desert", are especially relevant here) is inhabited by its own deities roughly typical of the environment, and by people following occupations adapted to the landscape. It can be shown that the theory has at least a great heuristic value in explaining the basic pattern of religious forms (Sontheimer 1985a: 131ff.) and can be applied to other parts of India at least until the *pax britannica* and the subsequent deforestation and systematic extension of agriculture on a scale never before experienced in Indian history. The contents of the *tiṇai* theory and of Caṅkam poetry reflect a rather "secular", though not irreligious, outlook on life.

The spatial dimension also plays a great role in Sanskrit culture and literature. I have called this Indian version of the "dichotomy" of "nature" and "culture" summarily and for the sake of simplicity *vana* and *kṣetra*, or "wilderness" and "settled space" (Sontheimer: 1994). I have avoided the terms "nature" and "culture" since *vana* and *kṣetra* may be partially co-extensive. As A. K. Ramanujan has said with reference to the classical Tamil poems (1985b: 286), nature and culture are in these poems not opposed but co-substantial. Between the two poles of *vana* and *kṣetra* there is a reversible, fluctuating continuity. A Brahmanical *kṣetra* with a purāṇic deity may relapse again into a locality where pastoral people and "predatory" people dominate. The deity is forgotten and is superseded by a folk deity attended by Guravs, a non-brahmanical caste (Sontheimer 1976: 23ff.). The forest with all its implications, e.g. social, mythological, ritual, philosophical and so on, was also, as we have said , very much a physical reality until the extension of agriculture in modern times. 150 years or so ago Rāma still would not have had to go very far from Ayodhyā to be in the midst of a forest. *Kṣetra* I would describe, in brief, as well-ordered space, the riverine agricultural nuclear area which is ideally ordered by the King, and by the Brahmans with their *dharmaśāstra*. If we speak in terms of settlement patterns, the two poles are demarcated by the "movable" tribal hamlet, the *halli* or *palli* (Sontheimer 1985a: 134) on the one hand and the ideal but static city of Ayodhyā as described in the *Rāmāyaṇa* (cf. Ramanujan 1970: 234).

2. The Five Components of Hinduism

1. The work and the teaching of the Brahmans

The Brahmans were the authors of authoritative scriptures which formed the elements of what is sometimes called codified Hinduism (Eschmann 1978: 82) or its normative ideology (Hardy 1984: 13ff), though we must remember that this normative Hinduism rather had only persuasive power and was no law in the Western sense. The basis of the Brahmans' belief and of their prestige was the eternal imperishable Veda (*śruti*), that is, texts which are not derived from God or Man (*apauruṣeya*). The Brahmans were the compilers of the *Dharmaśātras* (*smṛti*) in which they ordered life, teaching what was righteousness in their view. *Dharma* was strictly speaking to be interpreted according to the *mīmāṃsā* rules of the Vedic sacrifice. Accordingly all customs conflicting with *śruti* and *smṛti* were to be treated as void. The king was not obliged to follow *mīmāṃsā* rules: the Brahman, who advised him had no power to require him to follow their advice. In practice the public followed customs, even when repugnant to the *śāstra* (Derrett *et al.* 1976: 17ff, 57, 111). The Brahmanical world view in *Dharmaśāstras* may be seen as a ritual model of the universe expressed in social categories. The universe is a manifestation of Brahmā or a totality of ordered time and space. According to the organic model, society was found by Brahmā at the beginning of time and from him emerged the four *varṇas* (Burghart 1983: 637). Within this framework the Brahmans searched out and formulated the hidden values of human behaviour. They reflected on what were only human instincts. They were the great ritual experts, and they are still indispensable today, at least in the most important rites de passage (i.e. the *saṃskāras*), or, for example, in the *vastu-śānti-pūjā* for a new factory.

In the epics and the Purāṇas Brahmans gathered and reworked a part of the immense oral literature. They responded to the human inclination to assign the miraculous deeds of heroes and gods to the Golden Age of truth (*satyayuga*) and divided time into four cyclical ages. According to the Purāṇas the gods normally resided in heaven; only from time to time when *dharma* was in danger Viṣṇu descended as an *avatār* to restore *dharma.* The kings were not so much deities as in folk belief but rather had the *functions* of deities. What was alien to the epics and Purāṇas, which are also a part of *smṛti,* was a deity immediately accessible to man, "here and now". The gods who were part of the universe created by Brahmā became secondary in importance in the Vedic *yajña* of the *śrauta* ritual, and they were subordinated to the ritual act as such. When *mūrtis* became common the deity in the *mūrti* was not a visible, tangible manifestation of god as in the folk religion, but, as Śabara, the commentator on the *Pūrvamīmāṃsāsūtras,* argued: *na lokavat iha bhavitavyam, iha pūjyamāna pūjā pradhānam* (IX, 1,9; Sontheimer 1964: 50f). "The worshipping of the worshipped is the main factor in the ritual." This corresponds with the notion that the Brahmans are highest gods (Manu IX.317-19: *daivataṃ paramam*) on earth and that strictly speaking they should not serve as *devalakas*, i.e. as temple priests (Manu IX.152).

2. Asceticism and renunciation

Asceticism (*tapas*) and renunciation (*saṃnyās*) and resulting "sectarian movements" constitute another component. Asceticism and abstinence may have various aims, e.g. the achievement of the heightening of life-potentiality by the *tapasvin* (Piatigorsky 1985: 229-31), like the demon who performs *tapas* to obtain a boon of immortality from Brahmā. This kind of *tapas* brings the "yogī" close to the "warrior". Often juxtaposed in folk religion, both achieve superhuman feats (Sontheimer 1981: 15). Whereas in folk religion the aim of *tapas* is to acquire supernormal powers, side by side we find the effort to ethicise and spiritualise *tapas* (cf. Ruping 1977: 81-98).

The aim of asceticism may also be to renounce the life of the householder and caste. According to the *Dharmaśāstras* the ascetic renounces family and property, though not the world emanating from Brahmā: this he internalizes (Burghart 1983: 639). Standing apart from ordinary society, the ascetic lives a wandering life in the wilderness, at least during the initial phase of his carrier; he is beyond the plurality of phenomena and sees the unity of man, though he may visualize the *jīvas* caught in the cycle of rebirths bound by their *karman*. He discerns the unity of *ātman* and *brahman*. His discipline (*tapas*) may involve a wandering life in the forest (*vanavāsa*). This normally lasts twelve years, just as Cakradhara—to cite one example—wandered twelve years in the forest before he re-emerged and attracted followers who eventually formed the Mahānubhāv "sect" (Sontheimer 1982: 334). The preconditions of the ascetic's insights are not the performance of the *karmakāṇḍa* of the *Dharmaśāstra* but self-discipline and the pursuit of such ethical principles as *dama, satya, akrodha* and *dayā*. *Ahiṃsā* was another principle which was born in the realm of the ascetic renouncer who lives in harmony with the animals of the forest. The ascetic's *dharmas* also found a place as the *sādhāraṇa dharmas* in the *Dharmaśāstra*. Although they were subordinated to *varṇa* and caste *dharmas*, they made life in the *kṣetra* tolerable and acceptable, and made the *varṇa* ideology a viable proposition.

3. Tribal religion

As the third component I would like to consider tribal religion. One may object that postulating "tribal religion" means unnecessarily introducing an "etic" or "exocentric" category as a component which is not found in Hinduism. But the tribals are mentioned from the earliest times in texts and they stand in relationship to the social and ritual order of the plains, if only with an antithetical function as the necessary evil. As such they are referred to as robbers and even as demons (*piśācas* or *bhūtas*). At the same time we find seemingly paradoxical reference to their honesty, gratitude and innocence (Deliege 1985: 11f). This is reflected, e.g. in the famous episode when Śabarī, a women of the tribal forest-dwellers, offered Rāma berries which she had already tasted (*Rāmāyaṇa, Āraṇyakāṇḍa* 73). This notion of the tribals accords well with the image of their habitat amongst the people of the plains. The forest is as ambivalent as the tribal: fearsome and at the same time the source of renewal and "the seed of dharma". By tribal religion I mean not only the religion of the forest tribes, e.g. of the Murias and Marias of Bastar, but also the great, often nomadising pastoral groups who live, e.g. in Rajasthan and in the Deccan. Mountains, the termite mound, trees, animals of the forest, rivers, all characteristic of untamed, dangerous nature, are close to them and intrinsically divine. Religion reflects human life and the relation to deities is marked by intimate familiarity. Anthropomorphic *mūrtis* of deities are rare (Elwin 1955: 577; Eschmann 1978: 81f), because "shamans" get possessed by and deal with ancestors of the family, clan gods, or the earth-goddess, the *devī* of the village. For example the shrine of the goddess Danteśvarī at Chota Dongar in Bastar has no *image,* and the "seat" of the *devī* is empty. There are now often bell-metal *mūrtis* in temples, but the art of casting *mūrtis* is a relatively recent import to Bastar.

Drumming and dancing activate the spirits and divinities. Dance and music are also the expression of the deities (the marriage god) which grant fertility, as in the marriage dances of the Marias of Bastar. Part of the marriage dances may also be the enactment of encounters with bison. Similarly the bull-grappling of pastoralist preceding marriages is mentioned in early Tamil literature and bull-baiting is common in some parts of contemporary Tamilnadu (Hardy 1983: 616ff).

In the view of people adhering to other components, tribal

customs are reputed to be marked by sexual licentiousness and freedom. Misunderstood as these customs are by the people in the *kṣetra,* they contributed to the inversion in such tantric practices as the *śabarotsava* (*Kālikāpurāṇa* 63.17ff), in which the normal rules of hierarchy and sexual propriety are abandoned. Similarly the love of the *gopīs* for Kṛṣṇa is interpreted as erotic or it is interpreted as a pure example of emotional bhakti, or it is interpreted philosophically in terms of *yoga* or *advaita* (Hardy 1983: 494ff). Thus we must keep in mind that there was not only a process of "Hinduization" of tribes but also the influence of tribes on Hinduism (see Kulke 1979: 17ff).

4. Folk religion

A crucial ingredient in folk religion is the immediate presence and access to god or a goddess in the form of a *mūrti* or *mūrtis* which may be aniconic or iconic. The god exists "here and now", is earthbound, and does not live in some puraṇic *svarga.*

The folk deity is well-described in the view of the *pūrvapaksin* in the *devatādhikaraṇa* (IX.1.6-8) of the *Pūrvamīmāṃsāsūtras.* Of course, this view is unacceptable to the *siddhāntin,* who presents the "orthodox" interpretation of the Veda. The *pūrvapakṣin* suggests:

(a) *vigrahatva devatā:* the deity possesses corporality.
(b) *devata bhuṅkte:* the deity actually eats food in the form of offerings.
(c) *prasīdati devatā:* the deity is actually pleased by the offering.
(d) *pritā satī phalaṃ prayachati:* the deity rewards the worshipper with the desired fruit.
(e) *arthapati devatā:* the deity can be an owner of property.

The *mūrti* has as it were a living personality and is treated as a living person. Institutions like *prasād, darśan,* etc., indicate this. But there are many more terms in regional languages which form an unwritten inventory of folk cults. They point to a pervasive, coherent and conservative system of folk religion which is spread all over South Asia and which can never be expected to have been reproduced in its original form in Brahmanical texts. In practice the Brahmin would nevertheless often participate in folk-religion, and it would form the raw material for textual interpretation. Thus, the primordial cult of the mother goddess reappears in Māhatmyas and śaktic-tantric texts and ritual. We may cite *some* terms which are ubiquitous in the practice of Maharashtrian folk cults and which also have their equivalents in other regions and languages (cf., e.g. Höfer and Shrestha 1973: *passim*).

aṅgāt yeṇeṃ—possession by a deity or a *bhūt.* This normally does not happen in a Śiva or Viṣṇu temple with a purāṇic (*saumya*) emphasis.

devruṣi (Sanskrit *deva* + *ṛṣi*)—the medium who can get possessed by ancestors and god(s) and deal with them.

jāgṛt dev—the deity is alive, attentive, heedful and responsive, that is:

dev pāvto—the deity responds to the offerings and wishes of his devotees. Therefore one can make a vow:

navas—and the deity grants children, cattle, etc., and healing in return for the gift.

kaul lavṇeṃ—the deity when approached decides cases. This aspect is known even on the level of inscriptions, which even tell us that the deity's signature may be forged at times (cf. Derrett 1968: 484f, Sontheimer 1964; *passim*). A nineteenth-century Maratha document informs us that in villages where there is *jāgṛt daivat,* disputes have been settled with the help of the deity "since the beginning" (Pune Archives, Deccan Commissioner 1825, Rumal Nr. 151; I owe the reference to N.K. Wagle).

kheḷ—participation in the divine play of the deity. People get possessed by ancestral spirits or deities during a dance. Cp. kheḷ-Khaṇḍobā.

jatrā—participation in the god's divine play, e.g. in his hunting excursion or his marriage. In the Khaṇḍobā cult, for example, devotees act like horses and dogs of the god.

svayaṃbhū liṅg or *piṇḍ*—Unlike an image or a *liṅgam* and *yoni* installed in a ceremony (*prāṇapratiṣṭhā*), the god shows himself (*svarūpa*) for the first time spontaneously, to his devotee or to a cow, in the form of a stone, in an anthill, etc.

But the deity can be also a "walking and speaking god" like Cakradhara (*Līḷācaritra,* Uttarārdha 564). The deity may be like Rudra, the folk god (Sontheimer 1986a; 1985b), as reflected in the *Śatarudrīya* hymn. He is omnipresent and transcendent, but at the same time very much earthbound and very close to and similar to the folk; he has personal characteristics which distinguish him from other Vedic gods. Though incorporated into the Vedic ritual as Agni, Rudra was basically antagonistic to the Brahmanical outlook and ritual. Rudra was emulated by his followers. For example, the Ekavrātya or *sthāpati* of the Vrātyas became Rudra, Īśāna, Mahādeva, etc., in his cosmogonic ritual, just as even today the very similar *kāraṇikadevarus,* the chief Vaggayyas and devotees of Mailāra/ Khaṇḍobā, are possessed by the god and make their prophecies at the annual *jatrā* as Devaragudda and Mailar in Karnataka. Rudra appears as the leader of groups, just as Khaṇḍobā appears as the leader of particular groups on their terms, e.g. to the hunter he is a hunter, to the thief a lord of thieves, to the merchant he is the merchant *par excellence.* Similarly, Kṛṣṇa Gopāla lives among the *gopas* as a *gopa* ascending Govardhana with them to worship his *altar ego,* which was originally probably a mountain spirit (Vaudeville 1980: 1ff.). In Caṅkam literature the *vēlaṉ* is described. He dances the *veriyāṭu,* is a reflection of Murukaṉ, and in fact becomes *Vēlaṉ* with a capital 'V' in his frenzied dance (Ramanujan 1981: 115).

Charismatic persons endowed with *tejas* and considered divine were and are frequently found. After their death the surviving power of such persons or of those who had a premature or accidental death are still worshipped. In fact, after a premature or unnatural death, as well as a warrior's or *satī's* death, a person can be deified. But it is a formality or means of glorification rather than a necessary condition that the deified person should first be associated with a purāṇic heaven and deity (cf. Blackburn 1985: 259ff.). For example, a person may be famous as an animal doctor in his life, and after his death continue to be worshipped as a famous god without the need of ascending Kailās and returning as an *avatār* (Sontheimer 1976: 177).

In folk belief the king also tends to be identified as a god, with all the associations of fertility, heroship, and secular and divine powers. Especially the robber, or a hero rising from "obscure" origins, is such a king. His followers are heroes, for whom "the king is god" or "the god is king". Here the ethical considerations, the *dharmas* of the *kṣetra,* do not necessarily apply. The reaction in the Purāṇas or Māhātmyas would be to demonize these rulers for assuming the position of gods and for allowing themselves to be worshipped: e.g. the demons Maṇi and Malla called themselves *īśvara* and had to be killed by Khaṇḍobā (*Mallāri-Māhātmya* by Cintāmaṇi, 1.97), only to live on as devotees of Khaṇḍobā. In the *dharmaśāstra* the king tends to be subordinated to the *śāstric* order of world. He may be allowed to be considered a god in some contexts, but essentially he is given only the position of a god: here *kṣatra* may tend to be subordinated to *brahman*.

5. Bhakti

The emphasis of the fifth component is on devotion to a personal, single god (*iṣṭadevatā*) who on his part yearns (Marathi: *bhūkeḷā* = is hungry) for a true *bhakta* and supports him throughout his life. Pure love is emphasized, even if the god tends to be transcendent, as in the more philosophical or "intellectual" bhakti of the *Bhagavadgītā*. Bhakti, though heavily influenced by the sexual love-relationship, as illustrated by the tribal Kṛṣṇa Gopāla and the *gopīs* or the love between Murukaṉ and Vaḷḷi in the early *akam* poetry, transcends both "tribal" and "folk" religion. Bhakti poetry borrows from folk religion its metres and genres and the belief in the immediate presence of the deity, but rejects its "primitive" (*ugra*) features. The spontaneous, emotional bhakti movements of the Āḻvārs, Nāyaṉārs, Viraśaivas and Maharashtrian saints also reject and transcend caste barriers and the scriptural *karmakāṇḍa*, at least initially. It is the sincerity of devotion expressed through song-poetry, dance (as in *kīrtans* and *bhajans*), and the community of saints which matter, not the ritual as such. The saint or guru who has realized God may become the mediator between the *bhakta* and God, though in the monistic Śaivite bhakti the human guru tends to be obliterated. His only role is to make manifest the true nature of guruhood. This expresses itself in the divine *śabda* which participates in the transcendent nature of the *satguru* (Vaudeville 1974: 116f, 137).

3. The Khaṇḍobā Cult as a Mirrior of Hinduism

In order to illustrate our arguments we may again refer briefly to the cult of Khaṇḍobā. This is one of the most complex and widespread cults of Maharashtra and has equivalents in Karnataka and Andhra Pradesh. Basically Khaṇḍobā is a folk deity. He closely resembles the Vedic deity Rudra as reflected in texts of the Vedic period: the *Atharvaveda*, the *Brāhmaṇas* and the *Śrautasūtras*. There we find Rudra portrayed as an ambivalent folk deity who had to be integrated into the brahmanical *śrauta* ritual. It seems clear, however, that he belonged primarily to the Vrātyas and to the group mentioned in the *Śatarudrīya,* rather than to the Brahmanical sacrificial priests. In these early texts we also get a picture of a god who has not yet been dynamically interpreted by later epic and purāṇic authors nor by Śaivite "sectarians" with their own peculiar ritual and philosophy. The references to Rudra and his followers provide us with as it were a detailed checklist for describing the continuity of Rudra in the Khaṇḍobā cult (Sontheimer 1986a: *passim*). Rather than postulating a unilinear development from the Vedic Rudra to a purāṇic Śiva and eventually a parochialized Khaṇḍobā we are led to see a persistent continuity of *folk religion.* The least we may find is a structural identity between Rudra and Khaṇḍobā. For instance, the wandering Vrātya, Māgadha or Sūta (bard) who is joined by the *pumścalī* ("harlot") has his counterparts in the Vāghyās (Ma.) or Vaggayyas (Ka.), the special devotees (*devadāsīs*) of Khaṇḍobā, on their alms rounds (*vāri*). The Vāghyās are the poets and bards of Khaṇḍobā, who is considered to be a king. They sing his deeds during vigils (*jāgran*) while the Muraḷīs sing and accompany them with their dance. Like the Vrātyas, the Vāghyās are the "dogs" of the God. Whereas the *Mallāri-Māhātmya* (in Sanskrit and with Marathi versions) is much more "universalized", the contents of the Vāghyās' songs refer to historical events and specific locations and rituals. Unlike the written Sanskrit text, the contents and form of their songs are subjected to simplification and effacement on account of the general modernisation which nowadays is occurring in Maharashtra on an unprecedented scale (Sontheimer 1986b: *passim*).

Tribal groups equivalent to those mentioned in the *Śatarudrīya* are also represented. Not only were outlandish groups like thieves and robbers devotees of Khaṇḍobā but traditional tribal groups also form an important element in the cult (Koḷīs, Gavḷīs, and Dhangars in Maharashtra; Gollas, Kurumas, and Ceñcūs in Andhra Pradesh; Kurubas in Karnataka.). In accordance with this we also have, especially among the Dhangars, the "shaman" or *devruṣi* who gets possessed by Khaṇḍobā. The ritual hunt of the god on Somvatī Amāvāsyā, accompanied by hosts of Dhangars equipped with ceremonial spears, also reflects the tribal component.

Khaṇḍobā, the family god (*kulasvāmī*) of many different groups, is also the object of fervent devotion of individual devotees exceeding the normal loyalty shown by family members towards their *kulasvāmī.* Devotion expresses itself in the irresistible desire to be near and one with the god, even by imitating his dress and outfit (as Vrātyas did and the Vāghyās still do). This kind of bhakti could result in the self-sacrifice of the devotee. Self-mortification could elicit a boon from the deity. But "standard" bhakti would reject these rituals and attitudes as *ugra*, or reinterpret them. Tukārām, e.g. interprets Khaṇḍobā and the ritual objects of the cult as metaphors for his "inner" religion.

Like Rudra, Khaṇḍobā is the god of heroes (*vīras*) who are on that level not yet ethicised as rescuers of women, cows and Brahmans. Since the sixteenth century the *Mallāri-Māhātmya* gained importance as the Brahmanical-textual component. It would, however, be misleading to present the cult exclusively on the basis of this Brahmanical text: it is so far little known to those devotees who represent other components. If it is known, it tends to be subordinated to the folk religious point of view. On the whole the "ethicisation" of the cult by Liṅgāyats, Jains and Brahmans (though Khaṇḍobā is the *Kulasvāmī* of many Deśastha Brahmans) remains incomplete and partial. Nevertheless, the *Māhātmya* (said to be a part of the *Brahmāṇḍapurāṇa*) set the trend of purifying the cult and making it purāṇic: the demon is killed by Śiva who becomes (quite unusual for Śiva) a full *avatār* and not a partial manifestation called Khaṇḍobā or Mārtaṇḍa Bhairava. Śiva thus restores the *yajña* of the Brahmans and the dharmic order. He remains on earth as Khaṇḍobā for the sake of his *bhaktas.* While doing all this he assumes many of the attributes, weapons the *vāhanas* (horse, elephants, chariots) of his opponent, the demon king Malla or the two royal demon brothers Mani and Malla. Malla actually resembles the demonic Rudra much more than the epic or purāṇic Śiva. The folk deity, so to say, splits into two halves, the classical Śiva and the demon. Or we can say the *Māhātmya* implies that the god should transcend his own asuric form. But in Jejurī people still ardently worship the *mūrti* of the demon king who on his death became Khaṇḍobā's *bhakta,* before they proceed to worship Khaṇḍobā in the main temple.

The component of renunciation and asceticism is inherent in certain features already mentioned. The wandering habits of the Vāghyās (and also the Vaggayyas), the merit of doing *tapas* by going to the "*old*" temple far away on the distant mountain plateau rather than to the "*new*" temple (the "hill fort") just above the city, Khaṇḍobā's wife turning into Yogeśvarī, the *yogī* Śiva turning into a warrior, the influence of the Nāth sect—all this points to the fact that the component of *saṃnyās* and *tapas* is also present. Even the Muslims are reflected in a typical Hindu manner: Khaṇḍobā, the god on earth masquerading as a pragmatic king, welcomes them as *bhaktas* or loyal followers. On the other hand, according to a legend, the aggressive Aurangzeb and his army were driven away by 900,000 hornets sent by the god (Sontheimer 1986a).

Thus, we would suggest that a study of the Khaṇḍobā cult would yield a reflection of Hinduism as a whole if we keep in mind the different components and their dynamic interrelation. We cannot generalize on the basis of one component; this would be to assume *pars pro toto.*

4. Summary

This view of Hinduism emerged from an occupation with Indian texts of various periods and provenance, from field research, and only secondarily from modern theories and conceptualization. In the course of this procedure five components have time and again suggested themselves: (1) The work and the teaching of the Brahmans; (2) Asceticism and renunciation; (3) Tribal religion; (4) Folk religion; (5) Bhakti.

Though the emphasis here is on religion, these components may be seen to entail other aspects of culture, e.g. social, physical, linguistic, philosophical and ideological aspects. Each of these components—before it is compounded with others—has to be viewed in its own right in order to avoid monolithic conceptualizations or the indigenous self-images of a *single* group (e.g. the Brahmans). Once we have admitted the "simultaneous order" (A.K. Ramanujan *re* texts) of the components we can proceed to investigate a particular institution of Hinduism as a whole in terms of dynamic interrelations among the components. We can test, apply, and, if necessary, modify modern theories on interrelations (e.g. Srinivas, Dumont, Marriott, Staal, Hacker, Ramanujan, Burghart—to mention only a few) as well as indigenous concepts.

It may be that one or the other component received more or less emphasis and elaboration at a particular historical period, but all of them are present from Vedic times, even if they survive only as (possibly distorted) reflections in available written texts.

In this approach it seems unnecessary to split Hinduism into distinct though related religions. This splitting may serve the purposes of the comparative religionist, but ignores the fact that a particular religion or more appropriately a "sect" (in itself a problematic term in the Indian context) was never immutable, but would develop and revert to structures which it initially rejected (Ramanujan 1973: 34-6). The process of mutual interaction between the components is best described as "reflexivity", which takes many forms (Ramanujan), e.g. "Inklusivismus" (Hacker), or complete inversion, as in Tantrism. If phenomena of these components have reflected on each other for many centuries and oscillated between "divergence and convolution" (Derrett 1968: 437) we can expect a civilization which formed a close network or religious interaction and interdependence. This religious network cannot be refused the label Hinduism, even if it does not fit the definitions of religion deriving from the West. We would also not seem to be justified to foregoing the term just because modern self-interpretations called "Syndicated Hinduism" by Thapar, eclectically utilize, emphasize, and choose components or elements of components and neglect or even reject others, sometimes in order to create a dogmatic or fundamentalist Hinduism. One would think that this "Syndicated Hinduism" contradicts the essential character of Hinduism.

REFERENCES

Blackburn, S.H. 1985. Death and deification. Folk cults in Hinduism. In *History of Religions* 24/3, 225-74.

Burghart, R. 1978. Hierarchical models of the Hindu social system. In *Man* (N.S.) 13, 519-36.

———. 1983a. Renunciation in the religious traditions of South Asia. *Man* (N.S.) 18, 635-53.

———. 1983b. "For sociology of India: an intracultural approach to the study of "Hindu Society", *Contributions to Indian Sociology* (N.S.) 17/2, 275-94.

Burghart, R. and Cantlie, A. (eds.) 1985. *Indian Religion*. London.

Creel. A.B. 1977. *Dharma in Hindu ethics*. Calcutta.

Deliege, R. 1985. *The Bhils of Western India*. New Delhi.

Derrett, J.D.M.1968. *Religion, law and the state in India*. London.

———. 1976. Rājadharma. *Journal of Asian Studies* 25/4, 597-609.

———. Sontheimer, G.-D., Smith, Graham 1976. *Beiträge zu indischem Rechtsdenken*. Wiesbaden.

Elwin, Verrier 1955. *The religion of an Indian tribe*. OUP.

Eschmann, A., Kulke, H., Tripathi, G.C. (eds.) 1978. *The Cult of Jagannath and the regional tradition of Orissa.* Delhi: Manohar.

Eschmann, A. Hinduzation of tribal deities in Orissa: The śakta and śaiva typology . In (eds.) Eschmann/Kulke/Tripathi, 79-97.

Hacker, Paul 1983. Inklusivismus . In *Oberhammer* 1983, 11-28.

Hardy, F. 1983. *Viraha-Bhakti. The early history of Kṛṣṇa devotion in South India.* Delhi: OUP.

Hofer, Andras and Shreshta, B.P. 1973. Ghost exorcism among the Brahmans of Central Nepal. In *Central Asiatic Journal* 17/1, 51-77.

Kelkar, A.R. 1977. Bhakti in modern Marathi poetry: An essay (by Sadashiv S. Bhave). A response to Sadashiv S. Bhave's essay . In *South Asian Digest of Regional Writing* 7, 18ff, 24.

Kulke, H. 1979. *Jagannātha-Kult und Gajapati-Königtum. Ein Beitrag zur Geschichte religiöser Legitimation hinduistischer Herrscher.* Wiesbaden.

Kulke, H. und Rothermund, D. (eds.) 1985. *Regionale Tradition in Südasien.* Wiesbaden.

Marglin, F. Apffel, 1985. *Wives of the god-king.* Delhi: OUP.

Marriott, McKim 1965. Little Communities in an indigenous civilization. In *Village India* (ed.) McKim Marriott, 171-222. Chicago.

———. 1976. Interpreting Indian society: A monistic alternative to Dumount's dualism. In *Journal of Asian Studies*, 36/1, November, 189-95.

Molesworth, J.T. 1857. *A Ditionary, Marāṭhī and English.* Bombay.

Monier-Williams, Monier 1899. *A Sanskrit-English Dictionary.* Oxford.

Oberhammer, G. (ed.) 1983. *Inklusivismus. Eine indische Denkform.* Wien.

Piatigorsky, A. 1985. Some phenomenological observations on the study of Indian religion. In (ed.) Burghart and Cantlie, 208-58.

Ramanujan, A.K. 1970. Towards an anthology of city image . In *Urban India: Society, space and image.* Monograph Series (ed.) Richard G. Fox. Durham, N.C.: Duke University.

———. 1973. *Speaking of Śiva.* Penguin Books.

———. 1981. *Hymns for the drowning.* Princeton.

———. 1985a. Where mirrors are windows: Towards an anthology of reflections (unpublished MS.).

———. 1985b. *Poems of love and war.* New York: Columbia University Press.

Rüping, Klaus 1977. Zur Askese in indischen Religionen. In *Zeitschrift für Missonswissenschaft und Religionwissenschaft* 2, 81-98.

Sontheimer, G.D. 1964. Religious endowments in India: The juristic personality of Hindu deities. In *Zeitschrift für vergleichende Rechtswissenschaft*, 69/1, 45-100.

———. 1976. *Birobā, Mhaskobā und Khaṇḍobā: Ursprung, Geschichte und Umwelt von pastoralen Gottheiten in Mahārāṣṭra.* Wiesbaden.

———. 1981. Dasarā at Devaraguḍḍa. Ritual and play in the cult of Mailār/ Khaṇḍobā. In *South Asian Digest of Regional Writing*, 10, 1-28.

———. 1982. God, dharma and society in the Yādava kingdom of Devagri according to the *Līḷācaritra* of Cakradhar. In *Indology and Law. Studies in honour of professor J. Duncan M. Derrett,* (eds.) Günther-Dietz Sontheimer and Paramesvara Kota Aithal, 329-58. Wiesbaden.

———. 1985a. Cāturvarṇya, Bhakti und der Aufstieg von Volkskulten in Maharashtra: Religiongeschichtliche Skizze einer Region. In Kulke und Rothermund (eds.) 1985, 129-48.

———. 1985b. Folk deities in the Vijayanagara empire: Narasiṃha and Mallanna/Mailār. In *Vijayanagara—city and empire. New currents of research,* (ed.) A. Dallapiccola in collaboration with S. Zingel-Avé Lallement, 144-58. Wiesbaden.

———. 1985c. Bhakti in the Khaṇḍobā cult. Paper read at the third conference on early literature in new Indo-Aryan languages. Leiden.

———. 1986. Rudra and Khaṇḍobā: continuity in folk religion. In *Religion and society in Mahārashtra.* (eds.) Milton Israel and N.K. Wagle. Univ. of Toronto, Centre for South Asian Studies, 1-31.

———. 1994. The *vana* and the *kṣetra*: the tribal origins of some famous cults. In *Religion and society in eastern India,* Eschmann memorial lectures, (eds.) G.C. Tripathi and H. Kulke, Delhi: Manohar 1994, 117-64.

———. 1990. Between ghost and god: A folk deity of the Deccan. In *Gods and demon devotees.* (ed.) Alf Hiltebeitel. Albany

Srinivas, M.N. 1952. *Religion and society among the Coorgs of South India,* Oxford.

Staal, J.F. 1963. Sanskrit and Sanskritization. In *Journal of Asian Studies,* 12/3, 261-75.

Weber, Max 1920. *Gesammelte Aufsätze zur Religionssoziologie,* Vol. II. *Hinduismus und Buddhismus.* Tübingen.

Wezler, Albrecht 1983. Bemerkungen zum Inklusivismus-Begriff Paul Hackers. In *Oberhammer,* 61-91.

Vaudeville, Ch. 1974. *Kabīr,* Oxford.

———. 1980. Govardhana myth in northern India. In *Indo-Iranian Journal* 22, 1-45.

SOMETHING LOST, SOMETHING GAINED: TRANSLATIONS OF HINDUISM

Richard Burghart

The reconsideration of Hinduism has both an objective and a subjective movement; it leads one, perforce, to a consideration of Hinduism and to one's procedures of consideration. Yet each of these movements is bound up with the other; and in this essay I examine the nature of this entailment in the light of translation theory. Translation is central not only to our scholarly understanding of Hinduism but also to the perpetuation of Hinduism by Hindus themselves. It provides, therefore, a common ground on which to view the theoretical practices of those who speak both for and about Hinduism.

Translation and Tradition

To begin with some technical vocabulary, one might define translation as the specification in one code of a position which is equivalent to that in another. Following Jakobson (1959), there are three types of translation: inter-lingual, intra-lingual, and inter-semiotic. Inter-lingual translation (dog = *kuttā*) is "translation proper" for it entails the interpretation of a verbal sign by means of and in terms of another language. Intra-lingual translation (dog = canine) entails "rewording" within a language; and inter-semiotic translation (NO DOGS ALLOWED = 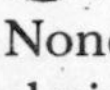) entails the "transmutation" of verbal signs by non-verbal ones. None of these categories denotes a type of message; rather each designates a lingual operation carried out on the message. For example, one occasionally sees over the entrance to cottage on the coast of Flanders a sign in wrought iron which reads:

The meaning of the message is arrived by a triple act of translation. First, one carries our inter-semiotic translation, rendering the non-verbal notation into the verbal signs of the musical scale: *do mi tsi la do re.* Second, one carried out intra-lingual translation, rendering the Latin-derived terms of French musical culture into French syllable: do mi ci la do ré. It does not require too much imagination to switch from a phonetic to a semantic frame: do-mi-cil a-do-ré. Bearing in mind that the sign has been placed over a house in Flanders, a native Flemish speaker requires a third act of inter-lingual translation before the expression evokes in his heart the same sentiment as "oost, west, thuis best".

Exact equivalence between codes is in some respects unattainable. Languages may vary in their sound systems as in their range of denotations; equivalent denotations within or between languages may have different connotations. But despite its theoretical impossibility, adequate translation can be achieved in two ways. First, an approximate equivalence may be attained which is sufficiently exact for the translator's purpose; that is, the translation is functional in the translator's management of the situation. Second, exact equivalence—or at least the awareness of a more exact equivalence—is realized meta-linguistically. This is the implication of the translator's assessment that something has been "lost" in translation. Such an assessment can be made only against the perception of an unattained equivalence. Conceived of in this way, translation presumably occurs in all societies, for no speech community lives in complete isolation from other communities; nor is a speech community so devoid of terminological substitutability and metaphorical convention that choices of rewording do not arise. While not as lurid as the incest taboo, translation merits anthropological interest as one of the very few "universals" of human existence.

At this level of analysis the attribution of universality does not require the complicity of other people; indeed the attribution could hardly survive with their complicity. We can assert that everyone is a translator, regardless of whether or not he knows it. Since translation is intrinsic to communication, it follows that it does not necessarily occur because of any specific intention, other than that of communication (this position is similar to that taken by Steiner 1975). By extension one can then conceive of a link between translation and tradition, or what one might call communication over time. This link is particularly marked in South Asia where the communication of knowledge over time is formally structured in pupillary traditions, called *sampradāya*. These self-conscious traditions include various Brahmanical schools of knowledge, redemptive traditions of ascetics, healing traditions, aesthetic traditions, and so on. More is known in the West of their textual basis than of the relation between text and practice or their social organization.

In this cultural context one might speak of a specifically Indian structure of tradition in which translation also takes on a particular character. The link between Indian tradition and translation is apparent in the way in which a notion of ontic identity undercuts historiography. Each historical displacement in the perpetuation of religious life is seen at some other level to be a successive instance of that which precedes it. One might refer, in illustration, to the statement that "the Purāṇas are the fifth Veda". On scholarly grounds, even those of a pandit, there are reasons for disputing this. The formal characteristics (*lakṣaṇa*) of a Purāṇa are rather different from those of the Vedas. Yet Puranic reciters, in proclaiming that the Purāṇas are the fifth Veda, set up an equivalence between these two religious genres. Furthermore, the number five signifies not only that the Purāṇas have temporally succeeded the Vedas (and hence are an equivalent unit in the series) but also that they have ontologically fulfilled them (for the same reason that the number five is identified with the zenith which surmounts the four cardinal directions). As the fifth Veda, the Purāṇas foreclose the future; the series is now complete. The numerology is, however, a side-issue. What is important for the present argument is the intra-lingual rewording. What might have been perceived as a different and "new" religious genre, is rendered as being equivalent to an "original" one. One might, as Dumont (1959) has done, construct a historiography in the development of Hindu religious traditions. But ritual spokesmen of Hinduism by means of intra-lingual translation see that "development" in their own characteristic manner: neither as a historiographical one defined by temporal displacements in consciousness, nor as a modernist one in which each personal link in the chain remakes the tradition and casts his shadow on his successor's ability to remake it.

Rather the "development" appears as a succession of formal resemblances. The present becomes an icon of the past.

Despite historical shifts and geographic variations, intra-religious translation enables Hindu ritual spokesmen—its Brahmins and ascetics—to bring into relation other systems of belief and practice as successive or variant instances of an everpresent or central ontic source. Any teaching or practice which derives from Brahma or aims towards Brahma shares a meta-perspective with other such teachings, and this meta-perspective enables a functional equivalence to be set up between lower level phenomena. An example of the way in which functional equivalence structures relations within a Hindu religious order may be taken from the Ramanandi *sampradāya*, one of the largest celibate ascetic orders in South Asia today. What unites all Ramanandis is that they see themselves as being vehicles of an identical Ram mantra and that they trace the transmission of this mantra by pupillary succession back to the fourteenth century saint Swami Ramanand. Despite their common ontic identity and historical source, there is considerable diversity in their methods of spiritual liberation. At present Ramanandis are more or less subdivided into two orders, each with its own method of spiritual liberation (for more details see Burghart 1983). After obtaining the initiatory mantra from their guru, some Ramanandis seek further instruction from another guru, the *sādhak guru*, who entitles his disciple to follow either the path of renunciation (*tyāg*) or that of sentiment (*ras*).

Ramanandis who are inclined to follow the former path seek secondary initiation from a renouncer guru who bestows upon his disciple the ashes of the Invisible Spirit. In the act of bestowal the disciple is instructed in the mode of consecrating the ashes; and having done so, the disciple henceforth smears his body twice daily with ashes. In the same way that the bath of water purifies the gross body, so the bath of ashes purifies the subtle body, sealing it from influences of the transient world. The renouncer Ramanandi is ordinarily itinerant and disciplines his body by means of *haṭha yoga* and *prāṇāyāma*. During the auspicious season he may also offer sacrifices and practice austerities.

Those who are inclined to follow the path of sentiment seek secondary initiation from a devotional Ramanandi who explains to his disciple the mystery of the *ātmā svarūp* and issues him with a certificate of affiliation (*sambandh patra*) whereby his intrinsic personal identity (*bhāv*) is used to form an expressive, redemptive relationship with Ram. The relationship so created—be it kin, affinal, or more rarely courtly—gives form and purpose to the ascetic's devotion and makes him an object of Ram's grace. In this way the devotee gains entry to Ram's celestial kingdom. Most devotional Ramanandis live in local rent-receiving or mendicant hermitages, which they liken to bowers within the celestial palace of Lord Ram.

The Ramanandi past is so obscure that it is difficult to understand how such different spiritual paths constitute the same religion. Indeed, even if we knew all the facts about the past, it would still be difficult to explain. Our difficulty is shared at times by the Ramanandis themselves, for they see their religious tradition to constitute in some sense a social body, yet the two suborders are so different that they do not even form a commensal unit. Devotionalists do not accept *kaccā* food from renouncers because renouncers smear ashes on their body, and ashes are an emblem of Shiva. The renouncers do not accept *kaccā* food from devotionalists, for the devotionalists are sedentary and therefore come into contact with desires which, when transmitted through the medium of food, would corrupt the desireless renouncers. Despite the absence of commensality (and the presence of considerable internal rivalry) all Ramanandis see themselves as vehicles of an identical Ram mantra and claim pupillary succession from Ramanand. Acceptance of this identity obliges Ramanandis to recognize that their two parts are equivalent in aim and efficacy; hence translation takes place such that the practices of the one are made equivalent to those of the other.

Most Ramanandis agree that the devotionalists serve Ram possessed of attributes (*saguṇa*) and renouncers meditate on Ram devoid of attributes (*nirguṇa*). The conventional attribute/attributeless distinction provides, therefore, a translation scheme whereby renouncers can identify the terms of their spiritual discipline with those of the devotionalists. In their code of ritual procedures, called *Siddhānt Paṭal*, renouncers offer their sensory perceptions in sacrifice to the attributeless Ram, called Niranjan. The *tulsī* of devotional Ramanandis is said to be a form (*rūp*) of Niranjan; the *śāli-grām*—the emblem of Vishnu Narayan—is situated by renouncers at the junction of the *iḍā, piṁglā* and *suṣumna nāḍī.* The distinction between attribute and attributeless is further worked out with reference to the means by which the religious subject comes into contact with the divine. Devotional Ramanandis seek physical contact with Ram and

Sita by establishing residence (*bās*) at abodes of eternal play, such as Ayodhya, Citrakut and Janakpur, where Ram and Sita sported in the Treta Age; the renouncers, leading an interior life, come into contact with the attributeless Ram by remembering (*smaran*) his internal presence. In this way formal differences between the two spiritual paths—residence and memory—are bridged by their functional equivalence. They both culminate in contact with the redeemer Ram. Reunion with Ram is not only the meta-position which renders equivalent the paths of renouncers and devotionalists; it is also the ontic aim which authenticates the difference as a valid equivalence.

The significance of translation in intra-religious contexts also holds true for inter-religious ones. It is by acts of inter-religious translation that ritual spokesmen at a particular time or place relate their religious traditions to a universal temporal or spatial context. For example, in Assam Vaishnavite devotees recall the words of Sankardeva (Sankardeva, *Pasanda Mordon*; cited in Cantlie 1984: 267):

> In the Iron Age by singing *kirttan*
> The thirty-four castes obtain heaven,
> In the Golden Age salvation was attained by knowledge,
> In the Silver Age it was sacrifices,
> In the Copper Age it was ritual,
> In the Iron Age it is *kirttan*.

A variation on this theme is uttered by tantrics in Bengal who claim that tantric spiritual practice, in particular the left-handed path, is the only appropriate method of liberation in the present Kali Age (Woodroffe 1953). Devotional Ramanandis hold similar beliefs in their claim that the practice of austerities (*tapas*) is equivalent to the repetition (*jap*) of Ram's name. In the Satya Age rishis possessed such spiritual energy that they mortified their flesh over thousands of years, storing up power and obtaining boons. In the Kali Age mankind is so constrained by his shortened life-span and spiritual feebleness that the austerities which were commonplace in the Satya Age are no longer practicable. The benefits of such austerities can still be obtained, however, by repetition of the name of Ram. Thus, a functional equivalence is set up between austerity and repetition. They are formally different spiritual methods of obtaining boons from gods, as the Satya Yuga is formally different from the Kali Age, yet they occupy functionally equivalent positions in respect of the common goal of both ages of man. By means of inter-religious translation, regionally diverse and historically different forms of Hinduism are perpetuated as if they were equivalent forms of religious life.

The Middle Ground

Because of the translator's commitment to the equivalence of çodes, his translation appears as a transparent activity. If something is unintentionally or regrettably lost in translation then it is still a translation, albeit an approximate or inadequate one. If something is intentionally distorted then the translator's purpose had not been the specification of equivalence; hence the translation does not count as a real translation. But who is to judge the adequacy of the translation or the authenticity of the translator's intention? How illusory this transparency is, shows up when translators hold different views on the nature of codes, the purpose of communication and the communicability of positions in a code. In Christian civilization the meaning of divine words is sacred, but language itself is not divine (Stall 1961: 15). Sanskrit mantras which "make sense" are usually translated semantically into European languages; ones which do not make sense, *faute de mieux,* are translated phonetically; that is to say, they are transliterated. Yet the Brahmanical sound-vibration theory of mantra may apply both to mantras which make sense and those which do not. Meanwhile a pandit might refrain from a word-for-word translation. Rather he will paraphrase the mantra in a vernacular language, leaving the formula in its original Sanskrit. His primary purpose is not to communicate an understanding of the mantra to practitioners, but to instruct practitioners in how to communicate with gods, whose mother-tongue is Sanskrit. The different commitment of translators raise questions about what is translatable in a text and what texts are untranslatable. Such controversies underscore the fact that—despite one's intentions—a translation is not a neutral activity. Consensus arises only when there is prior agreement on the purpose of translation. The translations carried out by spokesmen for Hinduism may be rather different from those of observers of Hinduism.

One way of focussing on this difference in the comparative terms of anthropology is to classify translation along somewhat different lines from those formulated by Jakobson. Rather than focus on translation as a lingual operation, one might consider instead the social context in which translation takes place. Here one might distinguish between two contexts: that in which source and target audiences do not know each other's codes and that in which they do. In the former context both inter- and intra-lingual translation may take place, and the translator aims to be a transparent personage standing between sender and receiver (e.g. a translator at a summit meeting of heads of state) or he may be a sender-receiver of messages in his own right (e.g. a lawyer who communicates back and forth between the professional language of the courts and the ordinary speech of his client). In the latter context both inter- and intra-lingual translation may also take place, but if target and source audiences know each other's codes, the translator's purpose cannot simply be communication. Nor is the translator any longer a privileged communicator of meanings. If anything, he is privileged communicator of media.

This second kind of translation was not unusual to pre-modern South Asia. At present ethnic rhetoric is central to South Asian politics; and language had become essentialized into thought such that a particular syntax and semantics are now seen to constitute the structure and content of a native speaker's consciousness. A Nepalese poet now writes in Nepali because it is only in his mother-tongue that he can express his "Nepaliness". The pre-modern Nepalese poet, however, might have written one poem in Nepali and the next in Maithili; and his audience—the royal court—would have been appreciative of both. In such multi-lingual contexts languages were valued aesthetically for their power to evoke a sentiment. One wrote in Maithili, not to communicate with Maithils, but to use the sweetness of Maithili in order to communicate a feeling to Nepalese. The translator is privileged, not because he communicates a literal meaning, but because he evokes by means of the entire code a feeling among those already familiar with the meaning. The implication here is that meaning is translingual or transcultural. For the poet this type of translation is not a problematic item by item restructuring of one thing in terms of another but a complete shift of code—each of which can be substituted for other in order to express a general meaning but only one of which is suitable to evoke a particular feeling.

Regardless of these two contexts, the translator occupies a middle position with respect of his audiences, but the middle position is differently constituted in each of the two contexts. In the former context of mutual unintelligibility the translator has a role, but one which does not necessarily privilege him, for he is a means to someone else's end. The authenticity of this work as a medium lies in his fidelity to the messages of others. The sender and receiver are the agents in this interaction; the translator remains their transparent, impartial instrument. In the latter context of mutual intelligibility the translator, if he is to exist at all, must come to play some special role which surpasses ordinary communication and the ordinary intelligibility of source and target audiences. Here the middle position becomes a privileged end in its own right.

In applying this contextual distinction to the case of Hinduism, scholarly spokesmen appear as translators where there is mutual unintelligibility between Hindus and "barbarians" and ritual spokesmen—Brahmans and ascetics—are translators in contexts of mutual intelligibility among Hindus. It follows that the middle grounds which they occupy are different, as are the methods they use to arrive at their respective middle positions. Brahmans take themselves to be the icons of Brahma and ascetics see themselves as "moving temples". It is by virtue of their divine nature that these persons are fit to speak with authority. The methods by which Brahmans and ascetics become fit include rituals of initiation, purification and concentration (it is for this methodological reason that I refer to them as "ritual spokesmen"). Brahmans speak with authority about Brahma by virtue of their initiation into Brahmanhood, their knowledge of divinely uttered texts and their procedures of textual interpretation (e.g. rules of evidence, logic). Ascetics speak with authority about Brahma by realizing Brahma in themselves. It cannot be said that Brahmans are the sole spokesmen for Hinduism, for ascetics of non-Brahman birth also do. But anyone who does speak for Hinduism, does claim the middle ground and does speak authoritatively from the point of view of Brahma. The scholarly understanding more or less accurately rewords the metaphysics of Hinduism but in gaining access through texts to divine knowledge, scholars perforce disregard the metaphysical basis of Hindu religious methodology. Scholars are not terrestrial gods; and they gain their knowledge by their objectivity, not their divinity.

The middle position of the translator as a master of codes may be illustrated with reference to Swami Ramanand, the founder of the Ramanandi *saṃpradāya* and one of the most successful of translators in medieval upper India. To Ramanand is attributed the statement: "Do not ask of anyone his caste or sect; whoever worships the Lord belongs to the Lord." According to Ramanandi exegesis, Swami Ramanand believed that the soul of each human being comprises a fraction of the universal soul of Ram. Because liberation from transience and reunion with Ram entails a union of souls, not of bodies or minds, caste status and redemptive path do not bar one from liberation. Humanistic Hindus today, bearing in mind the statutes concerning caste in the Indian constitution, take Swami Ramanand to have been a man ahead of his time, a "democrat" among medieval ascetics. This humanist interpretation overlook, however, the religious meaning of not asking anyone his caste or sect. The implication of the saying is not that "all may join"; but rather that "Ram transcends the differences among all joiners." All redemptive paths are equivalent, for they stem from Ram. Hence, their followers meet in Ram. Moreover, insofar as Ramanand is both the author of the statement and the founder of a redemptive path, then his famous dictum appears as if it were a self-referential paradox, as in "Disobey this command" or "All general statements are false." "Sects are not recognized in the Ramanandi sect." In fact, the statement is more a conundrum than a paradox, the apparent contradiction is sorted out in the different perceptives of subject and predicate. All religious traditions are equivalent because they stem from Ram. The Ramanandis recognize this; but other redemptive paths do not. They live in a world of differences. Hence, their paths are more worldly than that of the Ramanandis. Being more worldly, they are temporal, conditioned and spiritually inferior. In Hinduism acts of translation bridge differences at one level but set up ontic claims between levels.

Not only does inter-religious translation serve to advance claims, so also does intra-religious translation. To revert to the instances stated in the first section above, Ramanandi renouncers translate their *nirguṇa* terms into the *saguṇa* positions of devotional Ramanandis, but the *saguṇa* positions are part of the world of forms, not of the formless world of the renouncers. Renouncers respect devotional Ramanandis, but place them in an ontologically dependent context. Meanwhile, when devotional Ramanandis assert that repetition of the Ram mantra is an austerity of the Kali Age, they legitimate their spiritual discipline by claiming that it is functionally equivalent to the prestigious austerities carried out by ascetics in the Satya Age. But by the same token they imply that Ramanandi renouncers who bake in the sun, practising austerities all day, are disciplining themselves in a way which was efficacious in its time but inappropriate for the present Kali Age. Thus the devotional Ramanandis place the renouncers in temporally irrelevant context. The implication in Sankardeva's statement (cited earlier) is the same. When Assamese Vaishnavites claim that sacrifice and ritual are effective means of attaining Brahma, but appropriate only for the kind of men who lived in the Silver and Copper Ages, they are asserting the irrelevance of Brahmanical ritual duties in the present world period. Here reformed Vaishnavite ascetics claim the middle ground and in the same move annul the authority of Brahmans.

When two or more audiences are able to communicate directly with one another, the translator's fidelity shifts from the unbiased re-wording of sender-receiver messages to something else toward which he strives. Whether it be the poet's rendering into speech of the sublime or the ritual spokesman's knowledge of the formless Brahma, the translator communicates with both target and source audiences in such a way as to refine their sensibility and aptitude. Transparency and impartiality are no longer virtues of the translator. The ontic status of the middle position may be recognized only by the translator and his supporters in the audience. Inter- and intra-religious translation does not necessarily bring about a consensus in all audiences on the meta-term which transcends their differences. No Indian ascetic would disagree that his path culminates in release from transience, but not all Indian ascetics (e.g. Buddhist and Jains) would agree that the transcendent experience entails reunion with Brahma. Nor—to revert to the Ramanandi case—would all ascetics (e.g. Dasnamis and Nath Yogis) agree that Brahma, when possessed of attributes, takes on the form of Ram. In point of fact inter-religious translation in Hinduism often involve two translators talking past each other. There is no dialogue: only two mutually unreciprocated monologues.

The prospect of the middle ground has been variously observed by western scholars. Hacker's (1957) notion of inclusivism describes it as the integration of diverse redemptive paths with reference to their putative common purpose. Piatigorsky (1984) describes it phenomenologically in his observation that Hinduism is a religion which has already investigated itself. Comparative religion emerged in the West only when various religions could be compared from a non-religious (e.g. humanist) point of view. Indian religion is unique in that various dharmas are investigated and compared from a religious point of view, that of Brahma. In these scholarly observations, however, one reservation must be borne in mind. The middle ground is not a common ground. Its space is contested. All that is shared is agreement on the purpose that organizes the content. It follows that conflict occurs not on the existence of the absolute, but on its identity, its manifestations and the relative value of the ways of attaining it. It is not the absolute which is at issue, but the relativities. One can include everyone in the universe on the basis of common purpose or origin and then exclude them on the basis of an irrelevant spatio-temporal context. Beware of people who determine the context. It is better to be a translator than the object of someone else's translation. The resemblance does make a difference.

Manifestations and Understandings

Although translation is a universal activity of consciousness, scholars and ritual spokesmen conceive of the middle ground differently; and it is from this middle ground that the translation is validated. To take an example, from a scholarly point of view one might understand there to be an equivalence between Lord Krishna and Jesus Christ by virtue of their similar meaning in Indian and European civilization. The comprehension of this equivalence is achieved by an act of translation whereby Krishna and Christ are roughly equivalent instances of a meta-term, be it incarnation of god or whatever. Should a Vaishnavite ascetic find equivalence between Krishna and Christ, the scholar would take this to be a successful case of interlingual translation. Yet from the ascetic's point of view the equivalence of Krishna and Christ has nothing to do with human understanding, much less a meta-theory of meaning in the relations within and between cultures. Rather the universe is a materialization in time and space of Vishnu Narayan (or the primal Krishna, etc.). Krishna and Christ are but divine forms of the omnipresent formless Krishna. The meta-level which makes Krishna and Christ equivalent is ontic. It lies beyond time and space. It does not see itself as having anything to do with human understanding. Indeed, from the ascetic's point of view it would exist regardless of whether human beings understood it. The equivalence of Krishna and Christ in scholarship, however, is totally dependent on human understanding. If it does not exist in understanding, it simply does not exist.

In this way scholar and ascetic might concur that Krishna and Christ are equivalent terms/forms of god, but they would disagree on how they came to their agreement. Both spokesmen, in achieving their middle ground, distance themselves from their source and target positions and then proceed to carry out their translation. The scholar enters his field of study, rewords it in his meta-language and measures the adequacy of his representation by the extent to which it "fits" the facts. He works from the conviction that facts have some existence independent of his vision from the middle ground; and he adopts various empirical practices to guard this independence: suspension of personal belief, impartiality in recording opinion, awareness of the meta-terms of investigation, contextual re-ordering of testimony in the light of one's perception of the informant's motives, and so on. Insofar as these working practices give some semblance of independence, one can compare alternative representations in their degree of fitness. By contrast, the systematics of Brahmanical and ascetic spokesmen about dharma are rather different from the intellectual space conceived by Europeans for the description of "Hinduism". For Hinduism's ritual spokesmen knowledge stems from their cosmic function or divine realization, not from human understanding; and the adequacy of their translation is measured not against the facts but with respect to revealed knowledge and the realization of Brahma. Ritual spokesmen surmount the field from the middle ground, but their methodological concerns entail the iconography of Brahmanhood, the symptomology of really liberated ascetics, the ritual procedures by which one becomes a fit receptacle of knowledge, the rules of logic and evidence in religious discourse, and so on. For scholarly spokesmen of Hinduism the reality to be understood is the diverse beliefs and practices on the Indian subcontinent; for ritual spokesmen the reality to be understood is the ever present Brahma. For the scholar the Hindu universe is enclosed by the distribution of identifiably Hindu beliefs and practices; for the Brahman or ascetic the universe is enclosed by Brahma, not by Brahma's many forms—or what scholars would call beliefs and practices.

Although scholarly representations reword the views of ritual spokesmen, problems of translation inhere in the difference between representations which are a manifestation of Brahma and those which are objects of human consciousness. The former sense of representation emphasizes process: the unfolding of a manifestation and the tracing of it back to its authoritative original (e.g. Vedas) or everpresent (e.g. the primal Shiva) source. In either case the representation is definable as much in terms of its empirical distribution as of its essence. The essence figures as *dhātu* in Panini's "item and process" description of Sanskrit grammar (Emeneau 1955). It also figures in the *varṇa* conception of the universe as an exteriorization of the inner nature of Brahma. Such essentialism is intrinsic to Hindu religious discourse and finds focus in local determinations of who is a "real" renouncer or a "real" Brahman, and what are the qualities by which they may be known. These problems of ritual spokesmen refract differently in Western scholarship, for here the essentialism of ritual spokesmen, embedded in debates about the real (*asal*) and the false (*nakal*), is reworded as an empirical problem of the ideal and the real. Whereas Brahmanical spokesmen deal in the auspicious and voice their conception of social relations in the optative (the language of blessings and curses); empirically minded scholars deal in the normative (the ideal) and the normal (the real), and write their descriptions of social relations in pluralized forms of the declarative. Something becomes "lost" in translation. The ordinary Brahman, perpetually struggling with his self-esteem, becomes the real Brahman by virtue of his numerical superiority in Hindu society.

In enclosing and defining the Hindu universe, the scholar finds that his methodological neutrality is perpetually at risk of compromise. He aims to be a transparent translator of message, but in taking Hinduism as an "-ism"—that is, a discrete system of religious beliefs and practices with a community of believers—he puts himself in a more authoritative and interventionist role than he would wish. In the Kingdom of Nepal in the late eighteenth and nineteenth centuries certain "tribal" peoples became "Hindu" by administrative fiat, merely by promising the king to "respect Brahmans and not to yoke the cow". The upshot of this administrative arrangement was that these former tribal people could now be recruited by the state into the lower echelons of the civil and military administration. But such nominal conversions seem rather facile, even for atheist scholars. Without at least some "sincerity" nominal criteria are "open to abuse". General criteria, however, lead us to different impasse. What really is Hinduism? For Gujarati people vegetarianism is a hallmark of Hinduism. If we take vegetarianism as one of the defining characteristics of Hinduism then we are led down a path of seeming nonsense. The Brahmans of Bengal, Mithila and Nepal do not find their Brahmanical coinage debased by the consumption of fish and goat. Moreover, considered historically one could argue that the Gujarati inspiration for vegetarianism is of Jain provenance. The implication of vegetarianism as a defining feature of Hinduism is that the Jains of western India are Hindu and the Hindus of north-eastern India and the Himalaya are not. If we shift vantage point and look from the past to the present then we can conclude that in Gujarat Hinduism is a form of a crypto-Jainism. Similarly, one could argue (as Dutt 1962 does) that certain aspects of Hinduism are crypto-Buddhism. If we add to this the Christian and humanist influences of Hinduism, we eventually work ourselves into the position whereby Hinduism has almost entirely been reconstituted as some other religion. While the scholar ties himself in knots, the object of study slips loose. In the end it is the nominal criterion which come to the rescue. Gujarati Hindus are Hindu, not Jain, because that is how they call themselves.

On the one hand, Hinduism is recognized by virtue of the term which designates it. People who call themselves Hindu, or are called by others Hindu, are Hindu. On the other hand one recognizes Hinduism by virtue of the presence of certain general characteristics. Wherever and whenever these characteristics obtain, we identify the phenomenon as Hinduism. Taken on their own, each tack—the nominal and the general—has its problems, and the scholar is hard-pressed not to make some personal judgements about the proper ordering of relations among Hindus or the authenticity of the phenomenon that someone calls, or ought to call, Hinduism.

By virtue of these judgements, he becomes part of the very religious phenomenon that he investigates. Increasing numbers of anthropologists now report that, in carrying out their field inquiries concerning ritual procedure, caste-ranking, or whatever, informants have validated their testimony with reference to citations from anthropological monographs written by an earlier generation of fieldworkers in the region. In translating native belief and practice, the anthropological enterprise comes to take on the certifying function of ritual spokesmen in local society. Unfortunately, the methodological commitment to the detached observation of a detached people confines these anecdotes of anthropological self-awareness to the oral tradition of the profession.

Yet in this encounter a reverse transfer may also take place: the values and presuppositions of the scholar can be taken up by ritual spokesmen. It is commonplace in South Asian studies to note that the term "Hindu religion" is of non-Hindu coinage and that its use by "Hindus" was initially confined to descriptions of their external relations with Muslim "Turks" and Christian "Firangis". For the "Hindu", dharma was validated by its original and everpresent sources of divine authority; for the monotheist. "Turk" and Christian "Firangi" Hindu dharma only specified the religion of a people who *believed* such things to be true. For more than a millennium there existed, among foreigners at least, the notion that Hinduism had an ethnic constituency. And throughout this period dharma was the meta-term by which "Hindus" governed their religious relations with equivalent constituencies: e.g. Muslim dharma and Christian dharma. What seems different in recent times is the idea that the source of Hinduism lies in this very constituency. In addition to its divine origins, Hinduism has acquired a human source of authority. This other source appears in various guises, the most ironical of which (for the anthropologist) is that of culture. Since the early nineteenth century Indologists, historians and anthropologists have investigated South Asia and "discovered" that Hindu society is one of the world"s great civilization. Western influence on its "object of study" cannot be denied; and coming back to the West today is the self-definition of Hinduism as the "timeless spiritual culture" of a people. Culture, rather than dharma, has become the meta-term governing Hinduism's relations with the West. The essential characteristics of Hinduism (e.g. reverence for Mother Cow, tolerance, vegetarianism, non-violence) now mark a people in their capacity as subjects of culture.

The meta-position of culture in India's relations with the West is similar to that of science in the nineteenth century. Here again ritual spokesmen took on Western scholars in their own terms, interpreting Hindu, or proto-Hindu, religious practices in terms of rationalism. The example of Rammohun Roy is well-known. Influenced by the rationalist interpretation of faith, Roy was initially attracted to the Unitarian Church only to realize that Vedanta was similarly founded. Indeed, by virtue of its antiquity, Vedanta was superior to Christianity as the mother of world religions. In Vedanta lay the middle ground which served to bridge East and West (see Kopf 1979; and the interesting counter-responses documented by Young 1981). The Western scholar's methodological commitment to transparency leads him to see something inauthentic in his personal reflection in the native. Hence, the resort to such terms as humanistic Hinduism, neo-Hinduism or modern Hinduism to describe those religious forms which have become "contaminated", as it were, by Western values. Such terms imply, though, that there is a traditional Hinduism, or a Hinduism *tout court,* which has persisted on the subcontinent for the last two millennia, uncontaminated by Buddhist, Jain or Islamic preaching. Historical material, however, does not support such a view of the past. In the same way that "modern Hinduism" has defined itself in relations to the West so also did previous Hinduisms take their form in the meta-relations constituted by Brahmanical and ascetic spokesmen in response to other faiths. Fundamental to this encounter has been the practice of translation whereby rival religions are rendered equivalent to Hinduism in their being manifestations of the same universal source of authority and yet different from Hinduism, and inherently inferior to it, in their ontic and historical derivations.

Epilogue

Admittedly Brahmans and ascetics do not see themselves as translators; and it is only our modern, wordy sense of culture that leads me to attribute this role to them. By so doing, I am of course translating them as my counterpart—translating them as translators—even though we do not share common procedures and their translations are provoked by a ritual construction of religious purpose, not by a cultural construction of human understanding.

Yet they are translators of a kind, and by seeing Hinduism's spokesmen as translators, we are able to grasp at the very least why it is that ritual spokesmen in South Asia have enabled a certain kind of scholarly discourse to emerge in the West. In the academic division of labour indologists study antiquity, historians the past and anthropologists the present. But the fact that Brahmans and ascetics conceive of religious change emanating from a middle ground outside time and space has had the effect of creating a stability in the language of description of the diverse forms of Hinduism. It is from the perspective of this middle ground that ritual spokesmen translate the present in terms of the past, the "here" in terms of the "there", such that relations of equivalence are perceived in a world of appearances. The consequence of this for the scholar is that Indologists, historian and anthropologist may communicate with each other as if they had a common problem. Furthermore, by seeing ritual spokesmen as translators we are able to focus on the nexus of meta-relations in which the essential characteristics of Hinduism are defined in specific socio-historical context; and more particularly, on the way in which modern Hinduism is the outcome of acts of translation by ritual spokesmen as much as by scholarly spokesmen. Each has influenced the other in this religion doubly considered.

REFERENCES

Burghart, R. 1983. Renunciation in the religious traditions of South Asia. In *Man* (N.S.) 18, 635-53.

Cantlie, A. 1984. *The Assamese: Religion, caste and sect in an Indian village.* London: Curzon Press.

Dumont, L. 1959. Le renoncement dans les religions de l'Inde. In *Arch. Sociol. Relig.* 7, 45-69.

Dutt, S. 1962. *Buddhist monks and monasteries of India.* London: Allen and Unwin.

Emeneau, M.B. 1955. India and linguistics. In *Journal of the American Oriental Society* 75, 145-53.

Hacker, . 1957. Religiöse Toleranz und Intoleranz im Hinduismus. In *Saeculum* 8, 167-79.

Jakobson, R. 1959. On linguistic aspects of translation. In *On translation* (ed.) R.A. Brower, Cambridge (Mass.): Harvard University Press.

Kopf, D. 1979. *The Brahmo Samaj and the shaping of the modern Indian Mind.* Princeton: Princeton University Press.

Piatigorsky, A. 1984. Some phenomenological observations on the study of Indian religion. In *Indian Religion* (eds.) R. Burghart and A. Cantlie, London: Curzon Press.

Siddhānt Paṭal. n.d. Attributed to Ramanand by his followers. Benaras: Thakur Prasad and Sons.

Staal, J.F. 1961. *Nambudiri Veda recitation.* 'S-Gravenhage: Mouton.

Steiner, G. 1975. *After Babel: Aspects of language and translation.* London: Oxford University Press.

Woodroffe, J.G. 1953. *The Great Liberation, Mahanirvana Tantra.* Madras: Ganesa & Co.

Young, R.F. 1981. *Resistant Hinduism: Sanskrit sources on anti-Christian apologetics in early nineteenth century India.* Publications of the De Nobili Research Library, 8, Vienna: Gerold & Co.

CONTRIBUTORS

DR. SERGE BOUEZ, Dept. of Ethnology and Comparative Sociology, University of Paris X, Nanterre, France.

Fields of specialization: Munda-speaking tribes of India, especially the Ho and the Santal, Hindu religion in West Bengal.

PROF. RICHARD BURGHART, Dept. of Ethnology, South Asia Institute, University of Heidelberg, Germany.

Fields of specialization: North Indian Vaishnavism, the Hindu polity (Nepal), the Maithili language (died 1993).

PROF. GABRIELLA EICHINGER FERRO-LUZZI, Dipartimento di Studi Asiatici, Instituto Universitario Orientale, Naples, Italy.

Field of Specialization: Indian culture, modern Tamil literature.

DR. ANNCHARLOTT ESCHMANN, South Asia Institute, University of Heidelberg, Germany.

Fields of specialization: Comparative Religion, Hinduism, Orissa (died 1977).

PROF. ROBERT ERIC FRYKENBERG, Dept. of History and South Asian Studies, University of Wisconsin, Madison, WI 53706 (U.S.A.).

Fields of specialization: India under Company Raj and Hindu Nationalism.

MONIKA HORSTMANN (Prof. Dr. Monika Boehm-Tettelbach), Dept. of Modern Indology, South Asia Institute, University of Heidelberg, Im

Neuenheimer, Feld 330, 69120 Heidelberg, Germany.

Fields of specialization: Devotional Hinduism, Hindi literature and oral traditions.

DR. HORST KRÜGER, Academy of Science of the former GDR, Berlin, Germany.

Field of specialization: Modern Indian history (died 1989).

PROF. HERMANN KULKE, Dept. of History, Kiel University, Leibniz str. 8, 24098 Kiel, Germany.

Fields of specialization: History of India and Southeast Asia, Orissan Studies.

DR. ADITYA MALIK, Dept. of Indology, South Asia Institute, University of Heidelberg, Im Neuenheimer Feld 330, 69120 Heidelberg, Germany.

Fields of specialization: Hinduism, folk religion, pilgrimage studies, oral tradition, Rajasthan.

PROF. FRANÇOISE MALLISON, École pratique des Hautes Études, Section des Sciences historiques et philologiques, à la Sorbonne, 45-47 rue des Ecoles, 75005 Paris; and Les Montèzes, 30170 Monoblet, France.

Fields of specialization: History and philology of medieval western India, Gujarati.

PROF. GÜNTHER-DIETZ SONTHEIMER, Dept. of History of Religion and Philosophy of South Asia, South Asia Institute, University of Heidelberg, Germany.

Fields of specialization: South Asian religions, particularly folk religion, history of cults, Dharmaśāstra, Hinduism, Marathi language and literature (died 1992).

PROF. HEINRICH VON STIETENCRON, Seminar für Indologie und Vergleichende Religionswissenschaft (Indology and Comparative Religion), University of Tübingen, Münzgasse 30, 72070 Tübingen, Germany.

Fields of specialization: Indian religions and culture.

PROF. ROMILA THAPAR, Centre for Historical Studies, Jawaharlal Nehru University, New Delhi 110067, India.

Field of specialization: Indian History.

DR. GAYA CHARAN TRIPATHI, Principal, Ganganath Jha Kendriya Sanskrit Vidyapeetha, Chandrashekhar Azad Park, Allahabad 211002, India.

Fields of specialization: Indian Philosophy, Vedic Studies, Hinduism.

PROF. CHARLOTEE VAUDEVILLE, Professeur Emerite, Université de la Sorbonne Nouvelle, Paris, France; Directeur d' Etudes á la IV une Section de l'Ecole Pratique des Hautes Etudes, Paris.

Fields of specialization: Literature and religions of medieval India.

PROF. PETER VAN DER VEER, Research Centre of Religion and Society, University of Amsterdam, OZ Achterburgwal 185, 1012 DK Amsterdam, The Netherlands.

Fields of specialization: Hinduism, Sufism, Indian Overseas Communities, Indian nationalism.

DR. STEVEN VERTOVEC, Principal Research Fellow, Centre for Ethnic Relations, University of Warwick, Coventry CV 47 AL, England.

Fields of specialization: The South Asian diaspora, anthropology of religion and ethnicity.

PROF. NARENDRA K. WAGLE, Dept. of History, University of Toronto, Toronto, Ontario, Canada M5S 1A1.

Fields of specialization: Ancient and medieval Indian history, law and society of Maharashtra, Buddhism.

GENERAL INDEX

INDEX OF INDIAN TERMS

banana